*f*P

DIXIE LULLABY

★ A STORY of ★
MUSIC, RACE,
and
NEW BEGINNINGS
in a
NEW SOUTH

MARK KEMP

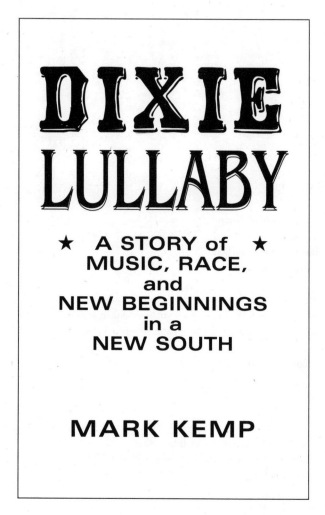

FREE PRESS

NEW YORK LONDON TORONTO SYDNEY

*f*P

FREE PRESS
A Division of Simon & Schuster, Inc.
1230 Avenue of the Americas
New York, NY 10020

The author gratefully acknowledges permission from the following sources: *The New York Times* to reprint an excerpt from a previously published article. *Rolling Stone* to reprint an excerpt from a previously published article. Little, Brown and Company to reprint parts of the essay "Southern Accents" from *Rolling Stone: The Seventies*, edited by Ashley Kahn, Shawn Dahl, and Holly George-Warren.

FREE PRESS and colophon are trademarks
of Simon & Schuster, Inc.

For information regarding special discounts for bulk purchases,
please contact Simon & Schuster Special Sales at 1-800-456-6798
or business@simonandschuster.com

Designed by Karolina Harris

Manufactured in the United States of America

10 9 8 7 6 5 4 3 2 1

Library of Congress Cataloging-in-Publication Data is available.

ISBN 0-7432-3794-3

For my dad,
Richard L. Kemp,
with deepest love and gratitude

★ Contents ★

"You people here have the same background, the same families, the same upbringing that I have—people from Alabama, Mississippi, Tennessee, Georgia, the Carolinas, Virginia, Florida. You share my past and my values, yes, but you also share my love of this country. . . ."

—PRESIDENT JIMMY CARTER, 1980

★ Preface ★

All right, then, I'll go to hell.
　　　　　　—HUCK FINN

On a brisk fall morning, the first day of the 1968 school year, some two hundred students of Lindley Park, one of five elementary schools in the small mill town of Asheboro, North Carolina, filed into the auditorium for what would be a historic announcement. From that day forward, the classes would be racially integrated. It had been a long time coming. In the previous four years, in accordance with Title VI of the 1964 Civil Rights Act, several other schools in this predominantly white, middle-class town nestled into the rolling hills halfway between the Blue Ridge Mountains and the Outer Banks had begun the process of desegregation. For the first time in history, black children were sitting alongside white children in classrooms all across the town and region, studying from the same books, learning from the same teachers, taking recess on the same playgrounds, eating from the same plates and utensils, sharing the same restrooms.

For a towheaded boy from a large extended family, many of whom called blacks "niggers" just as casually as they'd refer to the Reverend Charles White as a preacher, this news came as a shock. How do I know this? I was that towheaded boy—eight years old and entering my third year of public education.

I'd attended an all-white nursery school, an all-white kindergarten, an all-white church, and an all-white elementary school for the first two years of my formal education. I hardly knew what the words *integration* or *desegregation* meant. I'd heard them on TV and in conversations

among my parents and their friends. But before that day, the only blacks I'd known worked for my family. There was Dot, the woman who helped my grandmother with the housework; Sandy, Dot's tiny, rail-thin husband, who mowed my grandmother's lawn; Dorothy, the young woman who took care of me, loved me, and held me while my mama worked as a bookkeeper at the Asheboro Drug Store; and Emory, the gentleman with salt-and-pepper hair and a biting sense of humor who worked with my mama as a delivery man and often took me on his rounds in his sky-blue VW bug, carrying prescriptions to elderly white folks.

I genuinely loved Dot and Sandy and Dorothy and Emory, but the love I felt for them was confusing. At family reunions my aunts, uncles, and cousins spoke fondly of Dot and Sandy, but it was as though they were speaking of children. "Sandy," one of my aunts would say in her patronizing southern drawl, "he's that nice little nigger who cuts Mama Carlton's yard." I remember one night when that same aunt went with my mama and me to the Laundromat because it was raining and they couldn't hang their clothes on the line to dry. "I hate to come into this place," she told Mama, " 'cause, you know, niggers use these dryers." I don't recall my mama's response, but to my aunt, and to most members of my extended family, the following truths were held as self-evident: "Niggers" were inferior to whites; they were dirty, smelly, violent, unintelligent, and absolutely not to be trusted. My family wasn't unique: it was a microcosm of the rest of our town and region.

When we returned home from family gatherings, my mother and father would tell my sister and me that our relatives were wrong to use the "N" word. "Colored people," they told us, just weren't as fortunate as we were. Today I assume my parents' philosophical deviation from the viewpoints of the extended family was due, in part, to the fact that my father had risen from a tool-belt-wearing factory worker to a management position that involved world travel, and that this gave him an expanded view of different cultures. Also, his family members, who were Quakers, had always been more racially tolerant than my mother's family. Whatever the reasons for my parents' more progressive beliefs, and however seriously they took those beliefs, my sister and I were told not to judge or question the elders of our extended family. That would be disrespectful. To further complicate matters, at night, when my sister and I would turn on the TV, we'd get even more conflicting images: on one

news station, the grim-faced governor of Alabama, George Wallace, was telling the nation that under no circumstances would southerners allow Negroes to mingle with whites; on another was the peaceful yet determined face of a saintly looking black man who had a powerful, musical voice that trembled with conviction, compassion, and not just a little rage. It was the face of Dr. Martin Luther King Jr., who spoke of a future where Negro children would one day play with white children in peace, forever freed from the bondage of bigotry.

It was all very difficult to grasp at eight years old. Was this Dr. King one of those "nice niggers"—like Sandy? Did he smell bad? Was he to be mistrusted? I loved my family, but when Dr. King spoke, he seemed far more sophisticated than my aunts, uncles, cousins, and Governor Wallace. His unconditional love seemed genuine; his intelligence and sage demeanor allowed me to believe in him more than I could believe in anyone from my own bloodline. My family's racism baffled me, and Governor Wallace's speeches scared me. But Dr. King—his words and the cadence of his voice—held me in pure rapture. It reminded me of the way Dorothy would hold me in her arms as though I were her own son. And yet, even my own mother and father would tell us that Dr. King's actions were wrong; that one shouldn't break the law under any circumstance. To my young mind, that left only two choices: either blacks couldn't be trusted or laws couldn't be trusted. If I accepted the former, it validated every other prejudice that my extended family and community had programmed me to believe.

By age eleven, I had rejected the collective bigotry, and so had my older sister and a handful of our friends. It was 1971, and at school we'd been integrated with blacks for several years and had by now concluded that our elders had brought us up on lies. I had befriended the first black boy I'd met during my third year at Lindley Park. Martin Nicholson lived near my neighborhood, in an area of town across the proverbial tracks that white bigots referred to as "the Hill." Martin was a sensitive boy who smashed at least one stereotype that I had always heard from friends and family members: that the main thing blacks were good for was playing sports. Martin was as bad at playing sports as I was.

Even by 1971, racial mixing outside the classroom or organized sporting events was not considered proper in my hometown. And that meant that there were precious few places where my friends and I could find

validation for our unpopular behavior. At first, we turned to music. Hippie music. Music that embraced alternative lifestyles. Then we discovered marijuana. The combination of music and drugs took us far away from our dreary mill town lives. My favorite band was British—the Rolling Stones. I had no idea at the time that the Stones had been influenced by such southern American artists as black blues and rock & roll pioneers Robert Johnson, Willie Dixon, and Chuck Berry, and the white rockabilly and country musicians Carl Perkins, Buddy Holly, and George Jones. Those artists had made their careers in the very region that my friends and I found so suffocating. I completely missed the connection. Mick Jagger came from a land so far away that it didn't seem real. Jagger himself didn't seem real. He wore eyeliner and sequined jumpsuits, and strutted about the stage with effeminate gestures. In Asheboro, North Carolina, boys played football, chewed tobacco, graduated from high school to enter college or go into business, or quit school at sixteen to work for one of the local textile mills or furniture factories. I adored Mick Jagger, but to emulate him was to expose myself to ridicule. Besides, I couldn't really relate to him. He was so much larger than life.

Then I discovered the Allman Brothers Band, a mixed-race, blues-influenced rock group based in Macon, Georgia. The Allmans dressed in flannels and jeans, like I did. The singer, Gregg Allman, crooned with a melancholy I'd never before heard from someone who shared my reality. It was as though he were speaking directly to me. In the band's 1969 psychedelic-gospel dirge "Dreams," Allman moaned the words "I went up on the mountain / To see what I could see / The whole world was falling / Right down in front of me." I was only eleven years old the first time I heard that song, but I felt I knew what Gregg Allman was talking about. In the years following desegregation, the mood of the South was chaotic. Times were changing. Wrong seemed right and right seemed wrong. The Allmans embraced that chaos, combining country, blues, jazz, and gospel into an otherworldly musical stew that allowed me to feel conflicting emotions: sadness, joy, sorrow, pride. Between 1969 and 1973, the Allmans sang of what it felt like to be saddled with pain ("Dreams," "It's Not My Cross to Bear"); they sang of redemption ("Revival"); and they sang of falling in love with (and within) the awesome beauty of the rural South ("Blue Sky," "Southbound").

In those days, which side of the racial divide one stood on seemed just

a matter of a coin toss. Some of my peers mimicked the feelings of their forefathers, while others welcomed the monumental changes taking place. For my part, I loved the land that surrounded me but hated the history that haunted that land. And that history had a huge impact on the attitudes of the people around me. It was confusing. The Allman Brothers—and followers like Lynyrd Skynyrd, ZZ Top, Charlie Daniels, Wet Willie, and the Marshall Tucker Band—created a safe space within that confusion. Suddenly, we white southerners who were born between 1955 and 1965, and who questioned the status quo, didn't have to feel so alone during this traumatic transitional period of American history. While we fantasized about glamorous bands such as the Rolling Stones, the Who, and Led Zeppelin, we could directly relate to the Allman Brothers. They talked like us, they looked like us, they sang about issues and landscapes that we could feel and see, and they performed often enough in cities close to us that we could drive to their shows. For me and many kids like me, the Allman Brothers and the southern rock movement that they spawned in the early 1970s changed our lives and gave us a sense of community and purpose. We had southern rock, and therefore we had each other. We may have felt like freaks, but now we knew we weren't the only freaks.

I didn't realize it at the time, but the feeling of community that southern rock engendered during the early 1970s was the beginning of a healing process—in me and in many southerners of my generation—that continues to this day. That truth hit me like the rush of my first rock concert one evening, in 1998, when I was backstage at a Manhattan nightclub, talking with Mike Farris, the lead singer of the Tennessee band Screamin' Cheetah Wheelies. I had been living and working in New York City or Los Angeles for more than a decade, and as I spoke with Farris, I looked around the room. Standing nearby was Warren Haynes, the North Carolina–born guitarist for Gov't Mule and a sometime member of the Allman Brothers Band. Haynes was chatting with the Allmans' longtime road manager, Kirk West, who had come up from Georgia and decided to check out the Wheelies show. The vibe in that musty, beer-strewn dressing room felt as familiar as a family reunion, and at some point I noticed that my own North Carolina drawl had resurfaced.

Apparently, this bizarre behavioral reflex happens when southern transplants feel safe. Back in 1958, just four years after the U.S. Supreme

Court issued the landmark *Brown v. Board of Education* decision stating that segregation of public schools was a violation of the Fourteenth Amendment, another expatriate from Dixie, the historian C. Vann Woodward, posed an ominous question: "Has the southern heritage become an old hunting jacket that one slips on comfortably while at home but discards when he ventures abroad in favor of some more conventional or modish garb?" Sadly, in 1998, the answer to that question still seemed to be yes. When I moved to New York in the mid-1980s, I made a conscious effort to purge the southern vernacular from my speech. By then, the Allman Brothers Band had helped me feel the pain of my region's history, Lynyrd Skynyrd had articulated for me the anger of being branded a racist by nonsoutherners, and R.E.M.'s blurred musical paintings of southern landscapes and characters allowed me to take an intellectual step away from the pain and anger. But the healing was not yet complete.

What I realized in that nightclub was that while rock & roll may have saved my life, southern rock had made it worth living. This is not just melodramatic regional cheerleading. For white southerners like me, who began grade school in the wake of desegregation and came to embrace the rock counterculture as an alternative lifestyle, any declaration of ancestral pride carries a subtext of tremendous emotional weight. If rock & roll had initially provided refuge from the South's legacy of violence and bigotry, the music of the southern rock family tree—from the Allmans to Skynyrd, R.E.M. to Drive-By Truckers—offered an emotional process by which my generation could leave behind the burdens of guilt and disgrace and go home again. Step by step, the music has taken us down a path to self-awareness and forgiveness. Today, I am not compelled to suppress my identity, and for that I can thank not only the increasing predominance of southerners in American politics and culture but also bands like the Screamin' Cheetah Wheelies.

I was so excited by my epiphany that I wrote about it in *The New York Times*. Based on the feedback I received from that article, I learned that other white southerners had experienced similar feelings. What's more, many northerners told me they had no idea of the depth of the burden that southerners of my generation carry. A number of African-Americans called or wrote to me, congratulating me on my honesty. One prominent black music writer told me he was relieved to read a piece by a white

l bol-

in is
ed to
ers of
hern
anges
a vul-
ng of
aling
eone
I am
ngth-

and-
book
ners.
t led
f the
as an
: was
eady
ctiv-
and
pes-
ooks,
hern
y for
ash's
e an
hing

my
cted
past
who
me-

ne feel like a freak. Moreover, I've found that
here they were born or currently live, feel sim-
heir hometowns. That leads me to believe that
d his fellow southerners—resentment that has
again over the years—had less to do with his
n with his own feelings of both inferiority as a
ority as an intellectual. As Bertram Wyatt-Brown
"Indeed, although Cash struggled to achieve
shake off a deeply embedded sense of unwor-
own allows for validation of Cash's dilemma:
lienated from themselves projected their inner
at large, but not without some justice. Southern
e the solitariness of the thinker. Mistrust, not
e who preferred seclusion and time for reading

developed a sympathetic understanding of the
ly consider my home, and of the music that has
f self-discovery. Thomas Wolfe, another North
have been right when he determined that you
my journey has taught me that you can learn to

Mark Kemp
September 2001

writer that did not attempt to analyze the black experience. That ca
stered my determination to write this book.

My experience of suppressing my cultural identity in order to f
not unique. But in an era of lingering political correctness, it occu
me that many white writers are wary of treading the turbulent wa
this subject. After all, to some people the notion that young sou
whites might have suffered emotional trauma as a result of the cl
brought about by civil rights legislation might seem offensive — eve
gar. But to me, one man's suffering does not preclude the suffer
another, and any psychotherapist will tell you that wholesale h
requires treatment of all the affected parties. I feel it is time that sor
addresses these issues head on. For me, the process of accepting wh
and where I came from has been powerfully liberating and has str
ened my resolve to try and accept others unconditionally.

The most important thing that I hope this book affords is under
ing. In 1941, the southern journalist W. J. Cash wrote an importan
that continues to color people's opinions about white south
Interestingly, it is the brilliance of Cash's *The Mind of the South* th
to the preconceptions and misperceptions that have become part
mythology of southern small-mindedness and intolerance. Cash
intellectual from a small southern mill town, much like my own. I
reclusive, depressive, lacked self-esteem, and preferred more
endeavors, such as reading and studying, to the ordinary small-town
ities of his time. All of this made him an outcast in his communit
he developed a resentment toward his fellows that cast a cloud
simism over his ideas. "The pursuit of knowledge, the writing of
the painting of pictures, the life of the mind," he wrote of his sou
peers' attitudes, "seemed an anemic and despicable business, fit o
eunuchs." This resentment — some might say paranoia — distorts
otherwise keen cultural observations, and in the years since has ma
indelible imprint on outside perceptions of the South. Almost ever
written about the region cites Cash's work.

I feel a great kinship with Cash. I preferred listening to music
bedroom to playing sports or hunting, and I felt my behavior was re
by the community. But I moved away from the South, and for th
decade have cultivated friendships with people all over the count
share my aesthetic sensibilities. I'm no longer angry with those

★ Introduction ★

It was a weekend ritual. Sixteen-year-old Phil Walden and his buddies would amble over to the local YMCA in Macon, Georgia, to hang out with each other, play ball, and talk to girls. One weekend in 1956, Walden had another plan. Like always, he told his parents that he and the guys were going to the Y, but this time Walden made a beeline into the majestic, gold-domed Macon City Auditorium next door. "I had heard on the local R&B radio station that Little Richard was going to be playing," he remembered. That detour would change Phil Walden's life and chart the course for southern rock.

In 1956, Walden, who would later become the manager of soul legend Otis Redding and then of the Allman Brothers Band, was already crazy about music, specifically the black music he heard on his radio. Four years earlier, Walden had discovered the raw passion of rhythm & blues. "I was about eleven or twelve years old and my older brother had gradu-ated from college, in Bloomington, Indiana, and come back home with a batch of 78s—Hank Ballad, Joe Turner, the '5' Royales," said Walden. "I would sit there all day and play these things over and over." Walden's mother was nonplussed. "She said, 'What is it about this music?' I said, 'I don't know.' I couldn't explain it in words. There was just something real about it. I felt like those guys were singing to me."

Phil Walden wasn't the only young white southerner awed by African-American rhythm & blues in the mid-1950s. In 1954, during his first recording sessions for Sun Records, in Memphis, Tennessee, a teenaged

Elvis Presley blended the blues of his Mississippi roots with the hillbilly sounds of bluegrass king Bill Monroe. In May of that same year, U.S. Supreme Court Justice Earl Warren delivered a unanimous ruling in *Brown v. Board of Education* that ended state-sanctioned segregation of the public schools. By August, Elvis's first regional hit, "That's All Right," was blaring out of radios all across the South, and the swivel-hipped singer embarked on a tour of the southern states. Parents of white teenagers were outraged by this white singer who danced and sang like a black man. Within two years, RCA had signed Elvis and released his first national No. 1 pop single, "Heartbreak Hotel." It was 1956, and Bill Haley and the Comets' "Rock Around the Clock" was the smash theme song to a youth-culture movie of the same name. Rock & roll had established itself as a contender in American mainstream pop consciousness. The days of the romantic, silky-voiced crooners were over.

Before the mid-'50s, popular music in America was a wholly different beast from what it's been since. The white male stars that began making their mark during the waning years of World War II and into the postwar era—from Bing Crosby to Perry Como to Frank Sinatra—were mostly nonsouthern by birth, but they sometimes, to one degree or another, assimilated southern black or hillbilly styles into their music. Aside from Sinatra, though, these singers rarely let the grittier aspects of those styles clash with their own more polished sensibilities. Even popular black stars of the period, such as Nat King Cole, would soften the edges of jazz and blues to appeal to mainstream white audiences. Rock & roll let the styles clash, and many people were frightened by its dissonance, both musically and culturally. Prior to the '50s, about the only place you'd find real southern jazz, blues, or hillbilly music would be on regional independent or specialized record labels.

Jerry Wexler, cofounder of Atlantic Records, recalled the mood of the late '40s: "We were making black records, with black musicians and black singers for black buyers. It never occurred to us in the beginning that there were crossover possibilities."

For many young, adventurous southern whites, that crossover already had begun. In the late '40s, around the time Hank Williams was shaking up the country music establishment in Nashville, two radio stations— WDIA, in Memphis, and WOOK, in Washington, D.C.—were among the first to program black music exclusively. Other stations followed, and

by the early '50s, white teenagers across the South were tuning in to black-music radio stations. Niki Sullivan, a cousin of rock & roll pioneer Buddy Holly, recalled listening to black stations from as far away as Shreveport, Louisiana, more than five hundred miles from his hometown of Lubbock, Texas. "I started listening to rhythm & blues in high school," he said. "I can remember in my junior year, the Midnighters were very popular—where I ate lunch they had those records on the jukebox."

Rock & roll's roots in the South go further back than the '40s and '50s. Even though the region was known for its oppressive racial segregation, there were two places where poor blacks and poor whites could meet on common ground: work and church—two places where singing kept folks sane. And so it was here that music first began circulating from white hands to black hands and back again. Legend has it that in Western Kentucky in the 1920s, a black blues guitarist by the name of Arnold Schultz would get together with the young white mandolin picker Bill Monroe, and they would jam on Monroe's hillbilly music and Schultz's blues. What came out of those jam sessions was bluegrass, a lightning-speed blend of old-timey Irish and Scottish folk music particular to southern mountaineers, and pure, raw Kentucky blues.

This kind of musical miscegenation among the poorest African- and European-descended southerners goes even further back. For example, the banjo, one of the lead instruments in bluegrass and mountain music, is actually an African instrument, created by stretching a drumhead over a gourd and adding strings and tuning keys. The drumhead is what gives the instrument its distinctive twang. And then there's the guitar, the predominant instrument of the blues. The earliest evidence of guitar music is found in Spain, where the instrument's gently strummed strings give Spanish music its sweet, romantic melodicism. The point is that neither black blues nor white country would exist without this very important exchange, beginning in the early part of the twentieth century among the musicians and instruments of the two races that were not allowed to mingle in the United States when those musical genres were first born. And this happened primarily in the South.

There's a never-ending stereotype about southern race relations that keeps information about this important sharing of music one-sided and has led to the myth that white musicians habitually steal from black musicians. I've found that much of this one-sidedness has come not so much

from righteously angry blacks as from self-righteous white pop critics and political activists. I'm generalizing, of course, but this trend plays an important role in the development and evolution of southern rock and the mixed emotions the music validated during a traumatic period of our nation's history. While white critics generally praise the music of poor black southern musicians, many of those critics freely mock the music and character of working-class white southern artists.

Southern rock's heyday lasted from about 1969, when the Allman Brothers Band's first album was released, to about 1977, when Lynyrd Skynyrd's plane went down. It's ironic that the genesis of southern rock goes back to the British Invasion of the mid-1960s, when acts such as the Beatles, the Rolling Stones, the Yardbirds, the Animals, Cream, and Led Zeppelin took southern American musical traditions such as the blues, country, and early rock & roll, and transformed them into a new sound. It was an exciting new style of rock & roll that reintroduced southern musical traditions to a new generation of Americans, including young southerners, who were hungry for a sound of their own, a sound that was distinct from the music of their parents yet culturally familiar.

By 1964, when the Beatles arrived in the United States, young Americans were ready for this new style of music. Since 1959, when a plane crash killed Buddy Holly, rock & roll had been on a downward spiral. Around that same time, Elvis Presley joined the army, the careers of Chuck Berry and Jerry Lee Lewis had been stalled by sex-related scandals, and Little Richard turned to God. The record industry backed away from the gritty rock & roll of those musical giants and instead fed young America a steady diet of lightweight pop-rock by teen idols such as Pat Boone, Fabian, and Frankie Avalon. The rumble of urban folk music provided depth for young people who'd grown concerned about race relations in the South and the escalating war in Vietnam, but that music didn't have the force of electric guitars and drums. So when the Beatles' music hit the airwaves, it shook America like an earthquake, creating aftershocks from New York to California.

On their first U.S. tours, the Beatles and the Rolling Stones were stunned to find that Americans—particularly southern Americans—were ignorant of their own musical traditions. After all, since the late '50s, when the songs of Elvis Presley and Buddy Holly hit the U.K., young British musicians had been painstakingly schooling themselves on south-

ern American music. Guitarists George Harrison, Keith Richards, and Eric Clapton, and singers Mick Jagger, Eric Burdon, and Paul McCartney studied every guitar lick and vocal hiccup of artists ranging from blues guitarist Robert Johnson to rockabilly pioneer Carl Perkins to Presley and Holly.

In a 2002 television interview, original Rolling Stones bassist Bill Wyman talked about how surprised the group was during its first U.S. tour. "The white kids in America didn't really know much about the blues," he said. "The bizarre thing was that they used to say, 'Where can we hear this music?' We used to say, 'Well, it's right on your doorstep. Just go across the river and go to the clubs.' But of course, it was difficult in those days. There were a lot of problems, racially, in the early sixties, so they couldn't really just go."

Oblivious to the potential dangers, the Stones would spend their time off in the States during those early tours combing record stores on the proverbial wrong side of the tracks in towns across the South. "It was like treasure hunting," said Wyman. "I'll never forget those moments, because they were wonderful. And the guy [in the record stores] would be shocked when we came in the shop. But we found things that we would have never heard before. It was always really nice to come to these towns and just get the feeling of where it all began."

The Stones and the Beatles made the music of the South cool again, and future southern rock stars, including Duane and Gregg Allman, and Lynyrd Skynyrd founders Ronnie Van Zant and Gary Rossington, were taking notes. By the time they picked up instruments themselves and began writing songs based on growing up in the South, these musicians had been well schooled in the new southern-influenced rock music coming over from England. The Allman Brothers Band took the more traditional blues route of Britain's Cream; Skynyrd mimicked the grit and swagger of the Stones. After southern rock's initial attack, a string of other southern-based acts—from Charlie Daniels to Black Oak Arkansas, Wet Willie, and the Marshall Tucker Band—began filling in the stylistic gaps.

Since its heyday in the mid-1970s, southern rock has continued to influence new generations of musicians and touch new fans. The boogie-till-you-puke nature of the music's early days has evolved from arty to aggressive to sublime, but through it all—from R.E.M. to the B-52's, Jason and the Scorchers, Southern Culture on the Skids, the Black

Crowes, the Screamin' Cheetah Wheelies, Gov't Mule, and Drive-By Truckers—southern rock has maintained its sense of time and place and its cultural impact.

Southern rock's history, beginning as it did just after most public schools in the South had been desegregated, tells a story. It is a story of shame, of pain, of solitude, of anger, of acceptance, and, finally, of emotional and spiritual healing. In short, it is a story of change. Until now, southern rock has rarely been taken seriously as a pop-music movement, and I believe this is because many of the music journalists of the southern rock era looked down on the musicians as a bunch of wild-eyed, hell-raisin', redneck boogie boys. Luckily, life is not that simple, and neither is music.

This is not a story of black southern music (that story has been told many times, and rightly so); it is a story of white southern music. It's the story of a music that helped young white people heal at a time when we had no white role models who spoke as eloquently as Dr. Martin Luther King Jr. or Malcolm X. Instead, we had racist politicians such as Alabama Governor George Wallace and Georgia Governor Lester Maddox. If we were to learn tolerance, we had to look elsewhere, and many of us looked to rock stars like Gregg Allman and Ronnie Van Zant. Some of us came away with new feelings about our history; some of us did learn tolerance. Sadly, the sound and swagger of southern rock actually strengthened other peoples' deep-seated racism. Whatever the case, the music of southern rock bands defined my generation in the South and changed my culture. And in doing so, it changed America.

I

MOURNING IN AMERICA, 1968–1973

I ain't no psychiatrist,
I ain't no doctor with degrees.
But it don't take too much IQ
To see what you're doing to me.

—*Aretha Franklin, "Think"*

★ Chapter 1 ★

DEATH OF A KING

T HE *studio went silent.*

"That assassination changed everything."

The storyteller's warm Alabama drawl softened to a whisper, even though no one was in the room with us.

"We thought it was over," he said. "We really felt like we were done."

He'd been talking about all the great soul singers he played music with in the '60s, when all of a sudden he remembered that dark day, back in April 1968, when news traveled down from nearby Memphis, Tennessee, that the Reverend Martin Luther King Jr. was gunned down outside his room at the Lorraine Motel.

"As soon as that happened, whites were immediately shut out of black music," the storyteller said. "And rightfully so, to a certain extent. I mean, I backed them a hundred percent. They needed to take control of their music. But it was a sad time. And we were scared."

The storyteller paused and looked down at his hands, which were clasped together in his lap as if he were about to pray. Then he looked up again, furrowed his brow, and stared into my eyes, as if I might be able to help him in some small way.

"We gave our hearts and souls to those singers," he said.

It was nine o'clock at night and for several hours the storyteller had been taking me on a listening tour of his proudest moments as a recording studio session guitarist. There was that slinky shuffle he played on Wilson Pickett's "Mustang Sally," his funky rhythm part on Etta James's "Tell Mama," and

his subtle embellishments scattered throughout Aretha Franklin's 1967 mas-
terpiece, I Never Loved a Man the Way I Love You. *Each time he cued up a*
different track, the storyteller would stamp his feet to the music and flail his
arms about him like a spastic drummer, then bend forward in his chair, curl
his fingers, and play air guitar to the scratchy riffs.

"Listen, listen!" he barked during an instrumental break in Franklin's
"Do Right Woman, Do Right Man" as a blanket of churchlike organ
quivered beneath the singer's voice, followed by the sound of piano keys
pattering down around us like rain. The storyteller sat up in his chair and
pointed his index fingers skyward, as if he were preaching the gospel. "A
woman's only human," Aretha sang through a pair of speakers on the shelf
behind his head. "You should understand: She's not just a plaything. She's
flesh and blood, just like her man."

The storyteller leaned back in his chair again and smiled feverishly, his
eyes tightly shut and fists clenched. He looked like a man in the grips of
Pentecostal bliss. He was right there, in the moment—even though that
moment had come and gone more than thirty years before.

Jimmy Johnson was telling ghost stories he's told a million times before—
real-life yarns about the spirits that passed through this tiny section of
northwestern Alabama long ago, leaving an indelible mark on its landscape. An original member of the Muscle Shoals Rhythm Section,
Johnson helped put this river community, which serves as the headquarters of the Tennessee Valley Authority's Environmental Research Center,
on the map. His funky guitar licks appear on so many '60s and '70s rock
and soul classics that you can't turn on an oldies radio station without
hearing them at least once an hour. By the early '70s, Johnson and his fellow studio musicians had made Muscle Shoals, Alabama, the recording
mecca of American popular music.

As it turned out, the assassination of Martin Luther King Jr. did not
presage the end for Johnson and his colleagues. Within three years, a
peculiar thing happened. Young white rock stars whose lives had been
transformed by the sound of black American music—Boz Scaggs, Paul
Simon, even the Rolling Stones—descended on Muscle Shoals, hoping
to be inspired by the region's rich musical history.

"Man, I remember when Rod Stewart came over here from England to record with us," Johnson said. "He wanted us to make his music sound like all those great soul records. Well, when he got here and saw us—a bunch of white guys with guitars—he said, 'What the hell is this? Where's the band?'"

"We said, 'We *are* the band.'"

"He said, 'No, I mean the black guys that played on all those great Aretha records, Pickett and all that?'"

"We said, 'Well, that's us, but we're not black.'"

Johnson slapped both hands down on his knees and cackled. He was sitting at a sprawling soundboard inside his Swamper Studio, a ranch-style home he's converted into his current recording business. Johnson still works with the occasional big-name musician, but his profile today is much lower than it was in the '60s and '70s. Back then, the nation was in flux, and Jimmy Johnson's Alabama was right smack at the epicenter of change.

It only made sense that Johnson's talk of the golden years of southern soul would trigger thoughts of the King assassination. And when those thoughts came, they stopped him dead in his tracks. He had hit the volume controls on the tape machine, and for whatever reason, he felt it necessary to whisper. Maybe the spirits would hear him.

"During those civil rights years, music changed," he said. "We lived through those changes. We were *part* of the change. And we felt it."

As Johnson spoke, I checked to make sure the reels on my tape recorder were still rolling. I didn't want to miss this, because what he was talking about was the very genesis of southern rock, the music that, by the 1970s, had given a new identity to my friends and me back in North Carolina. In the early '70s, rock bands such as the Allman Brothers and Lynyrd Skynyrd articulated the confusion that we felt as twelve-year-olds growing up in a world in which black and white, old and young, wealthy and working class, hippie and redneck were becoming increasingly polarized. The South had changed dramatically in the '60s, and those of us who were too young to have experienced those changes with an adult consciousness were forced to find our place amid the fallout of cultural chaos. We were alone. Our parents couldn't help us. They didn't understand.

The white musicians who had worked alongside the South's most famous black singers during the civil rights years did understand. Their

music, and the music of those who followed them, would serve as a road map out of the chaos. It wouldn't be an easy journey, but it was a beginning.

That it took the assassination of America's greatest black leader to open the doors for those white southern musicians to step out from the shadows of the soul singers they had worked with, idolized, and emulated was a cruel twist of fate. King's death effectively provided a window of opportunity for young whites to begin expressing, through a new musical language, their own feelings of despair, gratitude, confusion, elation, guilt, and rage. This was not Elvis Presley's rock & roll—it was a mix and jumble of Elvis and Otis Redding, of Jimmie Rodgers and Robert Johnson, of Johnny Cash and Mississippi John Hurt, of Bob Dylan, Woody Guthrie, and Leadbelly, of the Beatles, the Stones, Little Richard, and Carl Perkins.

For Jimmy Johnson and the other white musicians who had backed black stars at Fame Studios in Muscle Shoals, 1968 was a year of soul searching. Rick Hall, the white producer and owner of Fame, looked back on that period in the 1995 PBS series *Rock & Roll*. "The mood of black music changed from that point on," he said. Suddenly, black singers stopped booking studio time at Fame. The goal of having their music cross over to the white pop charts was no longer important; in fact, it was a liability.

"The black musicians at that time were under a lot of pressure not to record with white people," said David Hood, Johnson's bass-playing partner in the Muscle Shoals Rhythm Section.

Hood and the other Alabama session players understood the reasoning behind that pressure, but they felt rejected by it nonetheless. After all, if black singers were now looking to record only with black musicians at black-run studios, the white musicians who had been playing with them throughout the '60s (and their youth) would have to find new outlets for their creativity—and new ways to make the rent.

"Here we were, cutting hit records for them," said Hood, over a plate of fried chicken at a soul food restaurant in nearby Florence, just down the road from the birthplace of blues legend W. C. Handy. "We loved working with them. I learned so much about music from Otis Redding and all the other artists I worked with. They taught me how to play. But it was different after the assassination. That was the turning point—that was when we started working with more white artists."

Jimmy Johnson decided to expand from being a musician to taking on the role of producer and artist representative. Three months after the assassination, he headed out to Los Angeles to try and land a record deal for a young black rhythm & blues singer from Canada. "I went up to Capitol Records and said, 'I got this record by this artist and I want to see if you'd be interested in releasing it,'" Johnson said. "Well, the guy at Capitol says to me, 'You're wasting your time.'

"I said, 'What are you talking about?'

"He said, 'You're the wrong color.'"

The following year, Johnson and Hood left Fame to open their own studio, Muscle Shoals Sound, where they worked predominantly with white rock bands.

At the hit-making Stax Records, in Memphis, the integrated Booker T. and the MG's, another group of studio players who backed a number of southern soul singers, consisted of two black musicians and two whites. The MG's were perhaps the first truly egalitarian rhythm section in rock & roll. In their heyday, they played on a string of hit records, from Rufus Thomas's "Walkin' the Dog" to Otis Redding's "(Sittin' on the) Dock of the Bay." But by the late '60s, the morale among the Stax studio brass, musicians, and other employees had reached an all-time low. In December 1967, Otis Redding died in a plane crash. When King was assassinated four months later, it only exacerbated the deepening rift at Stax.

"That was the turning point, the turning point for relations between the races in the South," Booker T. told Peter Guralnick in the book *Sweet Soul Music: Rhythm and Blues and the Southern Dream of Freedom.* "And it happened in Memphis."

White musicians continued to work with blacks, but to a much lesser degree, and the casual atmosphere of musical integration and experimentation had become tense, the relationships strained. Black stars became wary of any publicity linking them to their white colleagues. By late 1968, Booker T. and the MG's released a song fittingly titled "Soul Limbo."

With the rise of the civil rights movement in the early 1960s, blacks in the South and across the nation had already begun to take more control of

their lives. To the southern-based Martin Luther King Jr., control meant effecting change through steady, nonviolent confrontation; northeastern-based Malcolm X took a more do-it-yourself approach to activism, and his slogan advocating change "by any means necessary" was taken literally by some of his more militant followers. Those ostensibly conflicting outlooks from the two most eminent black leaders in America created tensions both within and between the races, and led, temporarily, to divisions that ran along racial, political, religious, and philosophical lines. During the civil rights years, things had to get worse before they could get better.

By the mid-1960s, a growing number of young African-Americans had begun to express their rage in ways that frightened whites. Any act or pose from an African-American male speaking out on issues of racism was perceived by Middle American whites as threatening; the image of the black man standing up to his captors had been branded into America's subconscious since the days of slavery, and it played straight into the white man's guilt. Consequently, violence broke out on both sides. The National Advisory Commission on Civil Disorders, appointed by President Lyndon Johnson, reported more than 150 riots between 1965 and 1968. In 1967, the year before the King assassination, 83 people were killed, 1,800 were injured, and more than $100 million in property was destroyed.

By the latter part of the decade, the civil rights movement itself had splintered into factions: on one side were those who continued to follow King's nonviolent route, on another were the more militant urban Black Nationalists who advocated direct confrontation. When King was assassinated, the floodgates opened for the more uncompromising activism, and the music business was caught in the undertow. Nowhere did this conflict manifest itself more than in the South. Within the music community, which for years had been one of the few shelters of interracial interaction, the divisions were devastating.

"It was a hard time," said Phil Walden, who in the early '60s managed a number of black artists in his hometown of Macon, Georgia, including Otis Redding. Walden went on to establish the preeminent southern rock record label of the '70s, Capricorn, and manage the Allman Brothers Band.

"It was through music that I had actually gotten to know black people," said Walden, sitting in the library of his home, which sits atop a hill

in the swanky Buckhead section of Atlanta, overlooking a winding, tree-lined road dotted with similarly huge southern mansions. "When you get to know a black person and become privy to their culture, their life, their lifestyle, it's like you suddenly realize that this person is a fucking human being. He can read just like me, he feels just like me, he's just got different-colored skin. So why in the hell have we been doing all this to these people for so long?"

It was the spring of 2002, and Walden was looking frailer than I'd ever seen him. He was completely bald, the result of treatments he'd undergone over the previous few months for cancer. Only a year earlier, I'd seen the veteran rock manager in a club in downtown New York City, dressed immaculately, his head full of wavy hair. If you took a photograph of Walden during his '70s heyday and placed it next to a young Bill Clinton, you'd think they were brothers. And when he smiled, Walden had the toothy sparkle of Jimmy Carter. Though Walden was looking in poor health on this breezy afternoon, he spoke with stiff-lipped determination and a passion for music that hasn't waned one iota. As delicate as his body was, Walden's booming Georgia drawl still resonated like that of an old-time southern politician.

Like most whites in the South, Walden was brought up to feel superior to blacks. "My father was a pretty avowed racist, because that's how he was raised," he said. "They were all raised that way—forever. I remember asking my mother why colored people were treated like that. She said it's not really right, it's just the way things are in the South."

Walden didn't buy it. When he listened to the music of black artists, he experienced feelings he'd never had. As a kid in the '50s, he would sneak off to performances by Macon's flamboyant rock & roller Little Richard. But it was Otis Redding who changed Walden's life. "I was real fortunate to discover a new way of seeing things through my relationship with Otis," he said. "He kind of walked me through his culture, and I kind of walked him through my side of it, and we were able to absorb and learn from each other. At some point I just became a total neoliberal and I thought—seeing the South, which I love very much, and the stupid stances people were taking, and the millions of dollars that were spent on antiquated laws—something is wrong here. You actually couldn't marry a black person back then. It was against the law."

Whites and blacks could discuss music together in the '50s and early

'60s, but only in management offices and back-alley clubs in progressive college towns or hidden behind the walls of a recording studio. Paul Hornsby, a former member of the band Hourglass, which also included Florida brothers Gregg and Duane Allman, remembered an incident in the early '60s when he and a college friend took a road trip. They were driving from the university town of Tuscaloosa, in northern Alabama, back to the southern part of the state where Hornsby's parents lived. Somewhere along the way, they spotted a VFW club with cars parked outside and music blaring. The two eighteen-year-old students stopped to see what was going on.

Inside, a black band was cranking out some heavy rhythm & blues. Hornsby, who was raised in a tiny Alabama backwater with bluegrass-picking kinfolk, was young and naïve. But he loved music and had begun to jam with black R&B bands at college frat parties.

"That band was just cookin'," Hornsby remembered. "I mean, they were good. So I thought, Hey, I sit in with bands all the time up in Tuscaloosa, I'd like to play with these guys. Well, I went up to the band when they took a break and we started braggin' on their music and everything. I said, 'Hey, if you don't mind, I'd like to sit in?'

"They looked kind of nervous, you know, and I couldn't understand why. And one of 'em, the leader, he says, 'You better ask the boss man.' Well, the manager of the club, he was a white guy, I said to him, 'Hey, do you mind if I sit in with that band? It's all right with them if it's all right with you.' And the man just looks at me and says, 'Probably better not do that.' "

Today, Hornsby runs a small recording studio in Macon, Georgia, where he's lived since he played with the Allmans in Hourglass. When that band broke up, Hornsby went to work for Phil Walden at Capricorn Records, where he produced hit records for the Charlie Daniels Band and Wet Willie. But to this day, that rural club owner's response still boggles his mind.

Unlike Walden, Hornsby grew up in the country, where he rarely came into contact with blacks, and his family never talked about race. He had no particular feelings one way or the other about racial issues; he just liked playing music. By the time he got to college, talk of civil rights was on the rise, but it all seemed academic to the young guitar player. Until that moment at the VFW club.

"I said to the club owner, 'Well, why not? Why can't we play with them?' And the guy just looked at me like he was surprised I even asked the question. He said, 'We just don't do that around here.' And I thought, Damn, ain't that weird? It's just music. I mean, I'm not trying to date their daughter or anything. We're breathing the same air, why can't we play music together? And all he could say was, 'We just don't do that around here.' "

It was a short, sharp education for the farm boy. "I guess we were just ignorant. You know, I always thought music transcended race. I thought race had no part among musicians. I knew there were problems back then, but until that night, I'd never seen it in a musical setting."

Neither had Mac Rebennack, better known by his stage name Dr. John, who had been recording and performing with blacks in New Orleans since 1954. "Back before integration, when the miscegenation laws was still in effect in New Orleans, the black and white thing was separated, but there was a lot of clubs where it was wide-open jam sessions all the time," said Rebennack, in his deep, bayou growl. "The gangsters owned the clubs anyway, so the police wasn't going to bother them."

Paradoxically, that changed when the civil rights movement gained momentum—and civil rights hit New Orleans relatively early on. The police, who had looked the other way in the pre-integration days, suddenly began bullying clubs where blacks and whites appeared onstage together. "They started coming in and stopping bands from having black-and-white jam sessions," said Rebennack. "Integration brought segregation to the clubs."

One of Malcolm John Rebennack Jr.'s earliest memories is of sitting on a front porch and hearing his grandfather sing, "I been hoodooed, I been hoodooed, I been hoodooed—somebody done put the jinx on me." It was an omen for the future Dr. John, who formed his first band, the Dominoes, when he was still attending New Orleans's Jesuit High School, the alma mater of Louis Prima. But Rebennack, whose father owned an appliance store and knew a local recording studio operator named Cosimo Matassa, wound up spending more of his teenage years hanging out with musicians and reading comic books than he did at school. Two of his biggest influences were Walter "Papoose" Nelson and Roy Montrell, both of whom played guitar with Fats Domino and taught the young Rebennack some of their tricks. Rebennack mimicked their

styles and eventually began playing on recording sessions for such legends as piano bluesman Professor Longhair and R&B singer Frankie Ford.

"Hell, I was fifteen years old when I started working in them studios," Rebennack said. By age seventeen, he had cowritten his first rock & roll song, "Lights Out," which became a regional hit for the white singer Jerry Byrne, on the Specialty Records label, in 1957.

By then, Rebennack had begun working as a producer for Ace Records, in nearby Jackson, Mississippi. From time to time, the small independent record company would put together package shows of its biggest acts and send them out on tour. Rebennack went along as a performer.

"When the civil rights movement heated up, it became more dangerous to travel as part of these package shows," said Rebennack. "Before then, we used to travel all over the South with no problem—me, Earl King, Guitar Slim, Chuck Berry, people like that—but then suddenly, we started getting hassled."

On one tour, the group was traveling a long stretch of Alabama highway when they saw a flashing light behind their car. "It was the Alabama State Police," said Rebennack. "They stopped us and came walking over to the car. And I mean, this was right around that time that all the bad shit, the lynchings and shit was going on. Well, the cop comes over and he says, 'I smell weed in this car.' And James Booker [the 'Piano Prince of New Orleans'], he says, 'Yes sir, I saw your lights and I threw the bag out the window. It's all over the highway back there.' " Rebennack let out a wheezy laugh, then continued: "You could say shit like that back then, because they didn't have a clue. Anyway, the cop, he says, 'Get the hell out of here, you crazy nigger.' But it's lucky he didn't see my ass sittin' back there in the car with them crazy sombitches, because that would have been worse than the weed. I mean, the police could have busted us for being in the car together."

Another frightening incident occurred when Rebennack was part of a tour headed for Harrisburg, Mississippi. "They'd just had this big famous lynching somewhere on the road between New Orleans and Harrisburg," he said. "So we heard about all this shit and here we are, a mixed group of guys on the road together in the deep South. It was scary. We was prime targets."

Os, but only in management offices and back-alley clubs in progressive college towns or hidden behind the walls of a recording studio. Paul Hornsby, a former member of the band Hourglass, which also included Florida brothers Gregg and Duane Allman, remembered an incident in the early '60s when he and a college friend took a road trip. They were driving from the university town of Tuscaloosa, in northern Alabama, back to the southern part of the state where Hornsby's parents lived. Somewhere along the way, they spotted a VFW club with cars parked outside and music blaring. The two eighteen-year-old students stopped to see what was going on.

Inside, a black band was cranking out some heavy rhythm & blues. Hornsby, who was raised in a tiny Alabama backwater with bluegrass-picking kinfolk, was young and naïve. But he loved music and had begun to jam with black R&B bands at college frat parties.

"That band was just cookin'," Hornsby remembered. "I mean, they were good. So I thought, Hey, I sit in with bands all the time up in Tuscaloosa, I'd like to play with these guys. Well, I went up to the band when they took a break and we started braggin' on their music and everything. I said, 'Hey, if you don't mind, I'd like to sit in?'

"They looked kind of nervous, you know, and I couldn't understand why. And one of 'em, the leader, he says, 'You better ask the boss man.' Well, the manager of the club, he was a white guy, I said to him, 'Hey, do you mind if I sit in with that band? It's all right with them if it's all right with you.' And the man just looks at me and says, 'Probably better not do that.'"

Today, Hornsby runs a small recording studio in Macon, Georgia, where he's lived since he played with the Allmans in Hourglass. When that band broke up, Hornsby went to work for Phil Walden at Capricorn Records, where he produced hit records for the Charlie Daniels Band and Wet Willie. But to this day, that rural club owner's response still boggles his mind.

Unlike Walden, Hornsby grew up in the country, where he rarely came into contact with blacks, and his family never talked about race. He had no particular feelings one way or the other about racial issues; he just liked playing music. By the time he got to college, talk of civil rights was on the rise, but it all seemed academic to the young guitar player. Until that moment at the VFW club.

"I said to the club owner, 'Well, why not? Why can't we play with them?' And the guy just looked at me like he was surprised I even asked the question. He said, 'We just don't do that around here.' And I thought, Damn, ain't that weird? It's just music. I mean, I'm not trying to date their daughter or anything. We're breathing the same air, why can't we play music together? And all he could say was, 'We just don't do that around here.'"

It was a short, sharp education for the farm boy. "I guess we were just ignorant. You know, I always thought music transcended race. I thought race had no part among musicians. I knew there were problems back then, but until that night, I'd never seen it in a musical setting."

Neither had Mac Rebennack, better known by his stage name Dr. John, who had been recording and performing with blacks in New Orleans since 1954. "Back before integration, when the miscegenation laws was still in effect in New Orleans, the black and white thing was separated, but there was a lot of clubs where it was wide-open jam sessions all the time," said Rebennack, in his deep, bayou growl. "The gangsters owned the clubs anyway, so the police wasn't going to bother them."

Paradoxically, that changed when the civil rights movement gained momentum—and civil rights hit New Orleans relatively early on. The police, who had looked the other way in the pre-integration days, suddenly began bullying clubs where blacks and whites appeared onstage together. "They started coming in and stopping bands from having black-and-white jam sessions," said Rebennack. "Integration brought segregation to the clubs."

One of Malcolm John Rebennack Jr.'s earliest memories is of sitting on a front porch and hearing his grandfather sing, "I been hoodooed, I been hoodooed, I been hoodooed—somebody done put the jinx on me." It was an omen for the future Dr. John, who formed his first band, the Dominoes, when he was still attending New Orleans's Jesuit High School, the alma mater of Louis Prima. But Rebennack, whose father owned an appliance store and knew a local recording studio operator named Cosimo Matassa, wound up spending more of his teenage years hanging out with musicians and reading comic books than he did at school. Two of his biggest influences were Walter "Papoose" Nelson and Roy Montrell, both of whom played guitar with Fats Domino and taught the young Rebennack some of their tricks. Rebennack mimicked their

styles and eventually began playing on recording sessions for such legends as piano bluesman Professor Longhair and R&B singer Frankie Ford.

"Hell, I was fifteen years old when I started working in them studios," Rebennack said. By age seventeen, he had cowritten his first rock & roll song, "Lights Out," which became a regional hit for the white singer Jerry Byrne, on the Specialty Records label, in 1957.

By then, Rebennack had begun working as a producer for Ace Records, in nearby Jackson, Mississippi. From time to time, the small independent record company would put together package shows of its biggest acts and send them out on tour. Rebennack went along as a performer.

"When the civil rights movement heated up, it became more dangerous to travel as part of these package shows," said Rebennack. "Before then, we used to travel all over the South with no problem—me, Earl King, Guitar Slim, Chuck Berry, people like that—but then suddenly, we started getting hassled."

On one tour, the group was traveling a long stretch of Alabama highway when they saw a flashing light behind their car. "It was the Alabama State Police," said Rebennack. "They stopped us and came walking over to the car. And I mean, this was right around that time that all the bad shit, the lynchings and shit was going on. Well, the cop comes over and he says, 'I smell weed in this car.' And James Booker [the 'Piano Prince of New Orleans'], he says, 'Yes sir, I saw your lights and I threw the bag out the window. It's all over the highway back there.'" Rebennack let out a wheezy laugh, then continued: "You could say shit like that back then, because they didn't have a clue. Anyway, the cop, he says, 'Get the hell out of here, you crazy nigger.' But it's lucky he didn't see my ass sittin' back there in the car with them crazy sombitches, because that would have been worse than the weed. I mean, the police could have busted us for being in the car together."

Another frightening incident occurred when Rebennack was part of a tour headed for Harrisburg, Mississippi. "They'd just had this big famous lynching somewhere on the road between New Orleans and Harrisburg," he said. "So we heard about all this shit and here we are, a mixed group of guys on the road together in the deep South. It was scary. We was prime targets."

in the swanky Buckhead section of Atlanta, overlooking a winding, tree-lined road dotted with similarly huge southern mansions. "When you get to know a black person and become privy to their culture, their life, their lifestyle, it's like you suddenly realize that this person is a fucking human being. He can read just like me, he feels just like me, he's just got different-colored skin. So why in the hell have we been doing all this to these people for so long?"

It was the spring of 2002, and Walden was looking frailer than I'd ever seen him. He was completely bald, the result of treatments he'd undergone over the previous few months for cancer. Only a year earlier, I'd seen the veteran rock manager in a club in downtown New York City, dressed immaculately, his head full of wavy hair. If you took a photograph of Walden during his '70s heyday and placed it next to a young Bill Clinton, you'd think they were brothers. And when he smiled, Walden had the toothy sparkle of Jimmy Carter. Though Walden was looking in poor health on this breezy afternoon, he spoke with stiff-lipped determination and a passion for music that hasn't waned one iota. As delicate as his body was, Walden's booming Georgia drawl still resonated like that of an old-time southern politician.

Like most whites in the South, Walden was brought up to feel superior to blacks. "My father was a pretty avowed racist, because that's how he was raised," he said. "They were all raised that way—forever. I remember asking my mother why colored people were treated like that. She said it's not really right, it's just the way things are in the South."

Walden didn't buy it. When he listened to the music of black artists, he experienced feelings he'd never had. As a kid in the '50s, he would sneak off to performances by Macon's flamboyant rock & roller Little Richard. But it was Otis Redding who changed Walden's life. "I was real fortunate to discover a new way of seeing things through my relationship with Otis," he said. "He kind of walked me through his culture, and I kind of walked him through my side of it, and we were able to absorb and learn from each other. At some point I just became a total neoliberal and I thought—seeing the South, which I love very much, and the stupid stances people were taking, and the millions of dollars that were spent on antiquated laws—something is wrong here. You actually couldn't marry a black person back then. It was against the law."

Whites and blacks could discuss music together in the '50s and early

Even in the more tolerant New Orleans, Rebennack found himself in some outrageous situations. "I remember a show with Bo Diddley at the Municipal Auditorium, which was a real segregated house," he said. "Bo's band didn't make it to the gig. Well, they wouldn't let us back him up. I mean, he was headlining this event and his band had got stuck somewhere else, and they made him go out and play that gig by himself because they wouldn't let a mixed band back him up. Here we were, a big seventeen-piece band, and we had to sit there and watch Bo Diddley play the gig all by himself."

Music was supposed to be the duty-free zone of racial interaction. In the parlance of today's kindergarten teachers, it was supposed to be the "time-out" corner. Even singer and fiddler Charlie Daniels, who wrote and sang the jaw-jutting southern rock anthem of the mid-'70s, "The South's Gonna Do It," and says he grew up with intensely racist views, would listen without judgment to African-American spirituals on the radio. "The one thing the South has always done is respect black music," said Daniels. "Whether you respected black *people* or not, you respected the music."

Daniels grew up in Wilmington, North Carolina, in the '40s and '50s, during a time when, as he says, "it was us against them." He graduated high school in 1955, a year after the first rumblings of civil rights legislation. "I never went to school with a black person one day in my life," he said. "My mind was conditioned in such a way that I felt they were an inferior race. That was just the way things were. And the thing about it is, when you're raised that way, when you're indoctrinated that way, it's not even a conscious thing to you. It was a cultural thing. No, it went deeper than a cultural thing: it was almost a fervent sort of belief that this was the way things were supposed to be."

Since there was no television in the '40s, Daniels listened to radio broadcasts of the Grand Ole Opry every Saturday night. In between the Opry and the local bluegrass stations on the dial, he would run across a black gospel station here and there. "A lot of black gospel music, a lot of blues, I was exposed to a lot of that kind of thing," he said. "You're not raised in the South at the time I came around without hearing black music. And I loved music, so I listened to all kinds of it."

That didn't immediately change his segregationist views. "For me, it was like this: they had their music and we had our music. And everybody

knew that black music was the pacesetter. Ever since it started getting any exposure at all, it's been the pacesetter. And, of course, that was the big change in music and culture—when black music began to get played on white radio stations and listened to by white kids, it just got bigger and bigger and bigger, and then, well, you know, rock & roll."

Daniels began his music career playing in a bluegrass band. In the late '50s, his tastes moved toward the burgeoning rock & roll of Elvis and Chuck Berry, and he formed an outfit called the Jaguars, which played cover versions as well as a few original tunes. It wasn't until Daniels left the South, though, that he began to understand the big lie he'd grown up with: that blacks were intellectually inferior. He was living in Washington, DC, and playing his music in clubs. There, he fell in love with jazz and began interacting with black musicians on a more intimate level.

"One of the hardest things about giving up any kind of prejudice is being honest with yourself," said Daniels. "It's not an easy thing to do. It's not easy to say, 'For nineteen years I've been living and believing a certain way and I'm beginning to wonder if what I believed is right.' Then you go a little further and start admitting, 'No, I *know* what I believed is not right. I have no right to feel that way.' And then you have to start working on your attitude. Because your mind has been so preconditioned to the them-versus-us mentality. It takes a while for things to kind of smooth out."

In the late '50s and early '60s, Daniels had begun to hear a lot about Martin Luther King Jr. and the nonviolent civil disobedience he was encouraging in the South. At first, Daniels's old ideas blinded him. "I just had him figured as a troublemaker," Daniels said. "I'd hear about them going down there and doing all this stuff and everything . . . I mean, the very audacity of them trying to become equal with white people was just beyond my comprehension. I couldn't imagine it."

By the time King graduated from small-town boycotts to national marches, though, Daniels was able to receive the message. "I had changed a lot by then. I'd already started having a tremendous respect for him. I mean, for years the guy just kept on and on and on. He never hurt anybody, never led violent marches, never burned anything down. He just kept coming and he kept coming and then, all of a sudden, there he is on TV. And he does this speech. He says he has a dream. And

it just knocked my socks off. I mean, he put it right exactly where it's supposed to be. He put it right in the middle. He was speaking the truth, and I heard it."

That was 1963. Five years later, King was dead. "I think he had a pretty good idea he wasn't going to make it through this thing," said Daniels. "When you listen to that last speech—the 'been to the mountaintop' speech—you get the idea he knew he was going to die. It would have been awfully easy for him to have pulled back much earlier and said, 'Okay, boys, I got you this far—I'm going back to Georgia, I'm going to preach in my little church, and I'm going to leave the rest of this civil rights stuff up to y'all.' But he didn't do that."

Daniels stared into my eyes with the cocky righteousness that fuels his biggest hit song, "The Devil Went Down to Georgia." He's a sermonizer by nature and by profession, and when he gets on a roll, his voice rises and his face reddens. "Right in the very face of death," he continued, "that man kept going. He walked into the valley of the shadow of death and then right into it. I mean, that man was a . . ." He trailed off, and his voice softened. "That man said he wasn't afraid of anything. He said, 'I fear no man.' Now, how can you not be affected by that? That, brother, is real faith."

Four days after the King assassination, more than one hundred blacks gathered at St. Luke's Methodist Church in my hometown of Asheboro, North Carolina, to march up Fayetteville Street, the town's main drag. It was a comparatively small demonstration, for sure, but Asheboro had never seen such a direct show of unity from its tiny black population. Onlookers, mostly white, gawked from the sidewalks as the demonstrators slowly rounded the corner onto Sunset Avenue. One of the marchers, a young black man, carried a hastily scrawled sign that read, WE WILL STILL LIVE!!! Another marcher, the Reverend Don Jackson, an elderly white man with sheet-white hair, held a Bible close to his chest.

Only four other whites participated in the march alongside the Reverend Jackson: W. R. (Sandy) Grey, the local chairman of the human relations committee, Grey's wife, and two other area ministers. To Grey, the march was a show of solidarity. "I never really thought about it being a protest march," said Grey in 2002 while sitting on the patio at the side

of his home in an upscale enclave of town. "I was just thinking it was to honor King and to show our disapproval of this way of handling racial matters."

At the time of the march, Grey was shocked that more whites didn't share his decision to march alongside Asheboro's black demonstrators. "I remember my wife and I feeling very alone out there," he said. "I swear, I never even thought about it being dangerous. I never thought that somebody might have taken a shot at us or anything like that. Until I got uptown. We were on Fayetteville Street turning onto Sunset, and I looked over and saw these white guys looking pretty hostile and making various comments. Somehow it hit me at that point that this was a little bit risky."

At the time, Grey was a thirty-year-old textile mill owner who'd been sheltered from the fear, resentment, and hostility of racial unrest. Though Grey owned a mill and was surrounded by punch-clock laborers, he was, by his own account, naïve to the ways of the working-class white South. The day after the march, Grey walked into a diner near his mill and sat down for some lunch.

"I guess it was a Monday," he recalled. "Our plant was down, and for lunch I used to walk to this diner to get my exercise. So I walked in and sat down, and there was this group of guys—various tradespeople I knew—sitting around a table and talking about the march. One of them said, 'Did you know there was a white woman marching with that bunch of niggers?' I thought, I wonder if I should tell them that that white woman was my wife?" His eyes wandered for a moment before he finished his thought: "I decided I would not."

The day after the march, the editorial page of the local newspaper made a desperate plea for a politically moderate solution to the tensions rising in Asheboro and across the South. The editorial suggested that citizens of Asheboro should steer clear of militant activists at both extremes of the racial divide, but the writer named only militant black activists who lived three thousand miles away from our small town. It didn't mention the Ku Klux Klan, which had chapters in our own backyard.

"If the reasoning men of both races fail to reaffirm a bond in the wake of the cowardly violence that snuffed out Dr. King's life," the paper declared, "then the Stokely Carmichaels and the Rap Browns of the future will be the Negro spokesmen, and the gun and police power will be the white man's." Later in the editorial, the newspaper showed its true

southern colors: "We don't harbor any such notions that the two races can live in placid harmony under the best of circumstances. . . . But with the assassination of the prime advocate of nonviolence, perhaps now the explicit lawlessness of 'black power' will appear more distinct, as a threat to permanent racial harmony. With violence as the alternative to Dr. King's way, perhaps more will view his passing as a dangerous sacrifice in the civil rights cause."

In another editorial, the paper praised the white citizens of the town for treating the marchers with respect. "If there was a single ugly word said, or a single epithet thrown all during the march, nobody heard it. . . ." the editorialist wrote. "Asheboro should be proud."

The day after the editorial ran, local Ku Klux Klansmen filed for permits in nearby Liberty and Siler City, to march through those towns later in the month. Citing a conflict with a local church event, Liberty's mayor gingerly rejected the Klan. "I would not want this board to encourage any extra activities that day by other groups."

Another editorial appeared later that week regarding the involvement of Grey and the other whites who joined Asheboro's black marchers. "Those white faces that braved criticism perhaps struck a chord of tolerance which we hope exists in abundance somewhere deep in the city's essence."

My parents don't remember the march. They'll tell you precisely where they were and what they were doing on November 22, 1963, when John F. Kennedy was gunned down in Texas, but Mom and Dad are fuzzy on the details of the King assassination. Dr. King was killed six days before my eighth birthday. My mom furrowed her brow when I asked her about that time. "I'm not sure what we were doing," she said. "We were probably helping you plan a birthday party."

The week of the march, Sly and the Family Stone were telling listeners of Top 40 radio in my hometown to "Dance to the Music"; Otis Redding was in the Top 10 with his posthumous "(Sittin' on the) Dock of the Bay"; and the Temptations were crooning their sad hit "I Wish It Would Rain." The Beatles were telling us to "take a sad song and make it better," and the rock band Blue Cheer was in the Top 40 with their bone-crushing, proto–heavy metal cover of Eddie Cochran's '50s rockabilly hit "Summertime Blues."

I remember hearing all of those songs blaring from a radio at the local

public swimming pool. But not long after the assassination, the mood of popular music would change. Aretha Franklin wrote and recorded her hard-driving funk hit "Think," which admonished America to "think about what you're trying to do to me." This sassy demand of a lover to her partner barely veiled the message Franklin was telling the South, specifically, and the nation at large: think about what you're doing to your country. It was one of the first protest songs to insinuate itself into my young psyche. Subconsciously, I must have picked up on the fact that I, too, was being told to think.

Franklin's hit song mingled with the music coming from other places in my hometown. In 1968, country music was king in the diners and factory parking lots around Asheboro. The town's country radio deejay, Perry Hunt, would spin the latest hits: Tammy Wynette's "Stand by Your Man," Sonny James's "Heaven Says Hello," and my favorite at the time, Jeannie C. Riley's sassy "Harper Valley P.T.A." In between those working-class anthems, though, another country singer, the little-known Henson Cargill, sneaked in a socially conscious song called "Skip a Rope," wherein he warns of hating your neighbor "for the shade of his skin." Things were changing, even on country radio in my hometown, and those of us who were listening to music could not escape its messages—even if we were too young to understand the significance of marching down Fayetteville Street.

Phil Walden looked out the back window of his home at the beautiful gardens that glistened in the spring breeze. He's proud of his home, those gardens, and the good life he has today as a result of his association with Otis Redding and all the other African-American artists with whom he came of age in Macon, Georgia.

"It was through my affiliation with musicians—with young black musicians, with Otis Redding, in particular—that I learned about life," said Walden. "Otis was my teacher, he was my preacher, he was my rabbi."

When the civil rights movement that Walden supported so vigorously forced him out of black music in the late '60s, he moved into the world of white rock & roll. This was ironic, considering Walden never really cared much for white music. But black singers no longer needed a white

Phil Walden to manage their careers. Walden, like the studio musicians who'd backed black stars in Muscle Shoals and Memphis, had to find a new place for himself in a rapidly changing world.

The assassination of Martin Luther King Jr. transformed Walden's life in ways he wouldn't have chosen. It transformed the lives of the musicians who worked with black stars. It transformed all of our lives. Like Jesus Christ, Martin Luther King Jr. died for our sins. He died so we could learn to live differently.

Walden put it this way: "Civil rights freed the white southerner, particularly the young white southerner. It gave us grace, it gave us an opportunity to escape the racism and politics of the Old South. We forget what a blessing Martin Luther King Jr. was to the South."

★ Chapter 2 ★

THE CROSSROADS

"**R**EMEMBER *the first time I brought you here?*"

My father and I were headed south on Northside Drive, in Atlanta, away from Phil Walden's home, when we approached the Atlanta Memorial Park, a two-hundred-acre recreational area adjoining the ritzy Bobby Jones Golf Course and Bitsy Grant Tennis Center. It was a bright spring afternoon in 2002, and Dad was feeling nostalgic about a family vacation we took here back in July 1968.

A breeze from the passenger window tousled Dad's helmet of white hair, and when he turned to me and smiled, his eyes squinted into little half-moons and his face glistened red in the sun, making him look like a happy Eskimo.

As we made a left onto Woodward Way and snaked around the park, the rolling hills, manicured sand traps, and velvety greens with flickering triangular flags resonated for my father. For one thing, he was an avid golfer and liked to admire beautiful golf courses; for another, this sprawling chunk of real estate was rich with history, and Dad loved to share history with me.

In July 1864, the patch of land that is now the Atlanta Memorial Park was a very different place. The wealth and grandeur of this tony neighborhood today obscures the bloodbath that occurred here during the Battle of Peachtree Creek, when the Confederate Army made a last-ditch attempt to keep the Union from tightening its grip on the city. It was a monumental defeat for the South: thousands were killed in the five-hour clash, and

*within weeks Union General William Tecumseh Sherman's troops occu-
pied Atlanta. By November, Sherman's soldiers had set fire to the city and
begun their devastating march to the sea.*

*Dad had come along with me on my journey through the South to keep
me company as I traveled from North Carolina to Florida, Georgia,
Alabama, Mississippi, Tennessee, and Kentucky to talk with the musicians
who sparked the southern rock movement and the everyday fans who
spurred its rise. When I was a teenager, Dad didn't understand my passion
for rock & roll. He was a moderate Republican and a sports enthusiast who
desperately wanted me to share with him his love of football and basket-
ball. He once told me in a rage that if I kept listening to the music of cross-
dressing rock stars like David Bowie and Alice Cooper, I'd probably wind
up homosexual.*

*Dad had spent my childhood and his young adulthood working through
the corporate maze of General Electric, trying to provide a better life for our
family than the one he had as a kid raised by a divorced mother. As he
climbed the ladder from a punch-clock tradesman to a management position, he found himself with less time for family outings. On his days off, he
played golf with his friends, and at nights he and my mother would attend
parties and community functions.*

By 1996, when I became music editor of Rolling Stone, *Dad had retired
from work and was beginning to show an interest in my career. Two years
later, when my college honored me as an outstanding alumnus, he was
right there in the front row, beaming as I delivered my acceptance speech.
Later, Dad told me he'd come to appreciate why I spent my teenage years
holed up in my bedroom with records and magazines. He finally saw that
I was learning from music what I couldn't learn from him.*

On that breezy spring day in 2002, we were learning from each other.

Three months after the assassination of Martin Luther King Jr., my family
loaded up the Ford station wagon and drove from our home in Asheboro
to Atlanta, to visit with relatives and see the city's historical sites. I'd never
been to Georgia before and was excited about the trip—more excited than
if we'd been going to the North Carolina mountains or to Myrtle Beach,
South Carolina, where we normally took our vacations.

It was an eight-hour drive, and what I remember most were the quiet miles, when no one was talking. The radio was on, and in each town along the way the deejays would spin music for the listeners in their particular neck of the woods. When we passed through the big cities, like Charlotte or Spartanburg, we'd get the 1968 Top 40—songs like "Mony, Mony," by Tommy James and the Shondells, "Yummy Yummy Yummy," by the Ohio Express, or "Jumpin' Jack Flash," by the Rolling Stones. But in the nooks and crannies—Harpers Ridge, South Carolina; Parkertown Mill, Georgia—it was pure country: Johnny Cash's "Folsom Prison Blues," Porter Wagoner's "Carroll County Accident," Merle Haggard's "The Legend of Bonnie and Clyde."

I processed every song in my head, trying to make sense of the words and the music and the different sounds used in them. Some of the singers had a whine to their voice, making them come off like a spoiled child throwing a temper tantrum; others sounded nasty, as if they were telling a locker-room joke to their friends; still others came off as tough and mean, as if they would pick a fight with you if you said something they didn't want to hear. The music ranged from sunny to dark. Some of the songs had a heavy bass foundation that rumbled in my stomach, even as the music played through tinny car radio speakers; others had a twang that pricked like a knife. I didn't know it at the time, but I was hearing the differences between rhythm & blues, country, and pop.

The drive to Atlanta itself was half the fun of the vacation, but still, I couldn't wait to get there. I was fascinated by Georgia. For all I knew, it could have been Oz, complete with poppy fields and flying monkeys. I'd learned in school about the Battle of Atlanta, how the city had been burned to the ground during the Civil War and then built up again from scratch; the way we learned about the Civil War in school was that it was a tale of working-class resilience as much as it was of victory over slavery. And Georgia was at the center of it all. There was a certain romance to the state: it was the sprawling backdrop to *Gone with the Wind*, it was a soulful song by Ray Charles. But most of all, it fascinated me because I'd always heard my mama call herself a Georgia peach.

She was born in the small town of Carrollton, a community just west of Atlanta where one of her three sisters, Christine, still had a home. Christine's daughter, Delores Garrett, lived with her husband, Bill, and their three children in the bedroom community of Dunwoody, fifteen

miles north of Atlanta. The Garretts were among the few families in our extended clan who were doing well for themselves. Bill was studying to be a lawyer, and within a few years he would move his family to the more upscale suburb of Alpharetta, one of the wealthier outposts of early-'70s white flight.

Bill Garrett was a loud, gregarious character whose later claim to fame was that he represented actor Junior Samples, the lamebrained used-car dealer on TV's *Hee-Haw,* who in real life had a habit of getting arrested on drunk-driving charges. I was impressed with Bill's connection to *Hee-Haw,* because I was a big fan of the country-music variety show. I laughed at the cornball jokes and goofy stereotypes, but most of all I looked forward to hearing Buck Owens, the veteran honky-tonk singer, perform his latest song on his red, white, and blue Mosrite acoustic guitar. I remember asking Bill about *Hee-Haw* once and being disappointed he didn't know much about the show or the stars who appeared on it. Instead, he would pontificate at length about his conservative political views and the virtues of General George Patton, the controversial World War II soldier and anti-Communist who once exclaimed, "Compared to war, all other forms of human endeavor shrink to insignificance."

When we arrived in Dunwoody on that muggy night in 1968, Delores took Mama into the kitchen to catch up on the family gossip while Bill and my father exchanged pleasantries and retreated to the living room. The eldest Garrett boy, Dudley, went into his bedroom and reemerged with his pet iguana. As the two of us played together on the floor, Daddy told Bill that he planned to take the family on a day trip into Atlanta the next day, before we headed to Six Flags that weekend. He asked if Bill had any suggestions as to what we should see. Bill looked at my father skeptically and warned him to be careful: the inner city, he said, had been taken over by blacks.

I don't remember the word Bill Garrett used for African-Americans that night, but I do remember being shocked by the comment. I was sitting on the floor of his living room playing with a prehistoric-looking creature, and this confident man who admired Patton was expressing a fear of other human beings. I didn't get it. And I didn't like it.

★ ★ ★

The next morning, Daddy said he was going to take me to see the Georgia state capitol while my mother and sister went shopping. As we drove into downtown Atlanta, I could see the building's gold dome shining above the city like a beacon. A fifteen-foot statue of Miss Freedom stood atop the dome, holding a torch above her head like the Statue of Liberty, looking as if she were piloting the sun, leading some kind of Apollonian march for redemption. We were at the crossroads of southern culture: the city Sherman burned to the ground on his way to making America at last free for all of its citizens—and horribly divided.

As we walked across the concrete plaza to the building's four-story portico supported by six massive Corinthian columns, I shivered with nervous energy. This was the most magnificent site I'd ever seen. When we entered the building, I stopped in the middle of the rotunda and looked around at the sweeping marble staircases; above me, the gold dome soared 240 feet high, like a giant umbrella. It made me feel dizzy.

"Look, son," Daddy said to me, pointing to a line of people forming outside a door. "It says here it's open-house Wednesday. Looks like we can go meet the governor today."

We took our place in line, and when it came our turn, we walked into a large room where a thin, bespectacled man stood up, smiled, and warmly welcomed us into his lair. It was the governor, and Daddy told him we had traveled all the way from North Carolina to see him. The governor motioned for a photographer to come over and snap a picture of us all together.

"Now, listen heeyah," he said in his big Georgia drawl. "You take this picture back to your governor over there in Raleigh, and you tell him I treated you right." It was all very exciting to me. I didn't know anything about this man, but I knew he was powerful, and I was thrilled by his doting attention.

His name was Lester Garfield Maddox. It wasn't until years later that I would learn more about this mousy-looking man with the trademark black-rimmed glasses. Four years before our visit, Maddox had become notorious for his zealous defiance of civil rights laws. When he was younger, he'd been known to brandish a gun and chase African-Americans out of his Atlanta short-order grill, the Pickrick. He even once took an ax handle to the hood of a black minister's car. His white customers were said to have stood behind him, with ax handles of their own,

as Maddox terrorized blacks. When the restaurant owner became governor, in 1967, his supporters and detractors alike called him Lester "Ax Handle" Maddox.

Later, my father and mother visited the governor's souvenir shop in the tourist ghetto of Underground Atlanta and were appalled to find that, in addition to all the Lester Maddox wristwatches and other tawdry ephemera, the store actually sold keepsake replicas of the ax handles of the governor's racist glory days.

"They were real, too. They weren't just little plastic toys," Dad tells me today. "And people were buying them."

Maddox always maintained that liberals and intellectuals misunderstood him. He was a populist politician, he said, who spoke for the workingman and believed in states' rights. He insisted that race wasn't the issue for him, that his concern was the federal government's meddling in local business practices. His justification for his behavior was all too common in the South in the mid-'60s, and when Maddox was elected governor with the backing of the Ku Klux Klan, Martin Luther King Jr. was moved to announce he was "ashamed to be a Georgian." The governor returned the barb, calling King an "enemy of our country." When Maddox whimpered away from office in January 1971, he and his fellow bully segregationists were fast becoming political dinosaurs.

On that hot August afternoon back in 1968, my dad and I left the Georgia state capitol building with a photograph and a memory that would haunt me as I became a teenager and my political views made a left turn.

That same summer, in Macon, about an hour and a half south of Atlanta, the deaths of Otis Redding and Dr. King weighed heavily on Phil Walden's mind. He'd valiantly managed Redding's career for years, but now that black musicians had decided to make a stronger political statement by pulling away from their white colleagues, Walden was looking for a new direction.

One idea he came up with was to start a recording studio in Macon, much like Rick Hall's Fame, over in Muscle Shoals. Walden decided to put together a studio band like the Muscle Shoals Rhythm Section and cut songs for his own label, which he would call Capricorn Records. But

Hall told Walden about a young and gangly white blues guitarist named Duane Allman, who'd been doing sessions at Fame. Walden listened to tapes of Allman's playing and was blown away by the young guitarist's soulful style of bottleneck slide guitar.

"I flew over to Muscle Shoals and when I walked in, they were taking a break," Walden remembered, recounting a story he's told countless times. "I saw this longhaired hippie boy sitting over in a corner by himself, just noodling on his guitar. Well, I walked over to him and I said, 'Are you Duane Allman?'

"He said, 'Yeah.'

"I said, 'Well, I'm Phil Walden.'

"He said, 'Yeah, man, I know all about you and everything. What are you doing over here?'

"I said, 'I was wondering if we could have lunch today. I got something I want to propose to you.'

"He said, 'What is it you want to propose?'

"I said, 'I've got an idea about putting together a band, and I want to be your manager.'

"He said, 'You got it.'

"I said, 'Well, now, hold on, let's talk about it at lunch.'

"He said, 'Naw, man, we don't need to talk about anything. I'm flattered. You managed Otis Redding.'"

Walden signed on as Allman's manager, but he didn't know exactly what he was going to do with him. Allman was too good a player to be just another anonymous member of a studio rhythm section, but he didn't have much marquee value on his own, aside from playing with the little-known band Hourglass with his brother, Gregg. Still, Walden took a gamble and talked the young guitarist into moving to Macon.

"People got very upset when I took Duane and said I was going to put together a band around him," said Walden. "I mean, he was the hottest session man in the country. But he had a bigger vision. It was so much bigger than playing behind a singer in a studio."

Walden saw the future of rock & roll and it was Duane Allman. If the veteran manager could put together a band of young, hungry, white rockers from the South who made music based on all the sounds and feelings and experiences they'd grown up with during the '50s and '60s, it just might hit a nerve in mainstream America.

"Duane was pure. What he was saying in his music—it had everything to do with the southern thing," Walden said. "He liked a lot of the Stax stuff and a lot of jazz stuff—Miles Davis, John Coltrane, and all that—but the times were changing, and Duane knew he needed to take all that stuff that was in him and create something new, give it a new sensibility."

First, Walden introduced Allman to a black percussionist from Gulfport, Mississippi, named Jai Johanny Johanson, who'd played behind Otis Redding. Then Allman enlisted a buddy of his own from Florida, bass player Berry Oakley, who in turn brought along a country-influenced guitarist named Dickey Betts. Allman's younger brother, Gregg, had returned to Los Angeles when Hourglass broke up.

The Hourglass had been disillusioned by the West Coast music establishment, which tried to siphon the "southern" out of the Allmans' sound. As Gregg Allman explained to *Rolling Stone* writer Cameron Crowe, "Duane got fed up, and when my brother got fed up, he got *fed up*. 'Fuck this!' he kept yelling. 'Fuck this whole thing. Fuck wearing these weird clothes. Fuck playing this "In-A-Gadda-Da-Vida" shit. Fuck it all!' "

Liberty Records, the Hourglass's label, wanted to turn the band into just another bluesy folk-pop combo in the mold of such L.A. acts as the Byrds or Buffalo Springfield. In 1967, the Byrds had run into a Georgia boy in Los Angeles, Gram Parsons, who encouraged the band to emphasize the country sound in its Beatlesque blend of folk and rock. That led to the Byrds' classic album *Sweetheart of the Rodeo*, which arguably was the first-ever popular fusion of rock and country. Another group, the Nitty Gritty Dirt Band, who had brought the Allmans to their label, Liberty Records, had been toying with country rock, too, though in more of a tongue-in-cheek way. Still, the Dirt Band's blending of banjo and fiddles into its '60s rock sound gave a certain legitimacy to southern country music. In 1967 the Dirt Band scored a modest hit with the gentle "Buy for Me the Rain."

The only other West Coast band with a real southern singer who'd left none of her musical roots behind was San Francisco's Big Brother & the Holding Company, whose front woman, Janis Joplin, sang with a soul-wrenching country-blues wail that evoked both the grit of Etta James and the twang of Loretta Lynn. On songs like "Down On Me" and "Easy Rider," from Big Brother's 1967 debut album, Joplin and her psychedelic cohorts performed what was perhaps the first real evidence of the south-

ern rock that would sweep the nation. Like Joplin, Gregg Allman had a gospel-tinged voice that was much too big for the folk-rock sound of Sunset Strip. So the Hourglass decided to hightail it back to the South.

Getting out of its record contract was not so easy for the band. Liberty wanted the good-looking Gregg Allman on its roster and threatened to sue the band. The company's lawyers forced Gregg to return to L.A. to fulfill the contract. Duane stayed behind as Gregg sat in L.A. recording sessions, listening to a twenty-six-piece orchestra ruin the songs he had written or chosen for the band to record. "Together," Gregg told Cameron Crowe of the music he and his brother released as the Hourglass, "those two records form what is known as a shit sandwich."

Meanwhile, Duane was traveling back and forth between Macon and the Allmans' hometown of Jacksonville, Florida. He told Phil Walden that Gregg would be the perfect singer for their new band and said he'd give his brother a call and try to get him to come back home. Feeling lonely and despondent in Los Angeles, Gregg Allman decided to give it a shot. "I had been building the nerve to put a pistol to my head," he later wrote in a letter to Crowe. "Then Duane called and told me he had a band. . . . I put my thumb out and caught the first thing smokin' for Jacksonville."

Former Hourglass members Paul Hornsby and Johnny Sandlin weren't so confident of the new group. "Rock bands from the South just didn't make it at that time," said Sandlin. Hornsby said he didn't want to get his hopes up just to be told once again that the music didn't fit into a corporate strategy. "Our spirits were pretty broken," he said. "That whole Hourglass thing left a pretty bad taste in our mouths." He and Sandlin stayed behind the scenes, working as producers, engineers, and musicians with Walden's Capricorn record company.

With the arrival of Gregg, the Allman Brothers' sound began to coalesce. Duane was clearly the leader, but it was the group's mix of musicians and styles—blues, soul, gospel, country, and jazz—that would ignite the fire that swept across the South in the early '70s.

The Allman Brothers' first album, released in 1969, redefined the boundaries of rock & roll. Its soulful blend of blues standards and original songs integrated the power of rock with jazzy improvisation and a hallucino-

genic swirl of effects. But the psychedelic sound that the Allman Brothers created in songs like "Dreams" had little to do with the loose improvisation of San Francisco's Grateful Dead or the studio wizardry of England's Pink Floyd. This psychedelic music conveyed the ambiance of the Deep South—the mournful echo of a country church choir, the lonesome moan of a Mississippi farmhand, the exasperated cry of a confused trailer boy. This was southern music, but it was like nothing that had ever been heard before.

The music knocked Charlie Daniels out of his rut. "Everybody had been kind of looking around for something to do, and here come the Allman Brothers," said Daniels, who had just put out his solo debut, a set of nondescript country-folk songs, when he first heard the Allmans. "They were like, 'To hell with everything, we're going to do it the way we want to do it.' And they were fantastic. I mean, that band just personified the South."

In 1970, the Allmans released an even stronger second album. If their self-titled debut had redefined rock's boundaries, *Idlewild South* stretched them further, bringing country music into the fusion of blues, rock, jazz, and gospel. By 1971, only three years into the group's existence, the Allman Brothers Band was the biggest and most influential rock act in America. That year, they put out a live album they'd recorded in New York City's East Village. *At Fillmore East* became one of the pivotal records of the rock era, kindling the coals of the southern rock explosion to come. Anyone who was young and conscious at that time heard the big, fat bottleneck slide-guitar lick that jump-starts "Statesboro Blues" and the chugging, Harley-engine bass line that gives the haunting "Whipping Post" its momentum.

This multiracial outfit of hippies and rednecks created a soundtrack that relieved young southerners of the weightiness of their guilt, fear, and economic insecurities: the family legacies of racism, the drudgeries of a rural, working-class existence. The Allmans' ambitious mix of musical styles was sonic integration at its purest. For restless young people all across the South, this music communicated stuff that couldn't be learned from books or from teachers, parents, or clergymen. This music went straight to the intuitive part of the human soul.

★ ★ ★

My sister got her driver's license in July 1971. Shortly thereafter, Daddy brought home a shiny blue Mustang Mach I for her birthday. I don't think Cheri ever liked the car all that much, but Daddy and I sure did. We'd stand out in the driveway, in our shorts and T-shirts, in the ninety-degree heat, and circle around it over and over, inspecting every curve and cleft of its lean and low body. We projected our latent NASCAR fantasies onto its powerful, 350 V-8 engine and soot-gray racing stripes that ran across its sides. When Daddy cranked her up, that Mach I's engine roared like one of those monster cars down at the Charlotte Motor Speedway.

Inside, it had deep bucket seats, an eight-track tape deck, and huge Pioneer speakers mounted into the back panel that blasted music much louder than the stereo in our house did. I loved that car. With my sister behind the wheel, it was a white-trash Cadillac piloted by a pot-smoking, bell-bottomed, blond-haired hippie girl whom I adored unconditionally.

When Cheri drove me to the swimming pool that summer, I'd crack the window to let the warm air blow in my face, close my eyes, lie back in the passenger seat, and soak in the music from whatever tape she shoved into the deck. One of her favorites was the T. Rex glam-rock classic *Electric Warrior*. She'd make me listen to the track "Jeepster," in which singer Marc Bolan grunted and groaned orgasmically at the end of the song: "Girl, I'm just a jeepster for your love." And then, with more attitude than I'd ever heard in a rock & roll song: "Girl, I'm just a *vampire* for your love—and I'm gonna suck yaahh! Oh, oh, oh."

Cheri would crank the volume way up for that vampire line and scream along with the words—". . . and I'm gonna suck yaahh!"—as loud as she could. Afterward, she'd turn to me with a devilish smile and say, "Isn't that just the coolest song in the world?"

It was cool, all right. And sexy. Aside from the Rolling Stones, T. Rex was the sexiest-sounding rock band of them all. But I was eleven years old and didn't understand the full implications of "sexy." I knew what it felt like, what it sounded like, and what it looked like, but I didn't have a word for it yet.

One day, Cheri tried to explain to me the difference between "sexy" and "cool." I had asked her why girls liked Mick Jagger so much, even though Keith Richards was clearly the cooler of the two Rolling Stones. I always loved Jagger, but I thought he was ugly and grotesque with his

protruding lips, awkward snarl, and spastic moves. It seemed to me that Richards was the good-looking one; he was cool, and I equated cool with desirable.

"You just don't get it," Cheri said to me. "Mick Jagger's not good-looking, but he's sexy."

I *didn't* get it. But if Jagger was sexy and sexy was desirable, then naturally I wanted to be Jagger, not Richards. I wanted to be the singer of a rock band and have girls swoon over my spastic moves. I could identify with spastic. I was never good at sports, because every time a ball came close to my face, I'd shut my eyes and recoil. The jocks laughed at me. That wasn't very cool. It drove me further into my own head.

I understood Mick Jagger. His gracelessness compelled me. What's more, in 1971 he sang lyrics such as, "Please, Sister Morphine, turn my nightmares into dreams." Those words spoke to me. Jagger was bigger than life, and he was singing about something that would turn my nightmares into dreams. I wanted whatever it was he was peddling. Life had become a major nightmare for me. I was ridiculed for wearing my hair longer than that of most of my fellow male classmates and mocked for my sensitivity to any disparaging word my classmates would say to me or some other poor soul who didn't fit the accepted mold. I was sensitive, all right—and angry.

At school, blacks had been integrated into the system for three years. I would see the white kids and coaches praise the black kids for their athletic abilities and then call them niggers behind their backs. I watched students terrorize the homely April Ragsdale and the athletically challenged Martin Nicholson more viciously than if they'd been white.

One day, Martin and I were among two of the last boys waiting to be picked for kickball. I don't recall why, but we got into an argument that led to a fistfight. Soon, Martin and I were rolling on the ground. The other guys stood over us, laughing and telling us we were fighting like girls. Martin and I became friends that day and have remained so throughout our lives. In later years, we'd do drugs together and talk about the injustice of the school's social and racial hierarchy. But in 1971, we were just scared.

In the South, my befriending a sensitive black boy and not liking sports meant one thing: I was a nigger-loving faggot. No one ever actually called *me* that, but as I internalized the behavior of the popular kids

and heard them use that kind of language to deride other kids, I came to the conclusion that something must be very wrong with me.

In my sixth-grade health class, we were learning about the dangers of drugs. With the rise of the hippies, drugs had become the talk of the decade and were showing up in every rural and suburban community in America. In class, we watched films of teenagers having "bad trips." They'd take LSD and sit in a corner with their hands to their faces, colors swirling around them, while the music of psychedelic rock bands like Jefferson Airplane reverberated all around them.

"Remember what the dormouse said: Feed your head," howled Jefferson Airplane's mystical front woman, Grace Slick. "Feed your head." Everything in my life seemed to be turning into one big ball of confusion, and those bad trips began to look pretty good to me. One day in the school bathroom, Michael Roper, one of the handful of black kids in my class, told me about heroin.

Michael Roper looked like the preteen Michael Jackson. He had a big Afro and a cocky strut. He put thumbtacks on the bottoms of his shoes so that when he swaggered down the halls, his feet would tap rhythmically with each step. Michael was the coolest guy I knew, but I was frightened of him. Frightened and intrigued. When he talked about heroin, it sounded pretty good, though it seemed to me that marijuana would be more accessible. As it turned out, Michael was all talk, but the seed was planted. I planned to find out where I could get some pot, and I would smoke it.

No one knew any of this, of course. I didn't talk about it with my parents or even my sister—yet. I would write school papers on the dangers of drugs, but my parents and teachers just thought I was interested in the topic and praised me for my impeccable research. I memorized every drug ever made—what each one would do to you, what classification it fell under: narcotic, amphetamine, hallucinogen. I was a virtual encyclopedia of drugs, but no one ever suspected that my curiosity might be a warning sign.

"Please, Sister Morphine, turn my nightmares into dreams," Mick Jagger pleaded in a voice that was at once innocent and corrupt. I understood innocent and corrupt. I *felt* innocent and corrupt. I wanted to be Mick Jagger.

Until I discovered Gregg Allman.

★　★　★

Cheri was taking me for a ride through the rolling hills between Asheboro and Charlotte one afternoon when she reached into the glove box, pulled out a brand-new eight-track tape, and held it in front of my face.

"Listen, Mark," she instructed, looking straight ahead at the narrow country road as though she were the keeper of all the world's knowledge. "It's this band; they're called the Allman Brothers." She turned to me and squinted her eyes: "They're from Georgia."

Georgia?

I couldn't picture a rock band from Georgia. The place had a lot of associations for me, but rock & roll wasn't one of them. To me, rock & roll was the stuff of modern British mythology, made by scrawny English guys like Mick Jagger and Marc Bolan, who wore frilly shirts, flashy boots, and skintight pants. Mama had told me that Elvis Presley was somehow connected to the birth of rock & roll, but in 1971, I couldn't see it. To me, Elvis was country, a hayseed from Mississippi.

Back then, though, that's how all southerners came off in the media. From as far back as I could remember, I'd watched sitcoms like *The Andy Griffith Show* and *The Beverly Hillbillies*, and howl at the ignorance and stupidity of the characters Gomer and Goober Pyle, Barney Fife, and Jethro Bodine. The real-life southern characters who appeared on the nightly news weren't much different—but their behavior wasn't so funny.

In the early 1960s, America watched as southern lawmen such as T. Eugene "Bull" Connor, a "public safety" officer in Birmingham, Alabama, unleashed vicious attack dogs and high-powered fire hoses on black demonstrators. In 1963, when I was three years old, George Wallace was voted governor of Alabama by the biggest margin for a gubernatorial election ever in that state's history. In his inaugural address, he claimed to speak for the entire South when he announced to the nation, "I draw the line in the dust and toss the gauntlet before the feet of tyranny, and I say segregation now, segregation tomorrow, segregation forever." Five months later, TV cameras captured a grotesque image of Wallace standing at the doors of the University of Alabama, refusing to allow entrance to two black students. The footage was beamed from New York to California and repeated over and over, well into my college years.

By 1971, those images were embedded in America's collective consciousness. For an eleven-year-old boy growing up in the South, the notion of a prominent white, male southern role model was one mess of

contradictions. So when my sister held up that Allman Brothers eight-track, I couldn't imagine what a rock & roll band from Georgia could offer me that the Rolling Stones wouldn't deliver with far more sympathy and taste.

We cruised further into the countryside, and the acoustic intro of the leadoff track, "Revival," gave way to dueling harmony guitars, a sweet, soulful organ part that sounded as though it was coming from one of the tiny churches at the side of the road we were traveling, and a funky foundation of bass and percussion. Toward the end of the song, the guitars and organ dropped out completely, leaving only bass and drums and a chorus of singers chanting the words "People can you feel it, love is everywhere." Damn, if I didn't feel it! I felt warm inside, as though everything would be all right. The music reminded me of the gospel songs I'd heard when my mama and I would pass by the old black tent revivals on Loach Street in the part of Asheboro that my grandmother referred to as "Colored Town."

I pulled the eight-track from the tape deck and studied the grainy group shot on the cover. There was Gregg Allman, his long blond hair parted down the middle, just like mine was beginning to do. His rapt blue eyes betrayed not the face of southern stupidity or intolerance, but they mirrored the resignation I would hear as he moaned the words to the album's final track: "Think I'll drink up a little more wine, to ease my worried mind / Walk down on the street, and leeeeeve my blues at home."

There were skeletons in this man's closet, just as there were skeletons in mine, even though I had yet to reach my teens. There were skeletons in the closet of the entire South, a truth that simultaneously fascinated and terrified me. It was too much for me to comprehend totally at eleven, and though I shared a lot of my feelings with my sister, I didn't feel comfortable telling her everything. I had no words for all of it. So I let the Allman Brothers Band hold it for me for a while.

★ Chapter 3 ★

DÉJÀ VOODOO

T HAT *summer, Patricia Fournier landed her first job.*

It was 1971, and Trish was between the eighth and ninth grades at Charles J. Colton Junior High School, in New Orleans. She and her older sister, Becky, had spent most of their summer break lazing around the house listening to music or hanging out in the steamy Louisiana heat with their best friends, Shaun and Derisue. One July afternoon, Shaun's mother approached the girls about a part-time job she'd heard of that would pay them ten bucks a week.

"She phoned up our mom and told her we'd be taking political contributions on the side of the road; they called it can shaking," said Fournier, who today works as an insurance adjuster in Atlanta and goes by her married name, Patricia Goddard. "My mom was like, 'Sure, that sounds great.' She thought it'd be good experience for us."

The girls were jazzed about the job. "Ten bucks a week—we'd never seen that kind of money in our lives," Goddard said. "Plus, they'd be paying for our lunch, which meant we could eat fast food every day. That was something our parents wouldn't let us do."

The morning of their first day of work, a friendly young couple, David and Chloe, came by to pick up Trish and Becky and take them on their rounds. They instructed the girls on what to do, how to act, and what to say to get the biggest donations. Trish and Becky weren't on the beat for long before they realized the money they were collecting was going to George Wallace's 1972 presidential campaign. They knew this wouldn't sit well

with their parents—McGovern Democrats who'd taught their daughters that whites were no better than blacks.

George Wallace represented everything that Lourdes and Barbara Fournier wanted to change about people's perceptions of the South. If they found out their girls were taking contributions for Alabama's notorious governor, Trish thought, they wouldn't let them go back the next day.

As Goddard related the story to me, her eyes widened and her speech became more animated: "But wait—it gets better."

"One day," she continued, "Chloe takes us over to their headquarters at this building in a part of town near the garage where my father worked as a mechanic. David was there, and Chloe had stopped by to pick him up. Well, when we walked into that place—holy shit!—there was all kinds of propaganda everywhere: literature and leaflets, the rebel flag, the Nazi flag. It was scary."

The girls lingered in the front room while Chloe went into the back to get David. Becky, the more daring of the two sisters, began stuffing things into her purse. "She picked up these tickets like you'd get at a movie theater or a carnival," said Goddard. "Only these tickets were free tickets back to Africa." She paused, lowered her voice, and continued in a slow, measured, and dramatic tone: "And on the back of those tickets, it said the bearer gets a free bunch of bananas, a spear, a tin of grease for their hair, and a few other horrible things."

Goddard stopped to check my reaction to the story. After I responded with a horrified "No shit," she continued in a rapid-fire delivery: "Well, I was totally scared, but my sister, she was like, 'Listen, Trish, we can't tell Mama, you hear me? Don't you say a word about this or I'll kick your ass, because we're making ten bucks a week and if you tell Mama and Daddy, you'll ruin it for us.'"

A few weeks later, police in neighboring Gulfport, Mississippi, caught up with the renegade can shakers and arrested Chloe and two other adults (David was not with the group on that trip). The girls were detained while their parents came to pick them up. Apparently, David and Chloe had been collecting the money fraudulently.

That day, the Fourniers found out David's last name. It was Duke. David Duke, former Grand Wizard of the Ku Klux Klan.

★ ★ ★

Patricia Goddard looked up from the bistro table where she was sitting in the lobby of the Atlanta hotel. The morning sun shone brightly through floor-to-ceiling windows, and when the forty-four-year-old mother of three smiled, her eyes sloped into little crinkles at the sides. Her long, straight, reddish-brown hair, streaked with blond highlights, lay gently on her loose-fitting blue turtleneck sweater.

"Wanna see something?" she asked, reaching into her bag and pulling out several old, tattered souvenirs her sister Becky had lifted from David Duke's headquarters all those years ago. She held up a red, white, and blue license plate that read, GEORGE WALLACE FOR PRESIDENT, then unrolled some of the bogus "back to Africa" tickets. "This is what we walked into that day."

Goddard, whom I had met on a Web site devoted to the Allman Brothers Band, agreed to come talk with me about her childhood in New Orleans, where she grew up with the sounds of jazz and blues and the rhythms of the Caribbean. She had moved to Georgia several years earlier, but the ordeal with the Dukes still haunted her. She told me it was one in a series of events that led to her earliest childhood awakening—the day she first heard Duane Allman play guitar.

It was a couple of months after the girls' showdown in Gulfport, and Trish, dressed in her usual patent-leather shoes and skirt, was lounging on the couch in the living room of the Fourniers' small shotgun house on Music Street. "My sister came running into the room with her little transistor radio, and she hands it over to me and says, 'Hurry up, put the earphone in and listen to this!' "

Becky had been listening to an FM rock radio station when the deejay announced he was getting ready to play a song she'd heard before by Derek and the Dominos, the early-'70s supergroup driven by the wailing guitars of Allman and Eric Clapton.

"She says, 'Now, go in Mama and Daddy's room and shut the doors and listen to this guy play guitar. Hurry!' " said Goddard. "So like always, I did what she told me: I went into my parents' bedroom, closed off the double doors, and laid down and listened to this song called 'Layla.' "

Trish was mesmerized. In all her thirteen years, she'd never heard anything like this. She'd heard the brassy sounds of Dixieland and the scratchy blues of the Mississippi Delta; she'd heard the one-step, two-step waltzes of Cajun and its Creole sister zydeco; and she'd heard the syrupy pop and country hits that played on the local AM stations. But she'd

never heard anything like the siren of guitars that kicked off "Layla." It was as though the song had been written specifically for little Trish Fournier.

"It made me want to hear more, immediately," said Goddard. "So my sister went out and bought the Allman Brothers' *Beginnings* and turned me on to songs like 'Whipping Post' and 'Dreams.' We had this little pink record player that we shared. I remember Becky used to say to me, 'If you scratch that record, your ass is grass.' "

The Allman Brothers Band changed Goddard's life. "This might sound dramatic, but to me, Duane Allman was like the Second Coming. When my sister and I would listen to that band, we were like . . ." She trailed off, shrugged her shoulders, and arched her eyebrows into a kind of "what can I say?" look. It was a knowing expression that she wouldn't have given to anyone who wasn't also born and raised south of the Mason-Dixon Line. Goddard sensed that I understood her feelings, and she trusted me, even though she'd met me little more than an hour earlier.

"*You* know what I mean," she continued. "Here's this lanky, skinny, red-haired, Tennessee-born, Florida-bred kid—poor, no money, daddy died—and the moment you heard him, you just knew he was going to change everything. He was speaking for us."

Allman wasn't the only guitarist on that FM station that made Trish and Becky's insides feel like Jell-O. The two sisters also liked the chunky, sexy riffs of Rolling Stones guitarist Keith Richards. "We loved the Stones. We really did," said Goddard. "But there was something about the Stones that didn't quite connect with my life. They played the right kind of music, but they never really affected me in that . . ." She trailed off again. "I don't know how to describe it. I can't put my finger on it. It just didn't totally speak to me. It didn't speak to us as a people."

The Stones' music did speak to some young southerners, though, particularly those who were a few years older than Goddard and me. For southern youths who had gone off to college or left the South, the Stones' "You Can't Always Get What You Want" spoke to their emotional and psychological yearnings in the waning days of the Vietnam War and civil rights movement. For those who were coming back from the war or who had friends who wouldn't be coming back, the Stones' music seemed more gritty and honest than the idealistic rhetoric of many of the hippie

rock bands of the period. For young southerners who'd grown up with the mixed messages coming from country music on the one hand and blues on the other, the Stones combined the deep feelings expressed in both forms of southern music and spat it back out in snarling sarcasm. These British thugs seemed to understand the absurdity and hypocrisy of the South better than any other young rock band of the era. And the images they presented in their songs were at once frightening and exhilarating.

In his book *The True Adventures of the Rolling Stones*, southern writer Stanley Booth wrote brilliantly and movingly about the Stones' impact on him when, as a young reporter for *Rolling Stone* magazine, he met the band and first heard a recording of their infamous rape song "Midnight Rambler": "As I sat on that Naugahyde couch, in crazy sixties-end Los Angeles, roaring from the speakers were such sounds, such low-down human groans and cries not new, old as time, almost, but never on a record had they seemed so threatening."

Booth described the music as an amalgamation of the noises he heard in the woods outside his bedroom window when he was a twelve-year-old boy growing up in the southern Georgia swampland: ". . . [T]he sounds of animals crying far off in the woods . . . the sounds the black woods hands made having what they called church, far off in the woods, the all-night drums, like the heartbeat of the dark swampy woods, *boom*dada *boom*dada . . ."

This British band had brought Booth full circle, back to the American South, back to the land he tromped as a child, back to his father and his grandfather and the frightening images of the black men whom young white southerners were warned never to trust. "If there had suddenly appeared before me one of the men my grandfather worked with and whom I loved so much," Booth wrote, "loved their voices and their looks, their yellow eyeballs and smooth bulging black muscles, transformed by poison whiskey . . . into a mad death-wielding animal, I could have stayed calm enough and steady enough in my terror to shoot him." For Booth, the Stones had re-created the terror of the deepest and darkest aspects of the South, the fear instilled in all of us raised in a culture that sought some kind of redemption in its fear of the black man.

For young southerners such as Patricia Goddard and me, though, the Stones were superstars, had always been superstars, and would always be superstars. By 1971, the Stones had hit the top of the pop charts with

"Brown Sugar" from *Sticky Fingers*, which they recorded in Muscle Shoals, with members of the Muscle Shoals Rhythm Section. Though it had the husky feel of southern soul, "Brown Sugar" was offensive on almost every level. Listening to it now, the song comes off more like minstrel music than an honest updating of the blues.

"Gold Coast slave ships bound for cotton fields," Mick Jagger sang, "sold in markets down in New Orleans . . . ooooh, Brown Sugar," he moaned, "how come you taste so good . . . just like a black girl should?"

When Jagger put his mocking twang to another song, "Dead Flowers," imitating a redneck in a heroin den, it came off like the stereotypes of every white, working-class southerner we'd ever seen on television. For young southerners who wanted to distance themselves from those stereotypes, these songs were panaceas. They provided a buffer between us and the rest of our culture, allowing us to compartmentalize any feelings of shame and inferiority we had, if only for four minutes at a time. If we listened to "Dead Flowers," we didn't have to think of ourselves as being those ignorant hillbillies on TV. We were different. We were Stones fans. We could laugh at those *other* southerners. Yet no matter how much we loved the sound of the Stones' music, it was ultimately window dressing, theater, comedy, a Band-Aid—there's no way it could ever touch us at our deepest core.

Even the more dignified Eric Clapton, who could out-technique many of the very Chicago and Mississippi bluesmen he aped, seemed more like a musicologist. When he performed blues standards such as "Sitting on Top of the World" or "Born Under a Bad Sign," it was as though he was giving us little lectures through the trebly sting of his Stratocaster.

But "Layla" was different. Duane Allman, the second guitarist on the song, seemed at once out of place in the music and right on target. When Clapton wailed, "What do you do when you get lonely," Allman's guitar made sounds that were empathetic to the lyrics' agony. What none of us knew when "Layla" first came out was that no one had planned for the young guitarist to play on the song in the first place.

Allman happened to be in Miami in late 1970, when Clapton's Derek and the Dominos were in town recording their debut album at Criteria Studios. He had come by the studio to meet his longtime British guitar hero. Clapton asked the younger musician to sit in on the session, and as

it turned out, Allman wound up playing on the whole album. The day he strapped on his guitar to rehearse what Clapton described as "a little ditty" called "Layla," it was as though the two had been working together all their lives. Allman suggested they speed up the song, then he tore into a twelve-note introduction that would become one of rock's most recognizable melodies.

"He wrote the riff," Clapton told biographer Michael Schumacher. "I just had the main body of the song and it wasn't enough."

Shortly after the album came out, Allman recalled the ease with which he and Clapton collaborated during the "Layla" sessions. "He greeted me like an old partner or something. . . ." Allman told *Guitar Player* magazine. "I was going to play on one or two, and then as we kept going, it kept developing. . . . I'm as satisfied with my work on that as I possibly could be."

So were young southerners such as Patricia Goddard and me. In those tumultuous years, Allman's guitar sound on "Layla"—as well as his work on his own band's renditions of "Stormy Monday" and "Statesboro Blues"—burned away some of the confusion. By then, several other songs on the free-form FM rock radio stations that had proliferated across the country beginning in the late '60s spoke to us, too: Leon Russell's "Shoot Out on the Plantation," the Band's "The Night They Drove Old Dixie Down," Janis Joplin's "Me and Bobby McGee," ZZ Top's "(Somebody Else Been) Shaking Your Tree," and the Allmans' "Revival (Love Is Everywhere)." Before long, FM radio became like twelve-step support groups for disaffected young people, where rock stars such as Duane Allman were our peers, sharing with us their experiences and their hopes through music.

In late 2001, three months before I began my journey across the southern states to talk with people like Patricia Goddard, I posted messages on several rock-band Web sites including those dedicated to the Allmans, Lynyrd Skynyrd, and the Charlie Daniels Band. I was looking to speak with people around my age about what this music meant to them then and how it has colored their views in the years since. I got all kinds of responses. Some were supportive, others were merely inquisitive, and still others expressed a leeriness of my motives.

Donnah Dunthorn, a forty-one-year-old librarian from Fort Myers, Florida, wondered if I was the kind of southern writer who had moved to New York City because I felt superior to my own people. "What I seek clarification of is your personal attitude towards us," she wrote to me. "I have noticed some writers from the South have internalized negative attitudes of others towards us: 'Yes, I'm from here, but I don't suck like they (other southerners) do; I am like you (northerners),' or 'We used to suck, but we've gotten past that now and no longer suck. We are *almost* like you now.'" Then she asked, "What's your take on this?"

The question was valid. I wrote back to Donnah Dunthorn, telling her that I hoped to work out my own feelings in the book. Part of me did feel superior, although deep down I knew better. I had to ask myself exactly what it was that made me feel this way. I had to ask myself why I felt the need to trash my Lynyrd Skynyrd albums and replace them with punk and art rock when I got to college. I had to ask myself why I chose to leave North Carolina in my midtwenties and run to New York City for a job that didn't yet exist. Was it all a reaction to my feelings of shame, guilt, and inadequacy? Or did I genuinely feel that the legacy of "my own people" had created an environment in which I could no longer live comfortably? These were things I planned to explore. I didn't have the answers.

I did know this: By the time I arrived in New York, in 1986, I had begun to drink so heavily that on particularly bad benders my behavior with regard to racial issues turned to the bizarre. One night, outside of King Tut's Wah-Wah Hut, a drinking hole in the East Village, I was so out of my mind that I began haranguing the bouncer for the bar's "racist policies." The Wah-Wah Hut happened to be one of the least racist establishments in the city. My reading of the atmosphere inside the bar that night was totally a product of my own mental and emotional confusion.

Before I arrived in New York, I had worked for three years as a newspaper reporter in Burlington, North Carolina. I covered the crime beat, and each morning I would go to the sheriff's office, police department, and 911 communications center to collect arrest records and ambulance reports from the previous night. At those offices, white cops, magistrates, and dispatchers sometimes would be standing around making racist jokes. This bothered me, and one day I asked one of the dispatchers if he minded not talking like that when I was in the room. He looked at me as though I was a party pooper, and it made me feel like I'd felt when I was

in the company of the jocks in high school—alienated and guilty. Experiences such as those led to my decision to move north. I didn't like what those experiences said about my culture—or me.

When I got to New York, I immersed myself in the city's developing hip-hop scene, writing about acts such as Public Enemy with a zeal that extended beyond my actual affinity for the music. I read the poems of Amiri Baraka and quoted the speeches of the Reverend Jesse Jackson. I picked arguments with people in bars who disagreed with Jackson's politics or didn't like hip-hop. I was on a one-drunk's crusade to rid the world of some notion of racism that I didn't even understand myself. It was a case of "the lady doth protest too much, methinks." There was something inside me that was eating me alive; there were racist feelings that had been programmed into me from an early age, and when those feelings surfaced, they frightened me. Rather than act on those feelings or accept them as feelings and not facts, I denied them or drank them away. I didn't want to deal with the darkness inside my own soul, so I embarked on a mission to purge myself of all aspects of my southern heritage. I hated who I was.

Within a couple of years, I gained a little clarity about myself and began talking with friends in New York who'd also grown up in the South. While only a few suffered the pangs of self-hatred as deeply as I did, all of them expressed some level of inferiority that colored their attitudes and behaviors. They rationalized or apologized for the South's political conservatism. They cracked jokes about inbreds and trailer trash. They idealized the artwork of southern eccentrics such as the Reverend Howard Finster without respect for the culture that nurtured the religious iconography of his paintings.

Donnah Dunthorn had a good point. There *is* a tendency among southerners who leave the South to internalize the bad feelings of others toward us. And there's a tendency among those who are not from the South to allow this behavior, indeed to encourage it. It's the human tendency to project one's bad feelings about oneself onto a safe target, and in America—whose history of displacing native peoples and taking Africans as slaves has left a deep psychological and spiritual wound—the South has long served as that safe target. At best, southern music, literature, and folk life are romanticized by those who don't live in the South; at worst, the romantic images of the region's religion, politics, work force,

and leisure activities often are caricatured. For some time, it's been acceptable to scoff at the folly of the "ignorant southerner."

When the caricatures are real people, however, the image is very different. Understandably, some southern clergymen and politicians—from nineteenth-century Presbyterian slavery advocate James H. Thornwell and early-twentieth-century racist Mississippi governor James Vardaman straight up to Jerry Falwell and Trent Lott—are not looked upon affectionately by many. Moreover, tobacco farming, once the economic lifeblood of my own home state—where, as a child, one of my former girlfriends worked side-by-side with her leather-handed aunts and uncles, pulling tobacco all day long during harvest season—has become more than simply a health issue; it's a southern issue. Generations of families have toiled in tobacco fields to feed their children, and yet the most vehement antitobacco advocates, many of whom probably never worked with their hands a full day in their lives, belittle those farmers beyond any sense of rationality.

Having talked with my southern friends who, like myself, left the region for the political and emotional sanctuary of New York City, I realized that from them I would get only part of the story of the South's tug-of-war with feelings of inferiority and superiority. For the full story, I would need to travel back down below the Mason-Dixon Line to talk and live with the folks who stayed.

Patricia Goddard had read my bulletin board posting on a site called Hittin' the Web with the Allman Brothers Band, and replied to it in December 2001. In her e-mail message to me, she opened up and expressed her innermost feelings about what being southern meant to her.

"I was born and raised in New Orleans, LA," Goddard began. "I can't ever recall a time when music was not a main force in our lives, particularly jazz, blues, and zydeco. In fact my childhood address was 1324 Music Street, New Orleans, LA. That may sound bizarre, but it is most definitely true."

She had a disarming tone, and as I traded e-mails with her, I began to see a rich and complex human being emerge. She was proud of her heritage, but she also was aware of our collective responsibility to acknowledge our culture's misdeeds while simultaneously forgiving ourselves for the dark feelings about race programmed into our consciousness from childhood. Not all southerners with whom I spoke were willing to talk about this stuff. It's messy. It leaves one vulnerable to attack from

the vocal but intellectually dishonest proselytes of political correctness.

When we met at the hotel, Goddard told me she had moved to Atlanta several years earlier and today lived there with her husband and three grown children. She told me she was glad that her children didn't have to grow up in a South that gave so many mixed messages about race, though she knew the healing was far from over.

"When I was a kid, I was always watching the news and you knew there was something about the South, that there was something going on in the South," Goddard said. "People were always talking about the South and you just felt vilified in some way. I'd get angry about it: Why do they keep talking about how bad we are? It was like we were all just terrible, terrible people, and I'd say, 'Well, all of us aren't terrible. We're not all terrible people. I don't get it.' "

Her mother helped her out. "She would say to me, 'Well, now, you really don't understand completely. There's a lot of history here, kid, and you don't understand that while some of what they're saying about the South is just a bunch of horse dookey, there's a lot that's justified, too. It's not that you can't be proud to be from the South, but we have to take responsibility for our history. If we can't do that, then we can't move on, we can't go forward.' "

Goddard brought along several items to our meeting in Atlanta: the David Duke propaganda, a 1972 album cover by the obscure southern glam band White Witch, and various other souvenirs from the time.

The Allmans, she told me, became a source of pride for her; they represented what was good about the South. For Goddard, Duane Allman personified the ideal southern man, almost Christlike with his long, messy hair and lanky body. "I was like, Okay, here's the man. He's the man who's going to turn things around, make the South come alive again," she said. "He's going to make it new again. He's going to bring people to the point that they are going to have to take a real look at us and delve more deeply into our history and our racial interaction, our roots and our music, and come out with a real sense of who we are."

She paused, brushed a few gray strands of hair out of her face, and fixed her gaze on the sky outside. "You know, I didn't really know who I was. I mean, New Orleans isn't exactly your typical southern town."

★   ★   ★

Driving south from my grandmother's hometown of Yazoo City, Mississippi, through the cotton fields of the Delta, past the "tall white mansions and little shacks" of the Neil Young song "Southern Man," and on down into Louisiana, you will at some point cross an invisible border into another country altogether. This country lies at the swirling mouth of the Mississippi River, below sea level, where mausoleums sit above-ground in the graveyards to keep the bodies from floating away, and where the religion is a mysterious jumble of Catholic, Protestant, vodoun, and Santeria. It's a country identified by its stately mansions with wraparound balconies, wrought-iron lacework, and big, thick columns; by its mammoth oak and magnolia trees, weeping lavender crape myrtles, cypress, and Spanish moss.

When the sun goes down in this exotic land, you hear the chatter and clatter of its citizens wobbling through the streets, drinking, dancing, celebrating; the rumble of drums and the lonely wail of a saxophone; the spooky nighttime hissing, growling, and chirping of creatures from the seething heat and mush of the Atchafalaya Swamp.

In many ways, New Orleans is neither American nor southern. It's a mix of Spanish, French, German, British, West African, and Acadian. It's the shotgun houses and Creole cottages along the streets of Esplanade Ridge, the old black neighborhood of Faubourg Tremé, and the antebellum pomp of the Garden District. It's the isolated outpost of Algiers Point, which is nestled into the bend of the Mississippi River only a ferryboat ride away from the tourist trap of the French Quarter.

New Orleans is the Voodoo Spiritual Temple, the Cafe du Monde, and the Louis Armstrong Park, where hustlers, pimps, prostitutes, thieves, and drug dealers practice their crafts. New Orleans is joyous and cynical, religious and hedonistic.

On a dark night in 1996, I pulled my rental car into the lot of a New Orleans convenience store and shut the engine. An old black man hurried over to the car and barked into the window, "No, man, you don't wanna stop here. You're in the wrong neighborhood." He pointed down the avenue: "Go that way. Now!"

In 1996, New Orleans had become the most violent town in America, with an average of one murder per day. "People were being killed in bunches," wrote Michael Perlstein in a *Times-Picayune* piece on the city's crime rate. "Residents in vulnerable neighborhoods bolted iron

bars across their windows and fell asleep to the nightly sounds of gun-fire."

By the middle 1800s, cotton was king in Louisiana and the port city of New Orleans boasted one of the largest slave markets in the United States—the phrase "sold down the river" is a direct reference to those markets. At the same time, the Big Easy also had the nation's largest population of free African-Americans and the South's broadest mix of immigrants. In the years following Reconstruction, the city flourished, its races mixing and mingling and making music together in ways unlike any other southern town. Because of its unique cultural makeup, New Orleans was one of the most racially tolerant cities in America, not to mention the South.

The Jim Crow laws of the latter part of the nineteenth century changed all of that, though, and for another several decades, the racial climate of New Orleans degenerated. By the 1960s, when the city began desegregating its public schools, racial tensions were high. Frightened white families began fleeing to communities such as St. Bernard, seventeen miles southeast of the Crescent City, so their children wouldn't have to attend schools with blacks. By the early '70s, most of the white families in Patricia Goddard's neighborhood were gone.

"When I was in grammar school, my classes were pretty mixed," said Goddard, "but as each year went by, there were fewer and fewer whites and more and more blacks. By the time I hit junior high, my sister and I were two of only a handful of white kids."

It was tough on the girls. When they walked down Music Street, toward their home, they were threatened by some of the black students. During African-American celebration days, such as Martin Luther King Jr.'s birthday, the girls had to have a police escort home.

"I don't know exactly how to say this, but those days were their days," said Goddard. "I mean, it was their day and if we walked by ourselves, they were going to take everything out on our hides the whole way home."

Goddard was frightened by the intimidation, but she wasn't angry. "I guess I just kind of understood," she said. "Unfortunately, we could never make friends with the black kids, because they didn't want to be our friends. I mean, think about it: we were the only white kids in the school. What if it had been reversed? Would the white kids befriend a handful of black kids? No. It was a role reversal."

Goddard was one of the lucky kids. She had parents who ran interference with the noise from the TV and the neighbors' racist remarks. Her mother was born in the South but spent much of her youth in Philadelphia, where she hung out in jazz clubs and saw performances by such music legends as Billy Eckstine, Gene Krupa, and John Coltrane.

"My mother was friendly with blacks," said Goddard. "When we were little girls, she and my father would go out to nightclubs to see jazz, and they'd invite all kinds of people over to the house all the time. Race was never a big issue for us—at least, not at home."

The Fourniers lived in a small home about a mile north of where rock & roll pioneer Fats Domino lived. "We'd take the bus to Bourbon Street on the weekends and just walk the streets of the French Quarter and listen to the music pouring out of the local clubs," said Goddard. "But at some point it got too dangerous for us to walk."

Eventually, even the Fourniers moved away from the city, but by then Trish and Becky were old enough to travel back into town for the music. They loved all of the characters—Allen Toussaint and his funk outfit the Meters, the eccentric Cajun fiddler Doug Kershaw—but one of Goddard's favorites, the man who made perhaps the greatest impact on other white, southern, jazz- and blues-influenced rock bands, was Mac Rebennack, better known as Dr. John. By 1973, this colorful piano player who called himself "the Night Tripper" had scored an unlikely pop hit with the song "Right Place, Wrong Time." In his performances he would don the ceremonial beads and feathers of Mardi Gras and wander out into his audiences sprinkling glitter onto the heads of his fans. With his mix of psychedelic rock and voodoo boogie-woogie, Dr. John was one of the most eclectic rock musicians from the South.

"He was everywhere," Goddard said. "And we loved him. One of the funny things he would do is he would take marijuana, roll it up, and tape the joints to playing cards, then he'd throw the cards out into the audience along with all the glitter and stuff. We'd all try to catch one of the cards; it was like catching balloons during Mardi Gras. It was a big deal if you were one of the lucky ones in the audience at a Dr. John show and got a joint."

Goddard laughed. "Oh my god," she said. "We'd all be up at the front yelling to each other, 'Get a card! Get a card!' "

★ ★ ★

On a Friday night in the summer of 2002, Mac Rebennack was sitting in the coffee room at Mirror Image Recording Studio, in midtown Manhattan, taking a break from producing an album by a young contemporary blues singer named Shemekia Copeland. A skeleton crew was gathered in the studio assisting Rebennack, helping him put the final touches to a scorching version of "Pie in the Sky," a song written by Copeland's father, Texas blues guitarist Johnny Copeland.

The next night, Rebennack would assume his Dr. John persona for a show at the glitzy B.B. King Blues Club & Grill in Times Square. When he performs these days, Rebennack leaves the feathers and glitter of his Night Tripper years at home; today, Dr. John is just a slightly jazzed-up version of Rebennack himself. He still carries his hand-carved walking cane onstage with him and props it up against the piano, and he still mixes spicy New Orleans funk with jazz, blues, soul, and a little bit of rock & roll. But like Rebennack, Dr. John has changed over the years. He's not as wild or spooky as he used to be. His life and shows are more manageable.

Rebennack spent his youth recording and performing with some of New Orleans's biggest music legends, and was barely out of his teens when he became a casualty of the business. The life of the traveling musician had gotten to him, and like so many of his fellow players, he became a heroin addict. At twenty-one, Rebennack had to switch from guitar to piano after his left index finger got shot off in a barroom brawl. The following year, he was busted on drug charges and sentenced to two years in a federal prison at Fort Worth, Texas. When he got out, in 1965, he decided to steer clear of his hometown.

"Hell, they kicked me out of New Orleans," Rebennack said. "They don't want me around them parts no more."

He hightailed it to California, where he'd heard that a musical renaissance was going on. But Los Angeles was a culture shock for the young piano player, who'd cut his teeth playing jazz and boogie-woogie in smoky, gangster-run clubs. In the City of Angels, he found himself in studios with psychedelic rock and pop bands such as the Strawberry Alarm Clock, whose guitarist, Ed King, would eventually move to the South and join a posse of ragtag southern rockers who called themselves Lynyrd Skynyrd.

Rebennack's experiences with longhaired musicians in California

prompted his metamorphosis into Dr. John, the Night Tripper, who played a combination of hippie rock and voodoo funk. His first Dr. John album, *Gris-Gris*, came out on Atco Records in 1968, and was a feast of Mardi Gras mysticism, tribal rhythms, and eerie, psychedelic effects. It included one bona-fide classic, "I Walk on Gilded Splinters," a spare, seven-minute groove of hypnotic conga drums, West African call-and-response vocals, and a Middle Eastern melodic touch that set the tone for Dr. John's eclectic bayou brew. At the time, no one knew exactly what to make of *Gris-Gris*; Atlantic president Ahmet Ertegun hated it, fearing the music was too exotic even for hippies.

It wasn't. The Mardi Gras rituals fit right into California's cosmic, LSD-fueled music scene, and Rebennack's shamanlike persona, with all the feathers, glitter, face paint, and mystic candles, became a favorite draw in clubs. On subsequent albums, Rebennack mined the entire musical map for inspiration and wound up becoming too eclectic for his own good. But by 1973, he'd found his place in music: Dr. John became underground rock's ambassador of New Orleans funk. Leon Russell, an Oklahoma-born studio musician, adopted and refined Rebennack's raspy bayou growl and became a rock star. Duane Allman had hooked up with Rebennack a few years earlier and the two became fast friends. An earthquake of southern music was about to erupt, and the strange and mystical musical mayhem of Dr. John was the rumble at its epicenter.

If you talk to any respectable southern musician of the '60s or '70s for any amount of time, the name Dr. John eventually comes up. But Rebennack is modest about his role in the southernization of post-'60s rock. Sitting in the coffee room at the Manhattan studio, with horns and guitars wailing in the background, he credited the Allman Brothers with everything.

"I tell you what, I owe them guys a lot," said Rebennack in his funky New Orleans patois. He took a drag from his cigarette and squinted his lazy eyes. These days he wears a beret on his head instead of feathers, and his long, stringy hair and beard are a mess of brown, black, and gray.

"You see, I used to always ask bands that opened for me, 'When you guys get over, remember to let me open for you.' Out of all the bands I ever said that to, the Allmans were the only ones that did it," said Rebennack. "They was good-hearted guys. They let me open up for them when they records started takin' off. I'll never forget 'em for that. I loved them guys."

He loved Duane best of all. Rebennack remembered a long talk he had with the guitarist on a beach one night when the two were in Miami, in 1970, working on an album by rockabilly singer Ronnie Hawkins. They'd been drinking heavily and Allman spilled his guts to the good doctor.

"Me and Duane hung out that whole day and he told me stuff that night—you know, personal stuff—that just blew my mind. I thought, Man, this guy's been through some shit in his life. You know what I'm sayin'? I had no idea."

Rebennack was referring to Allman's childhood, in which he and younger brother, Gregg, experienced the murder of their father, Willis, and then got shipped off to military school because their mother, Geraldine, was too poor to raise them alone. After she graduated from college, Geraldine took her sons back in and moved them to Daytona Beach. But without a father around and Geraldine often out of the house, the boys wound up raising themselves. Duane and Gregg befriended a black kid named Floyd Miles and began haunting local rhythm & blues clubs and jamming with some of the bands. By the mid-'60s, they had grown their hair and were getting in trouble. In the book *Midnight Riders: The Story of the Allman Brothers Band*, Miles told writer Scott Freeman that the brothers' outsider status gave them insight into black culture that most kids their age didn't have. "Gregg was a long-haired musician, so back then he was a freak," Miles remembered. "And I'm black. So we both knew what it was like to be discriminated against, which is probably why we got along so well."

Duane tried to step in as a father figure to Gregg, but he didn't have it in him. Another childhood friend, Sylvan Wells, remembered the guitarist as a high-strung teenager whose mood swings left him either elated or severely depressed. "He was absolutely on a self-destructive path. . . ." Wells told Freeman. "If you had a bike, a motorcycle, you wouldn't let Duane drive it. It's gone. Probably come back wrecked. Duane was on a destructive trip. The only question was how much life before he killed himself."

"That shit was tough on them boys," said Rebennack.

The night he and Allman sat together on that stretch of Miami sand, a hurricane was blowing into town. The alcohol probably fueled Allman's confessions, but Rebennack said he felt the guitarist honestly

needed to get things off his chest. "I mean, you know how it is," said Rebennack. "You're drunk, you're talking a lot of shit. But he was being real. And that's why I liked to hang out with him so much. He was real."

Rebennack was amused by the guitarist's wild streak. "You gotta understand—Duane was a crazy motherfucker. One time he took a test drive in one of them Opal cars that they said wouldn't turn over. Well, he turned it over." Rebennack leaned back on the couch and let out a big, wheezy belly laugh. "Duane come back and he say, 'Hey man, that damn car's no good. They said you can't turn it over, but I turned it over anyway.' "

On their walk back to the Thunderbird Hotel, where the two were sharing a room with Ronnie Hawkins, Allman had an idea. "Duane, he say, 'Let's go back to the hotel and roll that motherfucker'—he talkin' 'bout Ronnie. So we go back and Ronnie's lying on the bed with nothing on but his drawers and this big belt. We decided, 'Okay, we gonna roll his ass.' " Rebennack laughed again. "So we did. We rolled that motherfucker's ass."

Ronnie Hawkins had moved to Canada back in the late 1950s when his career stalled in his native Arkansas. By the early '70s he was still playing small clubs in the Great White North, but his influence on southern musicians was legendary. Everybody, it seemed, wanted to perform with this wild-eyed man who called himself "the Hawk." He billed himself as "the King of Rockabilly" and scored a hit in 1959 with his song "Mary Lou." Hawkins's high points were a rip-roaring update of Chuck Berry's "Thirty Days" called "Forty Days" in 1959 and a twisted 1963 cover of Bo Diddley's "Who Do You Love."

Hawkins has since made peace with his status as a footnote in American music. He was born in Huntsville, Arkansas, in January 1935, two days after Elvis Presley's birth in Tupelo, Mississippi. After Hawkins left the South, rock & roll suffered the temporary loss of Elvis to the army and Jerry Lee Lewis to a sex scandal. No one cared much about the Hawk. "Hell, I got more respect for my music ten years after it was popular than I did back in the '50s," he said from his ranch in Ontario. "I remember John Lennon and Yoko Ono coming up here to visit me one time. Well, John Lennon gets out of his limo and he's singing 'Forty Days.' He knew more about my music than I did."

The Hawk's importance to rock & roll has more to do with the albums that his backing band, the Hawks, made on their own. In the late '60s, his drummer, another Arkansas native named Levon Helm, took the young Canadian musicians in Hawkins's band—guitarist Robbie Robertson, bassist Rick Danko, and keyboardists Richard Manuel and Garth Hudson—and split from their leader. The group eventually relocated to the artists' colony of Woodstock, New York, where they holed up in a big pink house and wrote a set of songs that would give young rock fans a perspective of the South that was as accurate as anything ever recorded. Having been the backing band for Hawkins and later for Bob Dylan, the five musicians decided to call themselves simply the Band.

With the songwriting skills of Robertson and spiritual guidance of native southerner Helm, the Band's first two albums, Music from Big Pink and The Band, romanticized the South but never condescended to it. "The Night They Drove Old Dixie Down," from the Band's second album, released in 1969, was a populist anthem told from the bitter perspective of a proud but powerless young Civil War soldier named Virgil Kane. Helm's aching southern drawl on the song lent credibility to Robertson's words, and the growing movement of young American rebels, both northern and southern, who called themselves hippies and opposed the war in Vietnam, identified with its empathetic portrait of the frightened young man.

"It is hard for me to comprehend how any northerner, raised on a very different [idea of the Civil War] than Virgil Kane's, could listen to this song without finding himself changed," wrote pop-music sociologist and nonsoutherner Greil Marcus in his book Mystery Train. "You can't get out from under the singer's truth—not the whole truth, simply his truth—and the little autobiography closes the gap between us."

The Band wasn't as huge as the Allman Brothers in the early '70s, but the Band's music had at least as much of an influence on other rock acts. A few years later, when I first heard the group's self-titled second album, I was familiar with the Band mostly through the work they'd done with Dylan, and Joan Baez's No. 3 cover of "The Night They Drove Old Dixie Down" in 1971. That song had resonated for me, but it was another track on the album that spoke more directly to my reality.

"King Harvest" was a funky, countryish tune written from the point of

view of a southern mill worker who had joined a labor union but still mused over the farm he once worked. The mill worker of "King Harvest" could have been my grandfather, William Deforest Carlton, a former Mississippi cotton field worker who made the transition into the textile mills in the early twentieth century, when the Old South became the New South. Granddaddy Carlton eventually landed in North Carolina, not long after the big textile strike of 1929, in Gastonia, two hours southwest of my hometown. The strike put a permanent damper on union organizing in the South. Two people were killed in the violent skirmishes, one of whom was a young Woody Guthrie–like folk balladeer named Ella May Wiggins, shot while riding with fellow strikers to a union rally. When she died, so did the dreams of poor, white lintheads across the South, who were underpaid and forced to work in horribly abusive conditions.

"At the beginning, when the unions came in, they were a saving grace, a way of fighting the big-money people, and they affected everybody from the people that worked in the big cities all the way around to the farm people," said Robbie Robertson in the liner notes to the Band's *Anthology, Volume 1.*

But "King Harvest" is more than just the tale of failed unions. In a video documentary on the making of *The Band*, Robertson was more philosophical about the song. "In the story to me," he said, "it's another piece I remember from my youth, that [of] people looking forward, people out there in the country somewhere, in a place . . . we all know it, may have been there, may have not . . . but there's a lot of people that the idea of come autumn, come fall, that's when life begins. It is not the springtime where we kind of think it begins. It is the fall, because [that's when] the harvests come in."

The Band's music was a far cry from the rockabilly of Ronnie Hawkins, the boogie-woogie of Dr. John, or the psychedelic blues rock of the Allmans, and yet it encompassed all of that. It also was inspired by folk and country music; its lyrics painted portraits of the South that are more reminiscent of the character sketches of Mark Twain or John Steinbeck than the oral, backwoods blues tradition of Robert Johnson. The Band sketched a template for a musical appreciation of the South on the canvas to which southern musicians would begin adding their own brushstrokes.

None of that would have been possible were it not for Ronnie Hawkins. From his palette Robertson and company had blended their own musical colors. "I didn't want them to leave the band," Hawkins told me, "but it's not like I didn't know it was going to happen. There was an uneasiness about things. They weren't happy. I didn't know too much about all the stuff that was going on down in Woodstock. I didn't know anything about Bob Dylan. I'm a bar act, you know." He laughed. "I don't know about nothing but pussy and hockey. That's all you talk about in a bar. You don't talk about politics and culture and all that other shit."

When Hawkins finally heard the music his former sidemen were making, he supported them, albeit through clenched teeth. "Hell, I was happy for 'em," he said. "Besides, if it weren't for them moving down to Woodstock, I'd never have gotten to know people like John Lennon and Duane Allman."

In October 1971, not long after Duane Allman sat with Mac Rebennack on that Miami beach, the Allman Brothers Band took a much-needed break from two years of nonstop touring. By then, the Allmans were at the height of their first wave of popularity. Sick of the star treatment and fatigued from all the drugs they'd been consuming, Duane and Gregg Allman checked into a detox in New York but left early and eventually wound up back in Macon, Georgia.

A birthday party for a friend was scheduled for October 29 at the group's meeting place, known as the Big House, a fourteen-room, Grand Tudor–style home in a historic section of Macon. That afternoon, before the party, Duane cruised by the Big House for a visit, but he planned to go back home for a while before the party started. At around 5:30 P.M., he hopped on his Harley-Davidson Sportster and headed down the road. He was traveling on tree-lined Hillcrest Avenue when a flatbed truck made a left turn in front of him. Allman tried to maneuver around it, but he hit something that sent the bike into a crash. He was rushed to the hospital, where he underwent emergency surgery, but he didn't make it. At 8:40 that night, the twenty-four-year-old southern guitarist who was going to change the world was gone.

Rolling Stone ran Allman's obituary alongside a scathing feature story

on the band that depicted him and Gregg as doped-up rednecks and poked fun at their southern accents.

"It was just a weird scene altogether," remembered Rebennack, who was among the parade of musicians who attended Allman's star-studded funeral. "I remember all this shit went down—this weird shit about the mama and about Phil Walden, and all this shit about the way Duane died. There was just a whole bunch of scenes that went on down there. Everything was just nuts that whole year."

Duane Allman had been dead two years when his earlier support of Rebennack finally paid off for Dr. John. In November 1973, I was at home in Asheboro when I turned on my favorite late-night TV show, ABC's *In Concert*, and saw a leprechaun-like man onstage with a rainbow of feathers on his head and a big bowl of glitter in his arms. Every so often, he'd dip his hand into the bowl and sprinkle glitter out over the audience. It was Dr. John, and he was singing his big hit song, "Right Place, Wrong Time."

Thirteen years old and already a fan of Leon Russell and the Allman Brothers, I was mesmerized by this wild-haired shaman who looked like a cross between Ian Anderson of Jethro Tull and some crazy Indian rain dancer. I knew nothing about Mardi Gras or gris-gris. To me, New Orleans was simply the home of a football team called the Saints. But I liked the sandpaper grain of Dr. John's voice and the cosmic funk of his song. To me, "Right Place, Wrong Time" fit right in with two more of my favorite tunes: Russell's twisted, carnival-like "Tight Rope" and Dr. Hook & the Medicine Show's kooky "The Cover of Rolling Stone." Each of those songs had a gritty southern feel, with words that spoke to my small-town anxieties and zany music that mocked the darkness of the times. "I been in the right place," Dr. John sang, "but it must have been the wrong time . . . / Just need a little brain salad surgery / Got to cure my insecurity . . . / Refried confusion is making itself clear / Wonder which way do I go to get on out of here."

That night, I fell in love with Dr. John's music, and the next day I ran over to my friend Tim Womick's house to tell him about this new discovery. Tim, two years my senior, just laughed, sat down at his upright piano, and commenced playing the first few bars of "Right Place, Wrong

Time." I was devastated. I idolized Tim Womick. He knew everything about music. Of *course* he would already know who Dr. John was. What was I thinking?

"Man, he's the original," said Tim, with a shrug. "He started it all. There wouldn't be any Leon Russell or Allman Brothers if it weren't for Dr. John."

PRIDE
IN THE NAME
OF ANGER,
1974–1981

Hey! Said my name is called Disturbance.
I'll shout and scream, I'll kill the king, I'll rail at all
  his servants.
But what can a poor boy do,
'Cept to sing for a rock 'n' roll band?

—*The Rolling Stones, "Street Fighting Man"*

★ Chapter 4 ★

DOWN SOUTH BOOGIE

I was sitting in the top row of bleachers at the Charlotte Memorial Stadium when the shots rang out.

No one heard the crack of gunfire; the music drowned it out.

"What's going on down there?" asked a guy standing behind me on his tiptoes, craning to see over the back wall of the stadium. In the parking lot, a cluster of people gathered amid flashing police lights and an army of men in blue.

We were high above the fray.

"I dunno," I said. "They must have busted somebody."

It was Saturday, July 13, 1974, and I was one of twenty thousand kids who'd descended on downtown Charlotte, North Carolina, earlier in the day for a nine-hour southern rock bonanza. Leon Russell, ZZ Top, and a rising young Florida band called Lynyrd Skynyrd were sharing the bill with soul man Billy Preston and singer-songwriter Chris Jagger, the lookalike younger brother of Mick.

Five years earlier, the Woodstock era had screeched to a sudden and vicious halt during an outdoor concert at the Altamont Speedway, fifty miles east of San Francisco, when a Hell's Angel stabbed a black man to death right in front of the stage as the Rolling Stones attempted to perform "Under My Thumb." Mick Jagger, wearing an American flag top hat and black shirt emblazoned with an omega symbol, watched helplessly as chaos turned to anarchy. The killing, captured on film, was the focus of a feature-length documentary released the following year, Gimme Shelter.

Rock & roll had turned ugly. Peace, love, and good vibes had morphed into anger, resentment, and bad karma. Outdoor rock festivals were no longer innocent fantasylands where hippies gathered to seek temporary asylum from society's ills; the festivals themselves had become ill. They were now the stomping grounds of rage. The '60s were over. The hangover had begun.

Youth culture was no longer a single united front brought together by its opposition to the Vietnam War and utopian belief in equality for all people. Now bikers, hippies, rednecks, jocks, rich kids, poor kids, homosexuals, political activists, African-Americans, and other ethnic groups mingled together at these all-day Dionysian affairs with little or no security. Of course, it had always been that way at rock concerts, it's just that the drugs initially masked any disparities. But the drugs had stopped working.

On June 6, when Charlotte officials approved the Memorial Stadium concert, Chester Whelchel, a parks and recreation commissioner, warned his fellow board members that violence was on the rise at rock festivals. He had no idea how prophetic his warning would be. At 6 P.M., somewhere between Lynyrd Skynyrd's "Sweet Home Alabama" and Leon Russell's "Home Sweet Oklahoma," an angry young man who'd been kicked out of the show aimed a .25-caliber pistol at Police Sergeant Barry Worley and fired four shots. One bullet struck Worley's spinal column, then lodged in his chest a quarter-inch away from his heart. The twenty-seven-year-old officer was paralyzed for life.

"I don't know how many people have to get shot before we close these things down," Commission Chairman Eugene Warren said as he stood inside the stadium after the shooting.

Later that night, ZZ Top hit the stage and promised to donate part of its earnings to the fallen officer.

With all due respect to Hunter S. Thompson, we were somewhere around Richfield on the edge of the Uwharrie National Forest when the drugs began to take hold. Sixteen-year-old Tim Womick, his twenty-one-year-old brother, Chip, and I were on our way from Asheboro to Charlotte for a weekend of debauchery. Why my parents allowed their fourteen-year-old son to travel with two older, longhaired hippies to the

largest city in the state for the whole weekend to attend an all-day outdoor rock concert, I'll never know. But I wasn't asking questions. We had a fat bag of marijuana, a case of Budweiser, and Tim's mountain of eight-track tapes to get us in the mood: ZZ Top's *Tres Hombres*, Leon Russell's *Leon Live*, and of course the Allman Brothers' *At Fillmore East*. I probably brought along T. Rex's *Electric Warrior* and the Stones' *Sticky Fingers* as well, but I'm quite sure Tim wouldn't have let me play them.

"The Stones are bullshit," he once told me. "They're all show. You gotta listen to real music: the Allmans, Leon, ZZ Top."

I liked those bands, too, I said, but I would never kick my Stones habit. Maybe I could give up the lunkheaded metal bands and glitzy glam acts, but I'd never give up on the Rolling Stones. They were my heroes.

"Whatever," Tim said. "But you have to stop listening to that Alice Cooper crap. It's a waste of time."

The first time I met Tim Womick I thought I'd died and gone to heaven. It was late 1973, and I'd snuck off to have a cigarette in the woods at the corner of Dublin Road and Worth Street, about a block away from my parents' small, three-bedroom ranch-style house. I saw Tim off in the distance, a walking stick in his hand, his light coffee-colored German shepherd dog, Alice, sniffing the ground in front of them. I'd never seen this guy before; he must have just moved into the neighborhood. When he got within speaking distance, he walked straight up to me and told me I shouldn't be smoking. Then he started talking about music. It was as though my prayers had been answered—a new neighbor with a clue.

No one from my hometown looked like Tim did, with his waves of blond hair that draped down his back just above the beltline. He wore a crinkled, white, button-down shirt with a T-shirt underneath, a thick lumberjack's coat, faded Levi's blue jeans and a pair of old beat-up cow-boy boots. His jeans weren't flared like mine; they were straight-legged. He told me flared jeans and bell-bottoms were for sissies. Hanging from his back pocket was a dirty red bandanna—just like the one Janis Joplin sang about in her song "Me and Bobby McGee." To me, this pudgy, sixteen-year-old combination of Leon Russell and Gregg Allman was the most amazing guy I'd ever encountered. He was smart, witty, and cool, and he knew more about music than anyone I'd ever met.

I had friends who would listen to rock & roll with me, but most of them didn't know enough about music to suit me. We would talk about

bands like Deep Purple, Black Sabbath, Led Zeppelin, and Alice Cooper, and comb the pages of rock magazines such as *Creem* and *Circus*, picking out pictures of Zeppelin's Jimmy Page or Sabbath's Ozzy Osbourne to hang on our walls. Tim's knowledge of music ran much deeper than ours did. His tastes leaned more to the gritty, the organic. He'd sit for hours at the piano in his living room, banging out boogie-woogie tunes and belting songs with the gravelly yowl of Dr. John or Leon Russell. Tim was well schooled in the sounds of the South.

"Ever heard 'Will the Circle be Unbroken'?" he asked me one day, as winter turned to spring. He didn't leave space for an answer; he just started banging on the keys and singing the words to the old southern spiritual: "I was standing by my window on one cold and cloudy day / When I saw that hearse come rolling, for to carry my mother away." He called this the music for the salt of the earth. I didn't know what he was talking about. All I knew of "Salt of the Earth" was that it was the name of a Rolling Stones song.

"No, you little runt," he said. "It *means* something—the salt of the earth means real people."

That summer, Tim and I were inseparable.

When his older brother, Chip, moved to town, he told us about the big outdoor rock concert that would take place later in the summer in Charlotte. From the moment school let out in June, we sat around the carport of Tim's house and talked about the upcoming weekend of fun.

"This is going to be a big one for you, Mark," Tim said. "This is going to change your life."

When we arrived in Charlotte, Chip booked us into a cheap motel on Independence Boulevard. We tossed our duffel bags on the floor, popped a few beers, rolled all of the pot into little joints, and the party began. I don't remember the precise moment the police knocked at the door, but I do remember at some point running wildly around the motel swimming pool, hooting and hollering and laughing and letting out several loud rebel yells. I also remember being escorted back to the room and watching as the cops shined their flashlights into empty beer cans.

One officer looked at Chip's driver's license, pointed over at me, and then stared into Chip's face: "You know, we could arrest you for contributing to the delinquency of a minor," he said.

Like a jack-in-the-box, I popped up out of my daze and told the nice policeman, "Oh, officer, I don't mind."

Miraculously, we were simply asked to leave the motel. Tim and Chip had an uncle living in Charlotte who agreed to let us stay at his apartment that night and promised not to tell our folks about our little run-in with the law.

The next day, Tim, Chip and I jumped in the car and headed for the concert. A roar of Harley-Davidson engines followed us down Independence Boulevard to East Seventh Street in the heart of Charlotte, where a line of cars, motorcycles, and vans curled a quarter of a mile around the stadium. When we walked through a tunnel leading from the parking area to the entrance, we could hear Billy Preston and his band onstage performing their current hit, "Will It Go Round in Circles." Freaks were everywhere: guys with long hair, beards, and bell-bottoms; girls in halter-tops and skintight Landlubber jeans; leftover hippies in face paint and Indian prints, granny dresses, beads, leather vests, top hats, boots, sandals, bare feet. I was happy as a hound dog on his first hunt. This was where I was supposed to be. These were my people.

Around midafternoon, I was standing in front of the stage, the sun baking my back, as three guitars shot streams of sonic curlicues into the afternoon haze. The ground was shaking. The air was sweet with marijuana. A girl in front of me was jumping up and down at the lip of the stage, boobs shaking under her nearly transparent tube top, the crack of her ass showing just above the waistline of low-riding jeans. The sky was bluer than the ocean.

I had lost sight of Tim and Chip. I had no idea where they were, and frankly, I didn't give a damn. The alcohol and pot had me in a trance. The music was all that mattered. And it was intense, a frenzy of dueling harmony guitars, playing over and over, louder and louder, faster and faster, as if the song Lynyrd Skynyrd was performing in the hot July sun might just levitate the entire stadium and all of us who were inside it, writhing and sweating and puking on its playing field.

Allen Collins, the tallest and lankiest of Skynyrd's three guitar players, was jumping spastically into the air, doing moves that were somewhere between the cool splits of the Who's Pete Townshend and the pogo dancing of the punk rockers, who didn't even yet exist. Then there was the singer, Ronnie Van Zant, who just stood there at center stage, in the midst of all the noise, barefoot and hugging his microphone stand as if it were keeping him from falling forward into the crowd. I didn't know his name at the time. It didn't matter. To me, this band had been sent

straight down from heaven and was taking us back home on the wings of the free bird they were singing about.

I had heard the song before, but until that very moment, I hadn't realized the band that played it would be performing at this concert. A year earlier, my friend Bucky Parker had phoned me and said he had a new album he wanted me to hear. Bucky, who was two years my senior, picked me up and drove me over to his family's tiny mill house in a part of Asheboro where the poor white kids lived. When we got there, he wouldn't let me look at the cover of this new album. Instead, he cued up the last track and told me to guess what band it was.

The song began with an aching organ and slide-guitar part before a sweet, pensive voice began singing the words, "If I leave here tomorrow, would you still remember me?" I looked over at Bucky and with full confidence said, "Oh, it's the new Allman Brothers album." At the time, no one else made music that sounded like this.

"Nope," said Bucky with a knowing smirk on his pale, gaunt face. "It's this new band called Lynyrd Skynyrd." He grinned and brushed the stringy, white-blond hair out of his blue eyes. "But don't it sound just like the goddamn Allman Brothers?"

We listened to Skynyrd's first album (*pronounced leh-nerd skin-nerd*), all through that day and I immediately fell in love with its blend of country, hard rock, and southern blues. On the yawning "I Ain't the One," Van Zant drawled out a tale about a poor kid who falls in love with a rich girl, and in the white-trash boogie of "Gimme Three Steps," he sang a funny little story about a guy who nearly gets shot when he hits on another man's woman in a redneck bar. But that first tune Bucky had played me—the last track on the album—was the real gem.

In Memorial Stadium that afternoon in 1974, when the guitars eventually came to a halt and the crowd exploded into cheers and whistles, the bearded guy beside me turned and yelled into my ear, "Want some more?" When I nodded yes, he lifted up the pouch that was strapped around his shoulder, held it above my head for maybe the third time in an hour, and poured a warm clear liquid from its spout into my mouth. The first time he'd given me a hit from the pouch, I'd assumed it was water. But it wasn't water; it was vodka. And it was making me feel ten feet tall and bulletproof.

The girl beside me with the shaking boobs was seventeen. I was four-

teen going on twenty-one. But I told her I was sixteen, and even though I didn't look much older than twelve, she chose to believe me. We spent the rest of Lynyrd Skynyrd's set making out, sharing tokes off other people's joints, and occasionally rolling around on the ground together at the feet of all the freaks. Lynyrd Skynyrd made a man out of me that day.

Ed King's eyes lit up when I reminded him of his band's performance in Charlotte in the summer of '74. "Oh god, yes, I remember that gig very well," said King, the Skynyrd guitarist who came up with the immortal riffs for "Sweet Home Alabama" and "Saturday Night Special," two of the group's biggest songs. "Wasn't that the show where the cop got shot?"

King and I were sitting in a restaurant in downtown Nashville, in 2002, talking about the brief time he served as a member of Lynyrd Skynyrd during the group's formative years. He didn't look much different from the way he looked nearly three decades earlier. His hair was a little shorter and his beard was white, but other than that he was the same chubby guitarist who stood at the side of the stage at Memorial Stadium that day, unassumingly churning out the chunky riffs that would define the southern rock sound.

"That gig was exciting for us," said King. "We were on the bill with Leon Russell, and he was one of our biggest idols."

It was a heady time for Lynyrd Skynyrd. The band had performed in Charlotte on previous occasions, but only in small clubs. By late 1973, though, the group's first album had generated a big buzz in the music industry. The band had three dueling guitarists versus the Allmans' two, and *Creem*, the irreverent alternative to *Rolling Stone*, praised Skynyrd's machismo, writing that the band "possesses more wit and joy than the Allmans and more power pump whammo than the Stones." That fall, the band signed on as the opening act for some of the Who's *Quadrophenia* tour dates. When Skynyrd tore into "Free Bird" during those shows, the Who's audiences went wild, stomping their feet, raising cigarette lighters, and yelling for more. Even guitarist Pete Townshend took note of the Skynyrdmania, commenting during the crescendo of "Free Bird" at one show, "They're really quite good, aren't they?"

By the time of the Charlotte gig, the members of Lynyrd Skynyrd were headed for the big time. Only three months before the Memorial

Stadium show, the band had rushed out another album, *Second Helping*, whose first track, "Sweet Home Alabama," was riding at No. 8 on the *Billboard* singles chart. The song, a biting response to the wholesale accusations of racism that Neil Young leveled against the South in his famous tunes "Southern Man" and "Alabama," stuck out among the era's bombastic rock and wispy singer-songwriter music like Jerry Lee Lewis at a peace rally. One critic called *Second Helping* "remarkably refreshing in a time when much of rock seems at a standstill."

The praise was new for King, but the chart success was not. Although by the early '70s he was a key member of the group that would come to epitomize southern rock, Ed King actually was born in southern California. Unlike his Lynyrd Skynyrd bandmates, who'd grown up together as a gang of scrappy thugs in a poor section of Jacksonville, King was raised in the same San Fernando Valley suburban sprawl that produced the pristine harmonies of the Beach Boys and Jan and Dean. His first band, the Strawberry Alarm Clock, had a No. 1 hit in 1967 with the psychedelic pop song "Incense and Peppermints."

During the Alarm Clock's heyday, the band performed on a bill in Los Angeles with Gregg and Duane Allman's early group, the Hourglass. King was impressed by Duane Allman's guitar playing. A few years later, on October 9, 1971, King went to see the Allmans' new group perform at the Santa Monica Civic Center. King was so blown away by the Allman Brothers' ambitious mix of jazz improvisation and wailing blues that he went to see the group again, on October 12, at the Whisky-a-Go-Go on Hollywood's Sunset Strip.

"Those shows changed my life," he remembered. "There was just so much soul behind Duane Allman's music. It's hard to describe the feeling of watching him play. It was just so genuine."

Three weeks later, Duane Allman was dead and Ed King headed south, to the tobacco country of eastern North Carolina, where he hoped to absorb some of the southern magic that made Allman tick. "In my head . . ." King began, and then trailed off. "I don't know what I was thinking at the time, but I thought maybe I might try to do what I could to fill Duane Allman's shoes." He laughed. "What a bizarre thought! Looking back, that was pretty arrogant, but I was determined. That was my motivation. That's why I was there."

Ed King was falling in love with the South. He didn't know much

about his new mistress—how complicated she was, how unpredictable, and self-destructive she could be. To him, the South was beautiful and mysterious. "I was fascinated by it," he said. "It just had this real charm to me. There's something about the way southern people are brought up and all the things they go through in childhood and all the little things that they're surrounded by. . . ." He paused and looked down at his plate. "Actually, the music might even be the least of it."

His flirtation with the South had begun in 1968, when the Strawberry Alarm Clock went on the road with the Beach Boys. The tour was to start in Memphis, on April 4, the day a drifter and small-time criminal named James Earl Ray stood in the bathroom of a Memphis boardinghouse across from the Lorraine Motel and fired the deadly shot that silenced Dr. Martin Luther King Jr. "It was like, 'Welcome to the South,' " the guitarist recalled. "We were just a bunch of California guys; this was weird for us, just totally surreal."

The Beach Boys and the Alarm Clock were forced to change their plans. "We couldn't land in Memphis, so we had to fly over to Nashville and stay there for two or three days," said King. "It was crazy. There was a guy at the hotel where we were staying in Nashville going from room to room with this big flight case selling everybody handguns."

King bought himself a .38 Special that day, and each night thereafter he'd go onstage with the Alarm Clock and play songs like "World's On Fire" and "Go Back, You're Going the Wrong Way" with a handgun in his back pocket. "I remember the first time I shot it," he said. "We'd finally got out of the South and were in Pennsylvania at this hotel with a big field in the back of it. I went out there and shot the gun for the very first time. I couldn't hear for two weeks."

In 1971, when King and the Alarm Clock's keyboardist Mark Weitz heard that a bogus version of the band was playing gigs down South, they decided to go on tour again, to clear up any confusion over which band was the real one. In Florida, the Alarm Clock's opening act was a group of roughneck guys fronted by a short, scrappy singer named Ronnie Van Zant. At the time, Lynyrd Skynyrd fleshed out their sets of original music with covers of songs by Cream and Led Zeppelin.

"They were just borderline," King remembered. "They only had a few original tunes, one of which was 'Free Bird.' But Ronnie was already amazing. I'd never seen anybody with so much charisma. I made up my

mind right then and there that I'd do anything to play music with this guy."

When King and the Alarm Clock began their westward swing back toward California, the Florida boys helped steer them away from potentially dangerous southern backwaters where authorities would harass hippies for fun. "They'd tell us stuff like, 'Okay, you guys are gonna drive from Jacksonville to Mobile, Alabama. Well, after you pass through Tallahassee you'll go through a town called DeFuniak Springs. Make sure when you go through DeFuniak Springs you duck down in the car, because you guys have long hair and the cops will pull you over and they will throw you in jail and you'll be there for a while.'"

After a show in Alabama, the members of the Alarm Clock were packing up their gear when the proprietor of the club said he had another job for them: "He says, 'You guys are gonna sweep the floor now.' We were like, 'What? No way.' When we refused to do it, he ran us out at gunpoint."

On another occasion, when the Alarm Clock's regular van driver, a white guy, took a few weeks off for vacation, the band replaced him with a black man. The experience of having an African-American accompany the group through the South gave King and his cohorts a short education on the region's delicate racial dynamics. "We didn't think too much about this guy driving us around until we saw how he was being accepted by people at hotels, restaurants, gas stations, and little stores," said King. "But we quickly realized that a black guy running around with four longhairs was not cool in the South."

King was amazed at how deftly the driver was able to work the good old boys. "He instinctively knew how to act around white people," said King. "It just floored us. He knew what to do and say to bypass certain situations. This was stuff that, as a boy growing up in California, I'd never encountered. It was so bizarre. But it was very interesting."

Within months, Duane Allman was dead, the Alarm Clock had called it quits, and Ed King was living in Greenville, North Carolina. When he arrived in the small college town, nothing much happened at first. He joined a bar band that played at a student hangout called the Buccaneer Club, and he acclimated himself to southern culture by learning to love the spicy chopped pork served at Greenville's famous Parker's Barbecue. Then one day he got the phone call he'd been waiting for. It was Ronnie

Van Zant, from Jacksonville, Florida. He wondered if King would be interested in joining Lynyrd Skynyrd.

"I'll never forget that day," said King. "Ronnie and Gary Rossington drove up to Greenville in a little Toyota, picked me up, and took me away with them."

In early 1971, a few months before Ed King joined Lynyrd Skynyrd, Ronnie Van Zant and company packed up their gear and headed to Muscle Shoals to cut an album's worth of original songs with Jimmy Johnson. The producer, who'd heard a demo tape of the band, was impressed with the group's professionalism. "I was blown away by those guys," Johnson remembered. "They'd rehearsed this stuff to the tee; they had their solos down pat. Of course, as I came to find out later, they had to be good. If the guys in that band screwed up one little bit, Ronnie would kick their asses. He was hard on 'em."

Skynyrd's manager, Alan Walden, had known Johnson from his work with Aretha Franklin and Wilson Pickett. In the mid-'60s, Walden co-managed Otis Redding along with his brother Phil. After Redding died in December 1967, the brothers parted ways. When Phil began working with the Allman Brothers Band, Alan decided he'd audition some white rock acts of his own. The first time he heard Lynyrd Skynyrd, Alan was convinced the group could compete with his brother's new band.

"I heard them play 'Free Bird,' and I knew from that one song that they were on to something," said Walden, who today lives in a large home on a lake outside of Macon, Georgia, and spends much of his time helping the Georgia Music Hall of Fame keep Otis Redding's memory alive. Walden is close with Redding's widow, Zelma, and when I visited him in Macon, in the summer of 2002, he spoke with her on his cell phone twice in less than an hour.

"Zelma's an amazing lady," said Walden, sitting on a couch in his living room, surrounded by gold and platinum records of artists ranging from Redding to Skynyrd. "Her sons are amazing, too. Otis left us a wonderful legacy. He was one of the best friends I ever had."

A cursory look at Alan Walden—the big grin plastered across his round face; the countripolitan clothes he wears; his loud, booming southern drawl—would suggest he's the quintessential redneck made good. Even Walden admits that he and Skynyrd "were just a bunch of redneck hell-raisers." But the care and sensitivity he not only expresses,

but shows toward Zelma Redding and her children indicates he's more than just a hell-raising redneck. Walden is a complex man. He spins tall tales and brags about Lynyrd Skynyrd's drug-fueled exploits in the '70s. He tells off-color sexual jokes. He criticizes Yankees for not understanding the ways of the rural South, then criticizes fellow southerners who act like fools when they get around Yankees. He's not as urbane or polished as his brother Phil. In short, Alan Walden is to Phil what Lynyrd Skynyrd was to the Allmans—the scrappy kid brother; the less sophisticated black sheep of the southern rock family.

"We were the scourge of the South," Walden crowed. Even though he was fired by Lynyrd Skynyrd in 1974, around the time of the band's second album, Walden still sees the band as his own. "When I first met Ronnie Van Zant and those guys, they were totally independent from all the bullshit record-industry nonsense," said Walden. "Ronnie was a leader, he wasn't no follower. Other bands I'd auditioned had misconceptions about how to act. They'd follow the magazine stories to try to figure out what to say and do to be successful. Not Ronnie. He was totally down to earth."

When Skynyrd completed its recording sessions with Johnson, Walden began shopping the tapes to major labels but had a hard time endearing his new act to record executives. "We got turned down by nine different companies, and this was after they heard 'Free Bird,' 'Simple Man' and 'Gimme Three Steps.' " Walden reeled off the list—"Atlantic, Warner Bros., A&M, Columbia"—then paused, shaking his head. "Hell, even Capricorn, my own damn brother's label, turned 'em down."

The brothers were in a full-blown sibling rivalry.

Walden lowered his voice to a near whisper, as if Phil might walk into the house at any moment, even in 2002, and whup his butt. "Lemme tell you a story," Walden said. "We played Grand Slam right here in Macon, Georgia, right? Well, the Allman Brothers come out to hear Skynyrd play, and after they listen to the set, I walk up to Phil, start talking to him. Well, he's arrogant as hell, acting like he's the shit. He says, 'Your lead singer's too goddamn cocky, he can't sing, the songs are weak, and they sound too much like the Allman Brothers.'

"Of course, he says this loud enough to where Ronnie can hear it. Then he just walks away," Walden continued. "Well, Ronnie walks up to me and says, 'What'd he say?' I look Ronnie straight in the eye and I tell

him, 'Nothing important. Let's go have a drink.' And we went and had a drink—a whole bottle, actually. J&B Scotch."

By 1973, Yankee keyboardist Al Kooper—the guy whose Hammond B3 organ gave Bob Dylan's *Highway 61 Revisited* its signature sound— was living in Atlanta, scouring clubs for bands to sign to his new label, Sounds of the South. When the Allman Brothers arrived on the scene in the early '70s, Kooper saw the South as a potential hotbed of new rock & roll and decided to set up a label in the region. He figured his only competition would be Phil Walden's Capricorn Records, and Walden couldn't sign every good band below the Mason-Dixon Line. By the time Kooper saw Skynyrd perform at the Atlanta club Funnochios, the band had rehearsed its songs to perfection. At the end of Skynyrd's sets, club crowds were already yelling for "Free Bird."

"Al Kooper walked in and had this little dream of a southern label he wanted to start," said Alan Walden. "And I'll have to be honest with you, at that point we didn't have nowhere else to go. We had been fighting this thing for more than three years, trying to hold on to it. I finally reached a point where I felt the band would not survive had I not made a deal. So we signed a recording contract right out in the parking lot on the hood of my pickup truck."

Van Zant asked Walden what he thought of the contract. Walden said he told the singer it was the "worst piece of shit I ever seen—worse than any R&B contract I ever seen. Ronnie said, 'What else we got?' I said, 'Nothing.' He said, 'Give me the goddamn pen.' " According to Walden, Lynyrd Skynyrd "signed away two million dollars that day."

Kooper, whom Lynyrd Skynyrd would later immortalize as a "Yankee slicker," in the song "Workin' for MCA," remembers the deal differently. In his book *Backstage Passes & Backstabbing Bastards: Memoirs of a Rock 'n Roll Survivor*, Kooper wrote that he got a call late one night from Van Zant. The singer told him someone had broken into the band's van and stolen their equipment. The guys didn't have any money to replace it with and were worried about feeding their families. Van Zant asked Kooper if he would lend them $5,000. When the keyboardist agreed, Van Zant told him, "Al, you just bought yourself a band for five thousand dollars."

The keyboardist's impact on Lynyrd Skynyrd's sound was crucial, but according to Walden the members of the band weren't prepared for the

ways of this northeastern musician. "I have a favorite expression that I use when I introduce myself to record executives up north," said Walden. "I say, 'Now, don't you sit there and think we're all Bo and Duke Hazzard down here.' I have to take the approach of, hey, let's get past this dumbass southern thing right now. But really, you ought not have to do that. You ought to be able to go in there and be judged on your merits."

Kooper had a tough time adapting to the South, too. When he arrived in Atlanta, one of the first things he noticed was that most everybody had a handgun. He wrote in his memoirs that while there was certainly a presence of handguns in New York City, "it hadn't been in my face there as much as it was in Atlanta. For example: in twenty-seven years of living in New York, I never witnessed a shooting. In three months in Atlanta, I witnessed two." What's more, as Kooper got to know the members of Lynyrd Skynyrd, he quickly became aware of their fondness for getting into brawls. "If they couldn't find anyone to fight," Kooper wrote, "they'd fight each other."

Nothing Ed King experienced during his short stay in North Carolina prepared him for what he would encounter among the close-knit society of Lynyrd Skynyrd. "I had a real hard time with it," he said. "I couldn't put my finger on what exactly was different about the culture of that band, but it was way, way different. They all grew up together on the west side of Jacksonville in trailers and stuff. They'd been friends since childhood."

When I first contacted King by telephone to ask if he'd be willing to talk about his experiences as a member of the band, he pointed me to a photograph taken outside Skynyrd's infamous Hell House rehearsal space, a small cabin in the countryside south of Jacksonville. In the photo, taken in 1975, the members of the band are all lined up on one side of an open door, smoking cigarettes or standing with their hands in their pockets—all of them, that is, except for Ed King. He's standing at the opposite side of the door with his left hand to his mouth, taking a drag from a cigarette and gazing outside the picture's frame.

"Six guys on one side of the door and just me on the other side," King wrote to me. "That about says it all."

His discomfort among the good young boys of Lynyrd Skynyrd didn't

quash his curiosity about the South or his awe of Ronnie Van Zant. King had wanted to work with the singer for years and wasn't about to let a little alienation stop him. "Ronnie was the reason I joined that band," said King. "I didn't care anything about those other guys. I was always a better guitar player than any of them anyway, so . . ." He paused. "I mean, they wrote some good stuff, but Ronnie was the soul of that band."

To King, whose romance with southern characters and the region's nebulous soul bordered on obsession, Van Zant epitomized the simple yet complex southern man. His songs, like the Merle Haggard songs his father would listen to, were actually little short stories with themes based on distinctly southern experiences. One of Haggard's most famous tunes was "Mama Tried," about a young man who laments having not listened to his mother when he was a child and as a result was turning "twenty-one in prison doing life without parole." Lynyrd Skynyrd's "Simple Man," on the band's first album, was a variation on the same premise. Van Zant sings it from the perspective of a complicated young man reminiscing about the simple but profound wisdom of his mother: "Take your time, don't live too fast, / Troubles will come and they will pass, / Go find a woman and you'll find love, / And don't forget, son, that there's someone up above." Over a gently strummed electric guitar, Van Zant moans the words with a tender but nakedly raw gruffness. "Simple Man" is pure working-class white man's blues.

"When you get right down to it," said King, "Ronnie was a country singer fronting a rock band. He was writing country songs, because that's what he knew. His musical roots were very southern. But what I found even more interesting than Ronnie's musical roots was that he was the son of a truck driver."

King looked up at me, grinned, and asked rhetorically, "Have you ever met Lacy Van Zant, his father?" He didn't leave space for an answer. "Let me tell you about Lacy Van Zant: He was the kind of man who would tell you these long, rambling stories that would go on and on—he'd start at one place and go off on these wild tangents, then maybe two hours later he'd wind up right back where he started. He would take you on these fascinating, fantastic journeys. He was the quintessential southern man. And that's what Ronnie's songs were like. Ronnie was the spitting image of his dad."

I never got a chance to meet Lacy Van Zant, but I read his photo-

heavy memoirs, *The Van-Zant Family: Southern Music Scrapbook*, which he published himself. On the cover is a grainy black-and-white photograph of an elderly, burly, white-bearded man wearing a baseball cap, a cell phone to his ear. On the back are the words, "By Lacy Van Zant, Father of Southern Rock." Inside are rambling reminiscences of his childhood as the son of a logger in Putnam County, Florida; thumbnail biographies of his children; and snapshots of five generations of the Van Zant family, from Lacy's mother to the grandkids Ronnie has but never got a chance to meet. In the chapter on Lacy's most famous son, he remembered Ronnie as a child who "had a temper and a 'don't mess with me' attitude, which he would need growing up on the West Side of Jacksonville."

I caught up with Ronnie Van Zant's younger brother Johnny, on his cell phone one morning as he was driving his truck to his father's home in Jacksonville. It was a blistering day in May 2003, and Johnny had just bought some carpet for his dad and was sitting in the truck outside the old man's house, getting ready to go in and help him install it. Johnny let out a cackle when I told him some of the stories I'd heard about the former truck driver. "Hell, my father is eighty-eight years old and still full of piss and vinegar," Johnny said. "If he tells me to jump, man, I say, 'How high, sir?' "

Johnny Van Zant is the youngest of three brothers—in between him and Ronnie is Donnie, the leader of another southern rock band, 38 Special. When Johnny remembered the road trips his father took him and his brothers on during their youth, his voice softened. "Us kids used to go on the truck with him and we'd talk about all kinds of things while he was driving. When you're riding down the road, you have a lot of time to talk and"—he paused and laughed—"well, you know, my father's a real one-of-a-kind, he'll tell all kinds of stories. We heard some stuff, man, I can't even remember the details."

As Lacy drove his sons across what Woody Guthrie referred to as "that ribbon of highway" that curves and dips through all the nooks and crannies of the South, the elder Van Zant would listen to country music.

"That's what we grew up on—Gene Autry, Merle Haggard, Conway Twitty, Loretta Lynn. He'd listen to that kind of stuff. And then, of course, when Ronnie got a little older, he started getting into Elvis and the Beatles and us kids would listen to that. When I got older and Ronnie and

Lynyrd Skynyrd got big, I started listening to a lot of the British stuff, like Led Zeppelin and Free. But even then, we always loved country music. I think we had the best of both worlds and I think that's always shown up in Lynyrd Skynyrd's sound.

"You know, I'm sitting right in front of my father's house right now—the house where we all grew up—and it makes me think about how it was back then," he said, with a soft pensiveness in his voice. Johnny's southern accent is slightly less pronounced than Ronnie's was, but it's still there. When Lynyrd Skynyrd reunited ten years after the plane crash with Johnny stepping in as lead singer, he was able to give meaning to his late brother's words that another singer probably couldn't have mustered; he understood the spirit of the music. Though Johnny's own songs never had the resonance of Ronnie's, his later version of Lynyrd Skynyrd somehow didn't make a mockery of the original band.

"I remember we used to have a swing set right out here in the front yard and we'd get out here and sing all sorts of songs," he said. "I guess that's really how we got into this."

Ed King saw in Ronnie Van Zant what he'd seen in Duane Allman. Van Zant's soulful voice and narrative style of songwriting, like Allman's weepy guitar sound and improvisational playing, seemed like the real deal. It was emotional and immediate. It never even crossed Van Zant's mind to try and present a consistent, calculated image for himself or Lynyrd Skynyrd. He always worked purely on instinct. Van Zant was at once honest and wily, good-hearted and mean as a rattlesnake, sometimes innately progressive, other times as reactionary as George Wallace. If Van Zant contradicted himself from one song to the next, well, so be it. That's what most human beings do. Anyone who adheres strictly to one mode of thinking isn't being true to himself or his feelings. Van Zant wasn't a politician, he was a working front man for a rock & roll band.

In the terms of the blue-collar work ethic, Van Zant was the foreman of Lynyrd Skynyrd. He was the band's supervisor. By all accounts, if any of them were late to work or didn't perform up to his standards, Van Zant would take it out on their hides. "Every morning, we got in his car at seven-thirty on the dot—I mean, *every* morning!" said King. "It would be well over one hundred degrees in that space and he'd make us work our asses off. Don't get me wrong—we wanted to do it; it's not like Ronnie had to force us out there. But he definitely kept a handle on things, and

if you got out of line or if you got lazy, he'd be right there in your shit."

Kooper capitalized on the singer's hot-headed temperament. It wasn't Skynyrd's idea to use a skull-and-bones logo or to drape the controversial Confederate flag behind the band during its performances. These were the ideas of the Yankee slicker and the executives at MCA Records, the West Coast distributor of Skynyrd's albums. Before long, bass player Leon Wilkeson took to wearing a holster and guns during the band's performances. Kooper, in his memoirs, recalls a concert on New York's Long Island in which Skynyrd opened a show for the heavy metal band Black Sabbath, fronted by the English working-class singer Ozzy Osbourne. According to Kooper, Sabbath's fans heckled Skynyrd ruthlessly, yelling, "You guys suck! Get the fuck off the stage! Ozzy rules!" When Wilkeson pulled a gun out of his holster and fired off a few blanks, the audience, frightened, quieted down immediately.

Lynyrd Skynyrd was cultivating a reputation for being an intimidating and belligerent band of hard-drinking rednecks, and it began to work in the group's favor. Unfortunately, their image merely reinforced stereotypes of the South—not the aw-shucks sentimentalism of Andy Griffith's fictional TV character, but the ass-whupping aggression of the real-life Bull Connor.

For Skynyrd, the image was partly true. Like punch-clock workers, the members of the band worked hard in order to party and drink themselves silly during their off time. The problem was, when Van Zant drank, he became a monster. "All the stories about Ronnie are true," said King. "He was an outstanding bandleader, but towards the end of the time that I was in the group, he drank way too much. And when he drank, he was a totally different person. It runs in his family. No one in Ronnie's family can drink. They all turn into different people. It's just one of those things."

Van Zant seemed to recognize the problem. In "Poison Whiskey," another song from the band's first album, he sings about alcoholism among poor southerners with an authenticity that rings personal. "Daddy was a Cajun raised on southern land, / And so my kinfolks tell me, he was a street fightin' man," Van Zant groans over interlaced guitars and bass and a funky, gutbucket beat. "Well, they rushed him down to see the doctor: 'Hey doctor, won't you check his head?' / The only thing that was wrong with him was Johnny Walker's Red."

It's a story song, like "Simple Man," but in this yarn Van Zant reveals

an inherent understanding of alcoholism as a three-pronged disease of mental, physical, and spiritual breakdown. "It happened back in the bayou many years ago," he continues, offering some background to his tale. "Satan came to take him and did it real slow, / Well, they rushed back to see the doctor, but the doctor just shook his head: / 'Twenty years of rotgut whiskey done killed this poor man dead.' "

In February 1977, my uncle Wallace died homeless on the streets of Miami. He was fifty-six years old and had been rambling around the country for as long as I could remember. We'd see him from time to time over the years, when he'd run out of money and make his way back to Asheboro to recuperate. He would sleep in a dilapidated wooden shed behind my grandmother's house, where a small bedroom adjoined a larger workshop area. When he drank up the last of his whiskey, he'd call a cab and have the driver carry him over to the bootleg joint across the tracks, where he'd get another bottle. After he'd had enough of Asheboro and family—or after the family and Asheboro had had enough of him—Wallace would be off again, a hobo, drinking his way across the country.

Uncle Wallace had always been an enigma to me. My folks told me he was an alcoholic, but I didn't know exactly what that meant. In my hometown in the '60s and '70s, folks only whispered about people who drank too much. Hard drinkers were either considered funny, like the bumbling Otis Campbell character on The Andy Griffith Show, or depraved and bound for Hell. When Ronnie Van Zant sang about the toll of alcoholism in songs like "Poison Whiskey" or "The Ballad of Curtis Loew," he put a more complex and human face to the alcoholic.

My uncle Wallace suffered from a disease that runs through our bloodline like a predator, lying dormant for the most part but striking out at some of us like a deranged sniper picking off victims indiscriminately. Of my mother's four sisters and three brothers, Wallace was the only one whose drinking took him down. When he died, only a handful of us showed up for the funeral. It reminded me of the lyrics Van Zant sang in "Curtis Loew": "On the day old Curtis died, nobody came to pray."

"Like all alcoholics, Wallace was a good-hearted man," my dad remembers of my wayward uncle. "He just had really low self-esteem."

Three years before my uncle died, I formed my first garage band. My grandmother let us practice in the old workshop area of the shed where

Wallace's bedroom was. When we took breaks from rehearsing, my band-mates and I would take turns going into the bedroom with our girlfriends to fool around. I was in the bedroom rummaging through some old clothes hanging in a closet one day when I stumbled on a half-empty bottle of bourbon hidden in the pocket of a Navy jacket. Figuring it belonged to Wallace, I smiled and took a big slug in his honor.

It wasn't the first drink of whiskey I'd ever had and it wouldn't be the last. I suffered from Wallace's disease, too, although at the time I didn't know it. I've been luckier than my uncle. Although I've lost a great deal due to my alcoholism and hurt people deeply, I was able to find recovery. Why I was able to receive this gift while Wallace had to endure the worst of the worst of his disease and ultimately die from it, I'll never know. If I did know, I'd patent my knowledge and make a billion dollars.

One Saturday afternoon, my girlfriend, Kathy, had come to see my band rehearse. We were working up a version of "Can't You See," an acoustic-guitar ballad by the southern rock group the Marshall Tucker Band, from Spartanburg, South Carolina. I remember putting on a real show for Kathy that day, singing the words to the song—"I'm gonna find me a hole in the wall, gonna crawl inside and die . . . / Gonna take me southbound, all the way to Georgia, till the train run out of track"—with every ounce of passion I could squeeze out of my fourteen years of life.

Kathy was beautiful. She was a head taller than I was, with long blond hair, sharp blue eyes, and an already well-developed body. She was the new girl in town, and I had zeroed in on her the first day I saw her walk past me in the hall between classes.

That day at my band's rehearsal shed, though, Kathy had something she wanted to tell me. During a break, we headed into the bedroom next to the workshop. When I attempted to kiss her, she pulled away from me.

"You know that song by Lynyrd Skynyrd—'Free Bird'?" she asked.

"Yeah," I said. "Cool song."

"Well, you know that line about, 'I must be traveling on now, 'cause there's too many places I've gotta see'?"

"Um . . . yeah."

"And, uh, do you know that other part where he sings, 'Bye-bye, it's been a sweet love'?"

I was getting dumped. A fourteen-year-old girl was reciting words to me that a grown man had written for a woman. This was not acceptable.

It wasn't supposed to go down like this. I was crushed. My eyes welled up.

"And do you know that line where he says, 'Please don't take this so badly'?"

"Yeah," I said.

That night, for the first time, I drank with the full intention of snuffing out my feelings. Before then, I would have told you the reason I drank or smoked pot was to expand my worldview. But that night I was angry and hurt and filled with shame. So I drank to forget.

★ Chapter 5 ★

REDNECKS, WHITE SOCKS, AND HARD ROCK & ROLL

I N 2001, *printer and musician Jeff Brown and I took a day trip to Coleridge, a decaying mill village seventeen miles southeast of Asheboro on a particularly wide stretch of the muddy Deep River near the Chatham County line. In 1968, a film crew set up camp in this central North Carolina community to shoot a river scene for the* Bonnie and Clyde*–like crime drama* Killers Three, *a B-grade movie starring country singer Merle Haggard and featuring his classic prison song "Mama Tried." The film was a flop, but for a sliver of time the citizens of Randolph County felt mighty proud of this forgotten rural backwater.*

By the mid-'70s, most of the workers from the Coleridge textile mills had left town and the village began its slow decline. Still, some of the old brick mill buildings on the riverbanks were standing, and electricity flowed into at least one of them. That was where Jeff Brown's garage band, Stormwatch, practiced on weekends. During breaks from rehearsing songs such as Lynyrd Skynyrd's "Free Bird" and the Outlaws' "Green Grass and High Tides," Jeff and his bandmates would wander along the banks of the river, smoking marijuana and trying to come up with ideas for their own tunes.

As we walked west along the narrow and curvy Highway 42, which meets with Route 22 at the heart of the village where an old general store has stocked farm equipment and household items for local residents since 1898, Jeff spotted his old haunt. "It's over there," he said, pointing to a row of

boarded-up shacks girdled by kudzu, briars, and rusted beer cans. "That's where the infamous Stormwatch got our start."

Jeff has always camouflaged his prickly wit with a goofy grin and spastic wriggle of his shoulders and arms, and as he remembered his old band, his sense of humor went into overdrive. He motioned to the floor of the building, where broken glass, shards of moldy wood, insulation, and old, crumbling factory equipment surrounded a cracked shaft leading to the basement, Stormwatch's old rehearsal space.

"Right down there in that hole. We were the Kings of Coleridge," he said, and then went into an impersonation he used to do of a '70s-era Steve Martin routine.

"And we were really, really *small."*

Jeff Brown was my best friend in high school. I'd known him since we were babies. He lived with his parents, an older sister, and a younger brother in a three-bedroom house on Brookdale Drive, the street that ran parallel to Pepperidge Road, where my family lived until I was five years old. Back then, it seemed, everyone in the world inhabited those '50s-style rectangular, red-brick, ranch-style suburban homes. In 1965, when my parents moved into a new house in a different school district, Jeff and I lost contact for a few years, but by the mid-'70s we reconnected at Asheboro Junior High.

Jeff was the smart kid in school, and I was the daydreamer whose eyes would glaze over when the teachers quizzed me. In our second-period geometry class, I began to notice that Jeff had all the correct answers to Mrs. Warford's questions, so I moved to the desk behind his to look over his shoulder and copy his work. Our reunion was awkward at first. By the eighth grade, I fancied myself a badass. Gone were the days when jocks would make fun of me for my athletic ineptitude. Now I smoked cigarettes and got high, wore an old army jacket with peace-sign patches and scribbling all over it, listened to rock & roll, and had honed my powers of persuasion to a fine art. When I spotted sensitivity in Jeff, I pounced on it like a cat after a butterfly. I instructed him that come test time, he was to position his paper in such a way that I could see the answers.

In reality, I was hardly a badass. I just had a bad attitude. But Jeff was in-

timidated and grudgingly indulged my bullying. As time passed we began to talk about our respective roles as outcasts. With his curly, reddish brown hair and large, thick glasses, Jeff felt like a geek; with my long, straight blond hair, girlish features, and attention deficit (they didn't call it a disorder at the time, they called it a disciplinary problem), I felt like a freak.

One day, Jeff came to class with copies of the Beatles' *Sgt. Pepper's Lonely Hearts Club Band* and Frank Zappa's *Apostrophe* tucked under his arm. I decided Jeff was not a nerd but that he was secretly one of the cool students. I invited him into the culture of the "heads," the long-haired kids who dressed like hippies, smoked pot, and huddled together in the shadows of the tree-lined outskirts of the ball field during lunch. Initially, my friends were leery of Jeff; they told me that when push came to shove, he would probably tell on us for our punkish behavior. Jeff had never told on me for copying his math tests, so I assured them he was loyal, he could be trusted, that he was one of us.

Jeff Brown had something I wanted (intellectual discipline), and I had something he wanted (a sense of adventure). He introduced me to irony, to the offbeat humor of Monty Python and the Firesign Theatre, and to the brilliance of the Beatles, which had gone over my head when I heard Paul McCartney's quaint "Michelle" wafting from my sister's bedroom at night. I introduced Jeff to guitar playing, to the edginess of the Rolling Stones' *Exile on Main Street*, and to the allure of mind-expanding psychedelic drugs.

We were a team, Jeff and I. From 1974 until the turn of the decade, we played music together, talked about politics and the suffocating culture of our repressed mill town, took LSD trips, and wondered what life would be like if we moved away from Asheboro to a place like San Francisco, where alternative lifestyles seemed to be the rule rather than the exception. By the end of that school year, the music Jeff and I liked and the lifestyle we'd chosen were completely informed by what we read in *Rolling Stone* magazine or saw on the hip new late-night sketch-comedy TV show *Saturday Night Live*. We listened to the Beatles, the Stones, Bob Dylan, the Grateful Dead, Jefferson Airplane, Frank Zappa. But we were southern boys first, so whatever esoteric messages we absorbed from the outside world were filtered through our working-class, Bible-belt social environment: country music, the blues, the Allmans, Lynyrd Skynyrd, Charlie Daniels. Jeff and I were trying to find our place

among the sons and daughters of the mill owners, the day laborers, and the farmers. At fourteen, we were asking all kinds of questions: Who were we? Why were we here? What did it all mean? But as close as we were, there was an essential part of Jeff to which I was not privy. He was carrying a deep secret, a heavy burden.

Jeff Brown was gay.

"I remember my very first day at school, I felt like I didn't fit in," Jeff told me a few months after our trip to Coleridge. "There was a group of guys walking down the hall, locked arm in arm, and I was a part of that, but I pulled away from them. I just broke away from them and went off in my own direction. I don't know why, I just felt like I didn't fit in."

We were sitting in the apartment Jeff shares with his boyfriend, John, in the Fourth Ward district of Charlotte, North Carolina. The neighborhood, once a ghetto of run-down Victorian homes, has been painstakingly restored to its original form. Today, the Fourth Ward is a community of creative people from all walks of life. Many of those people are young, upwardly mobile gay men. Jeff's boyfriend works for one of the banks based in Charlotte, which by the 1990s had become the Wall Street of the South. Jeff works as a printer, but on weekends he plays his acoustic guitar in restaurants and wine bars.

In the mill town of Asheboro, seventy miles to the north, there was no context for Jeff's feelings. If I had felt alone with my general feelings of alienation, Jeff felt a million times more alone with his more specific ones. We never heard the words *homosexual* or *gay* in those days. It wasn't until we were in junior high that the word *queer* entered the locker-room lexicon.

"I ended up at some point joining the Boy Scouts, trying to figure out who I was," said Jeff. "And I had a lot of weird feelings there—I knew all along that I had this mysterious attraction that I was subjected to, I just didn't know what it was or why I felt ostracized. It was very difficult."

At home, Jeff's feelings were not validated in any way. His father, an insurance agent, was a severe man who couldn't express his feelings in any way other than through anger. Jeff's mother had died of cancer by the time he reached junior high. Jeff immersed himself in art, spending hours sketching and painting, activities his mother had pursued before she died.

"There was something wrong with me and I knew it," said Jeff, sitting

on his couch surrounded by various musical instruments, including a couple of guitars leaning against the furniture. "I remember the image that my father portrayed to me of men. It was rough and superficial and stereotypical of someone who grew up in the '50s. He was always bragging about what he could do—how many asses he could bust. And I resented that. I just hated that kind of arrogant talk, and it had a big impact on me from a very early age. I just feel like, god, that's so phony, it's so fake. It was the part of being a man that I never wanted to be like. But here I am, growing up in the South, where if you're a man, you have your gun and your truck and your woman, and I couldn't relate to any of that. So I built up a resentment towards my dad and isolated myself a lot. Especially when I got a guitar. I hid behind it."

Jeff got his guitar about a year before the two of us reconnected in junior high. When we began playing music together and talking about different ways of seeing the world, Jeff felt freed from the South's bondage.

Today Jeff will admit he cut his teeth on the guitar styles of Lynyrd Skynyrd and the Allman Brothers Band, but he tells me time and again when I ask what southern rock means to him that he's sure his ideas and opinions about the music and its impact on our culture would be of no use to anyone. Of course, he's wrong. Southern rock—the feelings and viewpoints reflected in the music, the attitudes of the people who performed it and listened to it, the putative freedom and individualism the bands promoted—has made an indelible mark on Jeff's psyche. When he talks about groups such as Lynyrd Skynyrd or the Charlie Daniels Band, he becomes visibly moved, but not in the wistfully nostalgic way other southern rock fans are moved. The veins in his forehead pop out and his face turns red.

On our way back from Coleridge on that hot summer day in 2001, Jeff became quiet and edgy when my talk turned to southern rock.

"I remember having always resented certain attitudes that I perceived as arrogant, narrow-minded, and somewhat simple among southern rock groups and the people who liked that kind of music," he said tersely, as we drove the narrow and curvy road back to Asheboro.

He was distant, speaking of the music and culture in a clinical tone, as though he had never been a part of it himself. He wasn't looking at me. For several miles we drove in silence, passing vast dairy farms and fine country homes followed by dark patches of woods with burned-out

trailers speckled with little cubes of light the sun produced as it passed through the tall oak and pine trees. Some of the trailers were so run-down they looked unlivable, and yet outside, in the front yard, would be an old rusted Plymouth or Dodge and a clothesline full of underwear, work shirts, and jeans. When Jeff finally looked over at me, his cool disdain had turned to angry condescension.

"I *hated* the songs 'The South's Gonna Do It Again' and 'The Devil Went Down to Georgia,' " he said, his voice rising as he spit out the titles to the Charlie Daniels Band's two biggest hits. "And the words to 'Sweet Home Alabama' really annoyed me, too. I just couldn't relate to gun-toting, tobacco-chewing rednecks. And that's exactly what I thought of them, you know? Rednecks. They made my life hell." As his anger turned to hurt, Jeff's voice softened: "The highest compliment someone could pay to me back then was: 'You don't sound like you're from the South.' "

The redneck stereotype is a complicated beast. Obviously, not every member of a southern rock band—or every citizen of the South—is of one mind-set. By the middle of the '70s, there was as much cognitive dissonance within southern rock and those who listened to the music as there was within southern culture at large. The mourning expressed by the Allman Brothers Band in songs like "Dreams" and "Whipping Post" had given way to righteous indignation. Lynyrd Skynyrd had hit the Top 10 with the regional cheerleading of "Sweet Home Alabama" and the Charlie Daniels Band had done the same with a song that urged southerners to "be proud you're a rebel 'cause the South's gonna do it again." Whether out of ignorance, frustration, or blind willfulness, many southerners then were angry and didn't know exactly how to express it, didn't know how to feel about themselves or the culture at large. Responding with violence and intolerance was the only way some people knew to deal with their feelings, and those behaviors were becoming passé, unacceptable except in scenes from black-and-white movies about tough guys and cowboys. The songs of rock groups like the Charlie Daniels Band and Lynyrd Skynyrd reflected a growing sense of insecurity in southern culture at large; they expressed feelings of anger and resentment in the way that many southerners had long communicated such feelings—passive-aggressively. Two of the songs that annoyed Jeff Brown so much—"Alabama" and "The South's Gonna Do It"—revealed a peculiarly vehement sense of regional pride.

Ed King, the Lynyrd Skynyrd guitarist who grew up in California, identifies with Jeff's feelings of alienation. When I asked King about southern rock and the culture that spawned it, like Jeff, he at first minimized his authority on the subject. In an e-mail message he sent to me after my initial contact with him, King wrote, "My perspective on 'southern rock' may be a bit skewed," but he added, "I'd be glad to offer some of my insights, as I have a few."

As the only nonsoutherner in Lynyrd Skynyrd, King was able to observe and process the intricacies of southern relationships and behaviors during this period of transition in the South in a way that no native could have done. He acknowledged this in a later correspondence. "Though I was an outsider," King wrote, "I could see the whole picture. And I don't mean to be too critical of the South—I love its charm and I do still live here—but, oh, the stupidity sometimes. It exceeds all ignorance."

Among the first things King noticed when he joined Lynyrd Skynyrd were the constant undertones of violence and the band members' bad treatment of women. "It was unbelievable," King told me during our lunch in Nashville. "The way they talked about women behind their backs, the way they treated them to their faces—where I grew up, that behavior was just . . ." he sighed. "Well, it was just unacceptable. You wouldn't even think about doing the kinds of things they did. I was appalled, man. I just thought it was the weirdest thing I'd ever encountered. And to them, it was like nothing."

As he spoke of his initiation into the world of Lynyrd Skynyrd, King constantly reminded me that he was grateful for the opportunity to have written and performed with the band. But there were shades of bitterness to his telling of stories. He would shake his head and sigh, trail off when he spoke, and pause to fiddle with the food on his plate. Some of the experiences King described were downright nightmarish. One night, for example, during a Lynyrd Skynyrd tour, Ronnie Van Zant walked into the hotel room he and King were sharing. The singer, King said, had dragged a young girl into the room with him and was beating her mercilessly.

"He threw her head into a nightstand three or four times. I mean, he really fucked her up," said King. "I said, 'Ronnie, what the hell did she do, man?' He said, 'She swallowed my yellow jacket [a speed pill].' "

By all accounts, Van Zant had the Jekyll and Hyde personality of a mean drunk. Ed King was not the only one to notice this. Original Lynyrd Skynyrd manager Alan Walden also witnessed the singer's scary side firsthand. "Oh man, he would kick your ass if you crossed him," said Walden when I visited him at his home in Macon, Georgia. "When he was drinking, ain't no telling what he'd do."

"Ronnie was one angry guy, particularly when he was drunk," said King. "I mean, he could be the nicest guy in the world, but when he was drunk he was a completely different person. There was something inside him that was just eating him up."

In the early part of the decade, the South had undergone a period of collective mourning over the loss of a bygone era, mixed with shame over its treatment of African-Americans. By raising issues that had been long buried or simply accepted as "the way it is down South," the civil rights era had exacerbated the collective bad feeling the white South had about itself. It had scratched a scab that had grown over the wound of slavery, and the South was bleeding again. But by the mid-'70s some southerners were tired of feeling guilty, tired of being told they were guilty by people in other parts of the country. White southerners wanted to get this thing behind them, but they were impatient with the process. Their rage wasn't essentially aimed at blacks—or at gays, or women, or Californians, for that matter—it was rage born of fear. Fear of change. Fear of outside perceptions of southern culture. Fear of interlopers coming in and taking over. Fear of perhaps never being able to heal. It was a primal fear that dated back to the Civil War.

By then, newly empowered blacks, gays, women, and outsiders came to personify what some born-and-bred straight white southern men perceived as the problem. Those groups were different from us. They didn't necessarily observe traditional notions of the white South regarding church, family, property, or work. The old thinking about these things was under attack as more and more blacks began exercising their new freedoms and working toward upward mobility, as gays began asserting their personalities through disco music and a newfound sense of validation and pride, as women began taking control of their lives and their careers, as the New South economic revival found outsiders moving in

with different perspectives on what America represents. For guys like Ronnie Van Zant, the prickly discomfort had to be expressed, and Van Zant expressed it in a song.

Ed King remembered the morning he woke up with a melody in his head. The day before, he'd worked up a duel guitar part with fellow Skynyrd guitarist Gary Rossington during the band's rehearsal.

"Gary was playing this one riff when I came in, and I picked up my guitar and immediately bounced my riff off his," said King. "Then I just finished writing the whole thing."

That night, King had a dream.

"I always sleep with my guitar next to my bed, and that night the whole guitar solo came to me in this dream. I didn't know what I was going to play but I knew it was my tune and I wanted to play it."

It was a catchy melody, and when Van Zant put words to it, the song came to represent everything Lynyrd Skynyrd and southern rock stood for. "Sweet home Alabama," Van Zant sang. "Lord, I'm coming home to you." For the first time in a post–civil rights–era rock & roll song, someone had the nerve to express southern pride. And that someone was Ronnie Van Zant.

By 1974, artists ranging from '60s protest singer Phil Ochs to '70s proto–grunge rocker Neil Young had consistently and vigorously harangued the South and its white citizens in song. In his 1964 ballad "Here's to the State of Mississippi," Ochs had unleashed a litany of charges against the citizens of that state: "Here's to the people of Mississippi . . . Oh, the sweating of their souls can't wash the blood from off their hands. . . . Where they smile and shrug their shoulders at the murder of a man." The singer ended each verse with the conclusion: "Here's to the land you've torn out the heart of: Mississippi, find yourself another country to be part of." It was harsh, but in 1964 most Americans saw only images of vicious southern lawmen and powerful politicians actively oppressing African-Americans. They didn't see the internal struggles that individual white southerners were going through.

When, in 1970, Neil Young released the first of two popular songs in which he also painted the entire South as a cesspool of racism, the badgering had become personal. "I saw cotton and I saw black / Tall white mansions and little shacks," sang Young in "Southern Man." Then he posed the question, "Southern man, when will you pay them back?" Two

years later, on his hugely popular album *Harvest*, Young returned to the subject, singing, "Alabama, you've got the weight on your shoulders." Then he posed another question: "What are you doing, Alabama? You got the rest of the Union to help you along. What's going wrong?"

To some southerners it seemed as though people in other parts of the country were projecting the sins of an entire nation's history on the South alone. Van Zant articulated the collective frustration in Ed King's new melody. Borrowing a line from an earlier song about the South—"Proud Mary," a huge hit for both Creedence Clearwater Revival and Ike and Tina Turner—Van Zant began his new song with the words, "Big wheels keep on turning." In "Proud Mary," John Fogerty had characterized working-class southerners of an undetermined race as compassionate people. The song suggested, however, that to understand this compassion, one had to visit the South and interact with its people. "If you come down to the river," Fogerty's lyrics invite, "bet you gonna find some people who live. / You don't have to worry 'cause you have no money, / People on the river are happy to give."

In "Sweet Home Alabama," Van Zant used the line from that song's refrain to stake his claim on his homeland. "Big wheels keep on turning," Van Zant sang, "carrying me home to see my kin." In the second verse, he moved in for the kill, aiming his rage squarely at Neil Young: "Well, I heard Mr. Young sing about her / Well, I heard ol' Neil put her down." With the same sweeping indictment that Ochs had leveled against the entire state of Mississippi, Van Zant continued, making Young a scapegoat for everyone who had ever painted the South with a broad stroke: "Well, I hope Neil Young will remember: Southern man don't need him around, anyhow." Van Zant's lyrics acknowledged the darkness of the civil rights–era South—"Now we all did what we could do," he sang—but they also posed a question to the rest of the nation: "Does your conscience bother you? Tell the truth."

The other members of Lynyrd Skynyrd were not aware how riled Van Zant was by Neil Young's songs, but they agreed with the sentiments their singer expressed in "Sweet Home Alabama."

"What Ronnie wrote about and what Ronnie talked about were two different things," said King. "There was never any talk about the lyrics."

There was not much talk among the members of Lynyrd Skynyrd about anything of global or political import, according to King. "The

other members of that band didn't think, period," he said. "There was nobody, to me, in that band who had a definitive viewpoint on anything." He paused. "But Ronnie was different. If you listen to his lyrics, he had a vocabulary that was very unusual for someone who had so little education. I'm not talking about just his storytelling—which was amazing—I'm talking about his words. He knew the right words to use to evoke specific feelings. I could never figure it out. It was totally incongruent with his upbringing."

When "Sweet Home Alabama" rocketed into the Billboard Top 10, in 1974, reporters and radio deejays inundated Van Zant with questions about the lyrics. In the '70s, rock stars weren't as media savvy as they would become after 1981, when MTV added a new dimension to public relations. Van Zant wasn't prepared to have to explain his motives, so he told the truth. He said he respected Neil Young's talent but resented the Canadian-born singer's point of view.

"We listen to Neil Young a lot, we love his music," Van Zant told a British radio reporter in 1976. "But he had this song called 'Alabama,' where he's putting down the whole state of Alabama. I mean, actually, he was just cutting down the governor—Governor Wallace—in a roundabout way, you know. But we just felt like he was shooting all of the dogs because some had the flu."

Van Zant attributed Young's ignorance of the South to his outsider status: "He's from California—they don't know nothin, you know?"

A month after I saw Lynyrd Skynyrd play that outdoor show in Charlotte, North Carolina, in the summer of '74, "Sweet Home Alabama" was blaring out of radios everywhere. That August, my family took a two-week vacation on the South Carolina coast.

Myrtle Beach was known as the Redneck Riviera. The midpoint of a sixty-mile stretch of shoreline, it was an endless whirl of trashy, neon decadence: wall-to-wall souvenir shops filled with cheap T-shirts with iron-ons, sunglasses, saltwater taffy, fake jewelry, and wacky postcards and trinkets emblazoned with "Greetings from Myrtle Beach." At night you'd hear the clanging of pinball arcades and the lilt of beach music wafting out of cheesy nightclubs with names like the Spanish Galleon. Along the boulevard a few blocks back from the ocean were Dixie Queens and Putt-

Putt courses, carnival rides, dirty motels, greasy-spoon cafes, loud Harley-Davidsons, and jacked-up muscle cars with Confederate flags draped across the back windows, their stereos pumping out thick slabs of Skynyrd, Zeppelin, or the Who. In those days a man could still walk the streets of Myrtle Beach barefoot and shirtless, with grease on his fingers, a can of Budweiser in his hand, and a dollar in his pocket, and feel like he was living the good life.

During colonial times, the South Carolina seaboard had been a sparsely populated no-man's-land where pirates terrorized the inhabitants. But by the 1700s, rice plantations popped up around the rivers and marshland of Georgetown, just north of Charleston. The plantation culture flourished in the late 1800s, around the time of the Civil War, and the beaches north of Georgetown became oases for wealthy planters and their families. By the turn of the century, a railroad made the coastline more accessible to vacationers, and oceanfront lots began selling for $25 a pop. Some forty miles north of Georgetown, Myrtle Beach, named for the wax myrtle trees that grew wild along its shores, became the epicenter of a growing strand of resort towns. With the construction of the Pine Lakes International Country Club, golf hit the beach community in the early '20s. At nights, wealthy families would stay at the elegant Ocean Forest Hotel, with its gold-domed gazebos and crystal chandeliers, swimming pools, horse stables, and lavish ballrooms.

Meanwhile, in the nightclubs of Columbia, one hundred fifty miles west of Myrtle Beach, a dance called the Big Apple hit like a tidal wave in the swinging '30s. Within a decade, this shuffling, slowed-down blend of northern jitterbug and southern square dance became known as the shag—the jitterbug with a southern drawl. Where northern swing dancers had bopped to big bands led by white musicians such as Benny Goodman and Glenn Miller, southern shaggers shimmied sensuously to black rhythm & blues. In the mid-'40s, South Carolina was rife with racial antagonism, but in Myrtle Beach, whites who normally wouldn't mingle with blacks felt free to mimic black dance moves. By the 1950s, Myrtle Beach had become an incorporated city where working folks rubbed shoulders with the wealthy, and shagging was the common denominator. When rock & roll hit later in the decade, the shag became a redneck dance sensation with moves that allowed the guy to lead his girl with one hand while the other was free to hold a beer and cigarette.

Shagging underwent a huge renaissance in the '70s, when aging rhythm & blues groups such as the Drifters began performing oldies shows at clubs along the South Carolina strand. By then, the high school and college students who flocked to the area during the summer months had grown weary of Vietnam and civil rights. At the beach, they could dance mindlessly to the songs of a bygone era: "Be Young, Be Foolish, Be Happy," by the Tams; "Under the Boardwalk," by the Drifters. The dancers began calling the R&B sound of these bands "beach music." Some of the white southern rock groups that performed in Myrtle Beach incorporated elements of beach music into their own sound. One of those bands was Alabama, which by the '80s would introduce a mix of meaty rock instrumentation and gentle pop harmonies to mainstream country music, selling more records than any other country band of the period.

Nearly every July or August, my family vacationed in Ocean Drive, a slightly less populated enclave just north of Myrtle Beach where the shag dance was born. I lived for those hot days and air-conditioned nights when the scent of suntan lotion and the taste of salty air filtered through all of our daily activities. In the daytime, I'd wander the streets of Ocean Drive with my sister, looking for iron-on images of the Allman Brothers or the Rolling Stones to put on a T-shirt. To me, those two weeks a year in a chain motel made me feel as though my family was the wealthiest, most privileged clan in the world. I had no concept of places like the Hamptons or Cape Cod, where real wealthy Americans sipped cocktails and discussed the relative merits of prep schools and Ivy League colleges. When my family visited Myrtle Beach, we discussed the relative merits of the fried fish restaurants in the nearby community of Calabash. As I sat on the white sand of the North Myrtle Beach dunes after nights of sneaking off and making out with some girl I'd met at the pinball arcade, I would daydream. I imagined taking a boat out into the sea and landing in a world much different from the one I lived in, a world peopled with longhaired rock stars, writers, poets, and beautiful groupies.

The summer of 1974 was different, though. I rarely ventured out of my family's motel room that year. Instead, I sat glued to the television, keeping up with the latest developments in the big national news story of the moment: Watergate. The previous summer I had watched the hearings play out like some extended daytime soap opera, with colorful characters acting out the downfall of an American president. There was Senator

Sam Ervin, quoting Shakespeare and admonishing witnesses like a Southern Baptist preacher forewarning of Armageddon. There was the nerdy, proto-yuppie John Dean, the young White House counsel who sat at a microphone answering questions like a kid who'd been caught with his hand in the cookie jar. By July 1974, the House Judiciary Committee had recommended the president himself face criminal charges and be impeached for his involvement in the cover-up of illegal activities. It was all very exciting. But what was even more exciting to me was that two young journalists—*Washington Post* reporters Bob Woodward and Carl Bernstein—had cracked open this dramatic case.

On August 8, the soap opera took a dramatic turn. The president was going to address the nation. That night, my family skipped dinner in Calabash to gather around the motel TV and watch Richard Milhous Nixon tell the nation he was resigning as president of the United States. I barely remembered a time when Nixon *wasn't* the president.

I began looking more closely at the newspapers I'd delivered since age ten. I was already a regular reader of *Rolling Stone*, the underground youth-culture magazine whose political reporter, Hunter S. Thompson, wrote about Nixon and politics in ways I'd never seen. To Thompson, one of the architects of the so-called New Journalism, politics, drugs, and the counterculture were all intricately connected; in his journalistic worldview, there was no such thing as objective reporting. Everybody was part of one big story. Thompson saw the Watergate hearings through the eyes of my generation, writing about "those hot summer mornings when John Dean's face lit my tube day after day." He described Dean as "a crafty little ferret going down the pike right in front of our eyes, and taking the President of the United States along with him." The fall of Nixon, he wrote, "was almost too good to be true"; the president "was walking the plank, on national TV, six hours a day—with the Whole World Watching, as it were."

My interest in politics was overshadowed only by my passion for music. As much as I loved reading about Thompson's hallucinogenic adventures in the theater of American politics, I positively consumed the meandering prose of music writers such as Lester Bangs and the young Cameron Crowe, who was close to my age. By fourteen, I knew what I wanted to be when I grew up: I wanted to be a music reporter for *Rolling Stone*.

The ocean at Myrtle Beach is the same vast swell of saltwater and bubbles that borders the posh Hamptons, eight hundred miles to the north,

at the far end of New York's Long Island. But the two beaches are completely different worlds. In the Hamptons, the drifting dunes and miles of sandy solitude provide sanctuary for famous Manhattanites; in Myrtle Beach, the wide, sandy coastline is a mosaic of tacky high-rise hotels filled with drunken college students and families with squalling kids. Many years later, I would live my dream, finding myself vacationing with my then-girlfriend Megan—the niece of *Rolling Stone* publisher Jann Wenner—at the family's sprawling compound in Amagansett, rubbing shoulders with many of the people about whom I'd fantasized during those fateful summers of my early teens.

"What's the most underrated band ever?" Wenner's fifteen-year-old son Theo asked me as we lay in the sun on a mild spring afternoon more than a quarter century later.

"Underrated by *Rolling Stone*?" I asked.

"Sure."

"Lynyrd Skynyrd," I said, looking for a reaction.

"No way!" Theo protested, scrunching up his cherubic face. "Those rednecks?"

I smiled, wondering if Theo, who was fascinated by the Confederate flag, had ever met a real redneck. It occurred to me that I might be the closest he'd get.

Later that night, before the help served dinner, Megan's aunt Jane showed me a rambling, incoherent dispatch that had rolled in via fax at some point from Woody Creek, Colorado. It was from Hunter S. Thompson.

My mind reeled back to Thompson's groundbreaking, drug-addled political tomes *Fear and Loathing: On the Campaign Trail '72* and *The Great Shark Hunt: Strange Tales from a Strange Time*, both of which had sent me into fits of laughter when I read them while in my teens. In them, Thompson wrote about "Yahoo Republicans and Redneck Southern Democrats," and dismissed then–Georgia governor Jimmy Carter as just another good ole boy southern politician. Four years after that '72 campaign—which pitted Nixon against George McGovern in a battle over whether the right or left, the old or new guard, would control the course of the nation—Carter was the Democratic presidential nominee. The mild-mannered former peanut farmer would have the strong backing not only of Thompson and *Rolling Stone*, but of every southern

rock act of note including the Allman Brothers, Skynyrd, and Charlie Daniels.

By 1974, America was at the tail end of a major cultural shift. Nixon was leaving. Carter was coming. And southern hippies—some of them groomed to be rednecks, others descendants of slaves or of wealthy slave owners—had joined together with hippies from New York, California, and beyond to create a new America. The common denominator was that we were all members of a new generation; we were hippies, radicals, longhairs, heads, freaks. Geography and economics no longer seemed to be a big issue. More than a century after the end of the Civil War, it looked as if the North and South were coming together again.

On a hazy spring morning in 2002, Charlie Daniels stood at a microphone in the recording studio on his ranch outside Nashville, laying down the vocal track for a new song called "Waco." Daniels was dressed in a white T-shirt, tan work pants, and black suede sneakers. The singer's face was flushed red and his hair white as cotton. When his producer punched a button on the soundboard, a thick honky-tonk guitar and bass line blasted out of the speakers. Daniels scrunched up his face, stuck out his jaw, and spit out the words with all the cocky attitude he'd put into "The South's Gonna Do It," back in the mid-'70s.

"Won't somebody somewhere come up here and take me to Waco," he sang, " 'cause I've got the blues, / these big city sidewalks just don't suit my shoes."

When Daniels was done, his producer asked him if he wanted a harmony part added to the song and the veteran country rocker shook his head.

"Naw, I'm hearing this as just straight-ahead, balls-to-the-wall," said Daniels. "Raw sounding—you know what I mean?—just me and somebody like Hank Williams Jr. singin' together on it."

When he speaks, Daniels's flat, eastern North Carolina drawl is still prominent, even though the sixty-six-year-old singer has lived in Tennessee for most of his professional career. But the cadence of his voice isn't slow or singsongy, like some TV caricature of a southern accent. Daniels speaks quickly and firmly, pronouncing each syllable as though he's absolutely certain of every word he utters. After a few more

takes of "Waco," the singer removed his headphones, walked out of the glassed-in recording booth, and grinned.

"All right now," he said to the producer, "let's listen to this bad boy."

Daniels was working on his twenty-eighth studio album, *Redneck Fiddlin' Man*, a return to the gritty southern boogie he helped make famous on his mid-'70s albums *Fire on the Mountain* and *Nightrider*. Ultimately, Daniels would not get his fellow outlaw rocker Williams, the son of country music's rebel pioneer Hank Sr., to sing on "Waco." Instead, Daniels would recruit a younger fan, Garth Brooks, the man whose fusion of cornball songs and rock-star pyrotechnics turned country music into a multiplatinum-selling pop sensation in the early '90s.

In the years since Daniels's southern-rock heyday, his music has made a much bigger impact on country than rock. You can hear it in the songs of stars such as Brooks, Alan Jackson, Travis Tritt, and Toby Keith. But Daniels himself has shunned the slick new country of the post-MTV generation. In the early '90s, when "alternative" became the mainstream rock sound of choice and "country" turned into a euphemism for slick, mushy ballads with a southern-rock swagger, Daniels's sound remained as raw and ornery as ever. After releasing *Renegade*, an aptly named collection of songs that included a cover of Duane Allman and Eric Clapton's "Layla" as well as Daniels's own patriotic "Let Freedom Ring," the singer's long-time record company, Epic, no longer knew how to sell his music. Daniels's sound was neither country nor rock, and by then, major labels wanted music to fit neatly into specific marketing niches: country, alternative, classic rock, hip-hop, metal. Daniels's brand of country music still rocked hard, and the singer continued to incorporate elements of jazz and blues into his extended live jams. After a short stint on Capitol Records, Daniels was forced to walk away from the mainstream music business, even though he had helped usher in the new era of country. In 1997, he formed his own independent record label, Blue Hat, so he could have the freedom to make the kind of music that came naturally to him.

"I don't fit into the whole Nashville thing," Daniels told me later, after his recording session, in a small break room. "I can't play that game. I never could."

By the 1990s, Daniels also had begun to incorporate his right-wing Christian beliefs into his lyrics, but his religious and political stances were as difficult to pigeonhole as his music. At a time when the Christian

right's agenda was as cookie-cutter as the sound of big-hat country pop, Daniels strayed on several fundamental issues—for example, the legacies of two American presidents: Richard Milhous Nixon and James Earl Carter Jr.

"Jimmy Carter is the most honorable man to hold the office of president of the United States of America in my lifetime," Daniels told me. It was not an offhand remark. The singer said it firmly and decisively.

Charlie Daniels well remembers the era of Watergate, Nixon, and Carter. For nearly two hours, we talked at length about the two former presidents, the rise of southern rock in the early 1970s, and the southernization of America as that decade lay its roots. At one point, during a discussion of Watergate and the nation's collective loss of innocence, Daniels looked up from the table where we were sitting and stared me straight in the eye with a look of genuine concern on his ruddy face.

"That was a pretty big crisis in our country," he said. "Until Nixon came around, we had not had a president come close to being impeached since Andrew Johnson, way back in the 1800s or something. Then all of a sudden, you had this guy sitting in the biggest chair in the world, and he's about to be impeached. And you thought, Wow, this is the United States of America—we're not supposed to have anything like that happen."

By then, Daniels, like many Americans, was disillusioned with his beloved country. He'd always had a strong faith in America and God, and believed in the collective feeling of righteousness on which the country had been founded. But like many of us who grew up in the South during civil rights, the singer wound up believing he had been lied to. After the assassination of Martin Luther King Jr. and Daniels's own personal transformation from a young racist into a thoughtful adult musician who combined black and white musical styles, the singer began to question the nation's sincerity. The Republican Nixon had won the traditionally Democratic South by a landslide, appealing to the region's strong sense of individuality. Daniels certainly fancied himself an individualist, but there was something about Nixon that didn't sit right with the singer. During Nixon's administration, the Vietnam War continued to drag on with no end in sight. What's more, the president displayed contempt for the feelings of many young Americans and African-Americans. When Nixon lied to the nation about his involvement in the attempted break-

in of the Democratic National Committee headquarters at the Watergate Hotel, Daniels's fears were validated: the house of cards that was the United States seemed to be crashing down.

In the South, the battle between longhairs and rednecks was nearly as heated as the battle between the races. At that time, having long hair in the South was only a notch above having black skin. Daniels, who by then had worked with Bob Dylan in Nashville, began to grow his hair long and shaggy and befriended other young southerners who also wore their hair longer than the norm. "Hair length had become just another form of discrimination, and a lot of people with long hair were easily intimidated by these redneck bullies," said Daniels. He laughed. "Heck, they'd grow out their hair and then feel intimidated. And then these redneck guys—they knew it. They preyed on it. But I didn't buy into that crap."

Daniels remembered an early incident that clued him in to the magnitude of the gap between hippies and rednecks: "I was recording with Roy Buchanan downtown [in Nashville] and I came out of the studio one night and went into this all-night place to get a sandwich. Well, I was just sitting there and this guy walked up to me and said, 'I reckon you think you look good with that old long hair, but I don't think you look worth a damn.' I looked at that fellow and I said, 'You know, if I live to be a hundred years old, do you think I could possibly give a damn what you think about my hair?' Well, of course, he just immediately backed off."

Daniels is a large, imposing man. He could get away with standing up to bullies. But not all longhaired musicians of the era felt so confident. Daniels remembered an event in Louisiana, just after the counterculture movie *Easy Rider* came out. The producers decided to hold the movie's premiere in Baton Rouge, and Daniels attended it. He was amused at the behavior of some of the nonsouthern hippies he'd met and befriended in California.

"Everybody from San Francisco was down there—the Grateful Dead, the Jefferson Airplane, the Youngbloods, all those bands, all those longhaired bands," Daniels said. "Well, I went into a restaurant one morning to eat and all those people were in there. Now, back then, you know, I got the impression that a lot of these guys were kind of paranoid, looking around at people, like, "Where's the redneck with the gun? Where's the guy with the scissors who's gonna try to cut my hair?" I thought it was kind of funny, you know, 'cause I was raised in the South and they

weren't. They didn't know what to think or expect, and they'd just seen *Easy Rider*, where those two characters get blown away by a couple of good ol' boys. And here they were, right in the belly of the beast."

By 1969, according to Daniels, the old-style redneck's bark was far worse than his bite. After several years of being rendered obsolete, bigoted rednecks had become fairly well emasculated, even on their own turf.

"But a lot of these kids from California during that time didn't know this," he said. "They were terrified of people like that. They didn't know that all you had to do was just turn around and stand up to them and say, 'Who the hell do you think you're talking to? I'll bust your nose if you don't get up outta my face.'"

The whole episode—the *Easy Rider* movie as well as the events surrounding the Baton Rouge premiere—inspired Daniels to write a funny song about a hippie who stands up to a bunch of rednecks in a Jackson, Mississippi, roadhouse. Called "Uneasy Rider," the country-folk story-song became Daniels's first hit single in 1973.

"The whole point of 'Uneasy Rider' was that you don't have to take crap from people," he said. "I was like, 'Are you gonna let some guy come up and shoot you like they did in that movie?' Hell no, I'm not gonna let some guy shoot me. I'll run over him in my car if I have to. Or I'll hit him in the head with a baseball bat or whatever else I can pick up. If I'm going down, he's going down with me. I'm not a sheep to be led to slaughter. That was the kind of impression I got from some of those longhaired kids from San Francisco—they were acting like sheep."

When Daniels performed in Mississippi after "Uneasy Rider" came out, he got death threats. "I heard the Ku Klux Klan had said we better not come down there. Of course, that made me want to go down just that much more. I was like, 'Ku Klux, hell! What are they gonna do?' I mean, they're just damn people. Put a sheet over your head and you're still just a man under there.

"Where I come from . . ." Daniels said, then paused and smiled. "Well, you come from the same place, so you know what I'm talking about. You just don't take stuff like that from people."

In 1973, Daniels represented a new brand of hippie, an edgier and more confident hippie than the peace-and-love crowd from the West Coast. He fell somewhere between the hawks and the doves, not totally at ease in either camp. When he first heard the Allman Brothers Band, Daniels said he

felt like he'd found his new family. He would soon be bonding with other southern musicians similarly inspired by the Allmans' rise.

By the mid-'70s, the locals around Macon, Georgia, were used to seeing longhaired hippies hanging around Phil Walden's recording studio. Ever since the Allman Brothers hit the big note, scrawny white rockers from all over the South, including the Marshall Tucker Band, from Spartanburg, South Carolina, and Wet Willie, from Mobile, Alabama, converged on the quiet town smack-dab in the middle of Georgia. When Daniels struck gold with "Uneasy Rider," he became just one more hippie to show up in Macon ready to jam with Walden's growing army of musicians. When it came time for him to record a new album, Daniels looked to Paul Hornsby, the former Hourglass guitarist, who was producing bands for Capricorn Records.

"Charlie had been out opening shows for the Allman Brothers and playing with the Tucker Band a lot, so we invited him to play fiddle on the second Tucker album," Hornsby remembered. "Well, we struck up a good friendship and Charlie wanted to know if I would consider producing his next album."

Daniels was already signed to another record label, but he felt such a strong kinship with Walden's roster of musicians that he thought recording in Macon might inspire him. He remembered the first time he met the guys in the Marshall Tucker Band: "I hadn't never met them in my life before, but I walked right into their dressing room that night and said, 'Somebody told me you sombitches are from Spartanburg, South Carolina,' and they just smiled at me."

Daniels shook his head and laughed. "Now, you just don't say that to people unless you know where they're coming from, and I instinctively knew," he said. "I mean, I didn't really know them yet, but I knew where they were coming from."

Hornsby needed to see the Charlie Daniels Band perform before he would commit to working with them. "I went over to Tuscaloosa, Alabama, to seem 'em play, and I thought they were good and all, but by that time they were almost too heavily influenced by the Allman Brothers," recalled Hornsby, sitting at his piano in his Macon recording studio. "I thought, there's already an Allman Brothers Band, we don't need another one."

In a recording studio, the producer's job is to look for that special qual-

ity in an artist's sound and bring it out in the music. Hornsby had brought out the jazzy elements in the Marshall Tucker Band's sound. In Daniels, he saw something else. "On the last song of his set that night," Hornsby continued, "Charlie brought out a fiddle. Well, when he played 'The Orange Blossom Special,' I tell you, the roof liked to have come offa that place. I mean, the crowd just went nuts. I remember telling him, 'Man, you don't need to hide that fiddle. That's what the people want to hear.' "

When Hornsby and the Daniels Band hunkered down in Macon, in 1974, to record *Fire on the Mountain*, the producer pressed Daniels for more fiddle. "It still wasn't the biggest thing in his music at that time," said Hornsby, "but I noticed that all throughout the session he kept playing this little song on that fiddle. We started referring to it as the 'fiddle boogie.' He didn't have no lyrics to it yet, it was just a little melody."

Daniels eventually came up with another story song, much like "Uneasy Rider," only this story was more of an allegory about a growing movement that had begun among his circle of musician friends. In "The South's Gonna Do It," the fiddle player name-checked every important southern musical character of the period, from the Allmans' Dickey Betts to Lynyrd Skynyrd to the Marshall Tucker Band, Wet Willie and ZZ Top.

In retrospect, the impact of 1974's "The South's Gonna Do It" across America was huge, and today Daniels is well aware of it. "You know, up until that time, people in the North never knew southerners very well," he said. "They still thought we were just a bunch of incestuous, uneducated people who didn't know anything. I think the Allman Brothers having a black guy in the group at that time was a real eye-opener for a lot of people outside the South. And nobody ever said anything bad about Jaimoe [the Allmans' African-American percussionist]. He is just one of the gentlest spirits you'd ever meet. He was one of the first people in the Allman Brothers that I really started getting tight with. He was always accessible. And I think people outside of the South looked at that band and said, 'Wow. This isn't something we expected.'

"The fact is, until then, neither the North nor the South knew much about each other. I remember working in Jacksonville, North Carolina, and some of these Marine kids would come down there from up north, and they didn't know nothing about southern people. But we didn't know much about them, either. So, I think this music and these bands kind of opened things up in terms of them understanding us and us understanding them."

Some of the Charlie Daniels Band's biggest audiences were in northern cities. "Our first big markets were in Long Island and the whole New York City area other than Manhattan—all those little cities in upstate New York," said Daniels. "People were fascinated by us up there. And I think it's because the music reflected a distinct lifestyle more than any other music that was going on at the time. Everything else in rock at that time was very cerebral—Jefferson Airplane, the Grateful Dead—you had to stop and think about it. But we talked about daily life."

Southern bands, said Daniels, spoke from the gut. "Take Lynyrd Skynyrd," he continued. "Ronnie was upset at something Neil Young wrote and he sang about it: 'Southern man don't need him around anyhow.' He just come right out and said what he meant. I think a lot of the kids up north were hungry for that kind of thing. That's when a lot of 'em started wearing cowboy hats and stuff." Daniels laughed. "I started seeing 'em come to our concerts with cowboy hats on. They looked pretty silly, actually."

The tables were turning. The South was coming into vogue. Charlie Daniels, Lynyrd Skynyrd, and the Allman Brothers were turning southern culture into a pop-culture phenomenon, and "The South's Gonna Do It" put it all into a little musical snapshot.

For Daniels, though, the song will always be "just a little fiddle tune" that expressed his delight at having found a group of musicians who shared his background—friends who identified with his long hair as well as his red neck.

"You know, I never looked at that song as a masterpiece or anything," said Daniels. "I just admired all those groups and I wanted to say it. This was the first time in my life where I felt like I could sit around with a bunch of musicians and be totally at home. When I met all those guys, it was just an instant friendship, instant bonding. It was like that with the Marshall Tucker Band and it was like that with all the rest of 'em."

Daniels lowered his voice. "You know, I could sit down with Ronnie Van Zant or with Dickey Betts of the Allman Brothers or with Jimmy Hall of Wet Willie, and we all liked the same things. We all ate grits for breakfast. We all went to basically the same kind of schools." He paused and shook his head. "I tell you, when people talk about southern rock, I say it's not a genre of music—it's a genre of people."

★ ★ ★

You could apply Charlie Daniels's definition of southern rock to my circle of friends in Asheboro, North Carolina, in 1974. There was Robert George, the budding sculptor with fire in his eyes, who would buzz into my front yard on his minibike on hot summer days, grinning like a Cheshire cat, and take me away from my lawn-mowing chores. There was Steve Kendrick, the preacher's kid who played bass in my junior high school rock band and talked with me into the wee hours about groups like Foghat and Deep Purple. There was Joey Jones, the redheaded troublemaker who'd get together with me on weekends to look for girls and play foosball at the local pool hall. There was Joey Moffitt, the older kid who'd swing by my house in his Triumph TR6, Lynyrd Skynyrd blasting on his stereo, and take me cruising through the countryside at eighty miles an hour. All those guys were among the "genre of people" about whom Daniels waxes so eloquently.

But Jeff Brown didn't feel a part of that "genre of people." Even though he hung out with us, performed in southern rock bands, and listened to the Allmans and the Outlaws, Jeff never felt the bond with us that Daniels experienced with the members of the Marshall Tucker Band and Lynyrd Skynyrd. Jeff didn't feel it because he was concealing the secret of his homosexuality. He didn't feel comfortable enough in Asheboro, North Carolina, to open up and talk about the very thing that informs our personalities, feeds our creativity, and inspires rock & roll songs: sex.

"I just couldn't, Mark," he told me many years later. "I didn't feel safe enough."

And for good reason. While Jeff's homosexuality might have been accepted by some of us, it certainly would not have been well received by a guy like Charlie Daniels. Fifteen years after "Uneasy Rider" rocketed into the Billboard Top 10—and a decade after the fellowship of southern rock fans at my high school graduated—Daniels recorded an update of his first hit song, renaming it "Uneasy Rider '88." In the new version, his protagonist walks into a punk-rock club rather than the redneck juke joint of his earlier song. At the bar inside, a gay man propositions him.

"He said, 'I love it when you get that fire in your eyes,' " Daniels sings. "I said, 'Well partner, try this on for size, / I unloaded on him and he went out like a light."

By the end of the song, the protagonist's buddy becomes physically ill when he inadvertently hooks up with a transvestite, and the final lines of Daniels's new song offers a twisted moral: "I done give up drinkin' and

I've give up bars, / And runnin' round the country in souped-up cars. / I'm goin' back to where the women are women and the men are men."

For nearly two hours, Daniels and I had been discussing the significance that southerners place on friends, family, integrity, and individuality. When I brought up the gay issue, he appeared insecure for the first time in our conversation.

This is how I broached the subject: "Charlie, we've been talking a lot about love and tolerance. I want to address something that bothers me about some things you've said in the past. You see, I have a good friend named Jeff Brown who always loved southern rock. We used to play in bands together and he developed into this amazing guitarist, totally inspired by the Allmans, Lynyrd Skynyrd, bands like that. We're real tight."

Daniels gave me the understanding smile of someone who identified with this kind of musical bonding with a fellow southern man.

Then I continued: "But Jeff has lost his love of that music, Charlie. You see, as a gay man, Jeff feels as though the music doesn't love him back."

Daniels furrowed his brow and looked down at his hands.

"And that makes Jeff very angry," I continued. "He feels alienated by the intolerance in songs like 'Uneasy Rider '88.' "

I paused, then asked: "What would you say to my old friend Jeff, from Asheboro, North Carolina?"

Daniels may have been taken off guard by the radical detour, but he was quick with a reply:

"You could tell him that I love him."

I didn't expect the response, although I don't know why. As contradictory as Charlie Daniels seems, there's a consistency to his overall worldview. As a Christian, he would be remiss in saying anything else about Jeff. He told me he would say the same of the rednecks in the original "Uneasy Rider."

"Look, I don't hate anybody," he said firmly. "That song's not about hating. That song's supposed to be funny. It's about a couple of old guys who end up in the wrong club. The earlier one was about a *young* guy who ends up in the wrong club."

Daniels leaned back in his chair and his face softened again. "I mean, we all have to laugh at ourselves," he said. "How many songs about fat

people have you ever heard? Look at me. I'm fat. I don't get upset about it. I laugh at it. What else am I gonna do? I'm not going to assume that because somebody makes up a funny song about fat people that they hate me or that they hate fat people in general. Fat people can be funny. Gay people can be funny.

"To me, it comes down to this: people can be very sensitive. They tend to take things all out of context. The first version of that song was funny, too. I made fun of a bunch of rednecks in a bar in Jackson, Mississippi."

Still, there was the nagging issue of the inflammatory editorials that Daniels regularly posts on his Web site. In 2001, the singer came under fire in his hometown of Wilmington, North Carolina, when the gay community there protested his induction into the city's Walk of Fame. Shortly after September 11, Daniels had posted a shrill editorial explaining why he believed God allowed terrorists to attack the United States. Daniels blamed abortion, "radical groups" such as the American Civil Liberties Union, and people living together out of wedlock. He even blamed former president Bill Clinton.

Finally, Daniels blamed gays.

"We have proclaimed that homosexuality is just another lifestyle, when the Bible clearly states that it is an abomination to God," he wrote.

When I brought up his editorial, Daniels cited the old adage about hating the sin but not the sinner. "Look, I'm not down on anybody, but I don't condone homosexuality. I'm a Christian; I can't condone it," he said. "But I'm as sinful as anybody else is. I know that. I can't go around pointing my finger at somebody else, but I can let you know how I feel about it. And I can write a funny song about it if I want to."

He was on a roll: "I can very easily be friends with homosexuals if they can be friends with me, man. I've corresponded with homosexuals and we get along great. But a lot of times the hostility reaches such a point that they just shut me out. To me, [shutting out Christians] is just as prejudiced as it would be if somebody were to shut out blacks or homosexuals or anybody else. It's closed-minded. And when people make statements like some of the things I've heard from so-called leaders in the homosexual community, they may as well expect people to look down on them. I've read statements like, 'We will rape your sons in the men's rooms of this country,' and when I hear that kind of thing . . . I mean, what do you expect?"

Surely, I pointed out, Daniels didn't believe that a statement such as that represents the feelings of the gay community any more than any statement of criminal intent represents any community. He concurred.

"Yeah, I try to look past that. I know that a lot of times the people who consider themselves leaders of a community don't necessarily reflect the attitudes of that community nearly as much as they'd like to think they do," Daniels said. "I know plenty of gay people who don't talk like that. Some of the gentlest people I've met are gays. I've sat down and talked with them and we've found common ground, you know. We might not find it in our sexuality."

I wondered how different the South would be today if Charlie Daniels had ever written *those* feelings into a song.

★ Chapter 6 ★

JIVE TALKIN'

On *a balmy weeknight in the spring of 1975 — a night warm enough for a T-shirt and cutoff jeans but not yet so hot that folks were complaining about it — I met up with Hubert Miller and Martin Nicholson next to a streetlight at the corner of Coleridge Road and East Salisbury Street in our hometown. The intersection served as the proverbial "tracks" in Asheboro. My family lived on the south side of Salisbury, the white side; Martin and Hubert's families lived on the north side, known as "the Hill" or "Colored Town."*

It was late, around midnight, and the three of us were not just a little freaked out. At school there was a riot going on. During lunch break earlier in the week, a white girl had been tackled on the playground by a black guy. When a group of white boys saw what happened, they pounced on the black kid and beat him with all the stored-up rage of several generations of white fear. The scuffle escalated into a schoolwide war. Although the black boy and white girl both were adamant that the tackle had been only horse-play, it was too late. As in Los Angeles in the wake of the O. J. Simpson trial many years later, the battle lines were drawn at Asheboro Junior High School.

For the next week, the school grounds became a combat zone. Whites and blacks released all the suppressed frustration that had been stirred up during the civil rights movement and left smoldering in the six years since the schools in my hometown had been completely integrated. The police were called in to mediate, and a few students were suspended or expelled

for the rest of the term. The kids who didn't want to be involved stayed home.

Martin, Hubert, and I skipped classes that week to avoid having to take sides. With nothing else to do, we roamed the streets of east Asheboro, throwing rocks up into the wiring of the streetlights to cause brief blackouts in the neighborhood. On this particular night, we eventually made our way to the home of Martin's aunt Peaches.

I brought along a copy of Keep On Smilin', *by the southern rock band Wet Willie. I wanted Martin and Hubert to hear the record, because one of the songs on it, "Soul Sister," was as funky as anything I'd ever heard by a black soul group. The song featured the vocals of the Williettes, two female backup singers whose voices resembled the sassy, gospel harmonies of the Sweet Inspirations.*

"Man, them dudes sound black. I think I like it," said Hubert, whom we called Tater for his round, potato-like body. Martin nodded in agreement.

They had an album for me, too.

"Get that Funkadelic record," Tater said to Martin, and the two grinned at each other as if they were about to open up Pandora's box. I'd heard the name Funkadelic, but was more familiar with leader George Clinton's other band, Parliament, whose album covers featured men and women in space-age outfits. Some of the black kids would bring Parliament's records to school and sing along to songs like "Up for the Down Stroke."

"Funkadelic's different," said Tater, pulling the record out of its sleeve. It had a disturbing cover image of a woman with a huge Afro buried to her neck in maggots. When Hubert put the needle to the grooves of the album, 1971's Maggot Brain, *the music was as bizarre as anything I'd ever heard by Pink Floyd or Frank Zappa. The wailing of lead guitar on the ten-minute title track made the noodling of the Grateful Dead's Jerry Garcia seem like quaint folk music by comparison. Things were going on in this funky, psychedelic mix that I never thought could occupy the same sonic space: heavy, fuzzy, hard-rock power chords; deep, funky bass; doo-wop and gospel vocals; gentle acoustic-folk guitar strumming. My bias had led me to assume that black musicians made only straightforward soul, funk, or rhythm & blues. I couldn't imagine they had the creative wherewithal to come up with such otherworldly sounds.*

At fifteen, I was slowly becoming aware of the limitations of my experience. In hindsight, having later discovered John Coltrane and Miles Davis,

and traced the music of the Allman Brothers Band back to its African-
American blues and free-jazz origins, my surprise upon hearing
Funkadelic's music that night is laughable. I'd heard the voices of the
singers in the black churches of my hometown and listened to the wisdom
of Martin Luther King Jr.'s speeches on television. But though I instinc-
tively knew blacks could do more than sweep floors or take care of white
babies, I'd never been taught as much. Neither Martin nor Tater had
learned until that night that southern whites could sing funky soul music
the way Jimmy Hall of Wet Willie did.

A quarter century later, when I was an editorial executive at MTV,
Martin came to visit me in New York. As we reminisced about our school
days, he asked me to play those Funkadelic and Wet Willie albums again.
When "Soul Sister" came on, Martin looked at me and smiled.

"Back then, man, I had no clue you people could sing like that," he said.

On that spring night in 1975, it took a race riot to bring Martin
Nicholson, Tater Miller, and me closer to each other's cultures.

A few weeks before the riot, Kathy, the girl who'd broken up with me
using lines from "Free Bird," came to school wearing a Kool and the
Gang T-shirt. To me, Kool and the Gang's "Jungle Boogie," released the
year before, represented the worst of a horrible new dance-music trend
called disco, and I ridiculed Kathy relentlessly, telling her disco was not
really music at all.

"Whatever," she said. "I like it. What's the big deal?"

The big deal was that Kathy had broken my heart and I wanted her to
hurt. In reality, Kool and the Gang played funk, not disco, but such subtleties went straight over my head. White stoner kids like my friends and
me, who preferred to sit around and listen to rock albums than to dance,
focused on disco's cheesy side. I would never have acknowledged it back
then, but my disdain of "Jungle Boogie"—the very image that its title sug-
gests—most likely had everything to do with race. As smart and open-
minded as I felt I was, this band of sexy, funky black men was somehow
threatening to me.

By the mid-'70s, the first rumblings of disco had reached Asheboro.
One Saturday morning I was watching the pop-music dance show

American Bandstand on TV and saw a wiry young white guy with an Afro shaking his booty to some new R&B hit. It could have been the Hues Corporation's "Rock the Boat" or Barry White's "You're the First, the Last, My Everything," I don't remember. But I do remember the dancer: he was wearing a skintight T-shirt emblazoned with the words LET'S GO DISCO, the name of a song by the Philadelphia funk band MFSB. I wasn't familiar with the song at that time, and I didn't know what the word *disco* meant.

Since the late '60s, MFSB (which stands for "Mother Father Sister Brother") had been the house band for Philadelphia producers Kenny Gamble and Leon Huff. Like the Muscle Shoals Rhythm Section, in Alabama, and Booker T. and the MGs, in Memphis, MFSB created a sound—heavy bass, funky guitars, organ, piano, horns, and lush strings—that informed the music of every hit-making soul ensemble that recorded for Philadelphia International Records: the O'Jays, the Spinners, Harold Melvin and the Blue Notes, Teddy Pendergrass, the Intruders, Billy Paul, Archie Bell and the Drells, the Trammps. In 1973, MFSB's instrumental "TSOP (The Sound of Philadelphia)" became the theme song for *Soul Train,* television's R&B answer to *American Bandstand.*

Late that same year, the first article on disco appeared in *Rolling Stone* magazine. Written by dance-music authority Vince Aletti, one of the first openly gay pop critics, the article described a growing trend in the predominantly gay New York City nightclubs that had sprung up across Manhattan in the years after the Stonewall uprising of 1969. That's when New York police raided a gay bar in Greenwich Village and relentlessly beat several patrons. The beatings led to rioting and demonstrations on the streets of the Village, which soon turned to open celebration of gay pride. That pride manifested itself on the dance floors of New York's gay nightclubs.

By the early '70s, people attending those clubs were not there to see musicians perform—they were there to create new dance moves and to see the deejays who were spinning the newest records. Many of those records happened to be by Philly soul bands such as the O'Jays and the Intruders. It seemed an unlikely alliance was forming among New York's glittery downtown gay scene and its uptown street culture.

Within two or three years, clubs such as Nicky Siano's the Gallery became meeting places for rock stars such as David Bowie and Mick

Jagger, who wanted to be seen by the hip and trendy. In 1975, Elton
John, who had gone from a piano-playing singer-songwriter to a full-
fledged pop star with his 1973 album *Goodbye Yellow Brick Road*, paid
tribute to the Philly sound with his pop/R&B crossover hit "Philadelphia
Freedom."

Disco and the Philly sound were making an impact on music fans of
all kinds, and southerners were no exception. But by the time the music
was beamed from the big cities into the small towns of the rural South,
its underground gay roots got lost in the transmission. In my hometown,
disco became the music of the popular kids at school: the jocks, the
cheerleaders, the preppies, the debutantes. It was hardly the sound of an
edgy political uprising; to my friends and me, it was music for mindless
materialists. Today, when revisionist pop critics look back on the "Disco
Sucks" movement, they often characterize it, rightly, as driven by homophobia and racism. On an institutional level, that's probably an accurate
interpretation, but on a populist level—that of the average music listener
in small towns across America in the mid-1970s—the homophobia argument is likely less true. Some of the most virulent homophobes of my
hometown were also the biggest fans of the new disco sound.

My best friend, Jeff Brown, who was secretly dealing with his own
homosexuality then, remembered, "To me, in the South, where we grew
up, disco was not the music of gay liberation or black power. It was the
music of the high school elite. Disco didn't make me feel empowered as
a gay man, it made me feel bad about who I was, because the people who
listened to disco made me feel bad about who I was.

"I listened to southern rock because it was good music, it sounded
good," Jeff went on. "I was a guitarist, you know, and southern rock had
great guitars in it."

Disco and funk, though, did inform some of the southern rock coming out by the mid-'70s. Wet Willie's big hit "Keep On Smilin' " was
driven by a funky, reggae-tinged groove, and inspired the band's further
flirtation with disco and funk on songs such as "Baby Fat," from *The
Wetter the Better*, in 1976. Wet Willie's keyboardist, percussionist, and
guitarist, John Anthony, even took to wearing the star-shaped sunglasses
made famous by Parliament-Funkadelic bassist Bootsy Collins.

★ ★ ★

By 1975, disco, funk, southern rock, and the rising outlaw country movement formed an unlikely coalition that would help elect a president. Southern rock was creeping ever higher into the American pop consciousness. Between 1973 and 1975, a slew of Dixie-centric songs—the Allmans' "Ramblin' Man," Skynyrd's "Sweet Home Alabama," Wet Willie's "Keep On Smilin' " the Atlanta Rhythm Section's "Doraville," Ozark Mountain Daredevils' "If You Wanna Get to Heaven," and the Charlie Daniels Band's "The South's Gonna Do It"—reached the Top 40 of *Billboard*'s singles charts. Phil Walden's Capricorn Records boasted twenty-seven acts ranging from the blues-based Allmans and country-tinged Marshall Tucker Band to the funky Wet Willie, jazz fusionists the Dixie Dregs, and blues-rock singer Bonnie Bramlett. Walden, now one of the most powerful men in the music business, had such a broad range of acts at his fingertips that when he began stumping for presidential hopeful Jimmy Carter, his youth-culture clout was formidable. Walden's benefit concerts for the Georgia governor featured a string of Capricorn acts as well as southern rockers on other labels.

Carter and Walden had become friends well before the governor became the Democratic presidential candidate. "We're still friends," Walden told me at his Atlanta home in 2002. "Hell, we went to see Bob Dylan together not too long ago and he was singing along to every song." In 1974, Walden brought Carter into a Macon studio to visit the Allmans' Dickey Betts while the guitarist was recording his first solo album, *Highway Call*. "He was very proud that a group of musicians from Georgia were reaching so many people," Betts recalled to Allmans biographer Scott Freeman. "He was just going to drop by the studio and say hello, and he stayed there for about four hours. He was really intrigued by it. He really is into music."

By all accounts, Carter's love of rock & roll was not just a ploy to secure the youth vote. In Kandy Stroud's book *How Jimmy Won*, the former president talked about his conversion from classical music to rock. ". . . I started listening to Bob Dylan's music primarily because of my sons," Carter said, "but I got to like it and I used to spend three or four hours a day listening to Paul Simon, Bob Dylan, and the Allman Brothers."

The Allmans liked Carter, too, and when the governor began his bid for the presidency, the group supported him wholeheartedly. Carter had

changed Georgia. When he became governor in 1971, ending Lester
Maddox's racist term, Carter immediately announced, to the consterna-
tion of many whites, "The time for racial discrimination is over." On May
31 of that same year, the former peanut farmer appeared on the cover of
Time magazine as one of the architects of the so-called New South.
According to Betts, "all of a sudden everybody started coming together—
the blacks and the longhairs and the musicians and the welders and the
mechanics. [Carter] made a misdemeanor out of reefer in Georgia before
they had it in California. It wasn't that he believed that smoking reefer
was out of sight, but he was sick and tired of seeing young kids sixteen and
eighteen years old going to jail with hardened criminals."

In early 1975, according to writer Freeman, the Allmans got an invitation to a party Carter was throwing for Bob Dylan at the governor's
mansion. The band arrived too late for the festivities, but Gregg Allman
asked the security guard to let the governor know they had dropped by.
As the Allmans' limo began to drive away, the guard yelled out, "Wait a
minute! The governor wants to see you on the steps of the mansion."
When the Allmans approached the mansion, Carter was waiting for
them, shirtless and shoeless, wearing just a pair of old blue jeans. "You
know, I'm going to be your next president," he told a dubious Gregg
Allman, who agreed to do whatever he could to help the campaign. On
October 6, the Allmans brought Carter along to introduce the band at a
performance at the Omni Theater, in Atlanta. The group's first real benefit for Carter came the following month, at the civic center in
Providence, Rhode Island. The show raised $40,000 for Carter's cam-
paign. It was one of five benefit concerts Walden would put on for Carter,
ultimately raising a total of $151,000.

The downside of Carter's association with the Allmans was drugs. By
the mid-'70s, Walden's Capricorn Records was nose-deep in cocaine.
Narcotics agents were swarming around the record company's Macon
headquarters like buzzards, and by the following year they would come
in for the kill. A prime target was Gregg Allman, who was severely weak-
ened by a heroin addiction that had him waking up each morning to a
blast of cocaine. Narcotics agents would eventually use Allman as a patsy
to bring down a bigger drug ring. Allman was a mess, and by the time the
band's sixth album, *Win, Lose or Draw*, came out in late 1975, his life was
falling apart.

"It was a terrible time for everybody," said Walden. "The drugs were so bad and everyone was so paranoid. Dickey Betts would be coming into the office all wild and saying, 'Johnny Sandlin [the producer] is going down there late at night and erasing all my guitar tracks.'

"I'd say, 'Well, now, why would he want to do that?'

"He'd say, 'I know he's erasing them, I know somebody was down there with him.'

"And I'd say, 'But Dickey, why would he want to do that? He's just trying to put an album together.'

"And he'd say, 'You motherfucker, I know you're on his side!' And then he'd jump up on my desk and want to fight and everything.' "

Walden shook his head: "All you gotta do is listen to *Win, Lose or Draw*—that son of a bitch was made with paste. The drummer would go down and make a drum track and then the other drummer would come in. They wouldn't want to be in there together. There's not a lot of feeling on that album. *Win, Lose or Draw* was definitely 'lose.' It was just an awful record."

The Allman Brothers Band hadn't released a new album since I was thirteen years old, and when you're only fifteen, two years is an eternity. In the summer of 1975, the main image I had of the Allmans came from a photograph on the back of the band's *Brothers and Sisters* album of 1973—that of an extended family of laid-back southern hippies, sitting on the front porch of a country home surrounded by wives, children, and dogs. The image couldn't have been further from the truth. One July afternoon, my friend Steve came over to my house to get high and play music. We rolled a few joints and walked into the woods to smoke them. I had a buzz on when Steve suddenly grinned and said he had some news for me.

"Gregg Allman married Cher," he said.

My first reaction was stoned silence. Shock. Open-mouthed disbelief. Denial came next.

I busted out laughing and asked him to repeat himself.

"It's true, man. He married Cher."

"No way," I said to Steve, whose grin now seemed to be splitting his face in half.

He reached into his back pocket and unfolded a newspaper clipping. Sure enough, according to the article, on June 30, 1975, Cher—the TV variety-show vamp ("and a bit of a tramp") who'd recently divorced her husband, Sonny ("I Got You Babe") Bono—had eloped with Gregg ("don't ask me to be Mr. Clean, 'cause baby I don't know how") Allman. The coolest man in the world had married a TV star who'd come into our living rooms for the past three years wearing outrageous headdresses and gawdy Bob Mackie gowns, singing off-key versions of cheesy pop songs like "Joy to the World" and "Bad, Bad Leroy Brown," and bantering with guests such as teen idol Bobby Sherman and television heartthrob Chad Everett.

"That's bullshit," I said, leery of the newspaper's accuracy. "Gregg Allman would never marry Cher."

Nine days later, Cher filed for divorce.

"Gregg and I made a mistake," Cher announced in a terse statement to the press. Within days, Allman was headed off to detox while Cher appeared with ex-husband Sonny on *The Tonight Show*. There was speculation of a Sonny and Cher reconciliation, but she was soon back in the news with Allman, appearing with him on the cover of *People* magazine under the headline: "She helps him stay off heroin."

Gregg Allman had become the butt of late-night TV jokes and a topic for the tabloids. He even later recorded a hideous album with Cher, *Allman and Woman: Two the Hard Way*. The singer whose deep, rich music had made me feel okay about being a small-town southern boy was turning out to be just another empty-headed rock star; Ozzy Osbourne with a southern drawl. I had idolized Allman, identified with him; he'd expressed my innermost feelings in his songs. But now, the guy who two years earlier had sung the Jackson Browne line "Please don't confront me with my failures" was failing in a big, public way. And young fans like me, who had put Allman on a pedestal, were disappointed. We had not factored failure into the equation. The greatest white soul singer alive was not supposed to marry the glitzy host of a bad TV variety show.

I turned my attention back to the Rolling Stones, my longtime English heroes who were touring America, performing on a giant, star-shaped stage. The Stones had announced the tour earlier in the summer from the back of a flatbed truck in the middle of Manhattan. It was a hell of a publicity stunt. Stunned New Yorkers watched as the Stones rolled down Fifth Avenue playing "Brown Sugar."

"Quick, Mark, come into the den," my mom called out to me the night the stunt hit the news. "You've got to see this. Hurry! Your boys are singing on the back of a truck in New York."

My mother and father had not let me go see the Stones in 1972, when I was twelve. I'd been allowed to see the Jackson Five in 1971 and never understood my folks' reasoning for not letting me see the Stones. They never gave me a clear answer, other than to say I was too young. But then they let me see the Allman Brothers shortly after I'd been to the Jacksons show, and of course they'd allowed me to attend that all-day southern rock festival when I was fourteen. I suspect they were afraid of the Stones. In 1972, the band's reputation among gullible adults in the South was comparable to that of shock rocker Marilyn Manson in the early '90s or rapper 50 Cent in the early 2000s. After the Stones' Altamont disaster in December 1969, the band had been linked to violence and chaos. The songs "Sympathy for the Devil" and "Midnight Rambler"—with lines like "I'll lay your soul to waste" and "I'll stick my knife right down your throat"—frightened parents in the Bible Belt. Though my folks weren't religious fanatics by any stretch, they were susceptible to the right-wing religious propaganda that branded the Stones as dangerous.

By 1975, though, it was pretty clear the Stones were harmless, and my mother was as intrigued with Mick Jagger as I was. She'd seen him interviewed on Tom Snyder's late-night talk show and began showing me articles about him in *People* magazine. Jagger's flirtation with New York's high society fascinated her, as did his 1971 marriage to the Nicaraguan political activist and beauty queen Bianca Rose Pérez Moreno de Macías. As we watched the Stones on the news that night, I told my mother that this time I couldn't miss the band when they stopped at the Greensboro Coliseum in late July. She agreed to take my friends and me to the show.

We arrived at the coliseum around 3:00 P.M. and waited in the parking lot along with several hundred other kids until the doors opened around 6:15 P.M. I whirled into the building with the flood of other fans and landed a spot right at the edge of the star-shaped stage. It was all very exciting to me; the newspaper had reported the week before that this would probably be the Stones' final American tour, and I was delighted to be a part of it. (In hindsight, the newspaper accounts are hilarious, as the Stones continued to tour America into the new millennium.)

The band's 1975 tour wasn't as jaw-droppingly intense as its '72 tour had been, but it was the first time I'd ever seen the Stones and I was awestruck. The opening act was Rufus with singer Chaka Khan, whose hit of the previous year, "Tell Me Something Good," was funky but with a cool rock edge. It reminded me of the Parliament/Funkadelic songs Martin and Tater had turned me on to when we skipped school during the riots. About half an hour after Rufus's set, Jagger pranced to the tip of the stage in loose-fitting pants and a striped shirt; on either side of him were the eternally cool Keith Richards and new guitarist Ron Wood. The stage's hydraulically controlled tips undulated as Richards opened the show with the deep, primal guitar riff of "Honky Tonk Women." The crowd of seventeen thousand behind me roared. Several songs later, during the infamous "Star Star"—in which Jagger spat out the words, "You're a star fucker, star fucker, star fucker"—a fifteen-foot-high inflatable penis rose up from the stage. Jagger grabbed it, jumped on it, straddled it, and rode it as if it were one of those mechanical bulls in an urban honky-tonk. The Stones ran through most of my favorite songs—"Get Off of My Cloud," "Rip This Joint," and of course, "Jumpin' Jack Flash."

I couldn't believe my idols were standing only a few feet in front of me. At one point between songs, guitarist Wood looked down at me and winked, then tossed me his half-smoked cigarette. I still have that nasty old butt safely sealed in a plastic sandwich bag along with some of the confetti spewed from a giant dragon Jagger brought onto the stage. Fuck Gregg Allman, I thought, as Jagger wiggled his way through "Midnight Rambler." At the end of the show, he tossed three buckets of water onto the heads of those of us in front of the stage and then one over himself. It was the wildest, wettest rock concert I'd ever seen. I was in heaven.

When the Allman Brothers' Win, Lose or Draw came out that year, my friends and I ignored it. The Allmans sucked. We hated them. Maybe, I thought, I'd been wrong all along. Maybe the band never did really speak to me. My dad had once told me that glittery acts like Alice Cooper were just taking my money; that they were phonies, that they were all show and no substance. What my dad didn't understand was that I never expected substance from Alice Cooper; I liked the show. But I began to wonder if I'd actually given too much of myself to bands like the Allman Brothers. At least Alice Cooper and even the Stones reveled in their flam-

boyance. Maybe the Allman Brothers were just as phony and only appeared to be honest.

Maybe, I thought, all rock bands were phony. Maybe all of them changed as they became more famous and desperate to remain popular. Maybe all of them became ugly parodies of themselves in the end. By 1975, rock & roll had become an Ouroboros, the ancient symbol of the snake that turns in on itself, devouring its own tail. What began as wild entertainment from acts like Little Richard and Jerry Lee Lewis and became a social movement with topical artists such as Bob Dylan and Joan Baez had come full circle. Former organic country rockers the Eagles and former earnest singer-songwriter Elton John had both put out slick, overproduced albums incorporating the worst elements of disco and flash. Led Zeppelin's bombastic two-record set, *Physical Graffiti*, lacked the raw, hungry edge of the band's earlier music. The Stones tossed out two crappy collections of old songs—a set of outtakes called *Metamorphosis* and the illogically conceived "greatest hits" album *Made in the Shade*—as well as a tepid new album of watered-down funk, disco, and reggae called *Black and Blue*. The Who's corny, locker-room joke of a hit single, "Squeeze Box," came off as lightweight pabulum on the heels of the band's two ambitious rock operas, *Tommy* and *Quadrophenia*. Even Bob Dylan was wearing makeup on his 1975 Rolling Thunder Revue tour.

By the mid-'70s, most rock bands were either making total idiots of themselves or taking themselves entirely too seriously. While Gregg Allman cavorted with Cher and the Eagles and Elton John dabbled in disco, a string of pretentious, classical-rock hybrid bands such as Yes, King Crimson, and Emerson, Lake and Palmer went off the deep end, producing overblown epics involving unicorns, elves, magic fairies, and moon children. Those acts led to a spate of dreadful new American bands such as Kansas, Styx, and Journey. This wasn't the rock & roll of Jerry Lee Lewis and Little Richard. It was J.R.R. Tolkien meets Andrew Lloyd Weber with loud guitars.

With the demise of the Allmans and the rise of disco and prog rock, it seemed that rock & roll was losing its soul. A new radio format called album-oriented rock began to use standardized playlists, and the top songs on AM pop stations ran from schmaltzy ballads by Barry Manilow and Neil Sedaka to lightweight singer-songwriter hits by John Denver,

disposable pop from forgettable acts like Captain and Tennille, and watered-down funk from groups such as the aptly named Average White Band. If it weren't for the southern rock bands that had sprung up in the wake of the Allmans—and the small group of Nashville insurgents led by Willie Nelson and Waylon Jennings—I would have given up on pop and rock altogether.

I almost did. Aside from attending that Stones concert, I spent much of the summer of '75 reading about hippies and the late '60s San Francisco sound—Jefferson Airplane, the Grateful Dead, and Quicksilver Messenger Service. Listening to those groups, I could escape into a psychedelic haze but still feel connected to reality by the outlaw characters in tunes such as the Dead's "Jack Straw" and "Tennessee Jed," or the pastoral setting of Airplane songs such as "The Farm." To me, outlaw country and older political folk and hippie music were more meaningful than the music of most new southern rock bands, and certainly better than the mainstream rock and pop. At fifteen, I was already beginning to feel like a crotchety middle-aged man, pining for the "old days"—the late '60s and early '70s, when rock was still daring and unpredictable.

I'd been reading in the rock magazine *Creem* about a new sound called punk, but I had only a vague idea what it was, and that idea was not a good one. Familiar names like Lou Reed and the Velvet Underground, the New York Dolls and David Bowie were mentioned in connection with a few unknown names: the Ramones, Patti Smith, Television, the Sex Pistols. But albums by those bands hadn't arrived in my part of the South yet, and the music didn't seem to have much to do with my reality. Beyond what I read about punk from the gonzo rock critic Lester Bangs, whom I felt was rather severe in his treatment of some of the music that I liked, I knew little about the actual sound of punk. From what I read, it seemed as if punk bands were just more amateurish versions of bands like Kiss. I was so ignorant of punk, in fact, that when I once read a blurb in *Creem* about P-Funk (shorthand for Parliament-Funkadelic), the connection to George Clinton went straight over my head. I didn't know this was the same group Martin and Tater had turned me on to that summer; I figured P-Funk was another one of the punk bands Lester Bangs liked.

The music that moved me most in 1975 was the old-time bluegrass and folk that I heard at a fiddlers' convention held each year in Union

Grove, North Carolina. My sister and her friends had told me about this festival, where young bikers and hippies gathered alongside farmers and factory workers to listen to organic acoustic songs on a sprawling farm. This was the music that my friend Tim Womick had introduced me to the summer before. When my dad bought me an old sunburst Gibson Hummingbird acoustic guitar, I began learning some of the traditional songs from my own region — songs by Doc Watson, Earl Scruggs, and Bill Monroe. I also learned to play tunes by artists such as John Prine, Dylan, and Phil Ochs, whom I'd read about in my school's library in a book called *Songs of Peace, Freedom and Protest*. If rock & roll was going down, I figured I'd jump ship before I drowned along with the rest of that Fellini-esque crowd.

By late 1975, a drug investigation was heating up in Macon, and Gregg Allman would soon be making headlines again. The news, combined with Allman's soap opera relationship with Cher, provided the final blow to his reputation. Facing charges, Allman was about to rat on his band's longtime dope dealer, Macon auto mechanic John Charles "Scooter" Herring. That was the clincher. It was unacceptable. If you were an Allman Brothers fan back then, you also were most likely a "head," one of the kids who got high and depended on the trust of fellow heads to stay out of trouble. If you considered yourself among the fellowship of heads, the worst thing someone could call you was a "narc." When Allman, dressed in fancy bell-bottoms and a rawhide jacket, walked into a Macon courtroom a few months later, on June 23, 1976, to testify against Herring, the singer was immediately branded a narc.

"He overstepped his boundaries when he got a man who saved his life more than once a seventy-five-year jail sentence," wrote Allman Brothers Band drummer Jaimoe Johnson in a letter to the editor of the *Macon News*. "I can no longer work with or for Gregg Allman, but I still pray for God to help him and all of us."

Guitarist Dickey Betts told *Rolling Stone*, "There's no way we can work with Gregg again. Ever."

"That was unbelievable," said my old schoolmate Debbie Higgins, who today goes by her married name Debbie Pickens. "It was totally uncool. Those were dark days for our southern rockers."

★   ★   ★

Debbie Higgins was the queen mama of the heads at my high school. At noon every day, you'd find her holding court on a little road behind the school where we all gathered during lunchtime to smoke pot and listen to music. Higgins was one of the few girls whom everyone referred to by her last name. She was too cool to be called Debbie.

I remember her telling me one day in 1976 about a regional band called Nantucket. I wasn't familiar with the group.

"You don't know who Nantucket is?" she said. "Jesus, Kemp."

I felt like an idiot.

"Nantucket Sleighride," she went on about the band, which hailed from the military town of Jacksonville, North Carolina, and would later sign to Epic Records. Apparently, Nantucket performed almost every weekend at some nearby nightclub that we were too young to get into.

But Higgins would get in.

"God, they rock, man," she said. "They got their name from that Mountain album, *Nantucket Sleighride*." She rolled her eyes and grimaced. "Jesus!"

Higgins seemed to know everything, and if she didn't, you'd never guess it, because she acted as if she did. We were buddies. We'd been buddies since my first semester at Asheboro Junior High, right across the street from the senior high school.

I had met Higgins in 1972, when George Harrison's *Concert for Bangladesh* film came to the only movie theater in town. I made plans to meet my friends Dean Needham and Craig King there. It was my first concert film and I couldn't wait to see big-screen performances of Harrison, Eric Clapton, Bob Dylan, and Leon Russell. When my mother dropped me off in front of Hop's Barbecue downtown, next to the theater, Dean and Craig were standing on the sidewalk, their shoulder-length hair blowing in the fall breeze. They were chatting up a trio of girls I didn't know. Everybody was smoking cigarettes, and when my mom's red VW bug rounded the corner and buzzed out of sight, I reached down and pulled a pack of Salems from my sock and lit up.

Higgins was talking when I approached the group. She had straight, strawberry-blond hair that fell halfway down her back, flared jeans, and a beanpole body that made her look a little like Jan from the Brady Bunch. Higgins was much cooler than Jan, though. She spoke in a loud, commanding voice and waved her hands about her as if she was making a

political speech. Though I already had a girlfriend, I was quietly smitten by this new girl who was a year my senior and seemed very worldly. She knew all about the rock stars in the movie we were about to see. Higgins said she didn't care much about the Beatle guy, but she loved Leon Russell and his trio of black female singers, known as the Shelter People, who danced in tandem and sang husky, gospelish backup vocals on Russell's songs.

We filed into the theater and planted ourselves in the first two rows. I ended up sitting next to Higgins and felt awkward when our shoulders touched. I don't remember what prompted it, but at some point I found myself explaining to her that I had a girlfriend. She looked at me, rolled her eyes, and with utter confidence asked, "Haven't you heard that song by Stephen Stills, 'If you can't be with the one you love, love the one you're with'?"

I didn't know what to say or do, but that afternoon, somewhere between Harrison's "Beware of Darkness" and Russell's "Youngblood," Higgins and I made out in that movie theater. At school the next week, she acted as if nothing had happened. I was a year behind her and back then, a year was a lifetime. Higgins hung out with an older crowd and I was just a kid. She knew all the cool rock bands and she knew where to get the best drugs. We remained friends throughout junior high and high school, but never again did Higgins and I make out in a movie theater.

For many years I lost contact with Higgins, but in 2002 I ran into her during a swing through my hometown doing research for my book. Both of us had survived serious alcohol and drug problems and were in recovery. I told her about the book I was writing and asked if she would talk to me about her experiences and how the music of the South fit into her life.

"Oh god, southern rock defined me," she said, laughing. "Sure, I'd love to talk about it with you. That'd be fun."

A few weeks later, I visited Debbie at her home deep in the woodsy countryside south of Asheboro. It was a mild evening and she was relaxing with a glass of iced tea on the deck behind her house after a day at the job. Today, Debbie Pickens works as an activities director at a maximum-security prison, and when she described the shock she felt back in 1976 when she heard Gregg Allman had ratted on his drug dealer, the juxtaposition of her appearance with the words coming from

her mouth was jarring. She was still dressed in her correctional officer's uniform, a state-issued prison badge dangling from her hip. In 2002, this former high school drug dealer looked like a cop.

"He really crossed the line when he did that," she said of Allman's indiscretion. "You just didn't go around narcing on people back then. You know what I mean?"

For hours Debbie and I looked through old photographs and concert ticket stubs. Since I last saw her, she'd been married, divorced, had two kids, and was married again, to a quiet, gentle guy named Don. Debbie had changed her life in many ways—she'd kicked drugs and alcohol— but some things remained the same. She was still the confident, boister- ous, animated, funny, and thoroughly engaging girl I'd met outside the Sunset Theater nearly thirty years earlier.

Debbie told me things about herself that I never knew. She grew up with two brothers and parents whose racial views were typical of blue- collar southerners in the 1960s. One day, when Debbie was about fifteen, her mother and a friend were sitting on the screened-in porch of her fam- ily's modest suburban home having iced tea. It was 1975 and Debbie's ordeals with drugs had already become an issue. Her mother was con- cerned about her daughter's drug problems, but was relieved Debbie's rebellion had not manifested itself in other ways.

"I remember her telling her friend, 'I'm so glad Debbie decided to rebel with drugs and not by dating black boys,' " she said.

"I thought, What? It's okay for me to do drugs as long as I don't have a black boyfriend? I could have OD'd on drugs, but to my mom, as long as I didn't date black boys, I was doing all right."

Debbie knew where her mother's racism came from. When Debbie was a little girl, her grandfather, a tobacco farmer, once took her for a ride into the countryside near Bennett, North Carolina, about an hour south- east of Asheboro. It was a rural area far away from any city.

"I was only six years old," she remembered, "and we drove out into the country and he took me to this tree where they had once hung a black man. He showed me that tree and he told me, 'They hung a nigger here,' and I was like, 'Wow, it's a hanging tree! That's wild.'

"He said, 'That man hung there for two weeks before anybody cut him down.'

"I said, 'Why?'

"He said, 'Runnin' with a white woman.' "

She looked up, still amazed that someone would say something like that in her lifetime, and that that someone had been her grandfather.

"I mean, I was just a little kid, and here I was visualizing this dead black man hanging from a tree."

Debbie looked around and lowered her voice, as if someone might be listening to us, even though we were sitting outside her home, in the middle of the woods, surrounded by the black of night and the chirping of crickets.

"I said, 'What happened to the *girl?*' "

She paused.

"Well, my grandfather, he just looked me dead in the eye and said, 'Nobody knows.' "

Years later, when Debbie and I were in our teens, someone burned crosses in the yards of a couple of high school girls who were known to date black guys.

"My mother thought that was acceptable," said Debbie. "She thought that was okay."

Debbie had attended the same all-white elementary school as my friend Jeff Brown, so when she arrived at Asheboro Junior High in the early '70s, she'd never encountered any black kids. Her father worked with a few black men at the Eveready plant in town, but he never talked about them. Debbie didn't know what to think of the kids at first, but eventually she befriended a few of the girls. It made her feel rebellious.

"I just didn't want to agree with my parents on anything back then, so I took a different opinion of blacks," she said. "But deep inside, I had feelings like they had. I mean, I was raised that way. I remember there were some black girls in school who had animosity towards me and they just wanted to pick fights with me because I was white. I didn't like it. I didn't understand it. So I didn't like them."

In the early '70s, drugs and music were the common denominators among the races. Debbie worked at a local pharmacy and had access to all kinds of pills—downers such as Quaalude, Seconol, Tuinal, and Valium; uppers like Dexedrine, Dexamyl, Fastin, and the most popular, biphetamine, known as black beauties. Her access to drugs made Debbie popular among the heads. And what she couldn't get from the drugstore, Debbie would find among her black girlfriends.

"Drugs were the great equalizers," she said. "Back then, blacks didn't have connections for pot, because white people controlled the pot trade in Asheboro. So I'd give my black girlfriends pot for other drugs. I was the little connection in that regard and I was young—I was only like fifteen when I started doing this."

When the race riot broke out at our school, Debbie was one of the kids who avoided the fray. "I remember everybody came to school with razor blades and stuff. It was awful," she said. "I had this black girlfriend and we were pretty good friends. It wasn't like she would ever call my house or anything, but we were friends and when the riot broke out, it got kind of weird."

Debbie remembered the first time she visited the home of a black friend.

"I'll never forget it," she said. "I'd never been to a black person's house in my life. So I'm going into her house and seeing all these velvet pictures of Jesus and eating peach cobbler that her mother had prepared and being so frightened to eat it. Because we were always told that blacks were dirty, you know." She laughs incredulously. "God, I just remember thinking how rebellious I was, sitting in a black family's house, eating peach cobbler and looking at velvet pictures of Jesus. I felt so cool."

Today, at the prison where she works, most of the inmates are young African-American men in their twenties who have no idea what Debbie is talking about when she quotes a song by one of the southern rock bands she grew up with. "I'll be walking on the cell block and I'll have a Lynyrd Skynyrd song or a Charlie Daniels song in my head, and it's funny, it's like armor to me. I get all cocky and feel all young again. One of the guys'll walk up and say, 'What you looking for?' "—she quoted a line from Daniels's "The Devil Went Down to Georgia"—"I'll say, 'I'm lookin' for a soul to steal.' I tell you, they think I'm crazy. I mean, I'm a lot older than most of them and those references are totally alien to them."

Debbie paused and furrowed her brow. "You know, the killers today are the children of our generation—their parents are our age," she said. "Most of those guys were born in 1976 or 1977. Their mothers were those poor women from our school who got pregnant and had to quit school."

She started thinking about her own boys, who are in their twenties and getting into a little trouble now and then, but not real serious trouble.

Though drugs and alcohol blurred her early years as a parent, Debbie was able to overcome her problems and her sons watched as she embarked on a journey of recovery.

Debbie has raised her boys very differently from the way her mother raised her. And the music she listened to played a part. It all started in the backseat of a car. "They were, like, three years old, and they knew every line to 'Curtis Loew,' " she said, referring to the Lynyrd Skynyrd ballad in which Ronnie Van Zant sings of an old black blues guitarist who teaches a young white boy about music and life. "I remember we'd be riding down the road and they'd be in their car seats in the back singing, 'Old Curt was a black man with white curly hair. . . . ' It was so funny.

"My oldest son, Jason, was born in 1979, but he really got into Skynyrd when he got older." She looked down at the faded concert tickets scattered on the table. "Hell, he has his own collection of ticket stubs from the postcrash Lynyrd Skynyrd reunion years. And he was into 'em, pretty much, until he moved out to California and got into something else — hip-hop, I think. He was living in Oakland and San Francisco, you know, where hip-hop is really huge. It's funny, his friends in California don't even call him Jason, they call him Southern. That's his nickname: Southern. I'll call out there and his roommates will answer the phone and if I ask for Jason, they don't know who I'm talking about at first. They'll say, 'Oh, you mean Southern.' "

One summer, back in our youth, Debbie Higgins began to think about her mortality. She and some friends were vacationing at the Pamlico Sound on the North Carolina coast, listening to an album by the Marshall Tucker Band. "We were laying out in the sun, smoking pot, and that song 'See You Later, I'm Gone' was playing. I remember it like it was yesterday — the suntan lotion, the heat. And I was thinking, damn, I'll never live past twenty-three.

"God, I still remember every word of that song," she said, then began reciting the lyrics: 'If I die at twenty-three, won't you bury me in the sunshine / Please let me know that you're still mine / Though I'm gone, my love for you is oh so strong / And when the grass grows over me, let me know that you still love me.'

"I told my friends, 'When I die, y'all, I want y'all to play that song at my funeral.' I was planning on it, man. There I was, still just a teenager, and I'd already decided that would be my funeral song."

A year before the Sex Pistols would hit America with their message of "No Future," and several years before the goth movement found teenagers across the country dressing in morbid black, seventeen-year-old Debbie Higgins was having her own holiday in the sun on the beach in North Carolina, unable to imagine living another decade. Two years before she would have her first child, the Marshall Tucker Band, from Spartanburg, South Carolina, expressed Debbie's hopelessness and nihilism just as surely as the minimalist moping of Joy Division or the Cure would for the next generation.

"My friends, they didn't think anything of it," said Debbie. "They were like, 'Okay, yeah, sure, we'll play that song at your funeral.'"

Gregg Allman's on-again, off-again relationship with Cher and his legal troubles continued to dog the Allman Brothers Band throughout the summer of '76, but the Jimmy Carter campaign trudged on. In June, *Rolling Stone* put a caricature of Carter on its cover, a toothy grin on his face, wrapped in a judge's robe with the Confederate flag draped over one shoulder. The cover line read: "Jimmy Carter and the Great Leap of Faith: An Endorsement with Fear and Loathing by Hunter S. Thompson." The "endorsement" part angered Thompson, who said journalists should never "endorse" a candidate. But the symbolism was set in stone, so to speak: Carter was the rock & roll candidate. In 1976, Thompson and *Rolling Stone* had perhaps a bigger influence on young voters than any other entity, and the endorsement was indispensable to Carter's campaign. By late summer the candidate was neck and neck with Gerald Ford, Nixon's former vice president, who'd assumed the presidency after Tricky Dick resigned. Americans wanted change and this Democratic peanut farmer from Georgia with a warm drawl and earnest smile seemed to be the panacea.

"Along comes old Jimmy Carter, from Plains, Georgia," said Charlie Daniels. "He didn't win by a landslide, he just slid in there, and everybody, even if they didn't agree with his politics, at least knew he could be trusted. That was a big, big thing at the time. It's something this country desperately needed. And he brought that to the presidency."

As the Allman Brothers Band imploded, other southern groups picked up the slack for Governor Carter. In July, a slew of southern rockers

played a benefit concert for the candidate at the Gator Bowl in Florida. Lynyrd Skynyrd, whose *Second Helping* album had sold more than a million copies, making them the second platinum-selling southern rock act behind the Allmans, was the big draw. On the day of the show, Ronnie Van Zant lost his voice, but Skynyrd soldiered on, playing with members of the other bands. Even the Allmans put aside their infighting to perform that day for Carter. The most important act on the bill, though, turned out to be Charlie Daniels, who until then had been the perennial opener for other southern rock bands. Daniels's hit "The South's Gonna Do It" was a showstopper at the Gator Bowl, and it became the Carter campaign's theme song.

The South itself had moved from cult status to superstar status. The days of backwoods lynchings were a distant, nightmarish memory. That year, RCA Records quietly put out an album by a racially mixed Atlanta-based band, Mother's Finest, that blended the grit of hard southern rock with deep funk and disco. Within the next twelve months, the band's provocative song "Niggizz Can't Sang Rock & Roll" blared from college dorms alongside Lynyrd Skynyrd's "Whiskey Rock-A-Roller." It was time to pick up the pieces. It was time to dance and sing, drink Jack Daniel's whiskey, and stop thinking so much. The party had begun. The Democratic Party, that is. Jimmy Carter's party.

"I think Jimmy Carter deserves a good bit of the credit for changing the way people viewed the South," said Daniels. "Everything was changing. All eyes turned to the South, man. The eyes of the United States turned in a southerly direction, and it was good, at least for a while."

★ Chapter 7 ★

SHUT UP AND GET ON THE PLANE

THE *news knocked me out of my stupor.*

It was a Friday night, late October 1977. As usual, my friends and I were hanging out at Crystal and Keith's place, a tiny, white clapboard house just north of downtown Asheboro. Crystal was seventeen and still in high school; Keith had quit school and was working a day job. They were trying to be adults, but they still lived like kids. On weekends we'd gather in their living room to drink beer, smoke pot, listen to music, and talk about how boring our lives were. It was an oasis from our nights spent cruising the quiet streets of our hometown in Toyotas, Trans Ams, and Z cars, playing foosball at the local game room, Carey's Place, or venturing into the countryside to find some hidden spot to party.

Suddenly, Marie burst into the house, the tears streaming down her face mingling with her blue eyeliner and strands of dirty-blond hair. She stood at the doorway of the living room in a tube top and frayed jeans looking vulnerable, wounded, as if some boy had just broken her heart.

"Skynyrd's plane," she began, hyperventilating between words. "It crashed. Ronnie's dead."

The moment of stunned silence was shattered by sobs from the girls and curses from the guys. Keith kicked the wall next to the back door and the impact of his motorcycle boot against the flimsy plasterboard made the entire house shake. The two Doberman pinschers lying on the floor raised their heads and pricked up their ears.

"*Goddamnit,*" Keith yelled, and then flopped back down on the easy chair he'd been sitting in.

No one said a word for what seemed like hours. The party was over.

I remained seated on the couch, in a daze, clutching the red bong that was positioned between my legs. It was the first rock & roll tragedy that actually affected me. I'd never known Duane Allman or Janis Joplin or Jimi Hendrix when they were alive. To me, those rock stars were forever frozen in time; icons all, eternally youthful, dead in their prime. I felt I'd known Ronnie Van Zant. I had seen him. He wasn't supposed to die.

We had no clue on that dark fall night that the death of Ronnie Van Zant would mark the end of southern rock's reign. And yet, by then the "southern" tag had become little more than a marketing tool, used by the major record companies to peddle a string of new bands like the Outlaws and 38 Special (led by Van Zant's younger brother Donnie), whose glossy, middle-of-the-road music blended in all too well with the blanched-out sounds of such interchangeable mainstream rock acts as Foreigner, Journey, and REO Speedwagon.

Even Ronnie Van Zant had expressed concern over the term's ghetto-izing effects: Five days before the crash, he told the *Miami Herald*, "Southern rock's a dead label, a hype thing for the magazines to blow out of proportion. We don't play like the Allmans did, or like Wet Willie. Southern groups are different."

Lynyrd Skynyrd had brought the sound of the New South full circle by adding the crunch of British hard rock to their distinctly southern blend of country, gospel, and blues. But there were no new bands to take Skynyrd's place. There were no new rock & roll songwriters with the angry edge of a Ronnie Van Zant, who wrote and performed on instinct rather than calculation. He'd spoken for young, disenfranchised southerners who had no future. He was a southern punk before "punk" carried the currency it would in the year following his death. Van Zant had bucked his corporate record label, singing "Workin' for MCA" with the same venom that working-class Brit Johnny Rotten would spit into the letters "EMI" on the Sex Pistols' landmark 1977 American debut, Never Mind the Bollocks, Here's the Sex Pistols.

Music was changing—and so was I. While some of my friends over at Crystal and Keith's place that night had left school to take jobs in local furniture factories or textile mills, I was thinking about college. I had already

begun to feel slightly self-conscious of my southern accent, embarrassed of those rabble-rousing redneck homeboys of Lynyrd Skynyrd, who sang of poison whiskey, simple men, and Georgia peaches. When punk hit, I initially resisted it. The first time I heard the Ramones' "Beat on the Brat," I didn't like it. The song sounded mean and violent to my laid-back southern hippie ears. And yet deep down, I knew this band had something new to say, something fresh and important. By 1977, Lynyrd Skynyrd's legacy had been reduced to one lone song title, shouted out as a drunken rebel yell at every bar band that passed through town:

"Freeeeeeee Birrrrrd!"

Before I left that night, my friends put "Free Bird" on the stereo and tearfully sang along to the words. Still in their teens, they were already reminiscing about the old days. It annoyed me. Though I was sad, I felt the ceremony had become mawkish. I was bored.

The backlash had begun.

On January 19, 1977—ten months before the Lynyrd Skynyrd plane crash—Jimmy Carter threw the hippest inaugural bash of any incoming commander-in-chief in the nation's history. It was the first such gala to be televised and Washington was hopping with rock stars and other celebrities. Cher and Gregg Allman were there, as were the Marshall Tucker Band, Charlie Daniels, Aretha Franklin, Linda Ronstadt, and Paul Simon. Former Beatle John Lennon, wearing a sheriff's badge, sat at a table at the Mayflower Hotel with his avant-garde artist wife, Yoko Ono, dressed elegantly in a fur coat, her hair pulled back into a tight bun. At one point the Ono-Lennons were photographed with boxer Muhammad Ali, the first sports figure to be treated like a rock star. Lennon, who had been out of the public eye for two years, was reportedly disappointed when Carter failed to recognize him.

Ronstadt, on her way to New York to visit friends at *Saturday Night Live*, swung through the nation's capital to perform at the inaugural concert. "I was so nervous," she told *Time* magazine a month later. "My God, I was awful!"

Aretha Franklin kicked off the proceedings with a stirring a cappella version of "God Bless America."

Carter's publicists called it the "People's Inaugural"—"black-tie optional." The 3,500 attendees at the Mayflower party came dressed in everything from tuxedoes to business suits to designer denim. When the incoming president walked down Pennsylvania Avenue the next day, the news media ate up the populist vibe. "Not since Andrew Jackson summoned all Americans to his oath-taking in 1829 has an inauguration been so open or freewheeling," wrote *Newsweek*. A few weeks later, the *National Journal* checked in with a story touting the new president's "refreshingly informal style."

Carter's mother, Lillian Gordy Carter, brought a little southern hospitality to 1600 Pennsylvania Avenue, making some of the famous guests— like Gregg and Cher—feel at home in Washington. "Gregory was from Georgia and we supported [Carter]," Cher told *Vanity Fair* in 1990. "So after the inauguration we were sort of just looking around the White House when Miz Lillian stuck her head out from around the corner and asked us to stay for dinner."

Overnight, the White House had become a warm and hospitable southern mansion, where a humble new First Family would begin healing the nation's post-Vietnam and post-Watergate wounds. But the Carter honeymoon didn't last long. The new president inherited a troubled economy and an unstable world. By the time he walked into the Oval Office in 1977, inflation was up, stiff economic competition was coming from Japan and Germany, the Middle East was in turmoil, and the oil crisis was about to spin out of control.

The former peanut farmer rose to the challenge at first, and the initial months of his presidency were successful. He met with Middle Eastern leaders to discuss peace in the region. He took proactive measures to end production of nuclear weapons and to ease the energy crisis. He signed the Panama Canal Treaty, giving back control over that land to the Panamanians. He signed the International Covenant on Human Rights. These measures made Carter popular among Arabs, Jews, Latin Americans, and European nations. Already well liked among African-Americans at home, the new president appointed Eleanor Holmes Norton, one of the key organizers of the 1963 civil rights march on Washington, to chair the Equal Employment Opportunity Commission.

Inside the Beltway, however, professional politicians were not so thrilled with the new president's unconventional ways. When it became

clear Carter would not play by Washington's rules, some insiders began a character assassination of the Carter family and the press ran with it. The same reporters who had gushed over the new president's freewheeling populism began hounding his family for quirky, *Beverly Hillbillies*–like stories. To be sure, the Carters offered plenty of fodder. The president's wisecracker brother Billy, who wore bib overalls, owned a gas station in Plains, Georgia, and considered himself a sort of benign redneck, began marketing his own Billy Beer. The president's sister, Ruth Carter Stapleton, was a motorcycle-riding evangelist who, in 1977, converted pornographer Larry Flynt to Christianity. Carter's mother expressed exasperation with her children's antics in a widely quoted quip, "Sometimes, when I look at all my children, I say to myself, 'Lillian, you should have stayed a virgin.' "

Southern rocker Charlie Daniels maintains that the reason anti-Carter forces chose to focus on the president's family was because they couldn't get anything on the president himself. "Jimmy Carter came along and, unfortunately, he was too good a man for the powers that be in Washington," Daniels told me. "Them and the press were just down on him from the get-go; they wouldn't let him do his job. But if history takes the right view of Jimmy Carter, it will say that he was the man who put decency back into the office of the president."

Carter's former chief of staff, Hamilton Jordan, concurs. "It seemed that Carter was a marked man as soon as he got to the White House," Jordan wrote in the book *Rolling Stone: The Seventies*. "The very qualities that had made him attractive to the American people were perceived as liabilities inside the Beltway. His southernness and his religious beliefs were poked fun at and said to be contrived."

It was classic southern stereotyping. The mostly northeastern-based media portrayed Carter and his family in a way that was mind-numbingly reminiscent of Hollywood's stereotypical characterizations of southerners in movies and on television. When the president's outspoken mother expressed her views in public, she was depicted as a loose cannon.

Throughout her life, Lillian Carter had set a powerful moral example for her children by fighting racism and bigotry of all kinds. In the 1920s, Miz Lillian crossed racial barriers when, as a nurse, she went into the homes of black women to teach them about health care. In June 1977, the Carter matriarch described wealthy northerners who

traveled to Plains just to rub shoulders with the new First Family as condescending hypocrites, as disrespectful toward blacks as any southern white trash.

"You know, some people come in with the idea that we are—that this is a hick town, and that, 'We're from the North and we're very wealthy,' " she said. "And I say, 'I'm sorry, honey, I see you're not in line. You have to get to the back of the line.' And, why, they resent more than anything if you have black people in the line."

Humorless political pundits quoted Miz Lillian as being serious when she made jokes about her family. On one occasion, a reporter knocked at her door wanting to talk to Miz Lillian about her son. He asked if Jimmy Carter was an honest man.

"Jimmy's always been an honest boy, and you can trust that he'll do what he said he would do."

The reporter pressed on, asking specifically if Carter had ever told a lie.

"Well, maybe a little white lie," she said.

The reporter instructed Lillian Carter to define "white lie."

Her answer came quickly: "That's just like what I said to you a while ago when I said I was glad to see you."

When anti-Carter forces weren't treating the new president's family like cartoon characters, they were accusing him of acting arrogant and "too smart" in press conferences. Carter was damned if he adhered to the stereotype of a dumb southerner, and damned if he didn't. What wasn't regularly reported until many years after he left office was Carter's statesmanlike behavior and the loyalty he showed to his friends.

Throughout his administration, Carter remained in close contact with Allman Brothers manager Phil Walden. When Walden's elder brother died in April 1977, the president sent a personal note. In addition to the obligatory condolences ("I was deeply saddened to learn of your brother's death. My prayers are with you"), Carter wrote, "Phil, I know that, like myself, you were very close to your brother. Your friend, J." In July, Walden fell ill and the president sent him a get-well note. That same month, Walden sent the president a copy of the Capricorn Records compilation, *The South's Greatest Hits*. Carter added it to his eclectic White House collection alongside works by Wagner and albums by Dylan, the Allmans, and outlaw country songwriter Billy Joe Shaver. At the Jimmy

Carter Library in Atlanta, Georgia, you'll find a photograph of the former president standing next to Walden, with the inscription: "To my great & early friend Phil Walden—Jimmy Carter."

To this day the politically conservative Charlie Daniels speaks of the former president with awe. Despite Carter's initial hurdles and the calamities of his later years in office, Daniels refuses to toe the conservative party line regarding the former president: that he was weak and ineffective.

"The Carter administration was a successful presidency, no matter what anybody tells you," said Daniels, who admits he differs with the former president on many specific issues. Daniels points to Carter's work for peace in the Middle East: "Look at the Camp David Accords—how many lives has that saved? If everything falls apart this afternoon and they go back to war again, how many lives did it save in the last quarter century?"

Charlie Daniels was on the road with his band the month Carter laid out his new vision to the American people in his first televised address to the nation as president. The singer was proud of the man he'd supported, but before Daniels could think much about the direction of the country, he was blindsided by some terrible news that hit closer to home. On October 20, 1977, Daniels was in St. Louis, preparing to play for an arena full of cheering fans, when a stranger walked into his dressing room.

"He said, 'There's a rumor going around that Lynyrd Skynyrd's plane crashed and everybody's dead,'" Daniels remembered.

"I said, 'Don't you come in here and tell me that kind of junk.'"

Daniels shook his head and looked down at his hands, which were clasped together on the table in front of him.

"I didn't believe it, so I went downstairs and [the host of a local radio show] was down there and I said to him, 'I just heard a terrible rumor and I want to know one way or the other if it's true: Did Skynyrd have a plane crash?'

"He said, 'I'll check on it and let you know.'

"Well, I went back upstairs and walked over to the wings of the stage—it was a sellout crowd that night and everybody in the audience was just hootin' and hollerin'—and my manager came up and told me it was true.

He said that Skynyrd had been in a plane crash and there were some fatalities, but they didn't know who was killed."

Daniels felt his whole body quake.

"That was about thirty seconds before we were supposed to go on, so I quickly called the guys up to my dressing room and told them we heard Skynyrd's plane went down and that I'd like to have a moment of silence for 'em.

"Ol' Tommy Crain [Daniels's guitarist], he came over and he said to me, 'I don't know what we're gonna do, man.'

"I said, 'I tell you what we're gonna do: We're gonna go out there and play our music.' If it were us, we wouldn't want them to blow off a show. So we went onstage that night, and I have no idea how long we played, but I know we played a lot and we played hard."

The magnitude of the loss didn't hit Daniels until later. Ronnie Van Zant had been like a little brother to the burly fiddler, and Daniels dearly loved the scrappy young singer who performed barefoot and got into too many fights. Daniels had counseled Van Zant on many occasions, talking with the singer on the phone well into the night about his restless spirit, his drinking, and basic issues relating to the music business. Daniels held his pain deep inside until he thought he was going to die.

"It just felt like there was something wrong all the time," said Daniels. "I mean, I knew what it was, but you just couldn't . . . I couldn't . . . It was just . . . depressing. It was like a weight mashing down on my head."

To make matters worse, Daniels was traveling separately from his bandmates. While they took the band's tour bus from show to show, Daniels had to fly to each gig to do advance publicity for the group's new album, *High Lonesome*, on which he'd sung about his own sweet home, "Carolina."

"I was away from the band for a lot of time right after the crash, and it wasn't a good time for me to be by myself," said Daniels. "I'm not much of a loner. I like to be around my friends. I'd be sitting in my hotel room and I'd hear the bus leave when I got up in the morning and I felt very alone."

Daniels was by himself when the words finally came to him. He sat down and wrote what would be the inscription on Ronnie Van Zant's grave:

My grandfather and grandmother in Mississippi, ca. 1914. (Author's collection)

My father and mother in Nashville in the late 1950s. (Author's collection)

Dad and me with Lester Maddox at the Governor's Mansion in Atlanta, 1968. (Author's collection)

Hourglass, 1967 or 1968. *Clockwise from top left:* Johnny Sandlin, Gregg Allman, Paul Hornsby, Pete Carr, and Duane Allman. (Courtesy of Paul Hornsby)

The road goes on forever:
The Allman Brothers begin their
journey by a railroad track
during the photo shoot for their
1969 debut album. *Left to right:*
Duane Allman, Dickey Betts,
Gregg Allman, Jai Johanny
Johanson, Berry Oakley, and
Butch Trucks. (Photo by
Stephen Paley/Michael Ochs
Archives.com)

Phil Walden Sr., Gregg Allman,
and Jimmy Carter *(left to right).*
(Courtesy of Philip Walden Jr.)

Thirteen years old and wearing my Leon Russell T-shirt,
1973. I thought I looked like Gregg Allman. Everyone else
in my hometown thought I was a girl. (Author's collection)

Johnson in 2003.
(Courtesy of Jimmy
Johnson)

Jimmy Johnson with Ronnie Van Zant, Gary Rossington, and Allen Collins of Lynyrd Skynyrd. At the mixing board is engineer Greg Hamm. The members of Skynyrd had reconvened in Muscle Shoals in 1976 to add overdubs to songs they recorded during their first Shoals sessions of 1971. (Photo by Tommy Wright/Universal Music)

Lynyrd Skynyrd in 1976, just after the departure of Ed King. Ronnie Van Zant is in a semi–sitting position in the middle row at right, wearing a top hat and a big grin, flanked by the band's three female backup singers. Van Zant's personality was much bigger than his actual physical stature. (Lynyrd Skynyrd publicity photo/Universal Music)

Far left: My best friend Jeff Brown's "infamous" band, Stormwatch, in 1978 (Jeff is the one with his finger to his nose)

. . . and Jeff in 2002. (Courtesy of Jeff Brown)

On the road to San Francisco, 1978, my friend Jeff Whisnant *(right)* and I mixed Jack Kerouac and Carlos Castaneda with all kinds of illicit substances. (Author's collection)

R.E.M. manager Jefferson Holt backstage at an outdoor show in Raleigh, 1985. (Photo courtesy of the *Times-News* of Burlington)

Michael Stipe of R.E.M. at Trask Coliseum in Wilmington, North Carolina, 1986. (Photo courtesy of the *Times-News* of Burlington)

The Right Profile in Winston-Salem, North Carolina, in 1986. Steve Dubner is wearing shades. (Photo by Mark Kemp)

Widespread Panic in the early days. (Flournoy Holmes/Courtesy of *The Charlotte Observer* publicity photo archives)

In my backyard in L.A. during the post-grunge hangover, *Option* magazine days, 1995. (Author's collection)

Warren Haynes and me in New York City, 1998. (Author's collection)

Eric Clapton and me in London, 1998. (Photo by Wayne Isaak/Author's collection)

Clapton let me strum a few chords on Brownie, the Fender Stratocaster guitar he used in his duals with Duane Allman in Derek and the Dominos. (Photo by Wayne Isaak/Author's collection)

Martin Nicholson, me, and Robert George *(clockwise from left)* at our twentieth high school reunion in 1998. (Author's collection)

Patterson Hood *(second from left)* with his band, the Drive-By Truckers. The group challenged stereotypes of the South and of Lynyrd Skynyrd on the 2001 concept album *Southern Rock Opera*. (Photo by Daniel Coston)

My dad and I took the following photos during our journey across the South in 2002:

Paul Hornsby at his Muscadine Recording Studio in Macon, Georgia.

Patricia Goddard outside the Atlanta hotel where we bonded over our shared experiences with southern music.

Charlie Daniels let me take a few snap-shots while he laid down the vocal track for "Waco" during the recording of his album *Redneck Fiddlin' Man* at his studio outside Lebanon, Tennessee.

Former Lynyrd Skynyrd guitarist Ed King outside Valentino's Ristorante in downtown Nashville.

Left: My old pal Debbie Pickens (née Higgins) with her husband, Don, and two German shepherds on the couple's sprawling land outside our hometown of Asheboro.

Crystal Carver (née Lunsford) in her home near Climax, North Carolina.

Me and Richard Young in front of the Kentucky Headhunters' practice shack in Metcalfe County, Kentucky.

Philip Walden Jr. in his office at Velocette Records in Atlanta.

Self-portrait at the Mason-Dixon Line on my way from New York back home to North Carolina.

The mill town I've made peace with.

My father and me in 2004.
(Photo by John Houston McJunkin)

SHUT UP AND GET ON THE PLANE

A brief candle both ends burning
An endless mile a bus wheel turning
A friend to share the lonesome times
A handshake and a sip of wine
So say it loud and let it ring
That we're all part of everything
The Present, Future and the Past
Fly on proud bird, you're free at last

"I guess I felt closure then," said Daniels. "Up until that time I couldn't feel anything. I just couldn't deal with it. I didn't know how to deal with it. And then when I wrote those words, I felt like I'd done all I could do. Words have a healing quality for me. So I just went to the funeral and read those words and I sang 'Peace in the Valley.' It was just, you know, a sad, sad time. It was bad."

Alan Walden saw the end coming long before the plane crash. Lynyrd Skynyrd's former manager was bitter about losing the band as a client, but he had moved on and was working with newcomers Molly Hatchet and the Outlaws. But by then, according to Walden, southern rock had lost its edge.

"Everybody got greedy," said Walden, sitting in the living room of his Macon home, surrounded by gold and platinum records and posters of the southern acts he'd worked with over the years. "Everybody wanted all the groupies and all the drugs and all the money!"

A born storyteller, Alan Walden is one of the more interesting characters of the southern rock movement. He's passionate, funny, angry, loud, engaging, and thoroughly entertaining. When he talks about music, he raises his voice and extends his Georgia drawl to make his grandest points, then he softens to a near-whisper when he speaks of the bond southern rockers shared during the music's heyday.

"There was a time," said Walden, "when the whole southern movement was one big family. We had the Allmans endorsing Skynyrd endorsing Marshall Tucker and Wet Willie and Charlie Daniels. We were all family. But then we made two fatal mistakes."

Walden spit out the words for what he claims ruined southern rock: "We made it sophisticated, we polished it all up."

His face became flushed as he jumped up from his couch and pounded his fists on the coffee table in front of him.

"We took the WHAM out of the music," he shouted. "Instead of play-ing BANG, we started playing . . . *zing*. We made it all purty; we got it all dressed up for the ball. We forgot about the rough and tough shit that made the music kick."

Jason Ringenberg remembered when he finally came around to punk rock.

"I'm not one of those people who can sit here and tell you the first Ramones album changed my life," said Ringenberg, the front man of the seminal country-punk band Jason and the Scorchers. We were sitting at a bistro table in a folk club called the Evening Muse, in Charlotte, North Carolina. It was the winter of 2003, and Ringenberg was telling me how he experienced the epic shift of popular culture in the late 1970s.

"I really didn't have any awareness of the Ramones until 1977, my first year of college," he went on. "And even then, it wasn't the Ramones that affected me so much as the Sex Pistols. I can certainly tell you that *Never Mind the Bollocks* changed my life forever. When I first heard that album, it was absolutely magical to me."

Ringenberg looked over at the tiny stage at the back of the room where a scruffy young alternative-country band was doing its sound check. The members were laughing and goofing around, clanging out a noisy, out-of-tune version of Commander Cody's old hippie-trucker chestnut, "Lost in the Ozone." Behind them, an exposed-brick wall showed the quirky works of local folk artists. Ringenberg smiled at the band's racket.

Around 1982, Jason and the Scorchers introduced a blend of punk energy and country twang that would make a huge impact on the sound of American independent rock. Within a decade, the Scorchers' music would inspire a generation of bands whose members had grown up on punk and alternative rock—Uncle Tupelo, the Bottle Rockets, Ryan Adams's Whiskeytown, Drive-By Truckers. Before the Scorchers' first widely distributed mini-album *Fervor* hit small record stores in college towns across America in 1983, punk and southern rock blended together about as well as oil and water. You were either a fan of the Ramones and the Sex Pistols or you were a fan of Lynyrd Skynyrd and the Outlaws. There was no in between. If you considered yourself a punk, you had to purge your record collection of all those old southern boogie and hippie country-rock albums.

Jason and the Scorchers changed all that with one song—a lightning-speed version of Bob Dylan's "Absolutely Sweet Marie" that revved into motion on the power and intensity of a Ramones riff but kicked redneck ass with the twangy, roadhouse swagger of Lynyrd Skynyrd's "What's Your Name?" The Scorchers had put the WHAM back into the music.

"I think it's very hard for kids nowadays to understand that line that separated punk rockers from old-style southern rockers during that time," said Ringenberg. "That was a real transitional time for rock & roll. We all carried the punk-rock flag at that time and we were willing to fight for that flag. Back then it was, essentially, you either got the Gun Club or you weren't my friend."

Ringenberg was born in 1959 and raised in northern Illinois. He was just five when his father put him to work on the family farm.

"When you have a thousand hogs and two hundred acres of corn on a farm, there's a lot of work to be done, and we worked very hard every day," said Ringenberg. "The concept of an allowance was alien to us. These townspeople would come to school and talk about getting their allowance for the week, and us farm kids, we were like, what's that?"

The closest town was Sheffield, whose population by the turn of the millennium still hovered at only about a thousand. Sheffield wasn't exactly the South, but it was country. "There weren't any racial tensions because there weren't any other races except for whites," said Ringenberg. "And my family was pretty nonracist. They never used the 'N' word or anything like that. It wasn't a matter of any big philosophy, they just weren't that kind of people. So I never was exposed to any serious racism when I was growing up, and I'm thankful for that."

He was exposed to country music, though, and he loved it. "My dad always had the farm station on and they'd do the weather report and the farm report, and then in between they played stone-cold country music. Whatever 45s they had lying around the station—Hank Williams Sr., Merle Haggard, all those guys. Old country. It sounded so good on that AM radio in the truck while we were working."

As I watched him pick at his salad and glance over the set list he would use later that night in his solo acoustic performance, it struck me how little he'd changed in the twenty years since I first interviewed him outside a punk club in nearby Greensboro before a Scorchers show. His facial features were rosy and smooth, and though his wispy, reddish-brown hair was graying a little, it was still cut just above the collar and combed back

behind his ears, just as it was during the Scorchers' mid-'80s heyday. He was wearing a faded blue, button-down denim shirt over a gray T-shirt with country legend Jimmie Rodgers on it. As he talked about his early exposure to country music, Ringenberg would pause and smile now and then, take off his black cowboy hat, and rub his forehead with his hand.

"I remember vividly the moment that music really hit me: We were out building a fence, the radio was playing in the truck, and I heard 'Golden Ring,' by George Jones and Tammy Wynette. I don't know why, but that song just really spoke to me that day. I was thinking, Man, this is so good. It's moving me in ways I've never been moved before. For me, it seemed like country music just came right out of the ground; like the ground was singing to me. It was natural and earthy and real. It just worked well when you were out there digging a posthole or getting ready to castrate a hog."

By the mid-'70s, Ringenberg's sisters had gone off to college. When they came home on breaks, they would play albums by Bob Dylan and other folksingers whose music had a political bite to it. "They had their little acoustic guitars and their hippie beads, and they'd been in sit-ins and stuff, protesting the migrant worker situation and stuff like that," Ringenberg remembered. "Those were brand-new concepts to me. I was fascinated by it."

He and his high school buddies liked rock with a harder edge—bands like Lynyrd Skynyrd and Black Oak Arkansas. "Where I came from, every farm kid who could drive a tractor liked Skynyrd. That music made sense to us. It was so radical and raw; it was country, but it was also rock & roll. It was something we could understand. We felt like the guys in Lynyrd Skynyrd could pick up a bale of hay and know what to do with it."

Inspired by the southern rock he and his friends listened to, the protest songs his sisters brought home, and the country music he'd heard as a child on the hog farm, Ringenberg began writing his own tunes. By the time he entered Southern Illinois University in the late '70s, he was doing solo acoustic gigs in local folk clubs and coffeehouses.

"That's when the South started to become more than just some sort of ephemeral place that I'd read about in history books," said Ringenberg. "When I was a kid and we were learning about the Civil War, it was always taught to us as this thing that we had won: we were from the land of Lincoln, we won the Civil War. But then, when I went to Southern

Illinois, which is right next to Kentucky, I started getting more exposure to the cultural South, to real southern people."

He paused, looked around the club, and motioned to the art hanging on the walls: "That's when I started thinking I just might want to live here for a while."

By 1978, I wanted to leave the South. My new friend Jeff Whisnant had introduced me to a guy whose musical tastes fascinated me and made me restless.

Richard Johnson had the biggest record collection I'd ever seen. The first time Jeff and I went together to his apartment near downtown Asheboro and walked in the front door, I was flabbergasted. There were albums everywhere—filed on shelves along with a copious book collection, stacked on the floor in front his stereo, scattered all over the couch and chairs. He had records lining the walls of his narrow hallway, records on his kitchen table. He even had them in his bathroom.

"Jeff tells me you like psychedelic music from San Francisco," Richard said to me after Jeff introduced us.

"Yeah," I said. "I like Jefferson Airplane, Quicksilver, the Dead."

When he smiled, Richard looked to me like a young college professor. He was tall, lanky, wore a beige herringbone newsboy cap, a T-shirt, and jeans. His hair was not real long, but it was messy, and he had a cropped beard that gave him a look of distinction. He certainly didn't look like a punk rocker.

"Jeff says you haven't really connected with the Ramones or the Sex Pistols yet," Richard said.

"Naw," I replied, sheepishly. "They just seem noisy and violent to me."

"Cool," he said, acceptingly. "You should listen to this, though."

He picked up an album and handed it to me. The cover was black with a stark, high-contrast image of the band on it. The members looked like heroin addicts, like they hadn't eaten in weeks. Their skin was pasty and their choppy hair looked greasy. At the bottom of the cover were the words *Marquee Moon*; at the top was the word Television.

"Here, I'll put it on," said Richard, very gently pulling the vinyl disc from its cover and placing it on the turntable. When the needle hit the grooves, a jagged, raw-sounding guitar chord knifed its way through the

quiet afternoon ambiance of Richard's apartment, followed by bass and a circular guitar part that repeated itself over and over like a chain saw. When the singer began spitting out the words—"What I want, I want now, and it's a whole lot more than 'anyhow'"—he sounded like he was having a seizure. His voice wasn't good, but it was urgent, as if what he was singing was somehow going to save his life. "I understand all destructive urges," the singer continued. "It seems so perfect—I see, I see no—evil."

Wow.

I wasn't sure I liked this music, but I was intrigued and not just a little frightened by it. Richard told me Television came out of the same downtown New York punk scene that spawned the Ramones, but what I heard on that record didn't sound anything like what I'd heard by the Ramones. Television didn't sing about beating on a brat with a baseball bat. To me, their music was smarter and more intense. It held me in thrall and broke down some of the barriers that had made punk rock initially distasteful to me. I was beginning to see the desperation in the music, the irony. Though I didn't become an immediate convert, I was beginning to see the light.

When "See No Evil" ended, Richard moved the needle to another track. The guitars again played off of each other in a circular motion; the music was syncopated, angular, with a groove that was totally different from the blues-based sound of southern rock or the San Francisco psychedelic music I'd been tripping to over the past couple of years. And yet the sound—the spacey, swirling curlicues of guitar shooting through all the syncopation—was not far removed from the space jams of the Grateful Dead's guitarist, Jerry Garcia.

This was a punk band?

"It's not really punk—it's new music," said Richard.

When Jeff and I left that day, I was changed. I wanted to visit Richard Johnson as often as possible and listen to as much "new music" as I could. And Jeff and I would do that. I didn't change overnight; I still listened to the Dead and the Airplane, to Neil Young and the Allman Brothers. I still had a negative reaction to the Sex Pistols and Ramones, but my record collection grew to include albums by Television, Talking Heads, and Elvis Costello. Within a year, even the Ramones and Sex Pistols would make sense to me, and when that happened, there would be no turning back.

Throughout our senior year of high school, Jeff and I visited Richard on a regular basis, absorbing more and more music that was new to our ears—everything from the raw, political folk songs of Phil Ochs to bizarre albums by Wire, Devo, and the B-52's. Richard opened our eyes to a whole new world of music. He brought to life the bands Lester Bangs wrote about in *Creem* magazine: older acts like Iggy Pop, the MC5, and Lou Reed's Velvet Underground, and new ones like X-Ray Spex and Richard Hell and the Voidoids. At first, I didn't know where he was finding all of these records. Then he introduced Jeff and me to his friend Joey, from Greensboro.

Joey had short hair and wore geeky, thick-rimmed glasses. You'd never see him in jeans or a T-shirt. His clothes looked like the kind of suits our dads would have worn to the office in the '50s—if they had been brainiac engineers or math professors. But Joey didn't exactly look like a '50s throwback, either; he didn't look like anything we'd ever seen, except maybe in one of the photos on those albums by Talking Heads or Devo.

One day Joey told us Devo was going to perform at an auditorium on the campus of the University of North Carolina in Greensboro. I was as excited by the prospect of seeing a "punk" band as I had been by my very first rock concert. When we arrived at the auditorium a few weeks later, Devo hit the stage in the yellow, postapocalyptic, nuclear-fallout lab outfits they wore in the photo inside their album *Q: Are We Not Men? A: We Are Devo!* The music they made that night was stripped of all emotion. It was the total opposite of the Allman Brothers or Lynyrd Skynyrd. It was clinical, computerized.

Devo performed a cover version of the Rolling Stones' "(I Can't Get No) Satisfaction" that sounded like it had been created by the computer character HAL in *2001: A Space Odyssey*. When the members of the band busted out of the lab outfits during one song and threw fragments of the garments into the audience, Joey got a pant leg. He treasured that scrap of yellow material as much as I did the cigarette butt that Ron Wood had tossed to me three years earlier at the Greensboro Coliseum. By the end of the night, I was at once repelled and captivated by Devo.

I was not yet a fan, though.

That summer, Jeff Whisnant and I graduated from high school and headed west, to San Francisco's Haight-Ashbury. We were on a pilgrimage to where the Summer of Love had unfolded a decade earlier. On the

road, we listened to eight-track tapes of everything from the obvious (Jefferson Airplane, the Grateful Dead, Commander Cody and His Lost Planet Airmen) to the not-so-obvious (country outlaws David Allan Coe and Johnny Paycheck) to the totally new and unusual (Elvis Costello, Patti Smith). We read and discussed the psychedelic writings of Timothy Leary and Tom Wolfe. We tripped on LSD and attempted to retrace the footsteps of the popular psychedelic anthropologist guru and literary con man Carlos Castaneda, writer of the hugely influential series of books on the teachings of a Mexican Indian shaman called don Juan.

The shaman had chosen Castaneda to serve as his apprentice, and Castaneda in turn passed his knowledge on to the young people of my generation. "I've made up my mind and I am going to teach you the secrets that make up the lot of a man of knowledge," don Juan told Castaneda in the first book of the series, but the shaman warned his young apprentice that he "would have to make a very deep commitment and that the training was long and arduous." That training involved large quantities of hallucinogenic drugs and a thoroughly open mind. Jeff and I felt qualified to begin the journey, though my only real *commitment* was to the drugs. Castaneda's program involved spiritual and psychological disciplines I wasn't capable of at eighteen. But it set Jeff and me on a path that would find us studying philosophy when we got to college that fall.

My head was reeling when we returned from San Francisco and began classes at East Carolina University. Punk rock, Timothy Leary, the Grateful Dead, Bertrand Russell, LSD, politics, *Rolling Stone*. Life was getting messy. Everything seemed to be in flux except for my old musical friends—southern rock, country, the blues. Those fundamental building blocks of rock & roll and of my youth were taking a backseat to the new clash of cultural differences. The world was changing. *My* world was changing. My mind was opening to new ideas. My impulsiveness was taking control. I was learning, growing, experimenting. And though I didn't yet know it, I was beginning to kill myself with drugs: the powerful depressant Quaalude, the intense speed rush of cocaine and crystal methamphetamine, and massive quantities of LSD, marijuana, and alcohol.

When I returned home to Asheboro on summer breaks from school in 1979, 1980, and 1981, I felt alienated from my old friends at Crystal and

Keith's place. When Jeff and I would go visit them, they were still drinking Jack Daniel's and playing "Free Bird." I felt as though I was in a prison, and I wanted out.

We'd go visit Richard and listen to psychedelic garage rock by obscure '60s bands the Electric Prunes and the 13th Floor Elevators. One night we listened to that Television album again and the lyrics suddenly made complete sense to me: "I get ideas, I get a notion. I want a nice little boat made out of ocean. . . . / I understand all destructive urges. It seems so perfect. I see—I see no—evil."

Meanwhile, in Washington, Jimmy Carter soldiered on, but a new resistance movement was simmering on the underground, its followers feeling the president was not delivering on his promises quickly enough. With this new movement came a new popular-music soundtrack.

Ronnie Van Zant had been dead a full year, the Allman Brothers were wounded road dogs, the Outlaws and 38 Special were rehashing old riffs with a new corporate-rock sheen. It took a punk band called the Clash to shake things up and create protest songs for a new era. Their music was edgy, dramatic, important.

Having flirted with the idea of punk for several years, I finally really got it when I heard the Clash's angry protest anthem "I'm So Bored with the U.S.A." I heard the song at Richard Johnson's apartment. Richard also had turned me on to some of the lesser-known '60s topical singer-songwriters after I discovered Phil Ochs's Vietnam-era "Draft Dodger Rag." I'd learned how to play it on my acoustic guitar, using chord diagrams, but I never actually heard the song until I saw the Ochs album *Chords of Fame* in Richard's collection. When he played it for me, I became an immediate convert. Excited by my interest in Ochs, Richard introduced me to a few politically oriented punk bands including Stiff Little Fingers, from Ireland, and Gang of Four, from Leeds, England. The best of the lot, though, was the Clash.

On Sunday, November 4, 1979, I was hanging around campus preparing for another week of classes, most likely watching the Robin Williams sitcom *Mork & Mindy* with my girlfriend Sharon, when everything crashed down on the Carter administration. Half a world away, a mob of angry Iranians had taken over the U.S. embassy in Tehran and

held seventy-one hostages. The following day the news was devastating, but no one thought it would last. It did. Within a few weeks, nineteen of the hostages were released but the other fifty-two remained captive for an agonizing 444 days. Carter froze Iranian assets, attempted a diplomatic solution through the United Nations. But by summer of 1980, it was clear the Iranian rebels were not going to budge. The president sent in a rescue unit by helicopter, but the mission was aborted when three helicopters failed before they reached Tehran. Eight Americans died in the rescue attempt.

Throughout late 1979 and 1980, Americans were angry and frustrated, and they took it out on Carter. The New South that the president had wanted to introduce to the nation was looking weak and ineffective. Americans turned again to the Republican Party for a fix. Southern conservatives dug their heels in deeper, putting their total support behind the smiling ex-actor Ronald Reagan's 1980 bid for the presidency. If the South was still in vogue at all, it wasn't the South that Carter and the Allman Brothers Band wanted America to see; it was the old conservative South, which was fast changing its affiliation from predominantly Democratic to predominantly Republican. Reagan won the election by a landslide, and on January 20, 1981, just hours after Carter left office, the fifty-two Americans who'd been held captive in Iran for more than a year were released. (A decade later it was revealed that the Reagan campaign had struck a deal with the Iranians to free the hostages on the new president's clock.)

Former Lynyrd Skynyrd manager Alan Walden sees the death of southern rock and the failure of the Carter administration as symptomatic of a bigger pattern for southerners. At his home in Macon, Georgia, he told me, "We southerners know how to rally around the pole, man, but can we hold on to the pole when we got it?"

He never answered the question, but I got the feeling he was talking about our general fickleness, our tendency to change directions when the going gets tough. We're a loyal lot—until things get too difficult or complicated. Then we run and hide and let someone else do the thinking and acting for us.

Walden cackled. "Hell, that's what made the South lose the damn Civil War," he said. "And that's what ended up destroying Jimmy Carter's candidacy when that second election came around."

★ ★ ★

It had been about a quarter century since I last saw Crystal Lunsford. By 2002, she and Keith, who lived together in the house where we were partying the night Lynyrd Skynyrd's plane went down, had been married and long divorced. In the intervening years, she had been Crystal Wood and Crystal Carver. Now she was single again, living in a small trailer near Climax, a little crossroads about twenty miles north of Asheboro just across the Randolph County line, not far from NASCAR legend Richard Petty's birthplace, where he still lives and maintains the racing dynasty's complex of garages, machine shops, offices, and a museum.

Driving up Route 22 was like taking a time machine back to my teenage years. I took the old roads through the villages of Central Falls, Gray's Chapel, Linberry, and Redcross. It's an area of snaky creeks and rivers and sprawling farms, separated by small houses, mobile homes, country stores, and rusty textile mills. When I was in high school, my friends and I would cruise these roads looking for spots by the river to stop, open the doors of our cars, blast Lynyrd Skynyrd, and party until a sheriff's deputy showed up. I'd fantasize about a time when I could have my own country home here, live out my life with a beautiful hippie girl, raise a kid or two, have some dogs, and play my guitar until . . . I don't know, until Jesus came back, I guess.

Crystal's trailer was hard to find. It was at the end of one of those blink-and-you'll-miss-it dirt roads off the main road out in the middle of nowhere. I missed her mailbox the first time I passed it and had to turn around at a house where a couple of tanned, shirtless, longhaired guys in their midthirties were hunched over the engine of an old Dodge. They squinted up at me suspiciously when I pulled into the driveway and threw the shiny white SUV I'd borrowed from my mom into reverse. When I nodded at them, they just glared.

Driving back to the road that Crystal lived on, I noticed a tattered Confederate flag waving ominously in the wind in front of a trailer. This was the South that New Yorkers thumb their noses at. The poor white South. The making-ends-meet South. The South of Skynyrd and Molly Hatchet. The South of Billy Ray Cyrus and Travis Tritt. The South of Ozzy Osbourne and Metallica. This was the dirt-track-racing South. The

right-to-own-firearms South. It was the real South, the sad South, the sometimes-scary South.

It was not the gauzy South of an R.E.M. song or the quirky, eccentric folk-art South of the hip and celebrated rural artist the Reverend Howard Finster. It wasn't the quaint, colloquial South of writer Fannie Flagg or the dramatic, pop-literary South of John Grisham. This was the South that survives unchanged by the election of a Jimmy Carter or a Bill Clinton. The South that goes unnoticed by magazines or television until a body shows up by some river, mutilated, with signs of satanic ritual, sexual foul play, or racial bias. This was the South I'd been embarrassed by when I moved away from North Carolina in the '80s. It was the South that folks like to mock but don't want to think about too much.

When I drove up the hill, Crystal was waiting for me, stooped on the back porch of her trailer holding on to the collar of a barking Dalmatian. Like Jason Ringenberg, she hadn't changed much over the years. Her face was thinner, with tiny crow's-feet creeping away from her eyes. She was still pretty, dressed in a cream-colored top, jeans, and sandals. She wore a Native American necklace and bracelet, and bead earrings dangled from her ears, mingling with her long, wavy brown hair.

"Goddamn it, Kemp," she barked as I got out of the truck. "You mean to tell me it takes a goddamn book for you to come see me after twenty years?"

She was still surly, still loud.

Crystal is not easy to pigeonhole: She likes to hunt and fish on weekends and said she hates "stupid" gun laws. She sees nothing wrong with flying the Confederate flag, likes to quote Janis Joplin, and longs for the old days of peace and love. She still parties, she told me, though not as hard as she used to. During the summer months, Crystal travels with friends to an annual hippie gathering called the Carolina Boogie, where Deadheads, jam-band fans and old southern rockers meet by invitation only to re-create the '60s and '70s at a secret spot out in the country somewhere in North Carolina.

"The first time I went, I'd never seen so many hippies with so much talent gathered together in one place," said Crystal. "It's so cool, like two thousand people or something. It's like this little Woodstock out in the country, once a year for a whole week."

She told me I ought to come along sometime. "We have something

similar to it right around here, one weekend out of every month of the summer. It's smaller, only about two hundred or so people, but for three days, man, you don't have no worries."

Crystal led me into the trailer and sat me down on the couch surrounded by her collection of Native American art and hunting trophies. She fixed me a glass of sweet iced tea and then, right off the bat, let me know she had a bone to pick with me. A handful of years earlier, our hometown newspaper had run a front-page article on me.

"It was right after you got that job at *Rolling Stone*," said Crystal. "You said in that interview, 'I *mourn* the loss of my southern accent.' I was like, Huh? He does what? He *mourns* the loss of his southern accent?"

She drew out the word *mourn* and repeated it several times.

"I thought, Damn, Kemp's got all uppity on us. That Yankee shit's rubbed off on him. He *mourns* the loss of his southern accent. Those were your exact words, man."

Crystal shook her head from side to side. "I don't know, Kemp, but that hit me hard. I'm not sure why. I guess it was your choice of words. It sounded like you'd gotten too sophisticated for us. I remember thinking, Could I still talk to this boy who used to come over to my house and get high with us?"

She winked at me and smiled, then sat down and slapped her hand down on my leg, cackling like Janis Joplin after a big slug of Southern Comfort. Crystal was ribbing me, but she was serious, too. I had crossed a line with my comment in that newspaper article. In waxing poetic about the loss of my accent, I had intellectually distanced myself from my upbringing. What I thought was an attempt at reconnecting with my hometown was really the exact opposite. I was building a wall between myself and Them—between my past and my present. I was saying, "Look at me. I used to be one of you, but now I'm better than you. I still remember you, though, and sometimes I think about you."

I was being a politician, not a friend. To Crystal, the comment was a slap in the face. What she was telling me in her trailer that day was the same thing Donnah Dunthorn from the Allman Brothers' chat-room board had expressed concern with. Was I one of those southerners who had internalized negative feelings about the South and moved away? Crystal's reaction to my comment in that newspaper article confirmed it: Yes, I was one of those southerners.

She grinned at me. "Aw, man, it's all right," she said, putting her arm around my neck and pulling my face tightly against hers. "You're here now. We still love you."

It's narcissistic to romanticize the South when you live in New York or Los Angeles; to listen to Lynyrd Skynyrd's "Sweet Home Alabama" in the abstract, marvel over the deep feelings expressed in the lyrics, and rationalize the problematical parts so that it fits your own lifestyle and worldview. That's what Yankee apologists do. That's what I had done. I lived away from home for so many years that the music began to take on a new meaning for me. After years of moshing to punk rock and analyzing hiphop, I began to reassess the worthiness of Lynyrd Skynyrd. The music had become nostalgic for me; it took me back home to the mountains, trees, rivers, lakes, farms, thunderstorms, and country stores; to going barefoot and shirtless on hot summer days. But in my writing about Lynyrd Skynyrd, I wouldn't admit to the element of nostalgia. Instead, I placed the music into some kind of historical context that fit my worldview.

By the time Lynyrd Skynyrd's plane went down in 1977, I had already left the South in my mind. Things had become too sticky, too complicated. I couldn't reconcile what I felt were intolerable contradictions: hikers, hunters, football, rock & roll, rednecks, hippies, fundamentalist Christians, philosophy professors, Jesse Helms, Jimmy Carter. Sometimes I wondered if I ever actually was a true southerner.

Crystal helped bring it all back home for me. She was not an apologist for her views; she did not attempt to be politically correct or consistent with her feelings. She was exactly who she was: a third-generation employee of the Eveready plant in Asheboro, North Carolina; the mother of a young man who was beginning to do his own youthful experimenting; a woman who'd been married a few times and now lived single in a trailer in rural Guilford County; a partyer who'd calmed down over the years but still liked to relax on the weekends by hunting deer or hanging out with friends at music festivals. She believed in the right to bear arms and talked of peace and love. She was a proud southerner who defended the flying of the Confederate flag. She got weepy when she saw New York City firefighters giving their lives to save the victims of the World Trade Center. But she would tell those very same firefighters where to put it if they bad-mouthed her home or her lifestyle.

" 'Sweet Home Alabama' — does that not do it to you?" Crystal asked

with a big grin on her face. "I mean, that song just about says it all. If you don't like 'Sweet Home Alabama,' you know what you can do with it, because this is where we live, this is who we are, there's nothing overly deep about it. We're southerners and we're proud of it. That's just the heart and soul of it. It's right there in the music. We don't mind saying it, and if you don't like it—well, take it back home, then."

Crystal sums up her idea of the South like this: "You know when you stop at the Quick Stop and a big four-wheel-drive truck pulls up beside you and the dude gets out and he struts up to the door? You just feel like he's telling you, 'This is me and if you don't like it, well, you can just take a walk, bad boy.' Is that not a reflection of the whole South right there in that one little moment? That's what it is. There's no dressing on it. You can try to explain it any old way you want to, but it is what it is."

By the 1990s, other rock critics besides me had begun to revise the image of southern rock, specifically of the late Ronnie Van Zant. We sanitized his image by presenting carefully considered apologies for the difficult stuff. We downplayed his reactionary side, dismissing the indisputable conservatism expressed in songs such as "Sweet Home Alabama." We projected our own political agendas onto the music, updating Van Zant's biting humor to the more politically correct status of irony. We hastened to point out his antihandgun sentiments in the song "Saturday Night Special" and the tenderness he expressed for the old black bluesman in "The Ballad of Curtis Loew."

Even when I began my journey across the South to look into the music that helped awaken me, I wanted to hear Van Zant's former colleagues tell me yes, he was more politically progressive than he originally got credited for. But they didn't tell me that, because it's not true. Those of us who have characterized the singer as a misunderstood liberal have done so only to placate our own irrational feelings of shame for responding to the passion in his music. We do the same with the violence and misogyny of hip-hop—or the drama of a Wagner symphony. When we can't separate the artist from the art, we make the art fit our own paradigms. Rather than accepting the art for what it is, allowing ourselves to feel it without letting it threaten our sense of self, we're dishonest in our examination of it.

Ronnie Van Zant wasn't antihandgun; he owned handguns. In "Saturday Night Special," he expressed a feeling of danger about guns,

not a political stance. But that truth doesn't fit the pattern some of us have created for rock & roll rebellion. For some reason, most (but not all) rock critics have decided that rock & roll should express a liberal or leftist viewpoint. When it doesn't, we either invalidate the music (just as some conservatives do with leftist musicians) or we revise it in a way that turns the artist's nonliberal or nonleftist position into something that feels liberal or leftist. We're like children playing with a puzzle: if we like something that doesn't quite fit into the landscape we've created, we get frustrated and force it into that landscape so we can walk away happy and satisfied with ourselves.

My friend Crystal does no such thing. "People in big cities don't understand why we have such a problem with stupid gun laws out here in the country," she told me. "To them, guns are used in crimes. Period. But I love guns. I hunt with them. You know, I love Ted Nugent and I hate that he isn't from the South because he's my man. To me, he's a southern rocker. He does benefits for hunters' rights and he advocates for responsible gun use, as opposed to that 'don't kill the animals' shit. Give me a break. There's an overpopulation of deer in this country and we need to balance it. Do you know how many deer would be running around downtown Asheboro right now if we weren't out there hunting them? They're like rodents."

Ronnie Van Zant wasn't vague about his views either, although he did become savvy to the ways of dealing with journalists without having to be dishonest. When reporters would ask him about his harsh criticism of Neil Young in "Sweet Home Alabama," Van Zant would say the song was simply a testament to his appreciation for Young's music. That was true enough. But Van Zant never said he *didn't* believe Governor George Wallace of Alabama wasn't good for the South. It was a clever maneuver on his part. It kept writers from hounding him with questions he didn't want to get into. When Skynyrd's apologists began to probe more deeply into Van Zant's songs years after his death, though, we rewrote the facts.

In his book *Lynyrd Skynyrd: An Oral History*, the politically progressive music writer Lee Ballinger found people who would perpetuate a popular "defense" of "Sweet Home Alabama" like this: The song's chorus of "boo, boo, boo," which follows the line, "In Birmingham, they love the governor," represents Van Zant's rejection of Wallace and those who shared the Alabama governor's politics. Some of Van Zant's old friends

have played into this modified interpretation. His widow, Judy, the northern-born Lynyrd Skynyrd producer Al Kooper, former Skynyrd drummer Artimus Pyle, and MCA Records all have worked to promote this revisionist image of Van Zant. Charlie Daniels and former Skynyrd guitarist Ed King, however, scoff at such fussy analysis, saying the rationalizations of Van Zant's conservative musings have little to do with the real man.

"He had great respect for George Wallace," said Daniels. "Ronnie was a southerner, man. I remember when we played in Tuscaloosa, Alabama, one time, and they all got declared honorary lieutenant colonels [in the Alabama State Militia]. They got plaques from the governor, and they were just tickled to death about it."

"Ronnie was a big fan of George Wallace," said King. "He totally supported him. We all did. We respected the way Wallace stood up for the South. Anybody who tells you any differently is lying."

The members of Lynyrd Skynyrd subscribed to Wallace's brand of populism, which by the mid-'70s had also gained the support of an overwhelming majority of African-Americans in Alabama. King doesn't see his band's backing of the former governor as racist. "It's just not that simple," said King. "To me, Ronnie was a proud working-class southern man, and George Wallace represented proud working-class southern people. To Ronnie, Wallace was not just a man who wouldn't let blacks into a college, he was a man who spoke for poor, uneducated people who didn't have a voice. It's right there in the song."

That position is messy and contradictory, but it ultimately represents Lynyrd Skynyrd. The band members were not politicians or political activists who followed political issues with a fine-toothed comb and tried to make rational arguments. "Basically," said King, "Ronnie didn't think real hard about what he was writing. He wrote from his heart; he was a guy who wrote his feelings into songs."

Any well-articulated assessment of southern music or the southern lifestyle should consider the facts, but that's not always the way it happens in music journalism. It's as though when discussing anything involving white southerners, our praise must be tempered by some kind of qualification, it must fit into an acceptable framework. After all, poor white southerners—or rednecks—can't possibly think for themselves. Right? Take this positive review of the 2001 album *Southern Rock Opera*, by the

southern band Drive-By Truckers. Music critic Roni Sarig notes that Truckers' front man, Patterson Hood, "may look the part of a textbook redneck, but his level of self-awareness and artistic sophistication make him, at the very least, a redneck savant, a roughened but enlightened bard who understands the world from which he came. . . ." Sarig's praise of Hood is of the astonishingly condescending nature against which the Drive-By Truckers' album rails.

Al Kooper, the northern musician who discovered Lynyrd Skynyrd in Atlanta and signed the band to a major-label deal, expresses a view of the South that mirrors Sarig's assessment of the Truckers' album. In *Backstage Passes & Backstabbing Bastards*, he wrote of his return to the South in the early '70s: "My band and I arrived in Atlanta for a few nights' engagement at a club in the Underground. . . . Things had changed! . . . It wasn't so . . . Southern. . . . There was a sociological gentrification in attitude that had taken place that was tangible to me. The rednecks had long hair now. They were no longer the enemy." In other words, to Kooper, the South was pretty great when it wasn't the South—when it was more like the North.

It's naïve to intellectualize about "rednecks" without considering class issues, to point a finger at the most obvious culprits of racism and judge them. Trying to understand someone's feelings is not so simple. It's uncomfortable to hear a poor white southerner express his rage at losing a job or not being able to get a job, just as it's uncomfortable to hear a poor black southerner express *his* rage at the same situation. When that poor, jobless southerner sees race as a factor in his predicament, his rage is that much more uncomfortable to endure. It's tempting to see the poor white man who expresses a racist feeling about his joblessness as the oppressor, but that poor white man by definition has no power to oppress. The oppressor is the wealthy system that drove the wedge between poor whites and poor blacks in the first place, creating a space for racism to pickle. In one song on Drive-By Truckers' *Southern Rock Opera*, Patterson Hood's protagonist sings, "Ain't about my pistol, ain't about my boots, ain't about no northern drives, ain't about my southern roots, ain't about my guitars, ain't about my big old amps . . . ain't about the races, the crying shame. To the fucking rich man, all poor people look the same."

Politicians such as George Wallace rose to power by exploiting this

racial dissonance. Southern whites from poor backgrounds, such as the members of Lynyrd Skynyrd, generally either ignored the political manipulation or were seduced by it. Whether an individual allows himself to be manipulated probably involves the views of his family and the immediate environment in which he was raised; whatever the case, the reasons are deep and complicated. But such subtleties are rarely talked about with regard to southern racism, because just the very act of entertaining them is considered either politically incorrect or just too emotionally charged. At one point during my conversation with Ed King, I asked a direct question about Skynyrd's behavior with regard to race: Did any of the members of Lynyrd Skynyrd express negative feelings toward blacks? When King's wife, who was sitting at the table with us, chimed in, saying, "Oh, please, I remember Gary [Rossington] making a comment just a few years ago—" King immediately interrupted her.

"I don't have any personal experience with that," he said. "But I can tell you this: unlike the Allman Brothers, we never had any black people hanging around Lynyrd Skynyrd at all. At all. I mean, none at all!"

My old friend Crystal treaded this topic gingerly, too. She doesn't hang out with blacks often, she told me, but it's not because she refuses to. It's just not an issue that comes up in her life. She offered a few details about her working-class background that shed a little light on why.

"My mother came from a mill-house town down in Stanly County, but she was pretty cool about that stuff," said Crystal. "She was, like, everybody's the same but there should be no racial intermarriage or anything like that. Because my mother believed that each race is unique and should be kept pure, which may be kind of Nazi-istic, but it's also very Southern Baptist. But if there was a special occasion where she wanted to hang out with one of her black girlfriends from work or something, she would. It was no issue. But my father, he was so prejudiced that you would never see him talking to a black person. And if you wanted to live, you would never date a black boy, because you knew that your father would kill you. I'm not so sure that he's mellowed all that much, either.

"I'll be the first to admit there's still problems with racism down here," Crystal went on, her voice rising. "There always will be, because it's human nature. But from what I understand, they got problems up north, too. If the South was as horrible—as rednecky and as white-trashy—as some of those TV shows make it seem, don't you think blacks would've

all left by now? Instead, blacks are coming back home and now we have Mexicans hauling ass over here because it's a great place to live."

Crystal climbed up onto her soapbox, and those age-old southern contradictions I remembered well from my own childhood experiences began to fill the room. Her conversation turned to the neutral ground of music. "How come you think music's so good in the South? It's because black people and white people worked together to make it so damn good, that's how come," Crystal said. "There's always been black people in white southern music and white people in black southern music. That's the way it works down here. We wouldn't have southern rock & roll without the black influence, but then, I don't think the blues and rock & roll would have been as accepted if it weren't for the white people down here who backed them and pushed them and recorded them. It took both races. Music has always been a universal thing down here. It goes beyond color. And that goes all the way back to slavery."

Her opinions on outside perceptions of the South were stronger than I would have guessed. I don't remember Crystal ever talking about these issues when we were teenagers. "When it comes to northerners making fun of southerners," she went on, "it's just a case of everybody wanting to have somebody to feel superior to. But that's human nature, too, isn't it? Everybody has to have a scapegoat and southerners are scapegoats for people in other parts of the country. Blacks were the scapegoats for whites in the South before civil rights. And now, guess what? The blacks down here have the Mexicans. The Mexicans have become the scapegoats for blacks in the South. What comes around, goes around. And that goes all the way back to Adam and Eve, man."

These distinctions, said Crystal, are things the media paint with big broad strokes. "Those people from up north who bad-mouth the South or who try to apologize for us don't know the South," she said. "And I'll be the first to admit that I don't know nothing about Yankees, either. I don't understand them. To me, northern people are like a whole different race. I feel much closer to a black southerner than I do a white northerner. It's not about color, man. There's a dividing line in this country and it's the Mason-Dixon Line. Lynyrd Skynyrd got it right: 'Southern man don't need 'em around, anyhow.' "

RECONSTRUCTION
OF THE FABLES,
1982–1992

We can reach our destination,
but we're still a ways away.

—R.E.M., *"Driver 8"*

★ Chapter 8 ★

PUNK ROCK
IN COWBOY BOOTS

Jason Ringenberg *had never felt so much like a damn Yankee.*

His band, Jason and the Scorchers, was playing at a club in Knoxville, Tennessee, in 1982, when a redneck-looking guy in the audience started to heckle the group's twangy punk-rock clamor and thrashing stage antics.

"He clearly didn't like us," Ringenberg remembered. "So Jeff, our bass player, he calls him a pussy."

It was an easy enough comment for Jeff Johnson to make from the pulpit of a dingy bar stage, with a bass guitar strapped across his skinny body like a shield, and a mosh pit full of punk rockers backing him up. Besides, Johnson, who wore his hair in a mohawk as pink as a preppy girl's sweater, felt qualified to call the guy a pussy. Unlike Ringenberg, Johnson was a bona-fide southerner, born and raised in Nashville. All of the guys in Jason and the Scorchers were from the South—except for Jason.

"They were punk rockers, but they were also southern boys," said Ringenberg. "Jeff grew up in a working-class area of Nashville and went to the rough West Nashville schools. Country, southern rock—that music was in his blood."

The redneck guy in the audience didn't know this, of course, and didn't care. All he knew was that the bass player with the pink hair had just called him a pussy—onstage, in front of a club full of people.

"He looked pretty mad," Ringenberg remembered. "But we just kept going."

In 1982, punk rock was all about confrontation. Bands would bait their audiences and the audiences would heckle back, calling them names, spitting at the stage, telling the musicians they sucked. The musicians would sometimes stop in the middle of a song to return the insults; they'd spit back, throw drumsticks and beer cans at the crowds. It was all in good fun; it was about getting out aggression.

The Scorchers were no different from any other punk band in that regard. When they performed, Ringenberg would pogo about the stage like a rockabilly ragdoll and hurl his microphone stand into the air. Guitarist Warner Hodges would stand with his legs apart, like Johnny Ramone, and bash out simple, staccato power chords and squalling leads. Occasionally, he'd leap up and do one of those midair splits, like Pete Townshend of the Who, only with less precision. His leather jacket and untamed mop of black hair made him look as much like an old-school biker as a Ramone or Sex Pistol. Drummer Perry Baggs had spiked hair, but also wore a sleeveless T-shirt with the Confederate stars and bars on it. Johnson preferred skinny ties and sport coats—and, of course, pink hair.

"In those days, we were a pretty violent band—I mean, the music was violent," said Ringenberg. "It was a very testosterone-fueled kind of thing, mixed with all kinds of artificial chemicals. On top of that, all these different kinds of people would come to our shows—punk-rock guys, bikers, what have you. So there were a few fights."

After the show ended and everybody cleared out of the club later that night, the Scorchers were out back loading their equipment into a Ford Econoline van when the redneck guy returned—with a posse of friends.

"We're out there with our gear and he comes up and says to us, 'Where's the guy with the pink mohawk?' Well, I see Jeff coming up through the alley and I say to him, 'Jeff, just go somewhere and hide—now!' There were twenty of them and just three of us and they were saying, 'We're gonna kick your asses unless you tell us where that guy with the mohawk went.'"

Ringenberg laughed, but he wasn't laughing at the time. "I don't know how we talked our way out of that one, but we did. They kicked over a few amps and smashed a guitar or two, but they didn't hurt us."

Jason Ringenberg arrived in Nashville on Independence Day 1981. In the years since he heard those old George Jones and Merle Haggard

songs on the radio in his father's pickup truck, Ringenberg's tastes had turned to early rockabilly and the kind of raw psychobilly that bands like the Cramps, in New York, and the Blasters, out in Los Angeles, were playing. He drove into Music City hoping to find guys like Carl Perkins, the '50s rockabilly cat who wrote "Blue Suede Shoes," hanging out at local diners and clubs. Instead, he saw a lot of young wannabe country singers who had just seen *Urban Cowboy* and figured they could be the next Kenny Rogers.

Nashville was in the business of making hits. In the early '80s, the music industry there cranked out sappy, corporate-sounding country pop that had little to do with the lonesome moan of Hank Williams. Some of the music was still good, but for every first-rate artist like George Jones or Tammy Wynette, there were ten cheesy Lee Greenwoods and Barbara Mandrells. By 1981, the outlaw country of Willie Nelson and Waylon Jennings had gone mainstream, and Nashville had softened its edges. The country pop of Alabama was the biggest thing that had hit Music City since—well, ever. The closest thing Nashville had to rockabilly was Eddie Rabbitt, a Brooklyn-born singer who'd moved south in the late '60s, wrote some songs for Elvis Presley, and eventually topped the charts himself with a string of easy-listening crossover songs such as "I Love a Rainy Night."

"Nashville was a real backwater place, much more than I would have thought," said Ringenberg. "There was that tiny little Music Row area, where the country music establishment did their business, and that was it. They had their little world and they were good at it—they were selling a quarter-million records, you know, but it had nothing to do with rock & roll. They didn't understand rock & roll. They didn't *want* to understand rock & roll."

Ringenberg fell in with a group of disaffected rockers and punks who hung out at bars where you wouldn't see many cowboy hats or snakeskin boots. Almost immediately he met Jeff Johnson, who introduced him to Warner Hodges and Perry Baggs. "They were the cream of the Nashville crop, playing in all these little bands. So we started jamming together, basically just getting drunk, raising hell, and causing a big stink around town."

Things happened fast for the Scorchers. It was late summer and hotter than two Julys when the band got together and started making noise out at Ringenberg's new place on Neighborly Avenue in a rough part of

town. "The first song we played was 'Gone Gone Gone,' by Carl Perkins, and I tell you, man, it was just magical," Ringenberg remembered. "It was a revelation to all of us; an epiphany. I remember it just felt like the walls were melting, it was so hot that summer. But there was a lot of energy in that place. We were bouncing off the walls."

In January, Jason and the Nashville Scorchers released a seven-inch extended single called *Reckless Country Soul*, on the tiny independent label Praxis. Among the songs on that record were a revved-up version of Hank Williams's "I'm So Lonesome I Could Cry," and an original tune, "Broken Whiskey Glass," that would become a staple of the Scorchers' shows.

"That was the first song I wrote, and it's still our most famous one," said Ringenberg. "I remember Jeff and his girlfriend had been out drinking all night long, and that morning they went to a black church, still dressed up from the night before. He had his crazy pink hair, and her makeup was all smudged. So I wrote the line, 'She went to church in her party dress.' "

By early 1982, Ringenberg had only been in Nashville for six months when the Scorchers began packing clubs.

Meanwhile, down in the college town of Athens, Georgia, the members of R.E.M. were living together in an abandoned church, writing dreamy songs that matched their name. The letters, some said, stood for the sleep state of rapid eye movement. At first, the band got lumped into Athens's new wave scene, which in 1979 had produced the kitschy, southern, pop-culture musings of the B-52's, whose two female members wore exaggerated beehive hairdos and whose musicians fused the angular, minimalist punk-funk sound of England's Gang of Four with surf-guitar licks and the apocalyptic sci-fi vibe of Devo.

R.E.M. was not that kind of novelty. When the band released its first independent single, "Radio Free Europe," in 1981, music critics well beyond Georgia loved it and the song showed up on several top ten lists in the *Village Voice*'s annual critics' poll. The band followed up in 1982 with a mini-album, *Chronic Town*, that established R.E.M. as a serious new rock & roll band. The group's sound wasn't like anything that had ever come out of the South, except for maybe the rough-hewn, Beatles-like pop of Big Star. R.E.M.'s songs droned like the Velvet Underground, but with chiming guitars reminiscent of the Byrds. Michael Stipe's mur-

mured vocals were nasal, hinting at country music, but his words—what you could make out of them—seemed more like the Beat poetry of Allen Ginsberg or the free association of Patti Smith.

The year before, the band had traveled to North Carolina to record *Chronic Town* with producer Mitch Easter, who ran a recording business called the Drive-In Studio out of his mother's garage near Winston-Salem. Easter was a regional underground celebrity of sorts associated with the dB's, an early new wave band that had formed in New York City but whose members were from North Carolina. When the dB's played a gig in my college town, their power pop failed to go over with the small crowd still yelling for "Free Bird." In early 1983, R.E.M. returned to North Carolina, this time to record at Reflection Sound Studios in Charlotte, a modest building on Central Avenue just southeast of downtown where most of the clients were gospel quartets from local churches. At Reflection, the band cut its first full-length album, *Murmur*, with Easter and a second producer, Don Dixon, who played in a regional pop-rock band called Arrogance.

"We wanted to make a non-cool, non-trendy record, and we particularly didn't want to go to Los Angeles or New York or London," R.E.M.'s guitarist, Peter Buck, told *Rolling Stone* when *Murmur* came out that summer. "We really wanted to do it in the South with people who were fresh at making rock & roll records."

R.E.M. didn't make the kind of southern rock that audiences were accustomed to, but the band's arty, punk-inspired sound was full of southern imagery. Stipe's words and vocal delivery conjured postcard images of rural landscapes, and guitarist Buck had a rowdy southern sensibility about him. "At [the University of] Georgia," he told *Rolling Stone*, "all you wanna do is avoid having a job for four years, so you drink and raise hell."

Stipe was an introspective art student and army brat who was born in Georgia but grew up all over the place, from Texas to Illinois to Germany. He was so shy and quiet that when he spoke you practically had to read his lips to make out what he was saying. He told *Rolling Stone* that his impressionistic lyrics came from his environment. "If we steal a lot from any one type of music, it's country," he said. "On the vocals . . . I go for what I call the acid *e* sound, which is that nasal thing where you take the sound of *e* and make it as terrible as you possibly can. Tammy Wynette and Patsy Cline knew a whole lot about it."

The other two members of R.E.M.—bassist Mike Mills and drummer Bill Berry—had played together in blues-based southern boogie bands as teenagers in Macon, Georgia. After high school, the two moved in together and Berry landed a job with a concert booking agency called Paragon, affiliated with Phil Walden's Capricorn Records. In 1977, the company hired a young hotshot named Ian Copeland, brother of Stewart Copeland, the American drummer of a new London-based trio called the Police. Paragon began booking a few punk bands along with its steady diet of southern rockers, and it caused a rift in the agency's management. But while other Paragon staffers scoffed at Copeland's "bad taste" in music, Berry ate it up.

"I thought he was the coolest guy in the world," Berry said. "Everyone else in Macon was still listening to the Outlaws and Marshall Tucker." Mills was equally enthusiastic: "We'd go over to his house and he'd start playing us the Damned, Chelsea, the Ramones, the Dead Boys, the Sex Pistols." Copeland, Berry, and Mills formed a trio called the Frustrations, for how they felt about living in the southern rock mecca of Macon. By 1979, they were frustrated with the band and called it quits. Copeland, the son of a CIA agent, set out for New York to start his own booking agency, FBI; a third brother, Miles, formed a record label called IRS. Meanwhile, Mills and Berry enrolled at the University of Georgia, up in Athens, where they met Stipe and Buck and formed R.E.M.

The first time I saw R.E.M. I thought they were awful. It was 1981 or 1982, just before or after the release of *Chronic Town*. I'd been following the development of punk rock in *The Village Voice* and a couple of magazines, *Trouser Press* and *New York Rocker*. By then, I was studying English at East Carolina University in Greenville, North Carolina, where Ronnie Van Zant had tracked down Ed King to join Lynyrd Skynyrd a decade earlier. Greenville was still a big southern rock town in those days, but by then I had seen Devo and was trying to expand my musical horizons. On breaks from school, I would drive from my parents' home in Asheboro to a little pizza joint in Greensboro called Friday's. Nestled into a small strip of shops on Tate Street near the University of North Carolina, Friday's was the first place I knew of that booked punk bands.

R.E.M.'s shows at the tiny hole in the wall had been getting a buzz, so when the band came to my college town I wasn't going to miss them. But that night in Greenville, R.E.M. didn't play what I considered punk;

what they played sounded to me more like amateurish noise. Stipe spent most of the show twirling about his microphone stand, mumbling and crooning bad cover versions of classic songs like "Gloria." If they did any original music—and I'm sure they probably did—I couldn't distinguish it from the covers. My friends and I were among only a handful of people to show up, and the consensus was that R.E.M. sucked.

The year before R.E.M.'s *Chronic Town* and the Scorchers' *Wreckless Country Soul* came out, British rocker Elvis Costello initiated punk's unlikely alliance with country music when he traveled to Nashville to record a bunch of classic American country songs for an album called *Almost Blue*. It was a major departure for the nerdy-looking new-wave singer who wore thick, black Buddy Holly glasses and wrote barbed songs like "I'm Not Angry," "Lipstick Vogue," and "Goon Squad." In 1979, Elvis Costello and the Attractions had introduced themselves to most Americans with a hostile performance on *Saturday Night Live*. Just seconds after they began playing "Watching the Detectives," the song they'd agreed to perform on the show, Costello stopped the music, huddled with his bandmates, and then tore into another song, "Radio, Radio," a scathing attack on the corporate dumbing-down of American pop. It was a landmark for both music and television, and neither would ever be the same.

Then came the infamous Ray Charles incident. Costello was on tour in America when he got into a row with a couple of old-style American rockers: Stephen Stills, of Crosby, Stills and Nash, and Bonnie Bramlett, the Delaney and Bonnie singer who'd worked with Ike Turner, the Allman Brothers, and Eric Clapton. Costello, drunk in a bar in Columbus, Ohio, and acting the part of the insolent punk rocker that his image required, goaded the musicians. He called Stills "old tin nose," then turned his rage on Bramlett. In an interview with British writer Nick Kent, Costello explained: "I said at one point . . . 'That woman has made one reputation off one E.C. [Eric Clapton], she's fuckin' well not going to get more publicity off of another one!' "

The argument escalated and the name of venerable R&B singer Ray Charles came up. Costello ignominiously called him a "blind, ignorant nigger." Bramlett took a slug at the young punk and the media had a field day with the incident. Costello's remark was offensive and hurtful, but what was less reported was the singer's track record on race: he was a

strong backer of the British organization Rock Against Racism, had just produced the debut album of two-toned ska band the Specials, and his own latest release, *Armed Forces*, was critical of the military and of British bigotry. Costello made a stupid comment designed to piss off two aging rockers, and he would pay for it.

In *Rolling Stone*, Costello apologized to Charles and tried to give some context to the brawl: ". . . What it was about was that I said the most outrageous thing I could possibly say to them—that I knew, in my drunken logic, would anger them more than anything else." Charles forgave Costello, commenting, "Drunken talk isn't meant to be printed in the paper." Still, Costello's momentum stalled, and all the apologies and forgiveness in the world couldn't fix the damage done to his career. To this day, some intelligent people I know still refer to Costello's "racism," which is about as absurd as talking about the other Elvis's racism—either you understand real racism or you don't, and if you don't, no stack of evidence exonerating either Elvis will ever convince you differently.

At the turn of the decade, Costello began to show signs of being more than just a belligerent, snot-nosed delinquent. On *Get Happy!!*, released in 1980, his songs paid homage to American soul and rhythm & blues. He may have been a punk in style and attitude, but he was also part of a new generation of British musicians who, like the Rolling Stones and Yardbirds before him, was able to experience southern musical styles outside their cultural context. When he wasn't drunk and disorderly, he seemed to genuinely appreciate the simplicity and soulfulness of American roots music. So in 1981, when the angry young rocker arrived in Nashville to record songs such as Merle Haggard's "Tonight the Bottle Let Me Down," it somehow made sense.

Costello didn't put a punk spin to the songs on *Almost Blue*; he performed most of them faithfully, with pedal steel guitar and a syrupy, old-style Nashville production. Once again, a new generation of American music fans who had lost sight of the South's rich traditions was reintroduced to its own music by a hip British rocker. "When I first heard *Almost Blue* I was floored," wrote an anonymous fan in a "customer review" of the album on Amazon.com. "Whereas the Stax Wall of Sound surprise of *Get Happy!!* seemed consistent with Elvis's musical sensibility . . . *Almost Blue* was COUNTRY . . . it seemed so out-of-synch back then . . ."

Costello got a sharp education on the gulf between country and rock

when he arrived in Music City. Johnny Cash and his wife, June Carter, welcomed him with open arms. June's daughter Carlene had recently married the British rock satirist Nick Lowe, Costello's friend from the London pubs who had produced his first five albums. But the Nashville studio vets who worked with Costello on *Almost Blue* played mind games with the four-eyed Brit. Producer Billy Sherrill, the man behind a string of country hits by the likes of George Jones, Tammy Wynette, and Charlie Rich, goaded Costello and called him a "limey punk."

In the liner notes to a reissue of *Almost Blue*, Costello reflected on the mood of the recording sessions: "My only uneasy moment was during one break when I came across Billy and [engineer Ron "Snake" Reynolds] discussing the merits of their handguns across the mixing console. . . . After a while it was less of a collaboration and more of a contest in cultural differences. . . ."

Costello had grown accustomed to getting high praise from the rock press, but the reviews of *Almost Blue* were lukewarm. In a three-star assessment of the album, *Rolling Stone* described Costello's foray into country music as having "no feeling of being on the edge"—hardly the way critics saw Costello's punk records. The influential *Village Voice* rock critic Robert Christgau warned, "Take it from me, EC fans, start with the Flying Burrito Brothers' *Gilded Palace of Sin*, then try *24 of Hank Williams' Greatest Hits*, then George Jones's All-Time Greatest Hits: Volume 1, and Merle Haggard's Songs I'll Always Sing . . ." Meanwhile, if Costello's southern fans appreciated the noble musical experiment, punk and southern rock remained as segregated in the South of the early '80s as the black and white bathrooms of the early '60s.

While Costello was recording *Almost Blue* in a slick Nashville studio, Jason and the Scorchers were tearing up clubs in rougher parts of town. They didn't exactly see their music as southern rock in 1981, but it was beginning to dawn on the Scorchers that the stuff they were playing was very different from most of the punk rock and new wave coming out of other cities during the period.

"At first, when I got all hip and cool and into punk rock, I thought Lynyrd Skynyrd wasn't cool anymore," said Ringenberg. "But that didn't last too long. Very early on with the Scorchers, we had these long raps in which we admitted to each other how cool we thought Skynyrd was. You have to understand: I may have been a farm boy from Illinois, but the

other guys were southern to the bone. They identified with Skynyrd big time. Jeff always said we should have covered 'Tuesday's Gone,' but we never got around to it."

When Ringenberg speaks, his voice occasionally breaks, making him sound a little like a teenager passing into young adulthood. That break in his voice was the hallmark of the Scorchers' sound. On "Absolutely Sweet Marie," the centerpiece of the band's 1983 major-label debut *Fervor*, Ringenberg came off like a cornball version of Joey Ramone, hiccupping Dylan's lines in mocking but loving tribute. Behind that hiccup, guitarist Hodges, a veteran of high school southern rock bands, cranked out guttural power chords that were thick and simple, like the riffs of the Sex Pistols but with a Stonesy swagger and a honky-tonk twang.

No one knew what to think of the Scorchers when they took their music out of Tennessee to punk clubs all across the Southeast. The first time I saw them, I wound up in a mosh pit among a group of skinheads and a few redneck types who were standing on the periphery looking confused. It was not a comfortable scene. At one point, I bumped into one of the rednecks and he wanted to kick my ass. He clearly didn't buy into the concept of friendly slam dancing.

By then, I'd been in a college punk band myself, but moved on to journalism. My group had done cover versions of songs by the Clash and the Jam and wrote a few of our own tunes. Back home, my friend Jeff Brown had been toying with new music, too, and wrote an angry song called "Dead Bird" for audience members who yelled for "Free Bird." One night, my band, also tired of hearing the persistent yelps for "Free Bird," decided to do our own interpretation of Jeff's idea, only we just played an amped-up version of the Lynyrd Skynyrd original and substituted the words, "I'm as dead as a bird now." To the southern rock fans who haunted the rock clubs of Greenville, my new lyrics went over about as well as a dead bird. One night, some guy threatened to kick my punk ass from here to Kalamazoo for "soiling" the memory of Ronnie Van Zant.

Around that time, the definition of redneck was changing. Ten to fifteen years earlier, a redneck was a fellow who wore his hair short and slicked back, was hostile to longhaired hippies who looked like Van Zant or Charlie Daniels, and was loath to accept new kinds of music or new ways of thinking. Now, many of the guys who looked like Van Zant and Charlie Daniels *were* the rednecks—guys who had long hair and beards,

wore Budweiser T-shirts and motorcycle boots. For the most part, they hated the rituals of punk rock and people who had multicolored hair. I didn't have multicolored hair at the time, but I liked to work up a good sweat in a mosh pit. That night at the Scorchers show, the guy standing next to me with the black motorcycle boots and greasy long hair didn't appreciate it when my arm clipped his elbow, and I got my second death threat in as many years for my punk-ass behavior.

Southerners are not known for our willingness to accept change quickly or easily. New lifestyles and traditions come slowly in the South. Ironically, considering our rigid, Bible Belt underpinnings, southerners are proof of evolution. We evolve from one thing into quite another without anyone having much noticed until the difference is staring them in the face. The transformation of rednecks into something that looked more like hippies had happened gradually, and the makeover was largely cosmetic. The look was different, the language was altered to fit the times, but the general mind-set remained the same: don't tread on us.

The same thing had happened in southern politics. It may have taken a long time for southerners to leave their staunchly Democratic affiliation behind, but in 1980, when Ronald Reagan beat Jimmy Carter by a landslide, the relationship between the South and the Democratic Party had soured. By then, it was evident that Carter's victory in 1977 had been little more than a reaction to Watergate and leftover resentment toward Nixon's handling of the Vietnam War. If my teenaged friends and I thought the Allman Brothers and Carter were ushering in a New South—one in which younger, more tolerant Democrats would suddenly replace the old-guard Dixiecrat segregationists—we were only partly right. It was true that whites were becoming more tolerant of blacks' integration into mainstream culture, and that more blacks and liberal whites were getting elected to important offices. In 1965, there were only seventy-two black elected officials in the entire South; by 1976, there were 1,944. In 1981, civil rights activist Andrew Young, the former ambassador to the United Nations under Jimmy Carter, became Atlanta's second black mayor. He would pave the way for other southern mayors including Charlotte's Harvey Gantt, who was elected in 1983.

Still, in the southern state legislatures of the 1980s, a full 90 percent

of elected black leaders came from districts in which blacks were the majority. Even well into the '90s, only two blacks in the South ever had been elected to Congress from districts in which the majority was white. According to a 1995 report by the American Civil Liberties Union, predominantly minority districts were "virtually the only ones that elect minority representatives." Thus, in most ways, the South of the late '70s, when Reagan began stumping for president, was as conservative as ever. What was happening was that the old Dixiecrats—the conservative southern Democrats—were switching political affiliation, and for the first time in history the Republican Party was growing in the South.

To my mother's generation, this shift in political affiliation was totally unexpected. I remember her being proud of me in 1978 when I turned eighteen and registered as a Democrat. Mama told me that my grandfather once said he would never vote Republican under any circumstances. I was continuing a family tradition. Though I was aware that not all Democrats supported a liberal agenda, by the time I came of voting age Carter was in office and I equated the Democratic Party with my own more liberal positions on issues. It was a generally reasonable conclusion: by the late '70s, most of the liberals in the South were Democrats and so were most black elected officials. That's just the opposite from the way it started out, though.

The South's Democratic stronghold had been in place since 1863, when the nation's first Republican president, Abraham Lincoln, signed the Emancipation Proclamation, freeing the slaves. The Republican Party had been formed in 1854 with the express purpose of stopping the spread of slavery beyond the southern states. It was the Republican Party that passed the first civil rights legislation in 1866 recognizing blacks as citizens. But exactly one hundred years after the party was formed, a rift among Republicans found right-wing activist Barry Goldwater of Arizona running a conservative presidential campaign against Democrat Lyndon B. Johnson. Johnson won the election, but the Republican Party seemed to be turning in a rightward direction. When Johnson pushed the 1964 civil rights agenda through congress, Dixiecrats began voting Republican or independent, although they didn't immediately leave the Democratic Party.

Richard Nixon added the final touches to the Republicans' new conservative face when his campaign crafted a southern strategy that put him

in office twice, once in 1968 and then again in 1972. Watergate put a temporary halt to Republican acceptance in the South and paved the way for Jimmy Carter's victory in 1976. But after Carter's troubled administration failed to keep the momentum going for a Democratic reemergence in the South, longtime southern Democrats began defecting to the Republican Party in droves.

Another group of Republican southerners with a staunchly conservative agenda began rising up in the late '70s and expanded its power outward to other parts of the American heartland. It was the growing evangelical Christian movement, led by a Southern Baptist television preacher named Jerry Falwell, who equated political conservatism with the Bible's teachings. In 1979, the National Christian Action Council invited Falwell to a meeting with right-wing strategists to push the issue of abortion, hoping it would encourage social conservatives to finally make a complete split from the Democratic Party. The group came up with the idea of a "Moral Majority," declaring that most people held traditional values and that those who didn't were out of touch with American mainstream life. Falwell launched a massive public relations campaign and an official Moral Majority organization that galvanized the fundamentalist Christian movement in the South and elsewhere.

The Christian right, led by Falwell and other influential right-wing preachers such as Pat Robertson, used the tactics of leftist '60s political activists to win support for its agenda. The Moral Majority organized, staged demonstrations, trained protesters in the civil disobedience, and persuaded working-class voters by using the populist rhetoric of the labor movement. Right-wing strategists began putting a negative spin on civil rights advances, using code words and phrases to conceal the underlying racism at the heart of their ideology. By lumping together ideas such as "affirmative action" with words like *quotas, preferential treatment,* and *reverse discrimination,* they made the very concepts that had brought about social change and a sense of racial justice in America seem unfair to working whites.

The rhetoric and political activism rang nostalgically familiar to some '60s-era political fence-sitters whose views had begun to turn to the right in the years after Vietnam. Many southern baby boomers were now married, raising families, and concerned about low-paying jobs, rising taxes, and big government. Some were feeling shame about their wild youth,

which for the first time in U.S. history had involved the use of drugs on a mass scale, sexual freedom, tolerance of homosexuality, and other issues that ran against the grain of a traditional upbringing—particularly a traditional *southern* upbringing. The born-again Christian movement capitalized on the vulnerability of these young, upwardly mobile back-sliders and won their support. The strategy worked. The shift in political ideology among rightward-turning baby boomers, coupled with the southern Democratic old guard's switch to the Republican Party, created just the right environment for the Reagan revolution.

By 1983, Reagan had been in office for three years and put a friendly face to political conservatism. His speeches weren't shrill like those of Goldwater, Lester Maddox, or George Wallace. He had a grandfatherly quality that made him seem wiser than Nixon and more understanding of human emotion than old-guard southern politicians such as South Carolina senator Strom Thurmond, one of the first high-profile Democrats to switch parties in 1964, or North Carolina Senator Jesse Helms, also a former Democrat. Reagan's soothing paternal demeanor translated well to television, and southerners who didn't see themselves as bigoted but also didn't want the government prying into their religious or social lives, loved him. He made the former conservative Democrats of the South feel comfortable in their new Republican duds.

Reagan was running for reelection when I left my punk band in Greenville to take a job as the police reporter for *The Daily Times-News* of Burlington, twenty-one miles east of Greensboro and about thirty miles northwest of the Research Triangle Area. I was not prepared for the move from a heady academic environment to the everyday life of a work-ing stiff in a conservative textile town. Each morning, I'd get up at seven o'clock and drive to the magistrate's office to comb through arrest records from the previous night. Each morning I'd read the same names and same charges: domestic violence, driving while impaired, carrying a con-cealed weapon.

The police beat and political climate of Burlington depressed me, and to keep my sanity I began writing a pop-music column on the side. After all, music was what I wanted to be writing about in the first place. Working the police beat was a means to an end. What happened, though, was that I was forced into seeing life beyond rock & roll. Covering crimes, fires, auto accidents, and the small-town council meetings in the

nearby community of Mebane helped me to understand the very real problems of everyday working people and ultimately gave me a better perspective of what was going on in the South and across America. In turn, I began to pay attention to why people gravitated to particular kinds of music.

I began reviewing big concerts that passed through Greensboro and Chapel Hill—everything from Willie Nelson, Reba McEntire, and contemporary Christian singer Amy Grant to Prince, Bruce Springsteen, Tina Turner, and Iron Maiden. I covered gospel-music events of both the black and white communities of Alamance County and the midlevel musicians who came through the local country-music club JR's Tavern: has-been rock and soul veterans from Leon Russell to Percy Sledge, as well as up-and-coming country singers such as Lacy J. Dalton.

By 1983, MTV had become a powerful force in popular music in the two years it had been in existence, and old-style artists who couldn't make the transition from radio to videos were left behind, just as the old-style, pre-Reagan conservative politicians had been. Content was quickly being overshadowed by image, and audiences began embracing whatever they saw on TV, whether a powerful negative campaign ad by Jesse Helms or a Bruce Springsteen video screaming, "I was born in the U.S.A."

In the '60s and '70s, you could fairly easily tell a person's politics by the music he or she listened to, but that was beginning to change. It didn't matter that Springsteen's hugely popular "Born in the U.S.A." was critical of blind patriotism, the only thing most Americans saw when the video came on MTV was a man singing that refrain over and over. In September of 1984, Reagan, obviously mindful of how the support of rock stars had helped Carter win the 1977 election and how pervasive MTV had become by the early '80s, dropped Springsteen's name on a campaign stop in New Jersey.

"America's future rests in a thousand dreams inside our hearts," the president said. "It rests in the message of hope so many young people admire: New Jersey's own Bruce Springsteen. And helping you make those dreams come true is what this job of mine is all about." Reagan's audience roared its approval.

A few days earlier, the conservative writer George Will had gone to a Springsteen concert and written a positive review of it in his column: "I have not got a clue about Springsteen's politics, if any, but flags get waved

at his concerts while he sings songs about hard times. He is no whiner, and the recitation of closed factories and other problems always seems punctuated by a grand, cheerful, affirmation: 'Born in the U.S.A.!' "

The impact of Reagan's name-dropping was remarkable. Conservative pundits twisted the hard-work ethic of Springsteen's music to fit their populist agenda.

Springsteen was livid; he, along with other left-leaning rock stars of the period including U2, Peter Gabriel, Bob Geldof of the Boomtown Rats, and Sting of the Police attempted to show they were not supporters of the president, but all the huggy-kissy Live Aid and Band Aid stunts in the world weren't making Reagan any less popular in the heartland. On CMT, the country-music version of MTV, conservative rock bands whose members sang with southern accents—updated southern rock, actually—were becoming the new country stars, attracting aging baby boomers whose ideas had turned to the right but who still liked the sound of rock guitars. There was no longer a rock & roll consensus in America. The perception of rock culture, as *Rolling Stone* pointed out in a mid-'80s ad campaign designed to attract advertising from huge corporations and maintain its readership in the era of the New Right, was out of sync with reality. The only rays of hope for an old-style rock & roll political consensus in 1984 had been Democratic Primary candidates Gary Hart, a Kennedy-style politician, and civil rights leader the Reverend Jesse Jackson, who looked promising until he made a costly mistake by calling New York City "Hymietown." On November 16, 1984, the Democratic blunders coupled with the Christian right's massively successful conservative public relations campaign put Ronald Reagan back in office in another landslide victory.

Meanwhile, a growing American postpunk movement was bubbling on small independent record labels across the country: SST Records, in Los Angeles; Alternative Tentacles, in San Francisco; Twin/Tone in Minneapolis; Touch & Go, in Chicago; Homestead, in New York, and Dischord, in Washington, DC. As bands from those labels crisscrossed America on inexpensive tours, stopping mostly in college towns and selling their albums at the shows, regional musical styles were blending and blurring together in a way that wouldn't have a real impact on mainstream popular culture until the early 1990s. Many of those bands, including Minor Threat and Minutemen, spoke for the political left. The

South's underground music scene was centered in Athens, Georgia, the college town that gave rise to R.E.M. and the B-52's. As R.E.M. began to gain more attention from the mainstream music press, the eyes of the American underground turned to the indie scenes of the South.

In North Carolina, Godfrey Cheshire, a film and music critic for a *Village Voice*–like alternative weekly out of the Research Triangle Area called *Spectator Magazine*, put out a three-cassette collection of new North Carolina bands. Called *Welcome to Comboland*, the compilation featured a wide variety of independent rock that put the state's fledgling music scene on the map. I began to moonlight for *Spectator* myself. When I wasn't chasing ambulances or writing reviews of mainstream pop concerts for the Burlington *Times-News*, I scoured the punk clubs in search of new music, covering local punk bands as well as new acts coming through from outside the region: Black Flag, Minutemen, Meat Puppets, Sonic Youth. I also quietly but diligently documented the rise of R.E.M.

Thunder and lightning ripped across the rainy southern skies outside War Memorial Auditorium in Greensboro on that hot July night in 1984. I was dripping wet when I arrived in the lobby of the concert hall lugging two cameras and a red backpack with extra notepads, pens, and a tape recorder. I was twenty-four years old, nervous and excited. This was the first big rock show to which I had backstage access.

R.E.M. had just released its second full-length album, *Reckoning*, which reached No. 27 on the *Billboard* chart and included a minor hit, "So. Central Rain (I'm Sorry)." The band had long outgrown Friday's, the little pizza joint down on Greensboro's Tate Street where it had gotten its start three years earlier. Since that first R.E.M. show I'd seen, the band had become my favorite new act. In the intervening years, I'd learned to appreciate R.E.M.'s hazy blend of folk, country, and punk. And the members were better musicians; they'd honed their sound and performances in a way that made them unlike any other rock band of the era, indie or mainstream.

By 1984, it was clear that something big was about to happen for R.E.M. For one thing, some of the more mainstream postpunk rock

bands of the early '80s had become more popular—and more overtly political. U.K. acts such as U2, the Alarm, and Big Country were popping up on MTV, singing folk-based new wave songs about social and political concerns in the U.K. Just before I graduated from college, I had seen U2 open for veteran pop-rock studio whiz Todd Rundgren at an outdoor concert in Chapel Hill. The first act on the bill that day was a curiosity called Grandmaster Flash and the Furious Five, a group that rapped over funky, minimalist beats and turntable scratching. I'd read about the burgeoning New York City hip-hop scene in *The Village Voice* and heard Kurtis Blow's hit "The Breaks," but I thought rap was just an interesting novelty that would eventually blow over.

Bands such as U2 and the Police, on the other hand, were creating a new mainstream arena-rock sound. Even though it was pouring rain by the time U2 hit the stage at Chapel Hill's Keenan Stadium that day, the group's performance was so intense, so passionate, and so big, and singer Bono was so charismatic, that no one seemed to care about the crashing thunder and blinding sheets of rain. U2 put on the best rock show I'd seen up to that point—better than the Rolling Stones, better than the Who or Eric Clapton. U2 was young, enthusiastic, on fire. Even as lightning bolts threatened to zap the towers and electrical equipment that surrounded the band, Bono, hoisting a white flag and wailing "Sunday Bloody Sunday," beckoned God and tempted Mother Nature, going so far as to scale the iron towers, waving his flag to the heavens as if rock & roll truly could save the world. He had a faith in the redeeming power of music that I'd always believed but never really seen until that moment.

When headliner Rundgren hit the stage and began singing his current hit, "Bang the Drum All Day," it was one of the most anticlimactic rock events I'd ever witnessed. Suddenly, the crowd was annoyed by the rain and people began filing out of the stadium in droves. I felt sorry for Rundgren. His music didn't matter. In Chapel Hill that day, no music that had come before U2 mattered.

By 1984, I saw U2 in relation to R.E.M. in the same way I'd seen the Rolling Stones in relation to the Allman Brothers. I put the Stones and U2 on a pedestal, but I directly identified with the Allmans and R.E.M. The themes in music were changing, though. R.E.M. didn't express the sense of sorrow or shame I'd heard in the Allman Brothers; U2 didn't incorporate southern music influences as obviously as the Stones did. Rock & roll

was growing up, expanding, changing. The pain of the blues and its social ramifications had merely become part of these bands' lives. The fact that the very different-sounding Grandmaster Flash played on the bill that day in Chapel Hill, and U2's later homage to B. B. King in the film *Rattle and Hum*, showed where Bono and his band stood in regard to racial and cultural issues, but their appreciation went beyond musical replication.

Likewise, R.E.M. had taken southern music beyond the moody blues of the Allman Brothers or the angry honky-tonk swagger of Lynyrd Skynyrd. The South of R.E.M. had an artistic and intellectually detached quality, its landscapes painted with the colors and hues of textured guitar tones and vocal nuances rather than emotionally reactive, blow-by-blow narratives. The band's sound captured the pastoral ambiance of southern life without all the social baggage. Stipe's impressionistic lyrics and garbled vocal delivery didn't reveal much about the singer's specific feelings. It wasn't that he lacked emotion—in fact, in some songs, such as the delicate "Camera," his voice positively bled—it's just that his enunciation was so vague that the songs offered only glimpses of his pain. Onstage Stipe communicated theatrically, wearing layers of clothing he would peel off, one item at a time, until he was left wearing little more than a T-shirt and baggy pants.

The following year, R.E.M. would release an album that hinted about their ideas of the South in an elliptical title that was more literary than literal. *Fables of the Reconstruction* was packed with quirky southern characters: an auctioneer selling off someone's property; an old man trapped in a "legend" and trying to find his way out; another man who wanted to paint signs but couldn't read; and still another who was "reared to give respect." The names of the characters had a distinctly southern feel as well: Old Man Kensey, Wendell Gee, Lawyer Jeff, Brother Ray. There were images of wheelbarrows, gardens, porches. Within this swirl of disembodied rural snapshots, Stipe offered cryptic captions. "The map that you painted didn't seem real / He just sings whatever he's seen." And then, in the same song, as if he'd reached some great epiphany, the singer added, "Maybe these maps and legends have been misunderstood." In a similar moment on *Fables*, Stipe used the sound and repetition of his words to offer a comforting message that rang loud and clear in the South of the mid-'80s: "Take a break, driver 8 / Driver 8, take a break / We can reach our destination," and then added, "but it's still a ways away."

If southern rock had been leading young southerners on a path to self-awareness in the years since desegregation changed our lives, R.E.M.'s music reflected one of the later stages of our journey. The Allmans had expressed melancholy, Skynyrd anger and resentment, Jason and the Scorchers a rambunctious sense of humor. R.E.M. was taking a step back from the emotional turmoil of its surroundings and setting the stage for real healing to begin. Still, in 1984, I wasn't there yet. I still had deep feelings of guilt, shame, and inadequacy, and from what I saw as a twenty-four-year-old newspaper reporter living in another southern textile town where police and emergency officials felt free to tell racist jokes even with a reporter in their midst, our culture wasn't there, either. We were still a ways away.

That night in Greensboro, I broached the subject of R.E.M.'s feelings about the South to Stipe backstage before the show. The band had recently returned from a European tour and I wondered if the trip had made Stipe feel homesick.

"I feel closer to home now," he told me. "You kind of gain this respect and feeling that you wouldn't have if you were here all year round. It's kind of like when your father dies, you realize just how much you have missed. You sometimes don't take advantage of it when you have it."

Later that night, when R.E.M. tore into "So. Central Rain" and "(Don't Go Back to) Rockville," I was in heaven. I watched Stipe peel off his layers of clothing, dance spastically about the stage, twirl like a dervish, grasp his microphone with both hands, and croon upward to reach the high notes. For the first encore, the band performed "Camera," Stipe's moving vignette in which he sees himself as a camera documenting one of life's small but significant events: a moment of loss. Behind the song's haunting melody and prominent but fragile bass line, he sang, "Will you be remembered? Will she be remembered? / Alone in a crowd, a bartered lantern borrowed. / If I'm to be your camera, then who will be your face?" The band followed with the Velvet Underground's equally beautiful and fragile "Pale Blue Eyes."

When R.E.M. was done, the feelings I had were about as close to homosexual as I had ever come, only it wasn't sexual. What I felt was an inner bonding of intellect and instinct inspired by a white southern man who was exactly my age. Though I didn't really know Stipe, I'd never in my life felt as deeply connected to another man. I didn't know why, exactly. I suppose it was partly the pure rush of rock & roll, but I'd felt

that before. Maybe it was the healing nature of Stipe's words and music and the way he communicated it in his performance. Maybe the very detached nature of his songs allowed me to project myself into the music. Stipe seemed to be expressing emotions I was having in a way that made me feel completely understood for the first time—more understood than I'd felt listening to the Allmans or Skynyrd. I felt understood on an intellectual as well as an emotional level. He stripped away all of the crap that comes along with being southern, and the only thing left was pure humanness. The artist in Michael Stipe seemed to have an understanding of humanity that transcended the burdens of our shared southern heritage. At the time I didn't feel as though anyone else in my environment had that understanding, though, of course, there were many of us.

I began to write about R.E.M. for the Burlington *Times-News*. I found out that the group's manager, Jefferson Holt, had grown up in Burlington and that his mother, Bertha "B" Holt, was one of the town's representatives in the state legislature. In 1985, just before *Fables* came out, I went to another R.E.M. show, this one outdoors in Raleigh, where I interviewed Holt for a profile to run on the paper's local page. He told me he'd met R.E.M. while working at School Kids Records, in Chapel Hill, the shop where I bought my first Elvis Costello album back in 1978.

"I always tried to convince the club owners in Chapel Hill to start getting these bands in town," said Holt, referring to regional new wave acts such as the B-52's and Pylon. On one occasion, a group that Holt had suggested to perform at a local club canceled; as a last resort, he recommended the little-known R.E.M. Holt became friendly with the band and eventually moved to Athens, where he opened a store called Foreign Legion Records. When the store went out of business, he started working full-time for R.E.M.

"When we started out, I did everything," said the lanky manager, with his long face, wire-rimmed glasses, and fine, bleached-blond hair. He wore a Dentzel Carousel T-shirt, tight black jeans, and tennis shoes, and when he spoke, his arms dangled puppetlike from his stringbean body. By 1985, the former record-store geek had made a career of managing R.E.M. and rarely had time to get back to Burlington to see his folks.

"If I had my way, I'd spend as much time as I could at home with my mom," he told me. "But with the records coming out, I can't." When I asked what it was like growing up in Burlington, Holt damned his home-

town with faint praise: "Burlington's a good place to grow up. I've found that incredibly boring places force people to create their own types of entertainment."

When R.E.M. returned to North Carolina for its *Lifes Rich Pageant* tour, in 1986, two of my reporter friends went with me to see the band play in Wilmington. A mutual friend of ours who had moved on to the Wilmington paper, told us he would be out of town that weekend but that we could stay at his apartment before heading back to Burlington the next day. At Wilmington's Trask Coliseum, we met up with Godfrey Cheshire of the *Spectator* and after the show invited him over to the apartment for some beers. He invited Stipe, and the five of us packed into my car and puttered off into the night. On the way, we stopped at a store to buy a few six-packs, then headed over to Kelvin's apartment, where we sat up all night talking.

Stipe told us about an experience he had at fifteen on a hilltop in the rain when he learned not to fear electrical storms. He told us he could tell when a major earthquake was going to happen because he'd get sick beforehand. He talked about influential early teachers, about how he liked to ride his bicycle around Athens, and about how the people of Athens still treated him like a regular guy and not a rock star. He showed us a tattered journal he carried to document all the changes that were going on in his life; in it, he'd scrawled notes, poems, and songs, and pasted photographs and drawings.

At one point, we heard voices outside the ground-floor apartment and saw what looked like faces at the window. I thought the alcohol had gone to our heads, but as we looked more closely, the faces were real. They were the faces of fans who had seen us at the store and followed us to the apartment. Stipe wasn't surprised, but I was. It dawned on me at that moment how big R.E.M. had become. By 1986, Michael Stipe was a bona-fide rock star who people followed just to get a glimpse of. I wondered what it was like to be someone people followed around just for a glimpse.

On our return to Burlington the following day, we took a major detour up to the rural town of Pinnacle, where a folk artist named James Harold Jennings lived in a compound of three old school buses. Stipe had told Godfrey about Jennings, whose work was similar to that of the Reverend Howard Finster, another folk artist Stipe helped bring to the attention of

the art world. Jennings carved wild, colorful whirligigs shaped like birds, cowboys, and Indians, and huge women sitting on tiny men. He was an eccentric, paranoid man who would ramble on about how people were out to get him. He was known to carry a gun and would sometimes shoo people away with it. On our visit, though, he was mellow and friendly. I bought two of his whirligigs, one for myself and another for my girlfriend. Sadly, Jennings would take his life in 1999, fearful of the looming Y2K scare.

The new southern rock was a far cry from the music of the old southern boogie bands. Brown leather vests, Jack Daniel's T-shirts, and Harley-Davidson insignias had given way to strange hairstyles and colorful rags bought at secondhand shops. Appreciation of the earthy wisdom of an old blues guitarist or banjo picker had given way to curiosity about the fanciful insights of eccentric folk artists who quoted the Bible and dreamed of space aliens. The love/hate relationship with blacks among young white musicians had given way to an exploration of whiteness—not as a racist exercise but as an honest investigation borne of curiosity. In the punk and postpunk years, opening up the old wounds and celebrating poor white cultural traditions didn't seem so scary or embarrassing anymore. White southern musicians suddenly reveled in their white-trash heritage: Elvis, rhinestones, bushy sideburns, MoonPies, beehive hairdos, Black Oak Arkansas, velvet Jesuses, trailer parks, Myrtle Beach postcards. This stuff was no longer something to apologize for, but a source of pride to be examined and played with in art, music, and performance.

Southern bands were cropping up all over North Carolina. In Charlotte, a group called Fetchin Bones dressed in thrift-store clothing and played a folky, punky sound that mixed Patti Smith–style stream-of-consciousness poetry with Kitty Wells's country twang and the B-52's' kitschy outrageousness. In Chapel Hill, Southern Culture on the Skids also drew from the B-52's' sense of kitsch but added a rockabilly chug to its music. The Flat Duo Jets, a combo that used cheap amps and battered guitars, played a cruder and noisier rockabilly sound. My favorite of the new bands was the Right Profile, a four-piece country-punk act that was more catholic in its style, blending the grit and spit of the Replacements with the ragged glory of Neil Young several years before Young would be hip again among the alternative-rock crowd. Like Jason and the Scorchers, the Right Profile, which got its name from a Clash song, was

an alternative-country band several years before the arrival of groups like Uncle Tupelo and, later, Whiskeytown.

On a breezy autumn day in 1986, a bright orange sun had begun to melt down into the rolling hills surrounding Winston-Salem as I drove into North Carolina's most famous tobacco town to visit with the members of the Right Profile. Steve Dubner, the band's leader, cocked his head to the side and gave me a fiendish grin as I pulled up to the corner of Main and Bank streets, in the city's historically preserved Old Salem district. We'd decided to meet there because it was a landmark I was familiar with.

Dubner's thick, curly black hair and long, scruffy sideburns stretched Elvis-like down his face, making the misplaced New Yorker look like a subversive parody of an old-style southern greaser. He was wearing black shades, black jeans, a white T-shirt, and a zip-up jacket. His bandmate Jeff Foster huddled with the other members on the sidewalk while Dubner walked up to my Toyota and hopped into the passenger seat.

"Wow, nice ride," Dubner deadpanned as he pulled the safety belt across his chest.

Meanwhile, Foster clicked open the door of his fire-engine-red 1962 Rambler station wagon parked on the side of the street in front of my car and hit the ignition. It growled and rumbled as the other two guys piled in behind him. We were off to the band's rehearsal space in another part of town.

The Right Profile was one of the most promising bands on North Carolina's fertile music scene. Dubner's whiny, punk-inspired vocals and keyboard playing blended well with Foster's raspy drawl, twangy guitar licks, and flair for a memorable rock melody. The band had all the ingredients that could have made them alt-rock superstars of the '90s, but they'd just signed a horrible deal with Clive Davis's Arista Records and recorded an album that would never see the light of day. Some of their music had surfaced on tiny independent compilations, including two classics on the *Welcome to Comboland* collection that hinted at why the Right Profile was such a popular live act: Foster's chiming, Gram Parsons–like anthem "God's Little Acre," a song about loss that was inspired by a graveyard in Old Salem; and Dubner's "Cosmopolitan

Lovesick Blues," a breathtaking play on Bob Dylan and Hank Williams that remains one of rock & roll's great lost classics.

The Dubner song brought together everything that was interesting about southern punk in one snotty line that he delivered Mick Jagger–like behind a charging beat and infectious melody: "I suppose you're living in a little trailer somewhere, with your husband and your eight or ten dirty little children, in a cotton dress, and I hope that you're absolutely miserable, yeah. . . ." It was actually a love song about a woman he'd lost and then found again, just like in the movies. But Dubner's white-trash imagery and kiss-off delivery offered a perfect snapshot of the southern punk scene of the mid- to late-'80s.

It was a Sunday afternoon and we stopped at a cafeteria for lunch before heading over to Dubner's place. Families still dressed up from church sat around tables eating fried chicken, mashed potatoes, black-eyed peas, turnip greens, and cornbread. I got the fried chicken; Dubner, Foster, and the other guys got the chicken pan pie. Dubner told me he and Foster had met at Western Carolina University in the mountains of North Carolina over "a mutual affection for chicken pan pie." It was a nice story, but the two actually met after Foster put up signs around the campus that read: LEAD GUITARIST AND DRUMMER NEEDED FOR BAND. INTERESTS: THE CLASH, BUDDY HOLLY, BOB DYLAN, BRUCE SPRINGSTEEN, STEVE FORBERT.

"I thought, Wow, that's for me. But I didn't play guitar or drums," said Dubner. He did play keyboards and accordion, though, and those instruments became central to the Right Profile's sound. I asked the two how they saw their music in relation to all the other new groups coming out of the Carolinas and Georgia at the time.

"Most of the South is perceived, especially by northeasterners, as kind of Podunk towns all strung together," said the northeastern-born Dubner.

"But we're not just a bunch of stupid cowboys or country boys," Foster piped in, then paused to reconsider his statement. "Of course, all my people on both sides of my family are pretty much like that, so I guess maybe we're more like that than we are citified."

Dubner preferred the word *rural* to *southern* in describing the band's sound. "Rural in the same way I think of the Band's music as rural," he said. "They had that little house up in Woodstock—that house out in the middle of the country where they recorded those great albums. Our

songs, like 'God's Little Acre,' sound like they could have been born sitting on some porch at twilight. They have a real homey sort of feel. But
when you say words like *homey* or *rural*, people think of folks who don't
know how to tie their shoes."

Dubner cited Lynyrd Skynyrd as an example of a band that never sold
its country soul. Today, the citation would be hip; it wasn't at all hip in
1986.

"Our songs that are real country sounding are going to stay that way,"
said Dubner. "We're not going to pretty them up. But then, our greasy,
Chicago-style bar-band blues songs are going to stay that way, too. We
don't plan to meld the whole thing into a slick, southern-rock production. We won't do that. We're happy sounding raw and different."

I spent the rest of the day and well into the night at the band's
rehearsal space, watching them work up songs that would never go anywhere. In hindsight, it's depressing to know that such a great band never
got its due attention and that Arista Records still has a full Right Profile
album that neither the band nor the company are willing to put out.

Years later Dubner would resurface as Stephen J. Dubner, a writer for
The New York Times Magazine who produced a groundbreaking article
about growing up in a Jewish family that converted to Catholicism before
he was born. His investigation of his cultural roots had a huge impact on
the Jewish and Catholic communities in New York and spurred a lively debate on authenticity. It was one of the inspirations for my own investigation
of my cultural heritage. Dubner went on to become a popular lecturer at
Jewish events and the author of the books *Turbulent Souls: A Catholic Son's
Return to His Jewish Family* and *Confessions of a Hero-Worshiper.*

In 2004, I called Dubner and asked him if he would reflect on his
time in the South: What was it like for a bright young kid who grew up
in a Catholic family in the rural northeast to move to the mountains of
North Carolina in the early 1980s? When he arrived at Western Carolina
University, Dubner told me, he knew little about the South other than
the images and stories from the civil rights era. "In my mind, that whole
Chaney-Goodman-Schwerner legacy had stayed with me," he said. "I
mean, even though the Right Profile didn't do drugs and were actually a
pretty straightlaced band, we were four scruffy-looking guys who rode
around in an old van late at night after shows. I was petrified that we'd
wind up facing some form of southern justice."

As he watched and listened and learned from the families of friends who were native southerners, Dubner saw a different South—one that he says "still remains a mystery to people in other parts of the country."

"Before I moved to the South, I didn't know anything about that whole cool strain of courtly, acerbic, fiercely independent southern writers—Flannery O'Connor and all that—and it fascinated me," he said. "I also had no idea about southern mores until I met Jeffrey [Foster] and visited his family. I learned so much from the Fosters and I really liked them a lot. They were very different from northern families. I don't want to say that northern families aren't loyal, but loyalty in the South is one of the real cornerstones of the culture." By the time he and Foster began writing music together, said Dubner, "Hank Williams was one of my favorite writers and the Fosters were one of my favorite families."

The weekend after my day with the Right Profile, I traveled to Charlotte to meet up with Hope Nicholls and Aaron Pitkin of Fetchin Bones. The couple had formed the band as a duo while attending Warren Wilson College, also in the North Carolina mountains. The Bones, whose first album, *Cabin Flounder,* came out in 1985 on the small Atlanta label DB Records, had been hailed as one of the best new southern bands since R.E.M. When I sat down with Nicholls and Pitkin, the Bones had just signed to Capitol Records and released their first major-label album *Bad Pumpkin,* whose mix of funky, white-trash kitsch was a far cry from their first album's folk- and country-inspired punk.

As Pitkin cooked dinner for the three of us, Nicholls and I sat in their living room and talked about southern music. "I never really considered us a country or southern rock band, per se," Nicholls said in a deep southern drawl as she stroked her two cats, Viva and Ico. That day, her hair was bleached blond, and when she gazed off from time to time, in deep thought, revealing only her profile, she looked like a young Robert Plant, of Led Zeppelin. "The only thing country about us is that I've got a southern accent," she said. "I mean, being from the South is just a fact for me. Does it mean that we should be chunked into this southern rock category along with all these other bands? I think not."

I thought *so.* Based on the themes of Fetchin Bones songs, here's what I wrote about the group in an article for *Option* magazine three years later: "Perhaps more than any band in southern rock's rich history—from the Crickets to Lynyrd Skynyrd to R.E.M.—Fetchin Bones defines the

South in the contradictory terms it is." I was referring to the band's juxtaposition of humor and sadness, decadence and religion, foolishness and wisdom. In their live performances, Nicholls would don skimpy halter tops and fluorescent bike-messenger shorts, or fluffy boas and sparkly, secondhand coats. Her hair would be jet black or bleached blond, and when she sang she looked and sounded somewhere between Plant and Janis Joplin.

In my *Option* article, I wrote about how the Bones had come from Charlotte, North Carolina, home of Jim and Tammy Bakker's P.T.L. religious empire, which, by the late '80s, had taken a high-profile fall into a sordid scandal that involved sexual impropriety and financial corruption. In an early draft of my article, I referred to Charlotte (where years later, perhaps ironically, I sit today writing this chapter) as a cesspool of denial, a growing banking town that desperately wanted to be like New York City and forget about its past both as a bastion of racism and the southern city where school busing eventually led to the end of classroom segregation. I put all of that weight on Fetchin Bones, referring to Nicholls as an "emotional oxymoron: a sort of blending of Patti Smith, Minnie Pearl, and Salt-n-Pepa." It was a bit dramatic, to be sure, but I wasn't just writing about Fetchin Bones: I was at the beginning of a journey that would lead me to this book.

Nicholls didn't exactly appreciate being used in this manner, but the band's music didn't do anything to discourage my analysis. She sang about chicken trucks and southern women trying to escape from the kitchen. The band's guitarist on *Bad Pumpkin*, Errol Stewart, was a Charlotte native who had moved to New York and gotten involved in the city's downtown art scene. He'd recently shown a southern-themed performance art piece in Atlanta called *Work, Lies and Noise*, which he described as "kind of droney and psychedelic."

"I managed to work into the piece these cutouts of all the articles that appeared in *The Charlotte Observer* right after the Jim and Tammy P.T.L. scandal," Stewart told me. "I'd already been collecting religious stuff while I was in New York and, amazingly, when I got back home, the Jim and Tammy thing broke within two weeks. It was great. I got to work it into my piece."

Fetchin Bones had taken the southern culture of the early 1980s—all the crazy shame and humor of sex, religion, race, and class—and formed

a pastiche that was at once fascinating and not totally successful. The band eventually broke up, but Nicholls continued making music, collaborating with members of the Chicago-based industrial-rock band Ministry and forming other Fetchin Bones–like bands along with Pitkin. By the early 2000s, the two were still well known in the Charlotte area as that zany art couple who threw the best parties in town. Nicholls later opened a boutique called Boris and Natasha's in the hip Plaza Midwood section of town, selling wild clothing and accessories, and her popular Ooo La La parties attracted a mishmash of creative people of all races and sexual orientation in a town known more for finance and religion than creativity or tolerance.

By the mid-'80s, bands such as Fetchin Bones, R.E.M., and Jason and the Scorchers had opened the doors for a reexamination of the South by more mainstream southern artists. In 1985, the massively successful Tom Petty wrote a totally unexpected concept album called *Southern Accents*.

When I first saw Petty on *Saturday Night Live* in 1980, performing his hit song "Refugee," I had no idea that he and his band were from the South. Their loud, chiming guitars came off more like a hard-rock version of the Byrds, and Petty had a voice that blended the angry attitude of a punk rocker with the nasal whine of Bob Dylan. At first, I thought "Refugee" was a political song, but when I listened more closely to the lyrics, it became clear that the singer was actually telling a wounded friend that she needn't feel like a refugee of love.

Petty and his band Mudcrutch had left the college town of Gainesville, Florida, in the early '70s and headed for the West Coast. After breaking up temporarily, they reunited as Tom Petty and the Heartbreakers. By 1979, the Heartbreakers had scored a few minor hits including "Breakdown" and "American Girl," but they were still relatively unknown. Then they put out *Damn the Torpedoes* in 1979, and by the following year it shot to No. 2 on the strength of "Refugee" and another single, "Don't Do Me Like That." When MTV began airing a year later, Tom Petty and the Heartbreakers became one of the few bands in the classic-rock mode to make the successful transition to videos. Petty also became known around L.A. for being a mainstream rock star with an uncompromising ethic. He fought with his record label, Lynyrd

Skynyrd's old nemesis MCA, threatening to withhold his 1981 album *Hard Promises* until the company agreed to keep the price down. MCA backed away and *Hard Promises* sold platinum.

By 1982, when the South began to rise again on the punk-rock underground, Petty started reflecting on his own southern upbringing and writing songs about it. He'd grown up in north Florida, which is closer to Georgia than it is to Miami, and culturally about as Deep South as it gets. Three years later, his ruminations became *Southern Accents*, a beautiful song cycle that was not like anything he'd done before. Petty took the project so seriously that at one point during the mixing of the album, he became so frustrated that he punched a wall and broke his hand. The album, produced by Dave Stewart of the Eurythmics, was a dazzling, ambitious work that sounded at once contemporary and deeply traditional. The centerpiece was the title song, with its immortal opening couplet that resonated strongly for those of us who were born and raised below the Mason-Dixon Line: "There's a southern accent where I come from, / The young 'uns call it country, the Yankees call it dumb."

Southern Accents was not unlike an earlier southern-themed concept album by New Orleans native Randy Newman. On *Good Old Boys*, Newman had presented a characteristically cynical take on southerners, and critics outside the South loved it. To be sure, the songs were powerful, but like W. J. Cash's *The Mind of the South*, Newman's album only served to reinforce stereotypes for intellectuals outside the region. *Southern Accents* took a less judgmental approach to the characters of Petty's youth. He sang from the differing perspectives of people he knew growing up. It wasn't a pretty view of the South, but it also wasn't as simplistic as some critics made it out to be. Unlike R.E.M.'s murky *Fables of the Reconstruction*, *Southern Accents'* narrative was straightforward.

In the song "Rebels," Petty's protagonist is a drunk and disillusioned husband; in "Spike," he tells of a gang of punk-bashing rednecks; in "Mary's New Car," he sings the simple, blissful feelings of a young, blue-collar kid excited about his girlfriend's new wheels. The album's MTV hit, "Don't Come Around Here No More," is a hypnotic song whose title sums up the collective mood of many southerners who feel infringed on by outsiders. *Southern Accents* was an eloquent portrait of the South, circa 1985, and a natural evolution from Skynyrd's "Sweet Home

Alabama" and Charlie Daniels's "The South's Gonna Do It." Predictably, Petty got slammed for his regionalistic identification.

"Petty's problem isn't that he's dumb, or even that people think he's dumb, although they have reason to," wrote Robert Christgau in an unbelievably harsh critique of *Southern Accents*. "It's that he feels so sorry for himself he can't think straight. Defending the South made sense back when Ronnie Van Zant was writing 'Sweet Home Alabama,' but in the Sun Belt era it's just pique."

In the early years of political correctness, Christgau's unbridled bigotry could have been written only about a white southern man. It was okay in 1985 for Christgau to call Petty dumb and to suggest southerners should just "get over" their feelings of pain and unease in the world. During that same period, if a conservative writer criticized an African-American artist or activist for not being able to "get over" his years of pre–civil rights mistreatment, that conservative writer would rightly have been dismissed as clueless (at best) or racist (at worst). Christgau, behind the veil of a presumably progressive outlook, was telling readers that while the raw, less sophisticated expressions of a Ronnie Van Zant were okay, Petty's more sophisticated expressions of those same feelings were not. The review rang similar to the rantings of folks who approved of blacks when they were minstrels but became defensive when African-Americans began expressing themselves in the language of the intellectual elite. It seems that *Southern Accents'* acerbic challenge to people from other parts of the country to reconsider their prejudices about the South was threatening to the rock intelligentsia.

In 1985, Petty talked with the *Los Angeles Times* about the people behind the songs on the album. "I was just thinking about the average young guy down there who is brought up in this tradition that tells you, 'This is the way it has always been and the way it should be.' I'm not just talking about jobs, but a whole way of living. That causes some real conflicts. In the song ["Rebel"], the guy is born with it all lined up against him, but for some reason he just can't get in line and play the way he's supposed to."

Petty identified with the feelings of his characters but not with their choices. "I never bought the idea of having your life laid out for you and I got out, but a lot of them never do," he said. "It's hard to understand why, but that tradition is so strong that they don't ever realize that two

hours in any direction gets you somewhere else. I could see the creases in the curtain at a real early age. One thing that helped me break away was music."

When I heard *Southern Accents*, I felt it was about time for me to leave the South, too, to bid farewell to the land I had such mixed feelings about. Within a little more than a year, I'd be living in New York, and the popular music world—from rock to country—would be primed for a new crop of southern artists to make their mark on music.

★ Chapter 9 ★

GUITAR TOWN

RICHARD YOUNG *can't go anywhere in Metcalfe County, Kentucky, without somebody wanting to talk to him.*

My dad and I were having lunch with the burly Kentucky Headhunters guitarist at Porter's Restaurant in the community of Sulphur Well when the waitress walked up to our table with a pitcher of sweet iced tea, giggled, and asked how Young was doing.

"I'm fine, baby, how are you?"

She giggled again. "Oh, I'm fine, too. Y'all want some more tea?"

Young looked up at her and winked. "Just set the whole pitcher down on the table," he said. "We'll be here for a while."

"Southern accent" is too subtle a description for the sound of Richard Young's voice. His warm, drawn-out, polysyllabic chatter just drips country. Kentucky country. Rural, small-village-in-the-middle-of-nowhere country. Green beans, mashed potatoes, country ham, and red-eye gravy country. That's what we were ordering that day in March 2002 when I started talking to Young about how weird it was that his ragtag band of longhaired, ugly-ass southern rockers managed to rise to the top of the country-music heap back in the early '90s.

"I tell you, man, to this day, I ain't figured that one out yet," he said. "It was unbelievable to us. It didn't make no sense, really."

He paused for a second to slice himself a slab of salty country ham. It was a long second. Young had been talking nonstop ever since my dad and I picked him up earlier that morning at his house in Wisdom, a little cross-

roads community just south of Sulphur Well and about forty-five minutes north of the Tennessee-Kentucky line.

The Young boys—Richard and his bald, mutton-chopped hillbilly-looking brother, Fred, the group's drummer—never left Wisdom for any length of time, not even back in the early '90s, when the Headhunters were the biggest band in country music. They put out Pickin' On Nashville in late 1989, and the album shot through the roof, becoming the fastest-selling debut ever by a country band. By the following year, the group had a string of hits: a revved-up version of Kentucky bluegrass king Bill Monroe's "Walk Softly on This Heart of Mine"; a novelty song called "Dumas Walker"; and Don Gibson's sweet, country-rockin' "Oh, Lonesome Me."

The Headhunters' gritty southern rock album wound up selling 2.4 million copies at a time when southern rock's shelf life had long expired. Even Alabama, the band that had brought a slick, Eagles-like pop-rock sound to country, didn't make music this rowdy. Now, it seemed, genuine southern rock was hip again—but this time as country. Ever since then, the dirty twang of southern-rock guitars has become as fundamental to country music as fiddles and pedal steel.

The Young boys hadn't done anything different from what they'd been doing since the early '70s, when they called themselves Itchy Brother and went down to Atlanta to see if Phil Walden would sign them to Capricorn Records. They were teenagers then, and Walden told them to skedaddle back up to Kentucky where they came from. A few years later, in 1977, Itchy Brother got a bite from Walden's former accountant, who planned to start up a Capricorn rival. Then Lynyrd Skynyrd's plane went down.

"It was over," Young remembered thinking. "I could just feel it. Nobody was going to sign a southern rock band after that."

Itchy Brother scratched its wounds and hightailed it back up to Metcalfe County, where the band continued to make music and play the club circuit. But by the early '80s, the members also had real jobs. Young was working down at Nashville's hit-making song factory Acuff-Rose, regularly traveling back and forth from Wisdom to Music City; brother Fred was part of the touring band for a flash-in-the-pan country singer named Sylvia.

Then Jason and the Scorchers hit town.

"I tell you this," said Young. "I think the Scorchers, the Georgia Satellites, Steve Earle, and Hank Williams Jr. opened the doors for us to make it when we did."

Those very different-sounding musical mavericks laid the groundwork for Nashville's return to an earthier country sound in the late '80s, a sound that called for musicians who didn't necessarily play by the rules. Whether Nashville liked it or not, country fans were ready for more than the steady diet of schlock they'd been fed since the Urban Cowboy days.

Young shook his head and let out a big Kentucky belly laugh.

"Who would have thought that more than ten years after we went down to Atlanta to try to make it as a southern rock band we'd come back up here and then make it down in Nashville as a country band?"

In the parking lot outside Porter's Restaurant, Young was showing my dad and me the old Beula Villa Hotel, a dilapidated structure across the road that was once the center of activity in Metcalfe County, when two girls walked up and asked him for an autograph.

"How y'all doin'?" Young said, and the girls giggled just like the waitress inside the restaurant had. "You tell your mama I said hello, hear?"

I asked if he knew the girls, wondering why they'd want his autograph if he did.

"Naw, I don't know 'em, per se," said Young. "But I'm sure I know their mama from somewhere. Everybody knows everybody in Metcalfe County."

In 1986, when Richard and Fred Young decided to put Itchy Brother back together again under the new name Kentucky Headhunters, Nashville had already begun to wake up from its doldrums. Jason and the Scorchers had been making a racket on the country-punk underground for five years and just released a second full-length album, *Still Standing*. The band's sound had become a little less punk and a little more southern rock & roll. In Georgia, land of the Allman Brothers and now R.E.M., a new southern rock band with a raw, punk edge, the Georgia Satellites, had managed to take its Stoneslike "Keep Your Hands to Yourself" to No. 2 on the pop chart. The only thing that kept it from No. 1 was Bon Jovi's slick pop-metal anthem "Livin' on a Prayer." All of this paved the way for a posse of edgy country acts to come out of the closet.

Steve Earle was one of those acts.

Born in Virginia but raised in Schertz, Texas, the thirty-one-year-old Earle arrived on the Nashville scene in the mid-'80s and put out an ex-

traordinary debut album, *Guitar Town*, that combined the angry snarl of punk with the rowdiness of outlaw country and the working-class poetic sense of Bruce Springsteen. But at its core, *Guitar Town* was unmistakably country. Earle was a hard drinker and a troublemaker, and his record company didn't know exactly what to do with him; MCA was so confused about this new country singer that the company had him playing with Dwight Yoakam on some dates and the Replacements on others.

"I am a country act and I am not ashamed of it. That's why I signed with the Nashville division of MCA," Earle told the *Los Angeles Times* shortly after *Guitar Town* came out. He also called Springsteen a country singer, saying the New Jersey singer's album *Nebraska* was "a hell of a hillbilly record" and suggesting "country radio stations ought to be playing records like that. It doesn't matter that they weren't recorded in Nashville."

Earle had an attitude. Some folks didn't like that about him. Others did. Truck drivers, pool players, punk rockers, and Springsteen fans all saw something in Steve Earle that had been missing in music for a long time. The album eventually reached No. 1 on the country charts and even edged its way onto the pop charts at No. 129. The title track became a pool-hall anthem with its singalong visions of wanderlust: "Nothin' ever happened 'round my hometown, and I ain't the kind to just hang around. . . . Everybody told me you can't get far on thirty-seven dollars and a Jap guitar." Blue-collar workers gravitated to "Good Ol' Boy (Gettin' Tough)," whose lyrics pretty much summed up the collective feeling of economic insecurity among working people in the Reagan years: "I got a job and it ain't nearly enough, a twenty-thousand-dollar pickup truck." Earle's early songs didn't touch on issues of race or intolerance, nor did he flaunt his southernness. He simply wrote and sang about the people he knew.

By 1986, white southern singers seemed confident enough to begin examining the complexities of their lives in relation to southern culture at large rather than feel bound by imported perceptions of the South. And they were beginning to export their own perspectives to other parts of the country. In Los Angeles, Dwight Yoakam was earning respect for his traditional country sound in punk clubs. Like the Young boys of the Headhunters, Yoakam was born in Kentucky, but he grew up four hours east of Metcalfe County in the coal-mining town of Pikeville, near West

Virginia. His relatives on his father's side had been miners, and Yoakam paid homage to them in a gorgeous old-time Appalachian ballad, "Miner's Prayer," from his 1986 debut *Guitars, Cadillacs, Etc. Etc.* The protagonist of the song is a proud, poor miner who prays to his savior: "I have no shame, I feel no sorrow, if on this earth not much I own. / I have the love of my sweet children, an old plow mule, a shovel and a hoe." Yoakam sings the words in a high-lonesome tenor behind crisp acoustic guitar and weeping dobro.

After his mother and father moved from Pike County, Kentucky, to Columbus, Ohio, Yoakam enrolled at Ohio State University to study philosophy. He didn't stay long, though; more interested in playing music, he eventually headed to Nashville. It was the early '80s, around the time Jason Ringenberg arrived in town, and ironically, the music executives in Nashville considered Yoakam's songs "too country." Rather than stick around and cause trouble as Ringenberg and Earle had done, Yoakam kept moving, eventually making his way to California, where Buck Owens had pioneered the late-'50s sound of honky-tonk in the Okie-transplant town of Bakersfield. Yoakam landed in nearby Los Angeles at a time when some West Coast bands playing the punk clubs, such as X, Los Lobos, Lone Justice, and the Blasters, had begun flirting with all kinds of rootsy American music styles.

"All those bands opened the door to us," Yoakam told the *Los Angeles Times* in 1986, after his first album came out. "I wanted to test the sincerity of the [punk] movement and play pure hillbilly music in front of that audience and they proved open to it."

Like the Allman Brothers, Tom Petty, and many other southern artists before him, Yoakam had to leave the South to find acceptance for his deeply southern sound. After his buzz in L.A. began reaching beyond the punk crowd, Music City decided Yoakam's music was no longer "too country." The Nashville division of Warner Bros. Records put out *Guitars, Cadillacs, Etc. Etc.*, and it went to No. 1 on *Billboard*'s country chart.

In 1986, the gritty new traditionalist movement led by Yoakam, Earle, and North Carolina native Randy Travis was making enough noise in Nashville that the country music industry could no longer ignore artists it deemed "too country." That year, Jack Hurst of the *Chicago Tribune* wrote a fascinating article about this new wave of country music, credit-

ing its mainstream appeal to the fact that many of the artists were more educated than previous generations. By the '80s, rural-born musicians who wouldn't have thought of going to college a generation earlier were coming into the business with undergraduate and even graduate degrees. Hurst's piece, whose condescending headline "Getting Smarter" undermined his premise, correctly pointed out that these new voices of country music were articulating the concerns of rural Americans in terms that people from more metropolitan areas could finally understand. Artists such as Earle and Yoakam wrote songs that didn't seem so alien or threatening to listeners who had more urbane tastes. The artists had a little intellectual distance from their poor backgrounds; unlike their parents' generation, they could see poverty as a matter of circumstance, not moral failure. Critics from other parts of the United States couldn't so easily write them off as goofy, quaint, redneck, or bigoted.

Though Earle was not college educated — he dropped out of school in the eighth grade — Hurst cited the singer's self-education as key to his progressive song lyrics and worldly outlook. "Texan Steve Earle, a well-read high school dropout who spent considerable time in an American artists' haven in Mexico, writes explosively about modern life; he views it through the eyes of a youngster aching to get out of one-lane backwaters and into the bright lights of metropolitan experience." Yoakam, Hurst wrote, "wants country music to become again the gutsy, gritty, somewhat rebellious music of rural-rooted but urban-reared people like himself, who take pride in the hardship and squalor their forebears endured and were ashamed of." What Hurst seemed to be describing was the southern rock of the previous generation.

This new "smart country" fit well with the new face Ronald Reagan gave conservative politics, even though most of the key players in the new-country movement were the opposite of conservative. Like Springsteen, Earle sang of blue-collar issues that, by the mid-1980s, were often mistaken or interpreted as populist conservative concerns. Of course, they were really the same concerns of leftist folksinger Woody Guthrie during the Great Depression.

"This guy in Boston thinks I am the Archie Bunker of rock or something," Earle told the *L.A. Times* in 1986. "He said I represented the new conservatism in rock. . . . He didn't even see [*Guitar Town*] as a country album."

Earle's reference to the provocative early-'70s TV sitcom made sense.
Born in Virginia in 1955, Earle was raised in Texas during the transi-
tional period that ushered in the civil rights movement, Vietnam, *Rolling
Stone* magazine, and Watergate. Like my sister and me in North
Carolina, Earle and his siblings grew up with mixed messages from adults
regarding race.

"I heard people say nigger, including, once in a while, my father when
he was around his brothers. And his brothers certainly said it," Earle told
his biographer, Lauren St. John. "But he tore us out if we ever said it to
a black person. There really wasn't any hate attached to it. A lot of black
people worked for my granddad whenever he was having a good year with
the peaches. There were a lot of black people at his funeral."

Earle began making music as an adolescent and gravitated to artists as
diverse as Elvis, the Beatles, Dylan, jazz-folk singer Tim Buckley, the San
Francisco psychedelic blues and rock bands, and progressive country-folk
legend Johnny Cash. Earle was only fourteen when he started performing in coffeehouses around San Antonio. That's where he was introduced
to the politics of the progressive folksingers of the day. Earle's mind was
opening up in the Texas of the early '70s. When he looked around at his
culture, he didn't like what he saw.

At school, Earle became known as a rabble-rouser who experimented
with marijuana and LSD. The students, he told his biographer, were
divided into factions: the cowboys, the kickers, and the freaks. In Texas,
the cowboys were the equivalent to rednecks in the part of North
Carolina where I was raised; the kickers were the popular kids; the freaks
were much like the heads of my school—longhaired kids who smoked
dope, listened to rock & roll, and challenged the racial status quo.

"It was a real division and it got violent. Kids fought about it. . . ." said
Earle. "I got beat half to death just because I had long hair."

He developed a strong opposition to the military and to capital punishment, and his views on those issues would make their way into his later
music, in particular his work on Tim Robbins's anti–capital punishment
film of 1995, *Dead Man Walking*, and the songs Earle wrote following
America's invasion of Iraq in 2003. Even early on, despite some people's
conservative interpretation of the populism in his mid-'80s music, Earle's
political leanings were clear.

"Reagan being in office has given many people in this country a false

idea of what is happening," he told the *L.A. Times* in 1986, just after the release of *Guitar Town*. "Springsteen said it in this show on his last tour. He was making this pitch for food banks and he said, 'There are a lot of folks out there that the trickle-down [economic] philosophy hasn't trickled down to yet.' I identify with a lot of that [frustration]. I have got an eighth-grade education, so when I have needed to do some [regular] work when I couldn't make it just with my music, I have a hard time finding something. I never made more than $7,000 a year in my life until about three or four years ago."

Steve Earle was the real deal. He was about as blue-collar country and southern rock as a singer could be. And yet his songs reflected the tolerance and open-mindedness of a blue-collar South that many people in other parts of the country had never seen or taken the time to notice. What's more, Earle was hugely successful. Not only did his debut album reach the top of the country charts, but rock critics hailed him as the savior of country music. In later years, drugs and alcohol would take all that success away for a few years, but in 1986, Steve Earle turned Music City into Guitar Town.

"In the end, you either cheer people up or help them exorcise some problems they have, and people need a bit of both right now," he told the *Times*. "The mood of the country as a whole is that things aren't as they are being advertised. Lots of people are going hungry. Even more have had to downscale their expectations. They are confused. They remember everything they heard about this country in school and they wonder what happened to it."

Ronald Reagan had two years left in his second term when country music's new traditionalist movement began paving the way for a new wave of old-style southern rock. In 1987, exactly ten years after the plane crash that killed Ronnie Van Zant and two other members of Lynyrd Skynyrd, the survivors got back together with Van Zant's younger brother Johnny stepping into his late brother's shoes. The reunion was a surprising success. A live album, released the following year, was well received and the band toured stadiums across America and played to sellout crowds.

When Johnny Van Zant was offered the job fronting his dead brother's

old band, he was initially apprehensive. In 2003, the younger Van Zant told me he agreed to give it a shot only after his father and other family members encouraged it. "It was a good three years before I felt comfortable in the situation, because you know, I just felt like people were dissecting the hell out of me," he said. "I mean, it would have been the same for anybody else, but I'm his brother. After about three years, people just kept coming back and kept coming back, and they knew the story of Lynyrd Skynyrd, they knew I wasn't Ronnie Van Zant. . . ." He trailed off and laughed. "It's been sixteen years now and yeah, I guess I feel like a real member of the band. If I were to go in the next thirty seconds, I'd know I made the right choice. This was the right thing to do."

Two years later, in 1989, the Allman Brothers Band reunited with a young powerhouse guitarist from the mountains of North Carolina. Warren Haynes and his bass-playing buddy Allen Woody brought new energy and verve to the Allman Brothers, and when the band members hit the road again, they began making their best music since Duane Allman died in 1971.

As a teenager in the 1970s, Haynes, who is exactly my age, was a huge fan of the Allmans. He grew up in Asheville, three hours west of my hometown, where his father Edward worked for the A&P grocery store chain. When A&P closed its stores in the Southeast, Edward Haynes chose not to move with the chain to another part of the country; instead he stayed in the same Robindale Avenue home in north Asheville where Warren grew up. "He had the choice of leaving Asheville or starting over," the guitarist once told his hometown newspaper. "And he started over, working in a factory. I'm sure it was a tough struggle."

In 2003, I talked to Haynes backstage at Bonnaroo, the Woodstock-like music festival held in rural Tennessee an hour south of Nashville. He had played with the Allmans the previous day and was scheduled to perform later that night with the Athens, Georgia, band Widespread Panic. He also sat in with New Orleans legends the Funky Meters during the festival and told me he would have enjoyed jamming with the hip-hop band the Roots, too, if they hadn't been playing on another stage at the same time the Allmans were performing.

Like his late inspiration Duane Allman, Haynes had become one of the most sought-after guitar players in any genre of music. In 2000, Allen Woody, who also played with Haynes in an Allmans side project, Gov't

Mule, died of a heroin overdose. At first, Haynes was so devastated he thought about giving up music altogether. Then he started getting phone calls from musicians whose bands had suffered similar losses, such as Dave Grohl of Nirvana and members of the Grateful Dead and Blues Traveler. That's when the miracles started happening: within weeks, some of the best bass players in music, young and old, from all over the map, began lining up to play with Haynes—John Entwistle of the Who, Bernie Worrell and Bootsy Collins of Parliament-Funkadelic fame, George Porter Jr. of the Meters, Jack Bruce of Cream, Jack Casady of Jefferson Airplane and Hot Tuna, Flea of the Red Hot Chili Peppers, Jason Newsted of Metallica, Les Claypool of Primus. Like the Muscle Shoals swampers who backed Otis Redding and Aretha Franklin in the mid-'60s, Haynes had become a musician's musician. Important people wanted to play with the amiable, open-minded southern guitarist for whom musical boundaries simply don't exist. Part of the reason for this is that Haynes, as talented and famous as he is, puts the music before his celebrity.

"When the Allman Brothers are up there playing, it's like we're teenagers in a garage," said Haynes, relaxing in jeans and a T-shirt on a couch inside the Bonnaroo press trailer set up in a patch of trees behind the festival's main stage. "When we're performing, we're looking at each other and we're communicating and playing for each other and, okay, yeah, there's eighty thousand people out there, but if they weren't there, it wouldn't matter. We'd still be doing the same thing."

The beefy, longhaired Haynes looks like the stereotypical badass biker, but he's actually a very warm and friendly man, with a smooth, easy North Carolina drawl that contrasts with his deep, gruff, often menacing singing voice. In the song "World of Difference," from Gov't Mule's 1995 debut, Haynes's vocals are as dark and creepy as a rural dirt road at night. Over a slow and snaky bass line, jazzy, syncopated drums, and quavering teardrops of bluesy guitar, his lyrics strip away the layers of southern politics and go straight to the core of racial antagonism in the South. At one point, Haynes angrily croons, "Black shoot black, white take all / Color will be our downfall. . . . / I hate you 'cause you hated my father / You hate him, his fathers raped your daughters / Hate breeds fear, fear breeds sin / Survival is your only friend / When we die, we're all the same."

Having grown up in the South at the same time, Haynes and I have a lot in common. We both come from families of modest to better-than-

average economic means and were integrated into the school system with black kids during those first few years of desegregation. Both of us were drawn to gritty, blues-based rock & roll. I asked how he felt growing up during that monumental shift in our culture. He didn't exactly answer the question; instead, he compared the old days with the present: "You know, that was back in the time when flying the rebel flag didn't seem to offend people as much as it did later, because at that time there were a lot bigger issues that needed to be dealt with," he said. "Now those issues have been dealt with, and so when I see these little towns in the South today still wanting to fly the Stars and Bars, I just think, My God, people, join the real world."

Like me, Haynes gravitated to the music of the Allman Brothers Band as a sort of safe haven, a place to go for some kind of answer. "I remember being a real young teenager and just thinking, you know, this is just so cool, they'd get up onstage and make this amazing music that was steeped in black blues and jazz and all these art forms that came from black heritage . . . and country music, too. It was all very southern and very new."

Haynes echoed what I'd heard from Patricia Goddard in New Orleans, Richard Young in Kentucky, and Crystal Lunsford in North Carolina, what I'd read in articles about Steve Earle in Texas and Tom Petty in his self-imposed exile on the West Coast. Like so many other white kids from the South looking for some kind of guidance in the early '70s, Haynes identified with the Allmans not so much as rock stars but as regular people. "They just got up there onstage and played music, and they were themselves, just jeans and T-shirts and long hair and . . . I don't know, I could relate with that," he said. "They looked like somebody in the crowd."

When he picked up his first guitar at age twelve, Haynes wanted to play like Duane Allman or Eric Clapton. By the time he reached his mid-teens, he'd become known in clubs around Asheville as the little guitar prodigy who could play with any band in town. Woody Mitchell, a *Charlotte Observer* copy editor and longtime North Carolina guitarist who played in a string of regional bands, remembered the teenaged Haynes as the kid who always wanted to get up and play with the big boys. "He was amazing," remembered Mitchell, who today leads two Charlotte-area bands, a country-swing band and an improvisational outfit in the Grate-

ful Dead vein. "But Warren, he was just this kid, you know. Who would have thought he'd end up in the Allman Brothers? I ain't surprised, though."

Haynes was nineteen when he began playing with notorious country singer David Allan Coe in 1980. By the tail end of the southern rock era and dawn of punk, Coe's provocative, often violent performances had become trendy among bikers and curious hippies in clubs across the Southeast. Coe had landed in Nashville in the late '60s, after a lifetime of reform schools and prison terms. In 1974, he made a name for himself with a sexually charged country ballad called "Would You Lay with Me (in a Field of Stone)," which sixteen-year-old Tanya Tucker took to the top of the country charts. The erotic lyrics and Tucker's Lolita image sparked outcry in the country world. It also landed the teenaged Tucker on the cover of *Rolling Stone*. Three years later, country singer Johnny Paycheck scored a No. 1 hit with Coe's blue-collar anthem "Take This Job and Shove It."

By the late '70s, Coe had aligned himself with the outlaw country movement and even wrote a song called "Willie, Waylon and Me," in which he name-checked artists as diverse as the Byrds, Janis Joplin, and the title characters, Willie Nelson and Waylon Jennings. He dressed in biker gear for the cover of his 1977 album *Rides Again*, on which he was pictured atop a Harley-Davidson. One of Coe's most popular club songs was "If That Ain't Country, I'll Kiss Your Ass."

Meanwhile, Coe also released several underground, "adults only" albums featuring his over-the-top racist, homophobic, and sexist humor. Curiously, some of the songs were in a talking-blues style that foreshadowed the cadence and foul language of gangsta rap. Coe's Triple X albums contained songs with titles like "Nigger Fucker," "Pussy Whipped Again," and "Cum Stains on the Pillow." It's ironic that by the early 2000s, an aging Coe had befriended rap rocker Kid Rock and wound up performing onstage with African-American musicians and deejays.

In 1979, the ever contradictory Coe was looking to add a rock punch to his honky-tonk sound and he called up the teenaged Warren Haynes. Coe's bass player had told him about the hot young North Carolina guitarist. "I didn't know much about Coe at the time," Haynes recalled. "I'd heard a couple of his songs and I knew he had a pretty large following,

but I didn't listen to much straight country music. Being young and cocky, I told him, 'Look, I'm not really a country guitar player and I'm not really interested in *being* a country guitar player.' He said, 'Well, I'm not looking for a country guitar player, I'm looking for a blues-rock guitar player to add an edge to my band.' "

Haynes had no idea what he was getting himself into. In the late '70s, Asheville, North Carolina, was an oasis for southern hippies, and Haynes was a peace-and-love kind of guy. Although Coe had toned down some of his more overtly racist tendencies by 1979, his behavior was still wild enough to make Ronnie Van Zant blush.

"There was some weird, harsh stuff," Haynes remembered. "But it was worse before I got there. I mean, even though it was still pretty crazy when I was in the band, all the stories I heard from the other guys was like, 'Oh, man, you ain't seen nothing.' "

Haynes was particularly put off by the violence. "There was a lot of violence, a lot of fights breaking out," he said. "I mean, it's hard to . . . you know, I don't know that I really want to be the one to go too much into that, but I'll tell you this: it got really weird at times. I remember fights breaking out in clubs where the band got involved. Not me, but I can remember Coe jumping out into the audiences and getting into it with people—from the stage. You hear those stories and all, and I'm telling you, they're true."

Haynes found himself torn between wanting to make it as a musician and wanting to get away from the chaos. "I was so young and coming from such a different place," he said. "I felt really uncomfortable being there, but I wanted to stick it out from a career standpoint and not give up or take a step backwards. But there were many times when I'd tell myself, 'Man, I can't deal with this, I got to get out of here.' And then he'd come up and say, 'We're going to Europe this month' or 'We're going to make a record next month,' and I'd say, 'Okay, well, I'll hold on a little bit longer.' "

Haynes lasted three years with Coe before he'd had enough and decided to go to work as a studio singer and guitarist in Nashville. That wasn't a good fit either. "You have to realize how sterile the times were in Nashville in 1983," said Haynes. "There wasn't much adventurous music going on at that time. But I had become brainwashed to the point that I thought, Hey, maybe I'll just be a studio musician. Why not? The money was good."

For young studio musicians such as Haynes, part of the Music Row program included scheduling songwriting sessions with fellow musicians. It worked much like the Brill Building era in New York City, where during the early days of rock & roll, songwriters such as Carole King, Neil Diamond, Neil Sedaka, and Burt Bacharach churned out songs in a factory-assembly-line manner. The Nashville songwriters would write dozens of tunes, most of which went nowhere. But Haynes and a couple of his Music Row cohorts wrote one that went somewhere. They hit pay dirt when a rising young singer named Garth Brooks decided to record their tune "Two of a Kind, Workin' on a Full House." The song and its album, No Fences, went to No. 1 on the country charts; the album reached No. 3 on the pop charts. Brooks became a household name.

Haynes's heart wasn't in writing songs for Garth Brooks, though. Outside of Music Row's hit-making factory, he began to notice a new band making a lot of noise in the clubs around town. The band was Jason and the Scorchers, and Warren Haynes's name sounded enough like that of Scorchers' guitarist Warner Hodges that people got them confused. "We got booked on the same session once and when we met, we were like, 'Oh, you're him,' and 'Yeah, and you're him!' We became good friends after that."

Haynes had never been much of a punk fan. "When punk rock first came out in the late '70s, I was a little allergic to it just because it wasn't where my head was at back then. But by the '80s, I'd listened to it a lot more and I thought, Wow, there really is something going on here that's different. Eventually, I came to really love Elvis Costello and the Police and a lot of what the Clash were doing."

By 1986, when Steve Earle and Dwight Yoakam put out their first albums, Haynes realized the studio music he was doing wasn't satisfying his creative needs. "Things were starting to happen on the fringes. The South still hadn't become completely in vogue again in a real acceptable way, but it was starting to happen," he said. "I mean, there was a time when everybody kind of wondered if there was any hope at all for the kind of southern rock we were doing, because it had become passé."

Right around that time he got a call from former Allman Brothers guitarist Dickey Betts, who wanted to re-create the Allmans' twin-lead guitar sound in his new band. Soon the Allman Brothers themselves were talking about getting back together, and it only made sense that Haynes

would stand in Duane Allman's extra-large shoes. That he wound up getting the same kind of respect was not anticipated.

By 2003, Haynes had been a member of the Allman Brothers Band seven times longer than Duane Allman had when he died in 1971. Hard as it is to believe, Haynes's version of the Allmans has made a bigger impact on subsequent generations of young southerners than the Allman Brothers Band that charted this path so many years ago. Haynes would never admit to such a thing, though. "For me, to be a southerner growing up as an Allman Brothers fan and now . . . to have been such a big part of the band for the past fourteen years . . ." Haynes trailed off and smiled: "I mean, think about it, man, that's pretty cool."

Three years before Warren Haynes joined up with the reunited Allmans, the band's former manager, Phil Walden, hit rock bottom. He was so consumed by drugs and alcohol that he hardly felt human anymore. "I'd come in, turn the TV on, turn the sound down, turn on the stereo," he told *The Atlanta Journal-Constitution* in the early '90s. "I'd pull a bag of dope out, get a bottle of cognac, get a pile of cocaine, and stare at the screen 'til four or five in the morning, then stumble into bed and would literally pray that I would not wake up." Walden later described how horrifying life was when he was in the grips of cocaine-induced psychosis: ". . . I would walk into a room and I would hear people whisper about how I used to be somebody. I was an absolute lunatic. By noon, I would be so paranoid that I was crawling around the floor peeking out of blinds."

His lavish lifestyle, the Allmans' very public fall from grace, and southern rock's waning popularity had forced Walden to pull the plug on Capricorn Records in 1979. By the mid-'80s, he was separated from his wife, Peggy, and living in a small efficiency apartment in Nashville. When Capricorn's assets were sold at a liquidation auction, Walden was left with little to show from his glory years: the gold and platinum records were gone; his financial statements, tapes, and other Capricorn-related ephemera, gone. By 1986, Phil Walden, once one of the most powerful men in the music business, had lost it all.

"I had gone from owning two of everything to owing two of everything," he said.

As Walden sank deeper into despair, his son was dealing with his own demons in the college town of Athens, Georgia. Born in 1959, Philip Walden Jr. had grown up around the Capricorn offices in Macon with the members of the Allmans serving as older-brother figures. When he was in his early teens, the younger Walden attended the inauguration of Jimmy Carter along with his dad's circle of rock star friends. He'd go to Capricorn's annual picnics, where he rubbed shoulders with the members of his father's bands as well as guests like David Bowie, Mick Jagger, and Andy Warhol. Walden Jr. grew up inside a southern clique in which racism and intolerance were old-fashioned, nearly nonexistent, though he realized that outside of that clique, in the rest of Macon's culture, racism existed.

"My grandfather had been a pretty typical crusty old racist guy until my dad started with Otis Redding," said Walden Jr. "That changed him. So by the time I came around, things were different."

His earliest memories are of the constant visits from music legends Otis Redding, Sam and Dave, and Arthur Conley. "That was our social circle. Those guys were at our house all the time, they were just part of my childhood growing up," he said. "I remember Redding's kids coming over all the time, and in fact they're still good friends of mine."

Phil Jr. led something of a double life, though. His mother was the polar opposite of his dad. She had divorced Walden years earlier, remarried a real estate man, and lived a typically conservative southern lifestyle in Macon. Walden Jr. remembered the difference being jarring for him when he was a child: "I'd stay with my dad and he'd take me to this store in Atlanta called Comes the Sun that sold hippie clothes—embroidered shirts, turquoise jewelry, that kind of thing. There's a picture of me in my fifth-grade annual where I have on a pair of these real conservative slacks that my mom bought me with an embroidered shirt and turquoise bracelet that my dad got me. It's like this total contradiction that pretty much summed up how I was raised."

At fourteen, he moved in with his father full time. During his later teens, Walden Jr. discovered LSD and would get together with older friends in Macon, trip on acid, and listen to the Grateful Dead. "As I got older, I started to understand that my family was not part of the normal country-club set in Macon," he said. "Not that I was all that different from any other kid who doesn't feel like he fits in." Still, in Macon,

Georgia, where deviation from the norm was not exactly valued highly, Phil Walden Jr.'s father was about as different as a man could be. Having worked with African-American musicians in the late '50s and early '60s, and having brought longhaired hippies to town in the late '60s and early '70s, Phil Walden had cultivated a bad reputation in Macon. When the world crashed down on him, there was no safety net. For Phil Jr., his dad's crash was difficult.

"My father had brought a high profile to the difference between the cultures in Macon, and a lot of people didn't like him. Most people were very happy to see him fail," said Phil Jr. "So when things went down the tubes, it was embarrassing."

By the early '80s, when his father was in Nashville contemplating suicide, Walden Jr. tried college but kept getting derailed by his own drug and alcohol problems. One night during a particularly crazed binge, he wound up at a house party in Athens where a band was playing cover versions of Grateful Dead songs in the backyard. At the time, Athens was in its heyday as the mecca for postpunk southern bands in the vein of the B-52's, Pylon, and R.E.M. The blues-based, acid-fueled improvisational music of a retro-hippie band seemed about as unhip and out of touch as could be, but Walden Jr. saw something special in the music of Widespread Panic.

"There was kind of a dividing line in Athens between the hippie crowd and the hipper R.E.M. crowd," said Walden Jr. "And I definitely wasn't very hip. It's not that I didn't buy into punk rock at that time, I was just so out of it that I wasn't paying attention. I missed the whole Athens music scene."

Well, kind of. Walden loved music. After all, he'd grown up around some of the greatest artists of the rock era. He may have missed the punk scene, but the scene he became involved with would begin to make a quiet and unlikely splash in the coming year and would be huge by the early 2000s. It isn't all that surprising that the younger Walden would gravitate to drugs and alcohol—or to the trippy music of a band that followed in the improvisational footsteps of the Grateful Dead and the Allmans rather than bands inspired by the Ramones and Patti Smith. "I never went to see R.E.M. or Pylon in Athens. I wish I had," said Walden. "I mean, I'd end up at parties late at night with that crowd, but it wasn't really my deal. I was more inclined to the stuff you go see when you do a lot of acid."

The night he stumbled into that party where Widespread Panic was playing in the backyard, Walden was drunk and high on acid. "Talk about being obnoxious—I could be really obnoxious back then," he said. "That night I was bragging about who I was, saying, 'Yeah, man, we got this studio down in Macon.' I was telling them all this stuff and they were like, 'Whatever.' Nothing happened right away." Shortly afterward, Walden went into rehab. When he got out, he returned home to Macon temporarily to recuperate. When he returned to Athens, he became Widespread Panic's manager.

"There was this guy, Tinsley Ellis, who was the big-shot blues guitarist in Athens back then, and he would sometimes come in and jam with Panic," Walden remembered. "They'd do songs like 'Key to the Highway' and it was just amazing. People loved it. So Tinsley gave me his list of clubs where he played around the Southeast and that's what we used to get Panic out of Athens and on the road."

When I met Phil Walden Jr. in 2002 he was no longer the arrogant kid who flaunted his connection to Capricorn Records. He didn't need to be. In the previous decade, he and his illustrious dad had both cleaned up and were back in business. I had come to his office at Velocette Records, an independent label he started with his father and sister Amantha. The company occupied three floors of a renovated 1916 building in the Fairlie-Poplar district of downtown Atlanta. The Waldens owned the whole building.

On the walls behind Walden Jr.'s desk were classic, Capricorn-era photos of the Allman Brothers that shared the space with quirky folk paintings and album art by hipper, postpunk bands such as Beulah and the Glands, both signed to Velocette. In the years since he managed Widespread Panic, Walden Jr. had come to appreciate R.E.M.-inspired indie rock. He looked up from his desk and laughed. "You know, once I actually listened to R.E.M., I thought they were phenomenal," he said.

As he talked with me, I saw his father in his eyes, good looks, and stylish but casual clothes. But that's about as far as the similarities went. Walden Jr.'s voice is smooth and measured. When he spoke of his musical connections, he came off as humble, not the slick, used-car-dealer personas of his father and uncle. If Phil Walden Sr. and his brother Alan are the kind of southern characters who will spin a tale as far out as it will go, Phil Walden Jr. is the exact opposite. Like many sons and daughters

of tall-tale-telling '60s-era baby boomers, Walden Jr. avoids romanticizing his lifestyle and past experiences. When I spoke appreciatively of all the music his family has funneled out to the world over the past forty years, he just looked down at his desk bashfully, as if he were slightly embarrassed. Phil Walden Jr. is, in fact, more modest than he should be.

"It wasn't because of my great skill as a manager that Widespread Panic got big," he said. "I'm telling you, I had no skill in that department. My dad and I have never had much skill in that department. I was just somebody who liked their music and took time with them during that one year and helped out as best I could, which wasn't much. So I'd like to go on the record as taking zero credit for any success they've had since then. They made it strictly because they're a great band."

After his brief stint as Widespread Panic's manager, he enrolled in law school at Mercer University in Macon. While he studied, Panic toured the Southeast and developed a growing fan base that wasn't being served by the alternative rock, hip-hop, and slick pop music on MTV, or the neotraditional country music coming out of Nashville. In 1988, Panic quietly released its first album, *Space Wrangler*, on the independent label Landslide Records. Neither the *Billboard* charts nor hip rock critics registered the band's popularity, but Panic's fans were already well familiar with jams like the loose, aw-shucks "Porch Song" and the spacey title track. Walden didn't return to the music business for a couple more years, but when he came back, he would wind up playing a much bigger role in Panic's career.

When Widespread Panic released its first album, I had already left my job as a newspaper reporter for *The Daily Times-News* in Burlington, North Carolina, and moved to New York City. I had no clue that a southern jam band was making waves in the clubs back home. In New York I got a job as an assistant editor at the science magazine *Discover* and wrote freelance music stories on the side.

Ronald Reagan was still in office when I arrived in Manhattan in 1987; within a year, Vice President George Bush would be running a close campaign for president against Democrat Michael Dukakis. The Democrats made a tactical error in running the Massachusetts governor in the waning days of the Reagan administration. Bush may not have had

much charisma, but at least he had Reagan stumping for him; Dukakis completely lacked charisma. What's more, the American heartland had taken such a conservative turn in the previous eight years that running a liberal candidate from the Northeast with an ethnic last name and look was political suicide. The Democratic primaries had been exciting, though, particularly in the South. Dukakis ran against a string of candidates including several promising southerners: Arkansas governor Bill Clinton, Tennessee senator Al Gore, and the fiery Reverend Jesse Jackson, the African-American minister and civil rights activist who also had run in 1984. Jackson lived in Chicago but had South Carolina roots and touted his connection to the Reverend Martin Luther King Jr.

The opposite of Dukakis in demeanor, Jackson came close to winning the nomination, compiling more delegates than almost any losing candidate in the history of the Democratic primaries. He won several states and trailed Dukakis right up to the finish line. Ultimately, though, Americans wanted something that seemed familiar, and with George Bush, we got it. We also got Lee Atwater, the Republican strategist who, predictably by 1988, got rock & roll into the inaugural festivities. Atwater was one of those yuppie music fans whose idea of the blues seemed to come from taking in a Nighthawks gig at a college blues bar catering to whites. At the Bush inaugural, he strapped a guitar onto the incoming president and had him pretend to play it. Like the blackface minstrels of less enlightened times, Bush protruded his lips and mimicked a clichéd image of an African-American bluesman. As vice president and now the incoming commander in chief, Bush proved to be at least as much of a caricature as Richard Nixon.

Still, those were heady years in America. With the fall of the Soviet Union, Republicans had no great Communist ogre hiding in the shadows. As Republicans searched for the next great enemy, average Americans were able to focus on issues at home: racism, drugs, and violence in the inner cities, AIDS, government funding of controversial art. By 1989, the music I once thought was just a fad, hip-hop, was in its golden age and the rappers of New York City were fast becoming more important to popular culture than any old rock & roll band.

In my first two years in the city, I was a confused and lonely young reporter trying to figure out how to achieve my dream of writing about music. I was in my late twenties, feeling like a naïve country boy and

struggling to acclimate to my new surroundings. Glad to be out of the cesspool of small-town southern racism, I was drawn to the postpunk and hip-hop scenes of Manhattan. I wrote stories about rising alternative rockers and rappers for a Los Angeles–based magazine called *Option*. I met a recording engineer named Bob Coulter, who worked with hip-hop groups and took me into Manhattan studios such as Greene Street Recording and Chung King House of Metal, where I met and talked with some of the most important hip-hop artists of the era, including Chuck D of Public Enemy and Daddy-O of Stetsasonic. I also sat in on or breezed through a few sessions for some of hip-hop's most groundbreaking albums: Stetsasonic's *In Full Gear*, Public Enemy's *It Takes a Nation of Millions to Hold Us Back*, Queen Latifah's *All Hail the Queen*, De La Soul's *3 Feet High and Rising*.

The years between 1987 and 1990 were among the more exciting of my life. Rap was the most explosive and meaningful music I'd heard since my childhood. During that time, I interviewed hip-hop pioneers Eric B. of Eric B. and Rakim; Parrish Smith of EPMD; Hank Shocklee of Public Enemy's Bomb Squad production team; Prince Paul, the whiz-kid producer of *3 Feet High and Rising*. But as music got more exciting and important in the late '80s, my life began to go down the tubes. Drugs and alcohol were keeping me from advancing as quickly as I wanted to. One night, in 1989, I was supposed to meet up with rapper L.L. Cool J at the star-studded record release party for De La Soul in New York's East Village. I was so drunk by the time the rapper arrived, I couldn't communicate with him. He smiled, patted me on the back, and told me to call him when I sobered up.

In November of that year, I found a support group for my addiction and my life changed dramatically. I began writing cover stories for *Option* on artists ranging from childhood heroes Lou Reed and John Cale to former Smiths singer Morrissey and rising alternative-rock band the Pixies. Life was good. I had put my emotional and psychological issues about my southern heritage—southern rock, the blues, country music, racism—on the back burner for a while. I was done worrying about where I came from; it wasn't worth the heartache. By then, America and its music was changing so fast that I considered quaint issues of southern pride and the roots of American music irrelevant. Communism had collapsed, the Cold War was over, the Berlin Wall had

been toppled—I even had a piece of it sitting on the computer where I wrote my articles for *Option*. I barely even noticed when a southern rock album with the smart-ass title *Pickin' On Nashville* shot to No. 1 on the country charts.

On the morning of March 14, 2002, my father and I left Nashville at about nine in the morning and drove the back roads up to Wisdom, Kentucky. We took Route 31 through Sumner County, Tennessee, passing Hendersonville, where Johnny Cash and his wife, June Carter, lived, then Gallatin, Desha, Bethpage, and Westmoreland. By the time we got to the Kentucky border, the small towns had all but disappeared and there was only rolling pastureland, corn and tobacco fields that reminded me of the North Carolina of my youth.

As I scanned the sprawling farmland—land that looked a lot like that of my own dairy-farming relatives—I began to understand why rural southerners feel such a strong bond with each other and such a powerful sense of possessiveness. The same families have worked these farms for generations. Not that it's any justification for the kind of provincial attitudes that foster racial intolerance and xenophobia; after all, if I were black and looking out on to the same land, my impressions would be quite different. But for me, on that spring morning, driving past the dairy farms of northern Tennessee and southern Kentucky, a window of empathy opened up in my heart and mind that I'd never felt in such a conscious way.

When Dad and I reached Route 68 headed into Wisdom, we began to look for Richard Young's house. As we approached it, the Kentucky Headhunter was sitting in a chair under a tree next to his back porch. He's an unmistakable presence: a big man with long ringlets of reddish hair, big, thick glasses, and a permanent grin plastered on his face. He was wearing a denim jacket over a white T-shirt, faded blue jeans, and sneakers. When he spotted our white Ford Explorer cruising slowly up the country road, Young began vigorously waving his arms to make sure we didn't pass the driveway.

There's not a warmer, friendlier, or more giving man in the world than Richard Young. If you spend any time with him at all, he makes you feel like he's known you all your life. He talks about the characters from his childhood as though you're as familiar with them as he is. There's old

Jakey, the black man who worked on the Young's farm and practically raised Richard and his brother, Fred; Grandma Effie, immortalized in "Shotgun Effie," a song by the Young boys' early band Itchy Brother; Uncle Fred, the farmer of the family, who grew tobacco, corn, wheat, sweet potatoes, and "pretty much anything else good to eat," according to Richard. He said his Uncle Fred would "roll over in his grave if he saw what we done to this land." It was more like what the Youngs had *not* done to the land. In the years since Richard and Fred became musicians, the amount of farming done on the family's enormous property had been significantly reduced.

After Young showed us through the family home that he and his wife had restored back to its antebellum splendor, he hopped into the truck with Dad and me and took us on a tour of Metcalfe County. We went down a winding dirt road and through the woods where Richard and Fred like to hunt, past all the old houses on the family's farmland, and on over to the Headhunters' practice shack in the middle of a cow pasture. Young rattled on about the crazy characters of Metcalfe County, such as Dewey Cooper, the fellow who puts up all the scary JESUS IS COMING signs on the sides of the roads.

"Look yonder," Young drawled as we passed one of Cooper's warnings. "He makes it sound like Godzilla's coming or something." Young slapped his knee and exploded in laughter that infected my dad and me, too. "Those signs like to have scared the hell out of me when I was a little boy." He got serious again: "You know, personally, I think it's a damn great thing if Jesus is coming. Why you wanna warn me about it? I thought it was supposed to be good."

The Young boys weren't raised in an overly religious environment. They went to church on Sundays, but not on Wednesdays and Saturdays, like some other families in small southern communities do. "We may not have been real religious, but we was real spiritual. And there's a difference," said Young. "We was close to God and very close to the people of this community, and that's more important to me than going to church all the time."

To this day, he said, the people of Wisdom call on the Youngs if they need something. "My family has a history of carrying a lot of the burden for the folks of this community, and maybe if we hadn't focused on that so much, our farms would look better than they do. But I don't feel bad

about it, because everybody's happy. Maybe the fields are all grown up now, but I don't think we were put here to be great farmers like Uncle Fred. I think we was put here to be good people. My dad's a great humanitarian. He's brought a lot to this community and my grandmother did, too."

When Richard was a little boy, he liked to go visit the Barracks family, descendants of former slaves who stayed on the Young's farm after the Civil War ended. "I just loved to go over there," said Young. "I remember how they talked and everything, it was so different from the way white families talked. They had these great old expressions. I remember the Barracks boys—Rob and Walter and Tom—they'd have all these little discussions about things, and I knew that they was talking about some girls they'd been out with that weekend. They'd talk about stackin' bricks with Essie Mae and I knew what they meant, even though I was just a little boy."

The best things about his visits with the Barracks family, said Young, was the peach pie and the music. "They'd be singing and playing these old spirituals and old blues songs and I was so intrigued with that. I remember the first race records I ever heard them play. I don't remember exactly who it was, it might have been Little Walter or B. B. King or somebody like that, I just don't know. But whatever it was, it was a lot more fun and interesting than what I was listening to."

Young heard a totally different style of music when he would visit another family who lived on the farm. The Fields boys were white and worked in the barn milking cows. "I liked to go in the milk barn with them 'cause they had cigarettes and I could smoke with them," Young remembered. "This was in the early '60s and they'd turn the radio on and it'd be country music. They'd roll me a cigarette and I'd be hearing country music. Then I'd go in the house and Daddy, he'd be listening to Lawrence Welk or Tommy Dorsey. It's a wonder I didn't go crazy with all them different kinds of music rolling around in my brain."

By the middle '60s, Richard's uncle Fred got the first color TV in Metcalfe County. When the Beatles performed on *Ed Sullivan* for the second time in 1964, the Youngs all went over to Fred's house to watch the new British pop stars.

"The Beatles had done been on once, but I'd missed 'em and I wanted to see 'em this time," said Young. "Even way out here in the country,

everybody was tuning in to *Ed Sullivan* that night to see these guys. It was like a phenomenon—like they was gonna bring Jesus or Godzilla out. Everybody had to be watching TV that night."

When the Beatles came on, Young said, it was like he was looking into a crystal ball. Already a big fan of Elvis Presley and Jerry Lee Lewis, Young felt a sense of dread for American rock & roll. "I just remember, the minute the Beatles hit the stage, I said, 'Well, this is it for Elvis.' I was actually afraid for his career. I knew these guys were it and that Elvis was pretty much over. I was like, 'Look at them girls screamin'. They were out of their minds. I said to myself, 'I gotta get into this—right now.' So I did."

He didn't immediately see that the Beatles were blending their English sensibilities with the sounds of the American South. "When the Beatles first came out, nobody was thinking about anything but the moment. But later, it came out that George liked Carl Perkins, Paul liked Little Richard, John listened to Chuck Berry and Johnny Johnson, and Ringo was the country guy who liked Buck Owens and Johnny Russell. Then it all made sense to me, and I started a band."

By the early '70s, the Young boys were playing in local bands and had gotten pretty good at it, absorbing all the new sounds filtering into rural Kentucky from England and the West Coast. "After we heard Jimi Hendrix and Eric Clapton, it was like somebody poured gasoline on the floor and lit it. All of a sudden we were overwhelmed—Hendrix and Cream and all that stuff. Hell, I was still trying to figure out George Harrison listening to Carl Perkins, but this new stuff was beyond the pale—these guys were playing guitar like they was the Devil or some-thing! Hendrix, man, he was just unbelievable."

Then came the Allman Brothers Band. "The first time I heard Duane Allman, it was a similar reaction, but Duane was different, he was one of us," said Young. "Duane and Gregg and those boys, they may have been a little older than we were, but we felt the connection."

By 1973, the Young boys had changed the name of their garage band from the Truce to Itchy Brother, a name they got from a TV cartoon called *King Leonardo and His Short Subjects*. Itchy Brother recorded "Shotgun Effie" and "Rock 'N' Roller," and released them together as a single on the regional record label King Fargo.

"We had a few other local bands from around here that did okay," Young remembered. "There was the Rugbys, they was probably the

biggest. It wasn't like they exploded or anything, but their song 'You, I' became the No. 1 song on the radio here."

Down a dirt road halfway between Young's restored country home and his parents' older, southern-style mansion, amid sprawling fields separated by small patches of woods, sat an old two-story farmhouse with a front porch supported by four columns. The white paint on the columns was peeling badly and some of the windows had plastic over them instead of glass panes. Two concrete steps led up to the porch, where a warped wooden chair sat alongside one of those steel-framed outdoor couches with removable pads. The pads were gone.

Above the door of the farmhouse was a green neon road sign with big bold white letters: KY HEADHUNTERS. The Young boys' bands have been rehearsing in this shack since the late '60s, and some of the ephemera on the walls of the main practice space (once a living room) prove it: album covers of the Beatles, the Rolling Stones, Cream, the Bluesbreakers, Joe Cocker, and Led Zeppelin; a picture of Robert Plant ripped out of a magazine, a poster of Lou Reed from his *Rock 'n' Roll Animal* days; drawings of John Lennon and Eric Clapton; photos of bluesmen Albert Collins and Sonny Boy Williamson, and, of course, homemade posters of old Itchy Brother shows and professional shots of the Kentucky Headhunters. It was a rock dude's paradise, and my father laughed as his eyes scanned the room.

"This looks just like your old practice space," he said.

"Yeah," I replied, "only I never made a platinum-selling record."

Young smiled and looked around at all the hero worship on his walls. "Obviously, we didn't either for a long, long time," he said.

The age difference between the Youngs and the Allmans may not be much, but in the early '70s it was enough to keep Itchy Brother from being professional contemporaries of the Allman Brothers Band or Lynyrd Skynyrd. "You know, when you're in your forties like we are, five or ten years doesn't sound like a whole lot," said Young. "But when you're a kid, the difference between being in the sixth grade and being a senior in high school—that's the widest age difference in our society. It might as well be thirty years. So we were just too young. Even the Lynyrd Skynyrd guys were four or five years older than we were."

The age difference, said Young, was significant in terms of the timing for Itchy Brother: "What it meant was that we missed the first comin' of southern rock. Even though we was good players and everything, we missed it. We were just too young."

As we talked, Young's brother, Fred, who had been out on a tractor plowing the field behind the house when we arrived, joined us in an office area next to the main rehearsal room. Fred wore jeans and a flannel shirt, and his graying muttonchops reached halfway down his chest. A green baseball cap covered his hairless head, and he sported round John Lennon–style wire-rimmed glasses.

The conversation turned to how the Young brothers saw the Allman Brothers Band in relation to Lynyrd Skynyrd in the early '70s. Back then, the difference between the two pioneering southern rock bands was a much more divisive topic than it was two decades later, though it remained an issue for some hard-core fans.

Richard explained: "The thing about the Allman Brothers is that the word *brother* meant something. They had a black dude in that band, and you knew that they all had to wash in the same water spigot. Well, that was a big deal back then. It meant something. It stood for something. We had a black guy in our first band, too, so we respected what they stood for."

Fred, whose slow, nasal southern drawl makes his brother's heavy accent seem nearly nonexistent by comparison, cut in: "The Awl-muns," he said, "had a little polish to 'em."

Richard continued, giving up any attempt to dance around the real issue he had with Ronnie Van Zant, Gary Rossington, and the other members of Lynyrd Skynyrd.

"Gary and them may whip my ass the next time they see me," he said, "but I tell you what it is: they got a redneck streak in 'em and they always did. And I don't think the Allman Brothers had that. I mean, Dickey [Betts] is a wild man, he likes to carry on and stuff, but he's not like those guys in Skynyrd."

The only way to truly blend black and white musical traditions is to have had an honest relationship with African-American families, according to the Young brothers. And the only way to have an honest relationship with an African-American family, they explained, is to spend a lot of time with them. There were subtle things that black folks would do, said

Fred, that you had to see and experience to really have context for how those things are manifested in the music.

Fred calls it the "umph" factor.

"If you didn't grow up around some really old-school black folk," he said, "ain't no way you could really understand or feel some of the things in the music the way we did. They'll go, 'umph'—like punctuation—after a line of lyrics. And when I hear that in a James Brown song or an Aretha Franklin song, I see old Jakey sittin' out there on the tractor and somebody walking by and he'll go, 'umph.' You have to have seen that kind of thing and really understood it in its context to understand it in the music. The Allman Brothers understood that. I don't think Skynyrd did or wanted to. And the English bands—well, they couldn't have understood it."

What Lynyrd Skynyrd, the Allmans, and the Young brothers had in common was an understanding of the ways of rural white people. But by the early 1980s, when Itchy Brother had already tried and failed to get signed as a southern rock band, the subtleties in the behavior of blue-collar southerners—black or white—had become obsolete. "You know, it's ironic but we never did attract people who understood that kind of stuff and appreciated it until after we moved into the country thing," said Fred. "Because by that time, R.E.M. and all those college bands were all the rage in rock. And their fans didn't care nothin' about that kind of thing."

By the late '80s, the Kentucky Headhunters had recorded a handful of songs, and some of Richard Young's friends in the music publishing business were playing the tapes to a few Nashville bigwigs. The music generated enough interest that the Headhunters eventually played an industry showcase in Nashville. The Youngs didn't get their hopes up. After all, they had long hair, played loud, rowdy, obsolete southern rock, and didn't look anything like the clean-cut country stars of the post–Urban Cowboy years. And yet, PolyGram executive Harold Shedd hung around until the Headhunters were done playing their show. He saw something bankable in this band of Kentucky hillbillies. The group signed a deal with PolyGram's Mercury label. Fred Young figures he knows what happened: country music had been trying to attract the yuppie set and there was nothing out there anymore for real working-class fans.

"We were playing music that by the '80s was attracting people who have a hard time getting by," said Fred. "Them was our biggest fans. Them's our biggest fans still, and the thing is, they just don't have too much money."

Said Richard: "I remember our manager, a nice Jewish boy from New York, once saying to us, 'I don't understand why we're selling so many T-shirts at the first of the month.' " The Young boys just howled. "I said, 'Let me explain something to you 'bout poor white trash: you get your paycheck at the first of the month.' "

Fred cut in: "It's like this, you ain't gonna walk in a place where we play and see a bunch of hip cats who go see R.E.M. and sit around and wanna be cool and analyze music and all that. We call that kind of music 'smarty pants music,' and the groups who play it, we call 'em 'light-pole poster bands.' That's because, back in the punk-rock days, you'd see their posters all over the light poles."

In 1990, the year after *Pickin' On Nashville* came out, the Headhunters' lead singer, Doug Phelps, told *The Orlando Sentinel* that the band's music fit the country format because that's the music that some southern rock fans gravitated to after new wave and punk left them behind. "Country is the closest thing to southern rock. They [the Allman Brothers, Lynyrd Skynyrd, et al.] were country boys, too. All of a sudden, a group like the Kentucky Headhunters comes along and reminds them, hey, that's what they used to listen to.

"We've always played what we play—it's just that country accepted us first," Phelps added. "We're very weird in country music, and I think we'd be just as weird in the rock field right now. Roots-oriented rock is kind of in a lull right now, and I think we could fit in there, too."

Actually, with Steve Earle and Dwight Yoakam shaking things up and the Allmans and Skynyrd back together again, the Headhunters' blend of country and rock in 1990 was well timed to attract fans of both blue-collar southern rock and the rootsy punk of all those "smarty pants" bands.

By 1990, R.E.M. had reached the *Billboard* Top 10 with *Green*, the band's sixth full-length album and first for Warner Bros. Records. *Rolling Stone* had dubbed the Georgia group "the best band in America." That

year, I found myself interviewing Michael Stipe yet again, at a small table in a Mexican restaurant in Manhattan's Chelsea neighborhood. When he heard I had moved to New York City, Stipe said it surprised him. I guess he had me pegged as a young, naïve, small-town lifer. I told him I'd become worn out by the South and didn't feel comfortable living there anymore. By 1990, though, I was missing a lot of the simple things about my home and I didn't particularly like the stereotypes I'd heard from many northerners about the ways of southerners. He said he understood.

"I think when R.E.M. first came out, people just didn't think worthwhile music or art could come out of somewhere that isn't a major metropolitan area," he said. "That's an incredibly stupid notion."

Though Stipe had acknowledged country music's influence on his vocal style, he had been reluctant in past interviews to really open up and talk about what the South meant to him personally. After a morning of hanging out on my rooftop in Brooklyn, noshing on bagels, and later looking at some films that his company C-00 Film Corp. had produced, Stipe became more comfortable discussing the region where he grew up.

"I have pride in where I live," he said, nursing a smoothie and picking at a plate of nachos. "I feel that the South, and particularly Georgia"—he paused and corrected himself—"no, not particularly Georgia: the entire Southeast has affected me deeply. It comes out in a number of ways, some very subtle, some more obvious. I think that most of it is in the pacing." He smiled. "*You* know what I'm talking about.

"I hate to use the word honesty, but I can't think of a better one," he continued. "It's an honesty that's just so real that it leaps out when you line people up and look at what they're doing—it's just really obvious who's honest and who falls short."

Many years later, when I telephoned Phil Walden for my *New York Times* article on the late-'90s return of southern rock in the music of bands such as Widespread Panic, the Black Crowes, Screamin' Cheetah Wheelies, Gov't Mule, and Hootie and the Blowfish, he used the word *honest*, too.

"There is something satisfying about the way this new music from the South connects with the old music from the South," said Walden in a comforting southern drawl that seemed to wrap itself around me like a blanket across the miles between his office in Atlanta and mine in New York City. At the time I was sitting in my office at MTV, high above mid-

town Manhattan. That morning I'd met with other executives at the network about possible names for a new daily show we were broadcasting from our new studio overlooking busy Times Square. We eventually decided on *Total Request Live*. The show wasn't about music so much as it was about style and mindless chatter. I wasn't feeling too honest.

I had drifted off, preoccupied with this *TRL* thing when Walden's homey drawl interrupted my anxiety. Still talking about the music of those new southern bands, he said to me, "It's a very honest, very powerful connection."

★ Chapter 10 ★

AGAIN . . . AND AGAIN . . .

H E *didn't want to talk about southern rock.*

"What do you mean by that?" the peeved singer asked when I brought up the term. He was pacing about his dressing room backstage at the Greek Theatre in Los Angeles, gesturing wildly with his hands, stopping now and then to take a sip from his Jamaican Red Star beer.

"Well, I mean, you named the album The Southern Harmony and Musical Companion," *I offered.*

Chris Robinson smirked. It was October 1992, and his band, the Black Crowes, was getting ready to play to a capacity crowd at the venerable outdoor amphitheater nestled in the blanket of hills above Hollywood. Robinson didn't like my line of questioning. To be honest, I wasn't being very nice.

"Yeah, well, our music is our music, not some copy of something that came out twenty years ago," he said, running a hand through his long, greasy hair.

"Just because we're from the South, everybody wants to call us a southern rock band or something," he went on. "We're a rock & roll band, that's it."

Two years earlier, the Black Crowes had soared out of Atlanta, Georgia, with a debut album that harked back to the southern boogie of Lynyrd Skynyrd and the raunchy, hard-rock strut of '70s-period Rolling Stones and Faces. Shake Your Money Maker *was a left-field smash, shooting into the Top Ten and selling more than three million copies. The only other bigname rockers that remotely resembled the Black Crowes in 1990 were Guns N' Roses, whose major-label debut three years earlier also drew from '70s*

rock & roll, and Lenny Kravitz, whose music had more of a '60s, hippie vibe. The Crowes' sound was raw and earthy. If Guns N' Roses were the '90s version of Aerosmith, the Black Crowes were the new Humble Pie, reclaiming that British band's soulful, southern musical sensibility just as Skynyrd had reclaimed the bluesy moan of Free and Cream.

The first time I saw a Black Crowes video, I racked my brain trying to figure out what old band it was. I thought MTV, which at the time often played clips of vintage rock bands in a segment called One from the Vaults, had unearthed some obscure gem.

The video was hot. Robinson wore a loose-fitting, Romantic-style shirt with puffy sleeves and danced about a barebones rock & roll stage mimicking the exaggerated hand claps of Mick Jagger; his guitar-playing brother, Rich, had on black shades and cranked out Keith Richards–style riffs on a blond Fender Telecaster. If the video had been old, I would have considered the Crowes a great lost rock & roll band; when I found out it was new and that the band members were actually in their twenties, I was unsympathetic to their retro-rock shtick.

Most young male rock critics of the early '90s had the same reaction I did. It was unfair of us. Whether the band in that video was vintage or contemporary, the music was the same. It's just that in 1990—with underground rockers such as Sonic Youth and political rappers like Public Enemy creating new sounds that reflected the mood of the times—these backward-looking cock rockers from Georgia seemed at best quaint; at worst, they represented everything modern rock sought to destroy.

By 1992, I was the editor of the alternative music magazine Option and had a girlfriend who often took me to task for my elitism. She was younger than I was and never listened to Humble Pie or the Faces. She didn't care that Robinson and company had adopted the sound and mannerisms of a musical style I had long ago dismissed as archaic. To her, the Black Crowes were simply a hot new band that brought a little sex back into rock & roll at a time when the geeky, ultrahip, indie-rock bands we were listening to were devoid of anything smacking of carnal pleasures.

Chris Robinson wasn't exactly patient with the criticism his band was getting from music journalists, particularly snobby ones like me. The year before our face-off at the Greek, Robinson and his brother had bonded with a female reporter from Rolling Stone whose article on the Crowes pooh-poohed the comparisons to older bands.

Robinson told her, "This guy at MTV got all upset because he read an interview where I called Ronnie Van Zant a redneck. He goes, 'Ronnie Van Zant was a great man.' I said, 'Look, I didn't say he was an asshole, I said he was a redneck.'

"I was born in the South," confided his brother, Rich, "and I'm very proud of that. But I'm not waving a rebel flag, you know?"

That seemed to be the rub for the Black Crowes. If you really listened to their music, you could tell they truly loved the sound of their southern fore-bears and wanted to recapture its passion and soul. But the Crowes had begun their career playing a hipper style of music that was more in the vein of R.E.M. They moved toward the blues-based hard rock sound that made them famous only after a record executive from the major label Def American spotted them playing in an Atlanta club. To some music critics, the change of direction looked awfully calculated. Now, with all the nit-picking over whether the Crowes' retro image was honest, the Robinson brothers seemed self-conscious of the social implications of being branded an old-style southern rock band.

At the Greek Theatre, Robinson was defensive from the moment I walked into the dressing room, but he became especially riled by the "southern" question. And yet, here we were, in decadent Los Angeles, with the Robinson brothers having just released a second album they chose to call The Southern Harmony and Musical Companion. It's like they just wanted to rub it in our faces and then throw up their arms and ask why we were asking them about it.

He looked at me with a fuck-you expression. "I grew up liking the same shit all those other bands listened to, man," he spat, elongating his sylla-bles like my cousins in Georgia did when we got into arguments as kids. Robinson had grown a beard in the year since Shake Your Money Maker came out, and it seemed an odd fit for the scrawny rocker with the long, thin face—like when sex symbols Jimmy Page and Mick Jagger briefly grew beards a generation earlier.

Robinson wanted me to know where his music came from: "I listened to Otis Redding more than I listened to Lynyrd Skynyrd."

Chris Robinson didn't have anything to be defensive about that day in 1992. I was playing the role of the smart, probing music journalist, but

deep down I knew where he was coming from. Though I questioned his honesty, I wasn't being completely honest with myself. I felt indignant and misunderstood about my southern heritage, too, and not nearly as cocksure of my role as the editor of a well-respected alternative-music magazine as I hoped others would believe. In the early '90s, I was torn between the underground music scene I had entrenched myself in and the mainstream rock & roll that still moved me as much as it did when I first heard the Rolling Stones as a child. I was in denial about it, though, and was conveniently putting all of my fears and insecurities on Chris Robinson's band.

To this day I believe with all my heart and soul that *Option*, the magazine I edited from 1991 to 1996, was the coolest music publication on the planet. We covered the spectrum of independent music, from melodic and fairly accessible groups like the Pixies, Sugar, and Teenage Fanclub to the difficult, noisy and unapproachable music of postpunk and avant-jazz bands with names like Throbbing Gristle and Naked City. I genuinely connected with many of the bands we covered—acts such as the Mekons, the Fall, Sonic Youth, Pavement, My Bloody Valentine—but I hated the droning, pretentious music of most of the avant-garde and industrial-pop bands *Option* featured. To me, acts like Controlled Bleeding, the Young Gods, and KMFDM were no less embarrassing than the popular L.A. hair-metal bands we considered ourselves too smart to acknowledge.

I was insecure in my role as the editor of such an important magazine, but I was also excited about it. The magazine's publisher, Scott Becker, was committed to covering interesting music of all genres that fell outside the narrow scope of mainstream pop. In addition to the alternative rock bands and bizarre fringe artists, *Option* published stories on new strains of hip-hop and electronic dance music emerging then: the Beat poetry–inspired rap of the East Coast Native Tongues collective of groups such as the Jungle Brothers and A Tribe Called Quest; the freestyle rap of crews coming out of small clubs in South Central Los Angeles, such as the Pharcyde; emerging rappers from other parts of the United States, such as Atlanta's Arrested Development; the adrenaline rush of new sounds made by deejays at underground rave parties and small chill-out cafes popping up from L.A. to London.

I looked forward to getting up each morning and going to work. Every day was a blur of heady discussions about new music and art, different cultures and lifestyles. For me, coming from the South, where new and

different was often equated with scary and threatening, *Option* was the head rush I had long been searching for. The most exciting part was learning about the music of cultures in other parts of the world. Our reporters filed stories from as far away as Mexico City, Africa, the Middle East, and India. We covered the gritty, rebellious *rai* music of Algeria; the Arabic-flavored hip-hop of Moroccan groups such as Ahlam and Aisha Kandisha's Jarring Effects; the mystical, devotional Sufi music of Pakistan's Nusrat Fateh Ali Khan. If I wanted to send a writer to Austin, Texas, to report on the latest crop of outlaw country songwriters, Scott would green-light it. If Scott heard about some Native American mini-malist flute player who incorporated synthesizers into his traditional music, I would call up a writer and put him on the story. If one of our gay, feminist, or African-American reporters saw a new trend developing in our blind spots, we encouraged a story about it. There weren't many rules at *Option*. The only thing we tried to avoid was too much coverage of music the mainstream press already covered heavily. Even that wasn't a rule, though. If something was making an interesting impact on popu-lar culture, our reporters were on top of it.

Nine months before my showdown with Chris Robinson, one of the indie-rock bands *Option* had been following, Nirvana, took its second album to No. 1. The gritty, passionate music on *Nevermind* had sur-passed new albums by both Michael Jackson and country superstar Garth Brooks. Nirvana's acceptance by mainstream rock fans was unprecedented for a group that made such dissonant, punk-inspired music. Those of us who had worked for years on rock's alternative fringes were giddy about Nirvana's success. One *Option* critic wrote an essay in another magazine that put the band's success in terms of a victory. "We won," wrote Gina Arnold, speaking for fellow geeks and punk rockers who had been championing this music ever since the Sex Pistols came out of England snarling "Anarchy in the U.K." In retrospect, I believe we may have been missing the point. Nirvana's success wasn't based so much on the fact that they were influenced by smart, experimental, postpunk bands such as Sonic Youth and the Pixies; it was based on front man Kurt Cobain's charisma and his anthemlike songs that expressed universal feelings of low self-esteem. Kids in small towns and rural areas across America could identify with those feelings. When *Rolling Stone* referred to Cobain's hometown of Aberdeen, Washington, as a "redneck logging

community," it hit me like a thunderbolt. Kurt Cobain had brought it all back home.

Like Gina Arnold, I also felt somehow that we had "won"—as if no other music except for what was being made by independent underground rock bands had any redeeming value at all. The problem was that my gut told me something very different. Outwardly, I criticized bands like the Black Crowes for crafting music that appealed to mainstream rock fans. Inwardly, I liked the Black Crowes; they made good, soulful rock & roll, the kind of music that had helped my culture get through its dark, racist past. Outwardly, I maintained that Chris Robinson was symbolic of everything alternative culture wanted to see dead and buried; his very image broke all the taboos of the times: he was a cocky, straight, white, male, southern rocker who flaunted his sexuality onstage. Inwardly, it moved me deeply to hear Robinson soulfully croon lines like, "My angels, my devils, a thorn in my pride." Outwardly, I wanted to take the rock-star scarf Robinson wore around his neck and choke him with it. Inwardly, I wanted to wear that scarf.

"Sometimes," Robinson sang, resignedly, "life is obscene."

In the years since punk had begun to emasculate the old-style rock star that Robinson mimicked, an array of new voices had flooded in to fill the void. They were the voices of strong female and gay rockers; sensitive male singer-songwriters; cocky and confident African-American rappers and self-loathing punk rockers; musicians from other parts of the world, such as Central America, Africa, Asia, and the Middle East. Hip-hop artists were manipulating old rock & roll records, turning them into sound collages and addressing important urban issues over skittering beats and chopped-up classic rock and soul. With AIDS having taken such a huge toll on the arts since the late '80s, young, out-of-the-closet gays were forming powerful punk bands rather than just novelty disco or glam acts.

By the early '90s, the old romantic image of a sexually charged straight, white southern male such as Chris Robinson no longer seemed to be a free and liberating fantasy; rather, it looked like a power move on the part of the Oppressor. Rock critics tended to slam anything that harked back to earlier times, whether the idealism of the '60s or the sexual bravado of the '70s. It seemed as if we were frightened of entertaining any feelings at all for the innocence and naïveté of a pre-AIDS world. Though themes of

sexual bondage were okay as a political statement by industrial art-rock bands or button-pushing pop stars like Madonna, the blatant display of sexual virility by a white, male rocker fronting a gritty southern boogie band was off limits. As a music critic, the only way I would give credence to such an image was to do so in a tongue-in-cheek manner. If I liked a Guns N' Roses song, for example, it was a "guilty pleasure." If I compared an Uncle Tupelo song to Lynyrd Skynyrd, it was "irony." I hid my sincere feelings for certain kinds of music behind the cool exterior of a hip, alternative magazine editor and music critic.

In many ways, alternative culture in the '90s was as prudish as the southern Bible Belt culture that once burned rock & roll records. The same image that in the '50s sent a chill through conservative white America and a tingle up the spines of young pop fans—Elvis shaking his hips onstage like a black man—was threatening again, but this time to those of us in the alternative-rock world. I'm sure that not all of my fellow music critics were as riddled with angst over this pop-cultural dichotomy as I was, but many were. And for those of us who were feeling this pinch, it was as though we were on pins and needles, looking over our shoulders to make sure that what we wrote about and listened to, how we walked and talked, was acceptable to our peers. Just like the suburban households of the '50s, we seemed to be asking: What will the neighbors think?

The upside to this collective insecurity was that the tables were turning for gender and racial roles in popular music. By the early part of the decade, women musicians, from underground acts like Bikini Kill to rap groups such as Salt-n-Pepa and mainstream pop singers like Madonna, were toying with sexual imagery and gender roles in ways that were once acceptable only from men. The downside was that the message to young boys coming of age during this period—particularly young white boys—was that they should feel guilty about their race and gender. That guilt began to show up in the music of budding alternative-rock bands and postpunk male singer-songwriters whose introspective music became known as emocore, short for emotional hardcore. One of the pioneers of this style was Fugazi, which in 1990 recorded a song called "Styrofoam," in which the band seemed paralyzed by its nihilism: "Everybody's down, we pulled each other down. . . . We are all bigots so full of hatred, we release our poisons like Styrofoam." Eventually, those self-loathing sentiments found their way into the gentler, more personal work of sensitive

songwriters like Lou Barlow of Sebadoh. "I'm not attractive today, I'm not a sight for sore eyes," Barlow sang on the group's 1994 album, *Bakesale*. "I'm not an Adam or Eve, I'm just a nervous young thing." Honesty and authenticity had become big buzzwords in the alternative-rock '90s, but beneath all the sensitivity and angst, it didn't feel as if many of us were being truly honest.

In the late 1980s, an insidious new form of intolerance had appeared from progressive quarters under the unbelievably arrogant description "politically correct." The first time I heard the phrase I was seeing a Yale graduate named Naomi Wolf, who would become famous for her pioneering book of popular political correctness, *The Beauty Myth: How Images of Beauty Are Used Against Women*. I don't recall the particular topic of conversation, but I do remember her looking at me with a straight face and telling me that I wasn't framing whatever issue it was we were discussing in a "politically correct" manner. The comment gave me pause. It was a brilliant display of rhetorical dexterity. I was impressed (and not just a little horrified) at the audaciousness of this new expression. I also bought into it.

The phrase "politically correct" came from '60s Leninists who used the shortened PC to describe their most committed fellow leftists. Eventually, young radicals in the United States began using PC to playfully characterize those among their ranks who conformed to the party line just a little too vigorously. By the early '90s, the vague and malleable term had made its way from the intellectual left to college campuses and on out into the popular vernacular. For the most part, the more earnest promoters of politically correct language and behavior were writers such as Wolf, who were making well-intentioned attempts to right intellectual wrongs—to bring a multicultural balance to the Eurocentric way that history for centuries has been recorded and taught in the West by mostly white, male scholars. In the popular media, liberal writers and thinkers attempted to balance and ferret out prejudices that had long excluded or downplayed the perspectives of women, blacks, and gays. What these popular progressives tended to ignore was the issue of class, and this error was a grave one. In boosting the points of view of women, blacks, and gays with little regard to class, the resulting

ideology began to look less like a leftist attempt to fight the power and more like an excuse to chastise the working class, whose voices on issues were no more powerful than the voices of women, blacks, or gays. Progressive arguments lost their firm grounding in leftist thought and opened the doors for valid criticism from the right, which since the Reagan years had been repositioning itself to appear as a friendly populist movement.

Between the late '80s and mid-'90s, liberal ideas in the popular media began to look very ugly. To working-class folks, particularly in the South, PC language appeared to give well-educated progressives carte blanche to express their own bigotry in ways that didn't allow for further discussion of an issue. To the "PC watchdogs," as they came to be known on the right, certain terms, images, and subject matter were unilaterally deemed either correct or incorrect. One could no longer freely argue, 'Well, gee, this is the way I see things,' for fear of being publicly rebuked as racist, sexist, or homophobic. If a writer or thinker (or rock critic) wanted to participate in a dialectic on a certain topic, he or she was vulnerable to severe censure. Some of the rules of political correctness seemed fair enough. For example, most intelligent people don't find it logical or moral to generalize or speak disparagingly of women, blacks, or gays. Other rules, though, seemed oppressive. To the most vocal overseers of progressive points of view, it became equally off limits to pose valid questions about the methods of certain organizations *representing* women, blacks, or gays. This form of "logic" made it hard for issues to be examined freely, and it led to deep resentments.

As it turned out, "politically correct" became more of a euphemism for cultural fascism than a rallying cry for cultural idealism or moralism. The phenomenon labeled PC by its critics was very Orwellian, with "language codes" that often made potential allies appear to be enemies. By 1998, Ruth Sherman, a teacher in a predominantly black and Hispanic elementary school in Brooklyn, came under fire when she read a book to her class entitled *Nappy Hair*. The book, written by an African-American author, was intended to boost students' self-esteem, but parents who had not read it called the white teacher a racist. Sherman volunteered to be transferred out of the school district. In 2002, Stephanie Bell, a white teacher in Wilmington, North Carolina, was reprimanded for defining for her fourth-grade students the word "nig-

gardly," which means miserly and is not related to the similar-sounding racial slur. Bell was ordered to attend "sensitivity training" and to apologize to the students' parents.

Most insidious of all was that white, working-class southern males—the same group of people whom the white, southern ruling class had used in its divide-and-conquer ploy from the earliest days of southern racism—were not protected under the unwritten rules of progressive language use. While the language codes forbade the use of certain terms to describe women, blacks, and gays, it was still okay to refer to working-class southerners—particularly southern males—as white trash, rednecks, and bubbas.

At *The Charlotte Observer*, one of my colleagues, Eric Frazier, wrote an elegant column in 2002 about why the South's racist past can't be forgotten. He got lots of negative feedback from intolerant white readers who regularly responded to columns they believed to be threatening to their way of life. In an otherwise solid follow-up piece in which Frazier enumerated the responses he got, he wound up undermining his own position by differentiating the smart respondents (read: educated or ruling class) from the stupid ones (read: working class). "The callers and correspondents," Frazier wrote, "have ranged from scholarly-sounding conservatives to foul-mouthed rednecks spitting the 'n-word' and other vulgarities into the phone line." I understood his annoyance, but the winner of that particular battle in the language wars was neither Frazier nor the working-class racists he referred to as "foul-mouthed rednecks." The winner was the same educated, wealthy racist Eurocentric southern ruling elite against which the popular progressive movement ideally should be focusing its arguments.

In popular culture, blue-collar southern rock and country fans have traditionally been easy targets for ridicule. They usually can't win the word game, because many haven't been afforded the arsenal of language necessary to prevail in that arena. So they use words and ideas handed down from previous generations and from the white ruling class. This gives progressives in the media plenty to hate, because the words some blue-collar folks use—even when not patently offensive—sometimes hark back to the South's legacy of slavery and defiance of civil rights. Their slow, twangy drawl and tendency to wear their economic burdens with an angry sense of cultural pride only adds fuel to the fire.

By the early '90s, the left itself had introduced a form of intolerance that was nearly as simplistic as the intolerance of its enemy, and it showed intolerance to be more than just a southern problem—not that it ever really was just a southern problem. Though white, working-class southerners were still burdened by the region's sketchy past, it was becoming clearer that when nonsoutherners—or "rehabilitated" southerners like myself—wrote or spoke mockingly of images associated with the blue-collar, white South, we were projecting onto an entire group of powerless people our collective shame and guilt over simply being American. The Black Crowes were not blue-collar southerners, but their music and style appealed to many of the same people who might also go to a Lynyrd Skynyrd concert. So when Chris Robinson used the word "redneck" to distance himself from Ronnie Van Zant in that 1991 *Rolling Stone* article, he was protecting himself from being identified with America's newest false villain: the white, working-class southern male.

On a sunny afternoon, a video camera catches the image of an obese man in a white T-shirt and bib overalls jogging up the center of a country road carrying an Olympic torch. He stops, struggles for a breath, then continues his journey, eventually making his way into a high-school football stadium. In the bleachers, a crowd of men and women, mostly overweight and wearing baseball caps, oversized T-shirts, cowboy hats, and tight jeans, cheer loudly as the celebratory sound of marching-band music bounces off the stadium walls. The camera pans the audience: there's a rotund woman with pink and yellow curlers in her hair, a scrawny man in a straw hat. The camera continues panning and then zooms in on a man with a moustache and mullet haircut standing on a ragtag stage in the middle of the ball field. He begins shouting into a microphone.

"Greetings, y'all," the man announces in a slow, Georgia lilt, "and welcome all you dang foreigners from other nations. Dear Lord, be with our guests and prepare them for the butt-whuppin' they're about to receive."

The twang of a country guitar and fiddles cuts in as the video fades to another image of the mulleted man with the moustache, who turns out to be comedian Jeff Foxworthy. He's sitting in a bar next to country-music singer Alan Jackson.

"The Olympics in Georgia!" Foxworthy says, incredulously, "God, you know we're gonna screw that up. I guarantee you, when they let those doves go at the opening ceremony there are gonna be guys in the parking lot with shotguns. . . ." His punch lines are punctuated by musical pauses. "Hell, the Olympic rings will be five old tires nailed together. . . ."

As Foxworthy delivers jokes in his video for *Redneck Games*, a parody of the 1996 Olympics, Jackson begins singing: "You can't blame them for the way they are / But you can sit back and grin. . . . / They just do things in a different way, all the games that the rednecks play. . . ."

Southern stereotyping clearly is not part of some great conspiracy from outside forces. By the early to mid-'90s, southerners continued to offer plenty of fodder for ridicule. Like President Jimmy Carter's family members back in the mid-'70s, we've happily perpetuated negative images of ourselves. If Andy Griffith began the South's tradition of spreading its self-deprecating humor via the broadcast media of the '50s with the dumb, country-boy skit "No Time for Sergeants" (which led to his successful TV sitcom of the '60s), others kept jumping on the bandwagon. Jerry Clower, whose loud, obnoxious, hootin' and hollerin' Southern Baptist preacher persona—"from Yaaaaaazoo City, Miss'sippi"—became a favorite on TV's *Hee Haw* in the late '60s and early '70s. By the '80s, Kentucky native Jim Varney introduced a dim-witted, southern blue-collar character named Ernest, who starred in a string of successful movies into the early '90s.

There was the newspaper-columnist-turned-stand-up-comic Lewis Grizzard, whose writing was sometimes erroneously compared to the musings of Mark Twain. Grizzard's quaint, sentimental humor lacked Twain's astute sense of social commentary. "I am the only person from Moreland, Georgia, who ever made the *New York Times* Bestseller List," Grizzard once said, adding the punch line: "I am the only person in Moreland, Georgia, who ever *heard* of the *New York Times* Bestseller List."

Grizzard's humor inspired Jeff Foxworthy, a young IBM employee from Atlanta who so dazzled his fellow workers with his redneck jokes that they convinced him to try them out at a local comedy club. The comic's "You Might Be a Redneck If . . ." routine cashed in on a popular Grizzard column called "Definition of a Redneck." Foxworthy released his album *You Might Be a Redneck If . . .* on the small Laughing Hyena

label in 1993, and it became a huge regional hit. Warner Bros. bought Foxworthy's contract in 1994, and the album shot to No. 3 on *Billboard*'s country chart the following year. It eventually sold more than four million copies, becoming the biggest-selling comedy album ever. By the late '90s, Foxworthy was one of America's most famous stand-up comics and he has inspired legions of similarly inclined southerners to keep on mocking themselves.

In 2003, I was talking with *The Charlotte Observer*'s pop-culture columnist Tonya Jameson about a board game that had recently come out called Ghettopoly, a parody of Monopoly created by an Asian-American hip-hop fan. In the middle of the board was a caricature of a black gang member with a bandana on his head, an Uzi in one hand, and a forty-ounce can of malt liquor in the other. The ad copy boasted: "Buying stolen properties, pimpin hoes, building crack houses and projects, paying protection fees and getting carjacked are some of the elements of the game." Ghettopoly sparked outrage among black leaders. But Tonya—a young, provocative African-American commentator who often wrote about negative portrayals of blacks in the media—took an interesting position with regard to the game.

"If it's the image that you put out there," she said, "then you shouldn't be surprised and upset when someone else takes that image and capitalizes on it."

Tonya had a good point. When the rappers of the '80s referred to themselves as "niggas" in their music, it was looked upon as a case of reclaiming a negative term and turning it on its head. By the late 1990s and early 2000s, after hip-hop had long been earning millions for artists and major media conglomerates, surpassing old-style rock & roll as the sound of mainstream popular music, the old rationalization for the negative images and terminology was no longer valid. If African-Americans didn't like the negative portrayals of hip-hop, the best way to get rid of those portrayals was to stop propagating them. What Tonya was suggesting was that the young Asian-American creator of Ghettopoly was not the culprit; he was just a fan of a culture he considered his own, that he'd been told was his own by the rappers of the entertainment industry since he was very young. The culprit was hip-hop itself. The old negative images and terms no longer served their original function; because they had not been taken to new levels of meaning, they only served to turn hip-hop into an ugly parody of itself.

The same could be said of "bubba" humor. When white southern indie-rock bands such as Fetchin Bones and Southern Culture on the Skids began toying with white-trash imagery in the early to mid-1980s, they, too, had reclaimed negative portrayals of southerners in a way that disarmed the stereotypes. By the early '90s, those images, coupled with the popularity of comedians like Jim Varney and Jeff Foxworthy, inspired young rock bands from other parts of the country to incorporate white-trash imagery into their music, too. The nonsouthern act Jon Spencer Blues Explosion exploited Elvis clichés in its noisy, experimental New York sound and got high critical praise for its avant-burlesque performances. To me, it wasn't funny or liberating anymore. I found myself intrigued by Spencer's music but annoyed with his caricature of a working-class southern singer. My feeling was: Who the hell is Jon Spencer, an Ivy League–educated indie rocker, to mock the eccentricities of my culture and extended family? It was one thing when Southern Culture on the Skids mocked those eccentricities; they understood the culture, they came from the South. It was quite another when writers and musicians from backgrounds that had no direct experience with working-class southerners mocked them. It served no discernable purpose, and it stung.

After Nirvana took alternative rock into the mainstream, the posturing of underground acts such as Jon Spencer Blues Explosion lost any irony it may have had originally; when the band's underground humor began to blend in with images coming from more literal, mainstream entertainment sources, such as Varney and Foxworthy, the result was that a new generation of young Americans felt okay about laughing at poor, blue-collar southerners. Naturally, major media outlets capitalized on the trend. But who was really to blame? After all, it was southerners who started it.

When I spoke with Warren Haynes of the Allman Brothers Band and Gov't Mule, our conversation turned to how others view the South. After joining the Allman Brothers in 1989, Haynes moved away from the South, to New York City. Unlike me, his move wasn't an attempt to escape his fears and insecurities about being southern; Haynes seems to be pretty secure with himself in that regard. And yet he, too, began to see how ignorance tinted outside perceptions of the South.

"It's funny, when I talk to some people from New York or the West Coast, they'll sometimes say things to me like, 'You know, I've never been to the South,'" Haynes told me. "And that always surprises me, because

they tend to have certain ideas about the South even though they've never been there. It's almost like they're scared of it. I'm like, 'What? What do you mean?' It's like they think the moment they get off the plane, there's going to be a Klan rally waiting for them."

In the early '90s, there was still reason for others to be dubious of the South. Between 1989 and 1992, former Ku Klux Klansman David Duke had repositioned himself as a mainstream politician. In 1988, Duke had run for president on the Populist Party ticket and enlisted former American Nazi leader Ralph Forbes to be his campaign manager. In 1989, Duke, now running as a Republican, won a runoff for Louisiana State House by a slim, 227-vote margin. He only served one term, and his bids for the governorship in 1991 and presidency in 1992 were dismal failures. By 2003, he'd been convicted of mail fraud and tax evasion and was sentenced to fifteen months in prison. His flirtation with mainstream politics was brief, but that a former Ku Klux Klansman could get that far was startling.

On the other hand, more and more black women from southern and heartland states were being voted into office. When Cynthia McKinney from Georgia was elected to Congress in 1992, she was one of six black women elected that year. "Cynthia means hope," Keysville, Georgia, mayor Emma Gresham told The Boston Globe. "She means progress, because she is a black woman who has beaten all the odds." Another member of McKinney's class of 1992, Carol Moseley Braun, a Democrat from Illinois, became the first and only black woman to serve in the Senate that year. Moseley Braun immediately initiated a debate that helped chip away at old-style institutional racism in the South.

By 1992, the South was in the midst of a fiery battle among blacks, whites, conservatives, and liberals over the meaning of the Confederate flag. When Moseley Braun took office the following year, she got into several high-profile clashes with the aging controversial conservative senator from North Carolina, Jesse Helms. She put a spotlight on Helms's racism that led to his political emasculation. On July 22, 1993, the Senate was to debate whether it should renew a design patent for the United Daughters of the Confederacy's emblem, which included the Confederate flag. Helms sponsored a measure that renewed it. In

response to the issue, Moseley Braun delivered one of the most memorable and emotionally charged speeches of the decade. She told her colleagues she had wanted to take an intellectual step back from the issue but was unable to do so. It was just too painful.

"The issue is whether or not Americans, such as myself . . . will have to suffer the indignity of being reminded time and time again that at one point in this country's history we were human chattel," she said. "We were property. We could be traded, bought, and sold." Moseley Braun, one of the more good-natured members of the Senate, reminded her colleagues that in the seven months she'd been in office, she was never one to shout or demand. But this issue cut to the heart of racial division in America. "It is an outrage. It is an insult," she said of the Confederate emblem. "It is absolutely unacceptable to me and to millions of Americans, black or white, that we would put the imprimatur of the United States Senate on a symbol of this kind."

The speech was persuasive, and Alabama senator Howell Heflin of Alabama, who spoke of his love of his sweet home Alabama in terms not unlike the Lynyrd Skynyrd song, backed Moseley Braun and reversed his previous support of the patent. "We live today in a different world," he said. "We live in a nation that every day is trying to heal the scars of racism. . . . We must get racism behind us, and we must move forward."

It marked a turning point in the debate over the crusty old Confederate flag. The debate still rages, but those in support are finding fewer and fewer rational reasons to keep it going. Even the most vigorous defenders were beginning to see that the rebel flag's meaning extended well beyond pride for one's southern heritage. People could hold on to their racist feelings, but they couldn't use government property to hatefully smear it in other people's faces.

Two years before Moseley Braun's impassioned speech, even June Leake, the South Carolina president of the United Daughters of the Confederacy, wearily told the *Atlanta Journal-Constitution*, "The world seems to have it out for the Confederate flag. I guess it's because of the slavery thing."

By the late 1980s and early 1990s, as southerners began coming to terms with the reality that racist symbols were as hurtful as violence, several unpleasant incidents in New York City and Los Angeles were telling another story about those regions. By the summer of 1992, when alter-

native rock and gangsta rap were screaming and shooting their way up the pop charts and onto MTV, racial unrest was literally tearing apart the inner cities of the Northeast and West Coast.

The following events happened after I decided to move to New York in the mid-1980s:

- On December 20, 1986, twenty-three-year-old black construction worker Michael Griffith and two friends, Cedric Sandiford and Timothy Grimes, were driving through Howard Beach, Queens, when their car broke down. After stopping at a pizza parlor to use the phone and get a slice of pizza, a gang of white guys wielding baseball bats harassed Griffith and his friends, called them niggers, and beat them up. Injured and frightened, Griffith staggered onto a nearby highway and was killed by a car.

- On August 23, 1989, sixteen-year-old Yusef Hawkins went to Bensonhurst, Queens, with three friends to look for a used car. A gang of thirty whites, some carrying bats and at least one with a gun, approached the teenagers. The whites were angry because one of their girlfriends had invited a black guy to her birthday party. Mistaking Hawkins and his friends for the black guys she invited, the gang beat up the teenagers. In the hubbub, Hawkins was shot and killed.

These incidents happened after I moved to Los Angeles in 1991:

- On March 3, 1991, police vehicles chased motorist Rodney G. King, a robbery parolee who was reportedly speeding. King drove through intersections but eventually was stopped. When he apparently refused to get out of the car, King was physically removed by police officers, who then struck King with their batons as many as fifty-six times. They also kicked him repeatedly and shot him with a stun gun. A police sergeant on the scene ordered the beating and twenty-three other officers witnessed it. King's skull was fractured and he received nerve damage to his face. A civilian bystander videotaped the beating, which was subsequently aired on television news stations. Citizens of Los Angeles and across the nation were stunned by the image of police brutally beating King.

- On March 16, thirteen days after the King incident, a Korean shop-keeper shot African-American teenager Latasha Harlins, fifteen, in the back of the head after the two got into an argument over a car-ton of orange juice. Although the shopkeeper was convicted of vol-untary manslaughter, he was set free on probation and ordered to do six months of community service.
- On April 29, 1992, an all-white jury in Los Angeles acquitted three of the four officers involved in the King beating. Announcement of the verdict sparked riots across L.A., from the South Central district, much of which was destroyed by fire, to parts of Hollywood near my apartment. For three days I watched as flames rose all around my area of the city. In the end, fifty-four people were dead, 500 fires were smoldering, and 4,500 stores were destroyed—many Korean-owned. More than 3,000 people were arrested during the uprising; half of them were Latino and about 40 percent were black. More than $900 million in damage was done.

On June 3, 1992, a little more than a month after the L.A. riots, Democratic presidential candidate Bill Clinton, the young, suave gover-nor of Arkansas, walked onstage at *The Arsenio Hall Show* with a tenor saxophone strapped to his chest. He blew into the mouthpiece, turning Elvis Presley's "Heartbreak Hotel" into a lament for early-'90s America. Clinton blew hard. He blew so hard that he became the president of the United States.

For Greil Marcus, one of popular music's most insightful sociologists, Clinton's appearance on that hip TV talk show in 1992 won him the election. The young baby boomer from a modest, blue-collar southern family had cleverly mainlined himself straight into the veins of popular culture.

America was primed for another southern president, and Bill Clinton was one savvy southern politician. His easy smile and confident, com-forting, sandy Arkansas drawl made him come off like the neighborhood good guy who'd lend you his lawnmower and ask how your family was doing. Clinton was much cooler than Jimmy Carter. He also came with much more baggage.

By early 1992, candidate Clinton seemed to be losing his connection with voters. His sex scandals as governor and his avoidance of the Vietnam

draft had caught up with him, and Americans were wondering if they could trust the southern charmer. Clinton's crack team of strategists, led by the crazy but brilliant political firecracker James Carville, put together a plan for the candidate that would turn him into an American Everyman and steer voters' attention toward his charm, not his contradictions.

Like publicists working with a rock star, Carville and his team transformed Bill Clinton from a man who sounded good but couldn't be trusted into a hardworking American who'd come from a humble, blue-collar family in the Deep South. Clinton was a loving husband and father whose own dad had died before he was born and whose mother struggled to provide for him and his brother. He was a strong young man who protected his mom and brother from an abusive, alcoholic stepfather. His heroes were Martin Luther King Jr., Abraham Lincoln, and John F. Kennedy. He despised institutional racism and worked to change a welfare system that no longer served its original goals. He was neither liberal nor conservative, but both at the same time. In short, Bill Clinton was an average guy for whom labels did not apply; he could identify with the struggles of all working people, black, white, poor, middle-class, young and old. He was part Elvis and part Ronald Reagan—a polite, soft-spoken populist from Anytown, U.S.A., who could charm the pants off an MTV audience as easily as he could a small-town garden club.

In *The Boston Globe*, southern political observer Curtis Wilkie described Clinton as "an avatar of Lyndon B. Johnson, whose style Theodore H. White wrote 'was shaped in the Old South where one runs man against man, with victory going to the man who can out-shout, out-dramatize, out-campaign, out-smile and out-entertain the raw voters until they feel in their hearts that . . . he understands them, he is one of them.'

"On the surface," Wilkie continued, "[Clinton's] childhood in rural Arkansas sounds as innocent as a scene from *American Graffiti*. As a little boy, he lived for a time with his grandparents in a town called Hope. . . ."

Clinton put a new face on poor white southerners. His ideas about race, he said, came from his grandparents, who were not the kind of people who saw blacks as their nemeses.

"There's that poor white southerner phenomenon where some of them were the most racist of all because they needed somebody to look

down on," Clinton told Wilkie. "But a lot of other poor whites in the South were real sympathetic with blacks because they knew them." Clinton described a black neighborhood behind a cemetery in Hope where "for the longest time the streets weren't paved, and I noticed that and I asked about it, and my grandparents said: 'It's not right.' "

The teenaged Bill Clinton liked jazz, played the saxophone, sang folk songs at the local ice-cream parlor, and was more sensitive than most other boys in the South, who gravitated to football rather than music. By then, Clinton had moved back in with his mother, Virginia Kelley, who had gone to nursing school to provide for her family. He and his brother spent their teen years in Hot Springs, Arkansas, where Clinton developed a passion for politics.

During the 1992 presidential campaign, Bill Clinton, forty-six, was shown to be the exact opposite of Republican incumbent George Bush. In some ways, the nation was in a similar place as it was back in 1976, when Jimmy Carter became the first presidential hopeful to tap the well of rock & roll. Republicans were coming under fire for the Reagan administration's shady dealings with Iran and the right-wing contras of Nicaragua, but unlike Reagan, Bush didn't have the personality to allay our fears about this new corruption in the government. Clinton sensed Bush's insecurity and pounced on it.

In his book *Double Trouble*, a collection of essays comparing the Clinton mystique to that of Presley, writer Greil Marcus notes that the King of Rock & Roll was often cited during the campaign.

"I guess you'd say his plan really is 'Elvis Economics,' " Bush had said of Clinton's economic plans during the sitting president's acceptance as the Republicans' nominee. "Americans will be checking into the 'Heartbreak Hotel.' "

"Bush is always comparing me to Elvis in sort of unflattering ways," Clinton retorted a month before the election. "Well, I don't think Bush would have liked Elvis very much."

On November 3, 1992, William Jefferson Clinton beat George Herbert Walker Bush, and a new kind of southerner marched into the White House.

Clinton's inauguration harked back to Carter's. Arkansas rockabilly legend Ronnie Hawkins was there, as were Bob Dylan and members of the Band, the old backing musicians for both the Hawk and Dylan. "It

was quite exciting," Hawkins wrote on his fan Web site. "Bob Dylan was there and so was Clinton's mother and his family. . . . It was crammed and a real rock & roll party. It was not a stuffy black-tie affair. . . ."

At the Blue Jean Bash the following night, Hollywood couple Melanie Griffith and Don Johnson appeared, and so did Dr. John and Stephen Stills. "Suddenly it was a good time to have been born and raised in Madison County, Arkansas," wrote Hawkins. "I got three letters from Bill Clinton himself. I'm getting them framed. It ain't every day that I get an invite from the President of the United States."

Throughout the '90s, it would become even clearer just how rock & roll the new southern president was. Clinton positively embodied popular culture, right down to the decadence of his crazy sex life. He was a baby boomer with a tongue as silver as Texas songwriter Kris Kristofferson's. Clinton was the guy who smoked pot but didn't inhale. He was slick Willie, the debonair don of progressive southern politics.

The rise of Bill Clinton coincided with the reemergence of Clinton's rock & roll look-alike from Georgia, Phil Walden. After Walden and his son cleaned up their acts in the late 1980s, the elder Walden started thinking about bringing Capricorn Records back from the dead. He wrote up a proposal and met with Warner Bros. Records executives Mo Ostin and Jim Ed Norman. Walden Jr. was supportive of his dad's idea. The first band to sign with the new Capricorn, in 1991, was Walden Jr.'s old Athens friends, Widespread Panic.

"I was in law school at Mercer in Macon when Panic started getting big and selling out the Cotton Club in Atlanta and doing really well in clubs all over the southeast," said Walden Jr. "So when my dad started the label back up, Panic wound up being the first band he signed to the new Capricorn. They were the only new Capricorn band for about a year." In keeping with the southern soap opera that Capricorn was, in later years, Widespread Panic would come to resent Walden Jr. just as the Allmans had resented Walden Sr.

"I think their beef is that they spent their entire formative years with Capricorn and made their best albums for Capricorn and maybe they think they should have done better," said Walden Jr. in 2002. "And I don't want to make it sound like we're enemies; I still regularly talk to some of the members of the band, but there are others who are kind of

bitter. But—whatever. I'll say this: I made sure they got treated like the Rolling Stones at Capricorn. I mean, the album packaging itself was always double the budget than what we should have been spending. We spared no expense when it came to Panic. I like to think that Capricorn helped contribute to their career in some way—we stuck with them when they were not selling that many records. But to me, they're the kind of band whose catalog will sell forever—like the Allman Brothers. Panic didn't have the immediate chart success, but that's not the kind of band they are."

Walden shook his head and laughed. "And now Widespread Panic hates me just like the Allman Brothers hate my dad. What a perfect little circle."

Widespread Panic was initially thrilled to sign with the Waldens. "We had no problems signing with Capricorn because we knew Phil had nothing to do with [the old] Capricorn losing money," Panic percussionist Domingo "Sonny" Ortiz told the *Chicago Tribune* in 1991. "In fact, we played a festival with the Allman Brothers Band and they said Capricorn really helped them grow and they had no hostilities toward it. That made us feel real good."

Walden Sr. gave Widespread Panic the same kind of artistic freedom he'd given the Allmans some two decades earlier. Capricorn even brought in one of its old employees, former Hourglass keyboardist and Allmans producer Johnny Sandlin, to preside over the recording. Sandlin found Widespread Panic refreshing.

Musically, Sandlin told me in 2002, "Panic would pick some of the things that you wouldn't have expected, some Meters' stuff, some Traffic songs. They had such a wide variety of influences, from country to funky stuff, but they had more to pick from in 1991 than the Allman Brothers did back in the early '70s. And the guys in Widespread Panic were much different people. The Brothers' sessions could get pretty hairy at times, but at Panic's sessions everyone was always having a good time. They enjoyed themselves. They worked hard, but they weren't fussing and fighting like the Brothers."

In the four years since Panic had released its independent-label debut, *Space Wrangler*, the band had developed a strong southeastern following of fans who called themselves Spreadheads. "In the South," Ortiz told the *Tribune*, "there wasn't a club owner alive that wouldn't take us.

"We've already sold more copies of our [Capricorn] album than the

first Allman Brothers album sold in its first year out," he added. "We're doing pretty good, and we've done it playing what we know is from the heart."

What Widespread Panic knew was that, by the early 1990s, a growing number of young music fans across America were turning away from alternative rock and hip-hop in favor of improvisational, blues-based jam music. As Bill Clinton crisscrossed the nation during his 1992 bid for the presidency, bringing southern hospitality back to politics and the American heartland, Widespread Panic joined a traveling road show of rock bands that were wholly dismissed by the hip music critics of the period and all but ignored by MTV. Young fans of the Grateful Dead—which was enjoying a surprising renaissance—were forming new groups that rejected the arch irony of alternative rock. In the summer of 1992, following the success of the alternative package tour Lollapalooza, the northeastern-based Blues Traveler put together a tour of its own featuring a few of the more popular underground jam bands.

The tour was called HORDE, an acronym for its endearingly clunky mission statement: Horizons of Rock Developing Everywhere. The first HORDE tour featured a mix of groups that included Widespread Panic and Phish, a Vermont band heavily influenced by the Dead. Panic brought along a legendary savant from Atlanta's psychedelic era who had been forgotten by the music industry. Colonel Bruce Hampton's late-'60s group, the Hampton Grease Band, had been the South's answer to Captain Beefheart, Frank Zappa, and the Grateful Dead—combined. By the early '90s, Hampton had formed the Aquarium Rescue Unit. Hampton's bizarre performances of southern rock, blues, funk, jazz, and psychedelia at those first HORDE dates inspired a thousand future jam bands.

The tour began quietly, with modest attendance by diehard fans. By the following year, when the newly reunited Allman Brothers Band head-lined HORDE, the tour became the model for every summer gathering of jam bands in America—and by then, they were proliferating like dandelions. "What we basically did," Blues Traveler's John Popper told the Web site jambands.com, "was just rip off the whole Lollapalooza idea. . . . You know, it just seemed right."

Whatever one feels about the noodling music of young bands that look to the Dead and the Allmans for inspiration, the jam-band scene, like Bill

Clinton, became a symbol of grassroots victory—much more so than the commercial success of alternative rock. The critically supported alternative rock movement may have broken into the pop charts without much help from corporate record labels, but the jam-band movement succeeded even without critical support. At a jam-band festival, the musicians and fans didn't worry about whether the music was clever or hip or popular. They didn't have to look over their shoulders to see if others approved of their tastes. If the old-style hippie vibe was sometimes annoying, the unbridled joy at the festivals was infectious. By the time of the Bonnaroo gatherings of the early 2000s, jam bands—many of them southern—had created an environment that welcomed artists as diverse as the Roots (hip-hop), the Flaming Lips (avant-pop), and Sonic Youth (New York noise rock). No one seemed to care whether any of the music was getting play on MTV Networks, or whether it got a rock critic's stamp of approval. The musicians were making music for each other and for their fans—and there were hundreds of thousands of fans across America going to similar concerts and festivals in similar rural nooks and crannies. At a time when the pop acts appearing regularly on MTV were having trouble selling concert tickets, jam bands that got little or no attention from TV, radio, or the music press were filling concert halls and sprawling meadows across the country.

With the slow rise of the jam-band movement, the comebacks of Lynyrd Skynyrd and the Allman Brothers, the success of the Black Crowes, and the election of Bill Clinton, the South and rock & roll had come full circle in 1992. Newer blues-based southern rock bands, such as Gov't Mule and Screamin' Cheetah Wheelies, were forming, and even the old Kentucky Headhunters were moving away from their garage-country sound and playing music that mixed Memphis and Muscle Shoals soul with the group's trademark Kentucky twang. By the 1990s, it was becoming safe again—even marginally hip—to be a visceral, long-haired rock star who strutted his stuff onstage or a beefy guitarist who played long, bluesy solos. But the music of the new southern bands of the jam-band scene was different from that of any other generation of southern rockers. These bands seemed at peace with their southernness—as sure of themselves as Bill Clinton had been on the campaign trail of 1992.

If the disaffected southern rockers of the '70s and '80s helped keep those of us who grew up in the South on an honest path to self-awareness

in the years since desegregation changed our lives, then the southern music of the Clinton '90s became, perhaps, the final stage in our emotional catharsis. Melancholy, anger, and intellectual detachment were necessary steps in that process, but acceptance was the ultimate goal. The bands that cropped up in the South of the post-Clinton years seemed to be headed in that direction. Both the Dave Matthews Band and Hootie and the Blowfish were racially mixed ensembles, though little was made of it. Widespread Panic and Gov't Mule took their cues from the Allman Brothers. Panic focused on the Allmans' improvisational side, while the Mule cranked out a heavy blues-rock sound colored by Warren Haynes's weeping, Duane Allman–style bottleneck slide guitar work, but neither band displayed the deep sense of cultural shame heard in Gregg Allman's voice.

And then there were the Screamin' Cheetah Wheelies, whose sassy, Black Crowes–like rock & roll sound conjured the heart and soul of Lynyrd Skynyrd. But there was a big difference between Wheelies' frontman, Mike Farris, and Skynyrd's Ronnie Van Zant. Farris's songs replaced anger with resolve. In fact, the Wheelies' self-titled debut album of 1994 includes one of the most powerful songs about southern pride since "Sweet Home Alabama." But in "Moses Brown," Farris takes a more spiritual approach than Van Zant had. Behind gentle acoustic guitar and conga drums, Farris sings: "Moses Brown told the children to sit down, please / He noticed that they had lost their identity." By the end, it's clear that no less than God himself is speaking through the song's biblically named protagonist.

"You must forget about hard times, they have ended," Farris continues in a soulful rasp inspired by nearly every previous southern singer of note, from Otis Redding straight up to Michael Stipe. "And if you ever need me to lean upon, reach to the sky and sing this song."

★ Postscript ★

LEARNING TO CRAWL

No snowflake in an avalanche ever feels responsible.
— Voltaire

Early one morning, in spring 2002, I looked into my father's seventy-year-old eyes and saw forgiveness. We were in a hotel room in Nashville, at the tail end of our monthlong jaunt across the South during my research for this book. Dad hadn't said anything in particular to me; I just saw it in his eyes. And when I saw it, I finally grasped how real the healing power of forgiveness is.

"Come on, son," he said, patting me on my back. "Let's go get us a Blizzard from the Dairy Queen."

Later that day, we would begin our journey back home again, to North Carolina, but at that moment Dad and I were going to walk across the street together and get us a Blizzard from the Dairy Queen.

"Don't tell your mother, now," he warned me, smiling. "She'd have my hide if she knew how many Blizzards I was having." I promised to keep it between us.

We laughed together like we'd never laughed before. We were buddies—best buddies—and having the time of our lives. We'd never had so much fun together, never spent so many hours with each other without getting into some ridiculous argument over political issues about which neither of us really felt so strongly. But there we were, on a bright spring morning, having been on the road for weeks, together at every waking hour, and not

once had we argued over anything. We didn't have time for arguing; we were too busy getting to know each other. And we liked the two men we were meeting.

In the previous three years, I had put my parents through pure hell. After staying sober and off drugs for several years in the early '90s, I made the arrogant mistake of thinking I was cured of my addiction and felt I could drink socially again. After all, I had become awfully successful in my career. By 1996, I had landed my dream job at Rolling Stone *and was about to be married to a fellow music journalist. Everything seemed to be right on schedule. I was on top of the world and about to blast off into the cosmos.*

For a while everything was generally okay. At first, I would drink responsibly during business functions, although I had to consciously force myself not to drink more than one or two glasses of wine. For an alcoholic, the most natural thing in the world is to keep drinking until there's nothing left, then search for more. Forcing myself to stop once I'd started was not just uncomfortable; it went against my very nature.

About a year after my arrival at Rolling Stone, *I had begun to drink heavily again, but it wasn't affecting my work yet. I negotiated cover features with artists such as U2 and sent journalists to report breaking news stories including the murder of Tupac Shakur. I organized the music editorial for* Rolling Stone's Thirtieth Anniversary *issue. I was nominated for a Grammy for liner notes I wrote for a CD collection by '60s political folksinger Phil Ochs. My college honored me as an outstanding alumnus. By 1998, when I was hired to help put the "M" back into MTV, my life had started to spin out of control. I wasn't blasting off anywhere anymore; I was fizzling out on the launchpad, drinking around the clock, and using drugs again. My marriage fell apart. I was unhappy in the world of celebrity television. My lifelong dream was becoming a living nightmare.*

At the dawn of the new millennium, as New York City prepared for the biggest New Year's Eve bash ever, I was holed up in my apartment next to the Chelsea Hotel, where punk rocker Sid Vicious and his girlfriend Nancy Spungen spent their final heroin binge before both died sad, pathetic deaths in 1979. In the previous year, I had overdosed twice and been rushed to the hospital; I'd been arrested for drugs and done several stints in rehab. That night, as the rest of the world celebrated the Y2K, I sat crouched in a corner of my apartment, alone and out of my mind on cocaine, so paranoid

I thought people were outside my window about to burst in and take my drugs. At thirty-nine, I'd become a middle-aged rock & roll cliché.

My folks were worried sick. I'd lost my respected, six-figure-a-year position as a vice president at MTV Networks and was about to lose my home. My friends in the music industry were worried, too. Some of them tried to help but ultimately realized they had no power to do so. If I was to live, it would have to be because I wanted to.

In Nashville on that morning in 2002, my father and I slurped our Blizzards down so far they made gurgling noises when we were done. At some point I sneaked the video camera out of its bag and caught Dad in the act.

"I'm gonna show Mom," I told him, and we laughed for what seemed like an eternity. I never want to forget that moment, because the relationship I developed with my father on the road across the South that spring is what I'd been searching for from rock & roll for most of my life.

While writing my proposal for this book I stumbled on to an album called *Southern Rock Opera* by the ragged, postpunk band Drive-By Truckers. In the three years since I had written my *New York Times* article on the reemergence of young southern rock bands, I knew something interesting was happening again in the South, but it certainly wasn't happening on MTV. When I listened to the story line of *Southern Rock Opera*, it blew my mind. It was as though the writer of these songs had gotten inside of my head—or into my computer—and wrote a musical version of what I'd been thinking about. In the booklet that came with the album, head Trucker Patterson Hood set the milieu:

"It's the summer after high school graduation and our hero hasn't played his guitar in two months. . . . It's 1979. The seventies' last rites are being read by the very same assholes who killed them."

I identified with the protagonist's rage; I graduated high school in 1978.

"By the early eighties," the story continued, "Skynyrd's crowd was being run out of town. There was no place for big, masculine-looking, hairy men with beards and guts and sweat and spit. Not on TV. Sure the hell not on MTV."

I couldn't believe what I was reading.

"Years pass. Our hero moved to the city, then a couple more cities. He got him a funny haircut or two. He became a punk rocker and tried to disassociate himself from his youthful transgressions. Much like so many well-meaning southern people who try to talk down their southern accents for fear of sounding 'too-southern'. . . ."

At the heart of Hood's song cycle is an idea he calls "the duality of the southern thing." In one song on *Southern Rock Opera*, he explains the concept in a scratchy voice that comes off like Paul Westerberg's of the Replacements: "You think I'm dumb, maybe not too bright / You wonder how I sleep at night / Proud of the glory, stare down the shame / It's the duality of the southern thing."

As it turned out, Hood's father is David Hood, the bass player for the legendary Muscle Shoals Rhythm Section, which had backed artists such as Otis Redding and Aretha Franklin in the 1960s. Patterson Hood grew up in Muscle Shoals around his father's music. He was a kid when Lynyrd Skynyrd came through town to record with his dad's partner, Jimmy Johnson, at Muscle Shoals Sound. But while Johnson's son went on to form a southern rock band in the Skynyrd vein, Patterson gravitated to punk. It wasn't until the mid-'90s that Patterson, like me, began to rethink the music and culture that shaped him. At first, his punk-rock friends told him he was nuts.

"People would give me this blank look when I tried to explain what I wanted to do with the album," Patterson said when I caught up with him at his home in Athens, Georgia. "They were like, 'God, that sounds like the worst idea in the world.' "

Southern Rock Opera isn't an opera like *Hair* or *Godspell*, or even the Who's *Tommy* or *Quadrophenia*. It's more of a concept album whose story line relates the fears and struggles of Lynyrd Skynyrd to the fears and struggles of a regular guy who grew up in the South of the 1970s. It was an ambitious project that could have been an embarrassing disaster; instead, it's a masterpiece of storytelling through ragged anthems inspired equally by gritty southern boogie and wailing punk.

The album floored me like no new music had in years. I already knew I wasn't alone in my feelings about my southernness, but the emotional integrity with which Hood tells his stories drove home for me how pervasive these feelings are among southerners of my generation. Hearing it

during the early stages of my writing renewed my energy and commitment. I phoned up my friend David Fricke, a writer for *Rolling Stone*, to see if he knew about the record. We met for lunch and he told me he'd just given the CD a four-star review. During my trek across the South with my dad, I decided to swing through Athens on our way from Macon to Atlanta.

Hood was waiting for me on the front porch when I drove up to his house just after noon on a Monday. He looked like he'd just jumped out of bed. His curly black hair was twisted and knotted, and his eyes had big bags under them. He was wearing a ratty T-shirt, jeans, and a pair of scuffed-up boots. On the steps of the house was an empty Pabst Blue Ribbon beer can. He invited me in, sat me on the couch, and offered me a glass of sweet iced tea.

I told him the gist of my book, and his eyes widened. "That's amazing," he said as Middle Eastern pop music wafted from his stereo. "It must be in the air."

Hood told me he'd been thinking about the topic of southern rock and its impact on us for the past six years. He wanted to make amends to the people of his hometown for a song he wrote when he was a kid in a Muscle Shoals punk band. "You know, the punk-rock thing was a generation gap between me and my dad's people," he said. "Dad didn't like punk rock, but he was more tolerant of it than Jimmy Johnson was. Jimmy was offended by my band."

Patterson had written a song about Muscle Shoals called "Buttholeville," which appeared on Drive-By Truckers' first album, *Gangstabilly*, in 1998. In the song, he expresses contempt for the mythology of his hometown: "Tired of living in Buttholeville / Tired of my job and my wife Lucille, / Tired of my kids Ronnie and Neil, / Tired of my 68 Bonneville, / Tired of working down at Billy Bob's Bar and Grille."

"You know, that song really hurt Jimmy," Patterson said. "To him, I was being a disrespectful little punk who was thumbing my nose at a place he helped to create, a place where all of his dreams had come true. He'd been able to do all this great stuff—play with soul legends, record Skynyrd and the Stones—without ever leaving there."

By the time Patterson and his punk friends had begun to make music, Muscle Shoals was a different place. Southern rock was over; the rush of bands coming to town to record with Aretha Franklin's old session musi-

cians had ended. People were packing up their studios and moving on to Nashville. Punk railed against the old music because the old music had become lame.

"There was a feeling among my friends that those guys had done what they did, and it was wonderful and all, but it was over," said Patterson. "So when we wrote that song, we were just kind of surveying the landscape, what was left of it, and it didn't look too good to us. Jimmy took it very personally. He wouldn't even speak to me for a long time."

Patterson truly loves Jimmy Johnson, and he was sorry he'd hurt him. "I wanted to sort of bridge that gap, I wanted to make peace with Jimmy," he said. "Jimmy's like a relative to me. He and my dad were partners for twenty-some years and he was always a presence in our lives. I felt he had taken my song the wrong way, that he didn't understand where I was coming from. I never meant it as a fuck-you to him, he just heard it that way."

By the early 2000s, Patterson, like me, was feeling that the indie and punk rock of the late '80s and early '90s may have taken its glib irony too far, causing unnecessary pain for people who didn't deserve it. "I mean, there's irony on *Southern Rock Opera*, too, but I don't think it's so extreme that it will turn off people who love southern rock and Lynyrd Skynyrd. I truly love Lynyrd Skynyrd. I hope that comes across."

He paused and glanced out the window, a look of concern on his face. "You know, I haven't talked with the guys in Lynyrd Skynyrd yet, but I will this weekend, because we're actually going to play with Skynyrd. I don't know how that's going to turn out; I hope they understand. I've heard through the grapevine that Gary Rossington didn't really appreciate the album, but I don't know. All I know is that we did it with respect and appreciation."

That much is very clear. Although Drive-By Truckers are not an old-style southern boogie band, their love of the music is written all over the sound and lyrics of *Southern Rock Opera*. When I talked to Johnny Van Zant a year later, Lynyrd Skynyrd had played several shows with the Truckers and Van Zant told me he approved of the band. "Those guys are cool guys," he said. "I think they're coming from the right place. We have the same management company and everything."

The lines had blurred. By the early 2000s, southern rock's biggest booster among music critics was a savvy young African-American writer

named Kandia Crazy Horse, who used her *Village Voice* review of the Kentucky Headhunters' 2003 album, *Soul,* to wax philosophical about the "redemption" of southern rock as well as its noteworthy impact on everything from country to the hip-hop of the rising Dirty South movement of rappers led by the great Atlanta outfits Goodie Mob and OutKast. One of those rappers was a white kid who called himself Bubba Sparxxx. "Unlike the Allmans and Skynyrd, who bore the onus of proving rednecks were not troglodytes," Crazy Horse wrote, "on *Soul* the Kentucky Headhunters easily draw on the rich legacies of Memphis and Muscle Shoals, recasting them for post-Carter freebirds and crunksters both."

Southern rock had indeed been making a comeback in some unlikely places. In 2001, Kid Rock put out *Cocky,* on which the rap-metal star name-checked Lynyrd Skynyrd over pounding hip-hop beats and chunky metal guitar riffs. "I make southern rock," he howled on one track, "and I mix it with the hip-hop." That same year, Sparxxx quietly put out his debut album on the major label Interscope Records. Sparxxx, whose real name is Warren Anderson Mathis, grew up on a dirt road outside LaGrange, Georgia, and had been turned on to rap by a black neighbor. Critics hailed his 2003 follow-up, *Deliverance,* for its organic-sounding blend of hip-hop with acoustic guitars, harmonica, and fiddle. The whole Dirty South hip-hop scene was not unlike what the Allmans, Skynyrd, and Wet Willie had done when they merged the blues and country to create the first wave of southern rock in the early '70s. When Kid Rock returned with a new, self-titled album in 2003, his transition to classic southern rock and country was complete. The new album found the rap-rocker singing duets with Billy Gibbons of ZZ Top, Hank Williams Jr., and Sheryl Crow. Hank Jr.'s son, Hank III, also was moving southern rock in new directions, making bona-fide country albums but performing shows in which he mixed songs that sounded eerily like his legendary grandfather with hard-core punk. Hip young southerners continued to crop up everywhere in rap and rock, from Mississippi rapper David Banner to singer-songwriter Ryan Adams and cool underground rockers such as Kings of Leon and My Morning Jacket. Like it had many times before, the South was doing it again.

★　★　★

Five months after my dad and I returned from our trip through the South, I was back at my apartment in New York, hard at work on this book but in a holding pattern. I needed something but didn't know exactly what. One day, I walked from the apartment in Greenwich Village over to the motorcycle garage in the East Village where I kept my Harley-Davidson. I hopped on the seat, fired up the bike, and drove back home to North Carolina. The only way I could finish this journey was to go back to the South and live there again.

As I headed across Lower Manhattan toward the Holland Tunnel, the bleating and blaring of New York whizzed through my helmet, making the noise of the city I had grown so familiar with seem surreal, like the sound of my blender mixing carrots, apples, and ginger into a pungent, brown-orange juice. When I emerged from the tunnel into New Jersey and headed up to the turnpike, I glanced back for one last look at the Manhattan skyline. It was very different from what I'd seen fifteen years earlier when I first arrived there, fresh-faced and still in my twenties, to find myself working in the industry that manufactured and marketed the music that I loved so much. In 2002, there was no longer a World Trade Center casting its great shadows over Manhattan. The world had changed dramatically in the previous year. By the end of my stay in New York, there was only heartache, much of it of my own making. I was going home again, Thomas Wolfe be damned.

I wasn't quitting; I haven't quit yet and probably never will. I just needed to come back to the source of it all, to figure out what led me on this musical journey in the first place. I realized I couldn't possibly do this story justice without experiencing life in the South on a daily basis again. It was a scary idea. After all, I'd left the South to get away from *its* great shadow. What would I be returning to?

I got a job as the entertainment editor for *The Charlotte Observer*—coincidentally, the same town where W. J. Cash, writer of *The Mind of the South*, had once worked as a journalist. My position at the paper was an interesting one for me. Of all the big cities in the South, Charlotte is least known for its support of gritty southern music. Legend has it that Bill Monroe recorded his first bluegrass songs in Charlotte, but Monroe was from Kentucky. Eighties country star Randy Travis came from the Charlotte area, but he found his success in Nashville. R.E.M. recorded its first album in Charlotte, but only because the band's Winston-Salem

producer knew of a good studio there where gospel artists recorded. Gospel music was huge in Charlotte, but the *Observer's* senior editors seemed unaware of, or disinterested in, the crucial influence of the region's black gospel on post-'50s popular music. In Charlotte, the big stories revolved around the professional football team, the Carolina Panthers, the city's importance as a banking center, and its desire to be seen as a sophisticated southern town with an appreciation for the arts.

In the fifteen years I'd lived away from North Carolina, the population of the Charlotte metropolitan area had shot from about 948,000 to 1.4 million. In 1995, Charlotte overtook San Francisco as the largest banking center in the United States outside of Wall Street. The city's famed love affair with NASCAR had exploded onto the national scene, and Charlotte touted racing's growing sophistication while downplaying its roots as a backwoods southern pastime that began in the '20s and '30s, when moonshiners souped up their cars to outrun the law. Charlotte wanted to retain its southern flavor but polish over the ugly stuff. City officials hyped its high arts and bragged of its multiculturalism. Officials seemed desperate to position Charlotte in a way that would make outsiders view the city as a clean version of New York. I got a sense that Charlotte officials just didn't get what made New York New York, nor what could make Charlotte Charlotte if they'd just relax a little. I found the words for my unease while editing an interview written by one of my reporters. She'd just chatted with a New York–based comic who would be appearing that weekend at a local comedy club.

"You've performed in Charlotte several times before," the reporter asked. "What do you think about our fair city?"

"You have the cleanest downtown I've ever seen," the comedian replied. "Your pigeons must be constipated, there's not even any bird poop."

Truth be told, there weren't even any pigeons. Charlotte was immaculate. Like the set of some '50s movie. It just wasn't natural.

At first, Charlotte's obsession with being seen as a sophisticated lady really bugged me. But after a while, I internalized the city's collective inferiority complex. Charlotte was suffering from growing pains. It was a fast-developing southern metropolis that still wore its small-town insecurities on its sleeve. I began to understand where my own liberal guilt and insecurities came from—they came from right here, seventy miles south

of my hometown. With this realization, I started to forgive both Charlotte and myself. We had grown up together, and growing up wasn't always so easy.

Some things looked very ominous. The month I began my new job at the *Observer*, the Charlotte-Mecklenburg school system was forced to stop its thirty-year social experiment that had ended segregation in the public schools. Robert D. Potter, a judge appointed to the bench by Ronald Reagan, had ruled three years earlier that racial discrimination was over in Charlotte. Despite several appeals, his ruling was upheld by higher courts, and at the beginning of the fall 2002 school year, Charlotte's pioneering antidiscrimination policies were gone.

Potter's decision wasn't out of character. In the late '60s, he had opposed the desegregation of schools, but his opposition couldn't stop the momentum of racial change. By the early '70s, Charlotte had become the poster city for desegregation. Its school busing policy was the model for other southern cities, and Charlotte's reputation as the harbinger of the New South attracted all the new business that made the city what it is today.

Potter's 1999 ruling was a major blow to Charlotte's carefully cultivated reputation, and it sparked an outcry among progressive whites and African-Americans. It looked as if clocks were about to run backward. Others cheered the decision, and seeing who was doing the cheering was an eye-opening experience. It wasn't so much old-style racists; they had little power. What happened is that in the years of new prosperity, scores of wealthy, predominantly white professionals had arrived in town from the Northeast, the Midwest, and the West Coast. To them, busing was a remnant from a bygone period of southern history. They didn't see it as necessary anymore. What they saw was that their children were being bused to parts of the city far from their homes, and they hired an attorney to represent their cause.

Sam Fulwood III, an African-American reporter for the *Los Angeles Times* who grew up in Charlotte, watched the development from three thousand miles away. In an article for his newspaper, Fulwood remembered the impact of busing on his childhood: "Among the first school children bused to integrate the Charlotte-Mecklenburg School District in 1970 was a fourteen-year-old black boy with thick glasses and no idea what awaited him in a white classroom on the other side of town," he

wrote. "As the bus rolled from his west side neighborhood, skirting the glass towers of uptown Charlotte and finally lurching to a stop forty-five minutes later at an east side junior high, he thought of himself as a soldier being mustered into some glorious army to wage war against segregation. . . . That bus ride was one of the most defining moments of my life."

In his article, Fulwood talked with Ron Thompson, the principal of Charlotte's East Mecklenburg High School. "If it hadn't been for busing to desegregate the schools, Charlotte wouldn't be the city it is today," Thompson told him. "The people who brought the recent lawsuit don't see that. They weren't a part of our past. They don't understand our history of struggle. We have allowed them to come into this community and be the prevailing voice. They have nothing to do with who we are and what we've come from."

To Fulwood, the comment was eerie. Thirty years earlier, he wrote, the principal would have been complaining to a white reporter about black parents and outsiders trying to force the issue of busing. Now the principal was complaining to a black reporter about white people coming in and trying to force the *end* of busing.

Other things about Charlotte and the South had not changed at all. Nearly every day the *Observer* received letters to the editor that made reference to liberals (in the negative), racism (either of the "You are" or "I'm not" variety), and the Civil War. When African-American columnists such as Mary Curtis, Tonya Jameson, Fannie Flono, or Eric Frazier mentioned race in their articles (and even when they didn't), many letter writers complained, "All they talk about is race"—a complaint that was so far from the truth it was laughable.

One of the first pieces I wrote for the *Observer* was a commentary on recent inductees into the Rock and Roll Hall of Fame. In it, I asked why, a quarter-century after Lynyrd Skynyrd's plane crashed in Mississippi, the band had been passed over yet again for induction into the hall. I got a few letters from sympathetic readers. One was from a guy who began his comments reasonably enough but then careened into a strange racist tirade. It was disconcertingly reminiscent of viewpoints prevalent during my childhood.

The issue of race was still on the front burner, as was the topic of the Civil War. I was depressed and not just a little disappointed. I assumed

things would have changed more. But then I began to get out and open my eyes. Each day I would walk into the city's downtown area for lunch and see numerous mixed-race couples confidently strolling hand-in-hand down the main drag. Even in the mid-'80s, that wasn't common in North Carolina. Nowadays there are Latinos living all across the state and in positions of power. That didn't exist at all in the South of the 1980s.

Living in the South again has been a bittersweet experience for me. It's helped me to fully come to terms with the music and people of my culture and my relation to it all. I'm not so sure I'll stay, but I'm glad I came back. It was essential to the telling of this story. And it's freed me up to feel love and forgiveness for myself and my culture—the kind of love and forgiveness my father and I shared that morning in Nashville at the end of our journey together through the music of the South.

★ Notes on Sources ★

Dixie Lullaby has been, for me, a work of love—love of music, of modern history and politics, and of the cultural smorgasbord that America is and always has been. I am not a historian or a sociologist, though; I'm a music journalist who has, since the early 1980s, had the privilege of covering a few other beats, too, from cops and courts to local government and even science. But mostly I've reported on popular music and popular culture, interviewing and observing the people who create, produce, and market what we hear on the radio and see on television, and trying to make some sense of it. This book is based on my personal experiences as an editor, reporter, and music critic, and as a southerner who just happened to grow up in a particularly interesting place during a particularly interesting time.

Some of the reporting in this book comes from stories I've done over the years for *Option, Rolling Stone, The New York Times, The Charlotte Observer,* the *Times-News* of Burlington, North Carolina, *L.A. Weekly, The Spectator Magazine* of Raleigh, North Carolina, and the book *Rolling Stone: The Seventies.* The majority of my reporting, however, comes from interviews I did specifically for this book while on the road with my father in spring 2002, when I traveled from my then-home in New York City to my hometown of Asheboro, North Carolina; then to Macon, Athens, and Atlanta, Georgia; Muscle Shoals, Alabama; Nashville, Tennessee; and several crossroads in between. What I didn't get on that journey, I got on subsequent trips to Jacksonville, Florida, and to Memphis; at rock clubs around North Carolina after I moved back home; from phone interviews and general conversations with folks in stores; at lunch counters, and at *The Charlotte Observer.*

While *Dixie Lullaby* is foremost a *story* told by a journalist, based on his experiences and observations, I could never have written it without help from other journalists whose work supplied me with observations by people I wasn't able to speak with; from historians, sociologists, and political theorists whose insights helped to strengthen or modify my ideas about the South; from librarians and archivists who sent me information and verified facts for me over the phone and via e-mail; and from family members and friends, whose recollections helped jog my own memories of people and events. Four books and one album stand out as huge inspirations for me: *Mystery Train: Images of America in Rock 'n' Roll Music,* by Greil Marcus; *Sweet Soul Music: Rhythm and Blues and the Southern Dream of Freedom,* by Peter Guralnick;

Dixie: A Personal Odyssey Through Events That Shaped the Modern South, by Curtis Wilkie; *Dixie Rising: How the South Is Shaping American Values, Politics, and Culture*, by Peter Applebome; and the concept album *Southern Rock Opera*, by Patterson Hood and his amazing band, Drive-By Truckers.

Although I have a vast knowledge of popular-music history, it's not infallible. So I checked and cross-referenced general historical facts about music and artists with several reference books, chiefly *The Rolling Stone Encyclopedia of Rock & Roll (Third Edition)*, edited by Holly George-Warren and Patricia Romanowski; *The Encyclopedia of Country Music*, edited by Paul Kingsbury; *The Billboard Book of Top 40 Hits* and other Billboard reference materials by Joel Whitburn; the All Music Guide's wealth of music information on the Web, www.allmusic.com; and my personal collection of about ten thousand albums and CDs. Two other indispensable reference books were the colossal, 1,634-page *Encyclopedia of Southern Culture*, by Charles Reagan Wilson and William Ferris, and the entertaining (and immanently useful) *1001 Things Everyone Should Know About the South*, by John Shelton Reed and Dale Volberg Reed. Any errors that may have slipped between the cracks are my own doing.

Because of the wide variety of sources used in *Dixie Lullaby*, I have chosen not to provide formal footnotes; that would wrongly imply that this is a scholarly work. Instead, I've opted to acknowledge my sources in a more informal, chapter-by-chapter manner. Wherever I have used direct quotes that are not widely known or that I didn't get firsthand, I have made every attempt to supply specific citations for them.

PREFACE

To help me bring to life my early childhood in Asheboro, I looked to several sources, the most important of which were my parents. I had long conversations with my mom and dad, who helped me with time frames and reminded me of the names of people, their personalities, and their dignity. I couldn't have painted an accurate picture of my elementary school and the educational system in my hometown without the help of Ross Holt, a librarian at the Asheboro Public Library whose family lived next door to mine when we were growing up. The daily reporting on desegregation by my hometown newspaper, *The Courier-Tribune*, was key to my understanding of the time line for decisions that were being made when I was a kid still learning to read. Also indispensable were my readings of the 1954 Supreme Court case *Brown v. Board of Education* (which can be found at the Web site www.nps.gov/brvb/pages/thecase.htm), and the Civil Rights Act of 1964 (usinfo.state.gov/usa/infousa/laws/majorlaw/civilr19.htm).

The section on the sense of community that southern rock created for young southerners in the early 1970s comes from an essay I wrote for the July 5, 1998, Sunday *New York Times* entitled "Coming Home to a New Strain of Southern Rock." I give much credit for the success of that piece to *Times* arts editor Fletcher Roberts, who helped me streamline my prose, and whose different perspective on the early seventies gave the piece a depth of insight it otherwise would have lacked.

Finally, no one can begin a thoughtful look at the South and its peculiarities without reading Wilbur J. Cash's *The Mind of the South* (with edification from Bertram Wyatt-Brown's new Introduction) and C. Vann Woodward's *The Burden of Southern History*. Any sense of humanity I may have brought to this writing should be credited

to my rereading of Thomas Wolfe's *You Can't Go Home Again*. (I hope my fate is not like that of Wolfe's character, the writer George Webber, who was startled to find that his friends were offended by his depictions of his hometown—although I realize that a writer has no power over the thoughts and feelings his stories may trigger in other people.) Each of these works served as crucial sources for my understanding of myself and my culture, not just in the Preface of *Dixie Lullaby*, but throughout the book.

INTRODUCTION

Peter Guralnick's excellent *Last Train to Memphis: The Rise of Elvis Presley* provided the background on Elvis Presley. The information about late-'40s and early-'50s popular music comes from a variety of sources, mainly Charlie Gillett's *The Sound of the City* and Brian Ward's *Just My Soul Responding*. Jerry Wexler's comment about recording black music in the late '40s comes from *Just My Soul Responding* (p. 29); the origin of the quote is a *Billboard* magazine interview from January 13, 1958 (he was referring to Stick McGhee's 1949 Atlantic Records single, "Drinkin' Wine Spo-Dee-O-Dee"). The Niki Sullivan quote, likewise, comes from the Ward book, but its origin is the Buddy Holly biography *Remembering Buddy*, by J. Goldrosen and J. Beecher (pp. 47–8).

The capsule history of guitars and banjos comes from various sources, including José L. Romanillos's exhaustive guitar reference, *Vihuela de Mano and the Spanish Guitar* (with Marian Harris Winspear) and Cecelia Conway's *African Banjo Echoes in Appalachia: A Study of Folk Traditions*.

The quotes from Bill Wyman of the Rolling Stones come from an interview he did with a local TV news crew following the publication of his book *Bill Wyman's Blues Odyssey: A Journey to Music's Heart & Soul*. (A few months after I transcribed that interview on Wyman's Web site via a link to the television channel, I returned to retrieve the information so I could credit the producers; unfortunately, the link had been eliminated. My sincere apologies to the producers of that interview; thank you, whoever you are.) Other references to early rock's time line from the fifties to the British Invasion of the sixties and its influence on early southern rock were culled from Robert Palmer's *Rock & Roll: An Unruly History*; Joe Nick Patoski's chapter on southern rock in *The Rolling Stone Illustrated History of Rock & Roll*, and Marley Brant's *Southern Rockers: The Roots and Legacy of Southern Rock*.

CHAPTER 1

The story of the assassination of Martin Luther King Jr. and its effect on music and the civil rights movement of the1960s is a combination of historical facts and my interpretation of them. The facts come from several sources, including the Martin Luther King Jr. Papers Project at Stanford University (www.stanford.edu/group/King) and the King Center Web site (www.thekingcenter.com); Stephen B. Oates's biography, *Let the Trumpet Sound: A Life of Martin Luther King, Jr.*; King's *Where Do We Go from Here: Chaos or Community?*; Malcolm X's *The Autobiography of Malcolm X*; and Louis E. Lomax's fascinating analysis of the two prime civil rights activists of the period, *To Kill a Black Man: The Shocking Parallel in the Lives of Malcolm X and Martin Luther King Jr.* Statistics on violence during the civil rights years come from the federal government–sponsored Kerner Commission's *Report of the National Advisory Commission on Civil Disorders* (March 1, 1968). Booker T. Jones's quote

about the mood at Memphis's Stax Records around the time of the King assassination comes from Guralnick's *Sweet Soul Music* (p. 355).

The details of what went on in my hometown in the days surrounding the King assassination come from a series of articles and editorials written in *The Courier-Tribune* of Asheboro between April 1 and April 10, 1968. I cross-referenced those accounts with articles from the nearby *Greensboro Daily News* during the same period. I couldn't have gotten the tenor of those times right, however, without talking at length with people of both races from my hometown, including Sandy Grey, Martin Nicholson, my grade school teacher Linda Isbell and her husband, Harold, and members of my family. I checked my recollections of songs that played on the radio in my hometown that summer with my parents and sister, but I also cross-referenced them with *The Billboard Book of Top 40 Hits* and *The Encyclopedia of Country Music*.

All of the anecdotes of Mac "Dr. John" Rebennack in this chapter come from my conversations with him in New York, but some of the background material on him also comes from his autobiography, *Under a Hoodoo Moon: The Life of Dr. John the Night Tripper*, including the direct quote from his grandfather ("Hoodoo Moon," p. 4).

CHAPTER 2

For details about the Atlanta Memorial Park, I looked to the Buckhead neighborhood Web site www.buckhead.net/parks/atlanta-memorial. I culled the historical information on the Battle of Peachtree Creek from numerous sources, including *Atlanta Will Fall*, by Stephen Davis; Shelby Foote's beautifully written trilogy, *The Civil War: A Narrative*; and two accounts from guys who were actually there: Union Major General Jacob D. Cox's *Sherman's Battle for Atlanta (Campaigns of the Civil War)* and Confederate soldier Sam R. Watkins's *Co. Aytch: A Confederate's Memoir of the Civil War*. The grand architecture of the Georgia State Capitol Building is something to behold; for details, I consulted the Georgia secretary of state's capitol guide at www.sos.state.ga.us/capitolguide.

There's been so much written on the colorful Lester Maddox that it's hard to know where to get the facts. For biographical information, the best source is Bob Short's *Everything Is Pickrick*, but that book, while thorough, is more sympathetic than most accounts. For an opposing view I looked to Hal Jacob's insightful article "Lester! The Strange but True Tale of Georgia's Unlikeliest Governor," from the Atlanta alternative weekly *Creative Loafing* (March 20, 1999). The direct quotes from my visit with Maddox when I was eight years old may not be word-for-word precise, but they're what my father and I remember him saying.

So far, the only full account of the Allman Brothers Band's story is Scott Freeman's *Midnight Riders*, which presents a balance of music, cultural history, and the scandals surrounding the band. I shied away from much of the infighting between original Allman Brothers manager Phil Walden and the band because it was not relevant to the group's impact on my friends and me, the culture of the South, or the period of southern history this book addresses. Still, the Freeman book provided a wealth of information for this section and other sections of *Dixie Lullaby*, as did my interviews with Walden and original Hourglass members (who were also Capricorn Records producers and players) Johnny Sandlin and Paul Hornsby.

The quote from Gregg Allman about his late brother, Duane, comes from a won-

derful story that writer/director Cameron Crowe wrote for *Rolling Stone* when he was just fifteen years old: "The Allman Brothers Story" (December 6, 1973, p. 54). The quote from Allman's letter to Crowe comes from Crowe's Web site, The Uncool (www.cameroncroweonline.com). I found that the honesty, idealism, passion, and enthusiasm of Crowe's take on the band made up for a terribly cynical piece by Grover Lewis that *Rolling Stone* published at the time of Duane Allman's death. A portion of my description of the Allmans' live album *At Fillmore East* comes from a review I wrote for *Rolling Stone*. Other parts of this chapter, particularly the scenes with my sister in the early 1970s, are based on a chapter I wrote for the book *Rolling Stone: The Seventies*.

The details about George Wallace come from Dan Carter's *The Politics of Rage*, as well as from a PBS *American Experience* episode, "George Wallace: Settin' the Woods on Fire," and its supplemental materials found at www.pbsvideodb.pbs.org.

CHAPTER 3

Patricia Goddard's story about her nightmarish childhood experience as a fundraiser for racist David Duke seems to check out in *The Rise of David Duke*, by Pulitzer prize–winning reporter Tyler Bridges, who once worked for *The Times-Picayune* of New Orleans. According to Bridges, the cops had long been on to Duke's questionable fund-raising activities. He and three others were arrested in 1972, the year after the incident Goddard described, for allegedly raising five hundred dollars for George Wallace's presidential campaign. Though Duke was accused of pocketing the money, the charges against him were dropped after a powerful friend persuaded the Wallace campaign to change its story about the incident.

The lengthy passages from writer Stanley Booth come from his groundbreaking book of rock writing, *The True Adventures of the Rolling Stones* (pp. 56–57). When I read this book at twenty-four, I not only identified with Booth's perspective as a southerner, but I wished I had been in his shoes during those crazy days of sixties rock & roll, before armies of publicists and MTV made spontaneity nearly impossible for music journalists. The Booth book is not just journalism, though; it's literature. And it remains, without a doubt, the best book ever written about a rock band.

The Eric Clapton quote about Duane Allman comes from Michael Schumacher's biography of Clapton, *Crossroads: The Life and Music of Eric Clapton*. The Duane Allman quote from *Guitar Player* about his first meeting with Clapton comes from the liner notes to the Allman Brothers box set, *Dreams*.

What limited knowledge I've offered about New Orleans in this chapter comes from my visits there, supplemented by a variety of sources ranging from the fun (*Frommer's Irreverent Guide to New Orleans*) and the practical (*The Unofficial Guide to New Orleans*) to the serious: Arnold Hirsch and Joseph Logsdon's *Creole New Orleans*; Adam Fairclough's *Race and Democracy: The Civil Rights Struggle in Louisiana*; Peter Kolchin's *American Slavery: 1619–1877*; and the Web site of the Louisiana State Museum (http://lsm.crt.state.la.us) and "The History of Jim Crow" (www.jimcrowhistory.org). The detail on the city's murder rate comes from reporter Michael Perlstein's New Orleans crime update, "Making His Marc: Crime Crackdown the Defining Issue of Moria's Tenure," in *The Times-Picayune* (October 9, 2001).

Details in this chapter about Duane and Gregg Allman's troubled childhood

come from *Midnight Riders*. Information about Ronnie Hawkins comes from a long, rambling phone conversation I had with the big-talking rockabilly cat in 2002, with additional details from his Web site, http://www.pipcom.com/fismthehawk. Additional information on him and the Band comes from Greil Marcus's *Mystery Train*.

I learned about Ella May Wiggins and the Gastonia strike of 1929 after moving back home to North Carolina and visiting the Levine Museum of the New South in Charlotte, where I met and had lunch with historian Tom Hanchett. I had read about and heard about Wiggins and the strike since I was in my teens and first discovered Woody Guthrie, but the Levine Museum filled me in on just how heroic she was.

CHAPTER 4

The specific details on the cop-shooting at the outdoor concert in Charlotte come from reports in *The Charlotte Observer* from July 14 and 15, 1974, by several reporters, including Nancy Brachey, who was still at the paper when I arrived there nearly thirty years later. (Thanks Nancy!) The rest comes from my memory and recent talks with my friends Chip and Tim Womick. The first line of the chapter (following the introductory anecdote) was inspired by Hunter S. Thompson's great *Fear and Loathing in Las Vegas*.

Most of the information on Lynyrd Skynyrd in this chapter comes from my conversations with the band's former guitarist Ed King, original manager Alan Walden, current singer Johnny Van Zant, and the late Ronnie Van Zant's friend and confidant Charlie Daniels. But many other sources were essential: The quote from the review of Skynyrd's first album comes from the December 1973 *Creem* magazine, and the quote about *Second Helping* comes from a 1974 *Billboard* review. Al Kooper's comments about Skynyrd come from his grumpy book, *Backstage Passes & Backstabbing Bastards: Memoirs of a Rock 'N Roll Survivor*. The quote about the young Ronnie Van Zant comes from his father Lacy's self-published *The Van-Zant Family: Southern Music Scrap Book*. I also got a wealth of information from stories in *Rolling Stone*; as well as Marley Brant's *Southern Rockers* and *Freebirds: The Lynyrd Skynyrd Story*; Gene Odom's *Lynyrd Skynyrd: Remembering the Free Birds of Southern Rock*; and Lee Ballinger's *Lynyrd Skynyrd: An Oral History*.

CHAPTER 5

Thanks to the All Music Guide's movie Web site (www.allmovie.com) for refreshing my memory of the lost B movie *Killers Three*. (An interesting note, given the nature of this chapter, which revolves around the difficulties suffered by my gay friend Jeff Brown, whose band rehearsed where that film was made: Bruce Kessler, the director of *Killers Three*, followed this flop with *The Gay Deceivers*, an irreverent, 1969 comedy about two guys who pretend to be homosexual to avoid the draft.) Historical information about the textile mills of Coleridge and Randolph County come from documents in the local research room of the Asheboro Public Library.

The 1976 quote from Ronnie Van Zant about Neil Young comes from a British radio interview I heard online. The interview was authentic, because I recognized the voices as being those of Van Zant and the other members of Lynyrd Skynyrd; unfortunately, there was no documentation of the interview's source. In the interview, Van Zant clearly compares Young's wholesale criticism of southerners to "shooting all the dogs because some had the flu." However, a *Rolling Stone* story by Tom Dupree in October 1974 quotes him as saying, "We thought Neil was shooting all the ducks in

order to kill one or two." I chose to go with the "dogs" quote because it makes more sense; I believe the *Rolling Stone* writer may have inadvertently misquoted Van Zant.

Historical info on Georgetown and Myrtle Beach, South Carolina, comes from Catherine Heniford Lewis's *Horry County, South Carolina: 1730–1993* and the Web site of the Myrtle Beach Chamber of Commerce, (www.myrtlebeach info.com/cvb/visit/rea_history.asp). Details on the shag dance style come from Bo Bryan's *Shag: The Legendary Dance of the South* as well as from other versions of shag history on enthusiast Web sites and in newspaper stories, including "Shagging vs. Clogging: Which One Really Gets Your Tar Heels Moving" (*The Charlotte Observer*, February 23, 1991) by my friend and colleague Dean Smith.

In the section on Watergate, Hunter Thompson's reference to John Dean as "a crafty little ferret" comes from p. 19 of *The Great Shark Hunt*; his description of Jimmy Carter as a "good ole boy" comes on p. 368 of *Fear and Loathing: On the Campaign Trail '72*; and the line "Yahoo Republicans and Redneck Southern Democrats" comes from p. 295 of *The Great Shark Hunt*.

CHAPTER 6

The history of disco as a social movement was culled from various sources, including an early report in *Rolling Stone*, "Discotheque Rock '72: Paaaaarty!" (September 13, 1973), by pioneering dance-music writer Vince Aletti, and Bill Brewster and Frank Broughton's eye-opening *Last Night a DJ Saved My Life: The History of the Disc Jockey*. For information on the Stonewall uprising, I looked to Martin Duberman's *Stonewall*, and to my good friend Jim Fouratt, a music historian and important political and gay-rights activist from the Stonewall days to the present. (Jim, you're the best!)

For the history of the Philadelphia Sound, I looked to another *Rolling Stone* article by Aletti, "Dancing Madness" (August 28, 1975), as well as the copious liner notes in the extraordinary three-CD Epic box set *The Philly Sound: Kenny Gamble, Leon Huff & the Story of Brotherly Love (1966–1976)*, by a who's who of dance-music experts including David Ritz, Carol Cooper, Barry Walters, Vernon Gibbs, and Brian Chin.

Jimmy Carter's quote about ending discrimination in Georgia comes from his first speech as the state's new governor, delivered January 12, 1971, after his defeat of Republican Hal Suit. His quote about liking Bob Dylan and the Allman Brothers comes from Kandy Stroud's *How Jimmy Won* (p. 148). The comments about Carter from Dickey Betts and Gregg Allman come from Freeman's *Midnight Riders* (p. 209), as does much of the other information in this chapter about the Allmans' relationship with Carter, and Gregg Allman's drug saga and relationship with Cher.

Information on the Rolling Stones' 1975 tour stop in Greensboro comes from two clippings from *The Greensboro Daily News* ("Stones Concert Packs Coliseum," by Brent Hackney, and "How the Town Went Bananas over Mick Jagger," by Charles Trueheart) and actual notes I took after the concert (I wasn't yet a reporter at fifteen), all of which I've saved in an old book on the group since 1975.

CHAPTER 7

The anecdote about my friends and me learning of the 1977 Lynyrd Skynyrd plane crash appeared in a slightly different form in the book *Rolling Stone: The Seventies*.

Info on the Carter inaugural and John Lennon and Yoko Ono's appearance there

comes from a variety of sources, including a shot of the couple taken that night with boxer Muhammad Ali by photographer Wally McNamee/CORBIS. The Linda Ronstadt quote about the inaugural comes from the *Time* magazine cover story "Linda Down the Wind" (February 28, 1977). Thanks to William Powers for the round-up of media quotes about presidential inaugurations in his funny (but conservative-leaning) commentary "Seven Rules of Inaugural Coverage: When a President is inaugurated, a funny thing happens to most media people. They turn soft and gooey. They act a lot like Larry King," from *The National Journal* (January 19, 2001). Comments from Cher about her experiences with Gregg Allman at the White House around the time of the inaugural come from Kevin Sessums's 1990 *Vanity Fair* cover story, "Cher: Her News, Her Blues, Her Six Tattoos."

Details about Jimmy Carter's successes and struggles as president come from a range of sources, including William Lee Miller's *Yankee from Georgia: The Emergence of Jimmy Carter,* Kandy Stroud's *How Jimmy Won,* Burton Kaufman's *The Presidency of James Earl Carter, Jr.,* and the former president's own *Turning Point: A Candidate, a State, and a Nation Come of Age; Keeping Faith: Memoirs of a President*; and *The Blood of Abraham: Insights into the Middle East.* Additional information was culled from the Carter Library Web site (www.jimmycarterlibrary.org), the Carter Center Web site (www.cartercenter.org), and *Rolling Stone: The Seventies.* (I got the Hamilton Jordan quote from his essay in that book on page 191, "On Walking to the White House").

The president's comment on the press's treatment of his family comes from *Keeping Faith.* I got Lillian Carter's comments on "dressed-up" northerners from a link on the PBS series *The American President* (www.americanpresident.org), in a section called "Presidential Moments" related to the Carter segment ("Jimmy Carter: 1977–81: The Outsider"). The anecdote about Lillian Carter's visit from a nasty *Washington Post* reporter comes from a speech that former Carter press secretary Jody Powell gave in 1986 to students at the University of Tennessee. Thanks a million to Carter Library archivist Keith J. Shuler, who was kind enough to supply me with a pile of documents pertaining to the former president's relationship with Walden and southern music notables. The correspondences between Carter and Walden come from the Carter Presidential Papers, White House Central File—Name File, "Walden, Philip M." In this chapter, I quote from documents dated April 15, 1977; June 15, 1977; and July 5 and 25, 1977.

Information about the Reagan campaign's deal making with the Iranians comes from an April 15, 1991, *New York Times* editorial, "The Election Story of the Decade," by Gary Sick, National Security Council Middle East adviser for presidents Ford, Carter, and Reagan. Sick followed that editorial with an in-depth book about the Iranian deal, *October Surprise: America's Hostages in Iran and the Election of Ronald Reagan.*

The quotes from pop anthropologist and new-age pioneer Carlos Castaneda and his shaman don Juan come from pages 2 and 34 of *The Teachings of Don Juan:A Yaqui Way of Knowledge.* The book of protest music in which I first discovered Phil Ochs's antiwar ballad "Draft Dodger Rag" is Tom Glazer's *Songs of Peace, Freedom and Protest* (p. 92).

I used statements from Lee Ballinger's *Lynyrd Skynyrd: An Oral History* to show the revisionist characterizations of Ronnie Van Zant, but arguments suggesting Van

Zant was a closet liberal have been repeated in many other books and essays. I found the figure on mid-'70s African-American support for George Wallace in a September 5, 1991, article in *The Washington Post*, "The Rehabilitation of George Wallace," by Carl T. Rowan. He cites a 1974 poll commissioned by the *Birmingham News* and University of Alabama showing 74 percent of blacks considered Wallace "the best governor the state ever had." The quote about Drive-By Truckers' *Southern Rock Opera* comes from writer Roni Sarig's review of the album, "Exhuming the Ghosts of Southern Rock," in the Atlanta weekly *Creative Loafing* (September 26, 2001).

CHAPTER 8

Much of the background info on R.E.M. comes from stories I've written on the band over the years, but several books filled in my blank spots, including *R.E.M. Inside Out: The Stories Behind Every Song*, by Craig Rosen; *Talk About the Passion: An Oral History*, by Denise Sullivan; and *An R.E.M. Companion: It Crawled from the South*, by Marcus Gray. The quotes from Peter Buck and Michael Stipe about why R.E.M. chose to record in North Carolina come from an article by Parke Puterbaugh, "R.E.M.'s Southern Rock Revival," in *Rolling Stone* (June 9, 1983). Bill Berry's and Mike Mills's comments on their pre-R.E.M. days come from Gray's *It Crawled from the South* (p. 22).

In the section on Elvis Costello, the British rocker's account of the drunken bar-room argument that led to his offensive remarks about Ray Charles comes from a Nick Kent magazine article: "Murder on the Liverpool Express: Nick Kent Takes a Train. E. Costello Takes the Strain," (*New Musical Express*, June 9, 1979). Costello's subsequent apology and rationalization for the incident come from Greil Marcus's interview with the rocker in *Rolling Stone* (September 2, 1982). I found the Ray Charles quote, in which he forgives Costello, in the Brian Hinton book *Elvis Costello: Let Them All Talk* (p. 151).

I took Costello's comments on his experiences in Nashville from liner notes he wrote for a reissued version of his 1981 album *Almost Blue* (Rykodisc, 1993). The *Rolling Stone* review of the album was written by Martha Hume and appeared in the December 10, 1981, issue. The Robert Christgau review appeared in his *Village Voice* "Consumer Guide" column (November 30, 1981).

The numbers of African-American-elected officials from the '60s to the '80s come from the public policy report "Reaffirmation or Requiem for the Voting Rights Act? The Court Will Decide," released by the American Civil Liberties Union (May 1995). Four recent books—all great resources for politics junkies—helped me to characterize the shifting nature of the two dominant American political parties: Lewis Gold's *Grand Old Party: A History of the Republicans*; Jules Witcover's *Party of the People: A History of the Democrats*; Kari Frederickson's *The Dixiecrat Revolt and the End of the Solid South, 1932–1968*; and Earle and Merle Black's *The Rise of Southern Republicans*.

To get an idea of how the Christian right gained power just prior to the Reagan years, I looked to three books: Dinesh D'Souza's *Falwell: Before the Millennium*, William Martin's *With God on Our Side*, and Sara Diamond's *Spiritual Warfare*. I also had lengthy conversations with my friend Jeff Brown about the tactics of the born-again movement on a smaller, church-by-church level. (In the early 1980s, Jeff joined the Assemblies of God sect of the Pentecostal church and for about a decade

lived as a born-again Christian. He came out of the closet in the mid-nineties, at which time he felt compelled to leave the church.) Additionally, out of a personal intrigue with televangelists since I was a teenager, I periodically watch them on TV and browse fundamentalist Web sites to look into their current methods, ideologies, and politics.

My ideas about formerly left-leaning baby boomers being partly responsible for the rise of Reagan come from conversations I've had with old friends whose politics have turned rightward as they've begun to shoulder more day-to-day responsibilities. Three books by a couple of prominent ex–sixties radicals offered even more insight into this phenomenon: *Destructive Generation: Second Thoughts About the '60s*, by Peter Collier and David Horowitz; *Radical Son: A Generational Odyssey*, by David Horowitz; and *Second Thoughts: Former Radicals Look Back at the Sixties*, a volume of essays, edited by Collier and Horowitz, which includes testimonials by twenty other former radicals.

Ronald Reagan's quote about Bruce Springsteen comes from a speech he made on September 9, 1984, at a Reagan-Bush rally in Hammonton, New Jersey; the full text can be found at the Ronald Reagan Presidential Library Web site (www.reagan.utexas.edu). The quote from George Will's review of Springsteen comes from his syndicated column of September 14, 1984. Within months of Reagan and Will's rather cavalier support of Springsteen, *Rolling Stone* rolled out the "Perception vs. Reality" ad campaign I allude to in this chapter, which capitalized on the sort of misperceptions that led to Reagan's infamous Springsteen comment. The ad campaign juxtaposed the trappings of stereotypical *Rolling Stone* readers (psychedelic clothing, a VW microbus) against '80s designer products (business suits, a BMW) on opposing pages. The campaign worked like a charm, and *Rolling Stone* prospered; but in the process the magazine forever lost the level of credibility and cultural impact it once had, and the stage was set for the rise of edgier and more up-to-date youth-culture publications such as *Spin* and *Vibe*.

The quotes from Michael Stipe backstage in Greensboro in 1984 come from an article I wrote for the *Times-News* of Burlington, North Carolina ("R.E.M., a Favorite Band in This Area, Returns for Concert," August 2, 1984). The quotes from Jefferson Holt come from another piece I wrote for that paper (" 'Jefferson, I Think We're Lost': Burlington Native Jefferson Holt Manages Rock Band R.E.M.," June 5, 1985). For another view of the richness of southern imagery in R.E.M.'s music, I looked to Phillip L. Beard's essay " 'Can't Get There from Here': R.E.M.'s Early Indiscernibility," from *Crossroads: A Journal of Southern Culture* (vol. 5, no. 2, spring 1998), published by the Center for the Study of Southern Culture at the University of Mississippi, Oxford.

The mid-'80s quotes from Steve Dubner and Jeff Foster of the Right Profile are from an interview I did with the band for a story that never ran. The more recent remarks from Dubner are from an interview I did with him specifically for this book, in early 2004. Hope Nicholls and Aaron Pitkin of the band Fetchin Bones spoke with me for an *Option* magazine story I wrote on the band: "Charlotte Ruse: The Tricky Tunes of N.C.'s Fetchin' Bones" (May/June 1988).

The background on Tom Petty and the Heartbreakers comes from a variety of music references including *The Rolling Stone Encyclopedia of Rock & Roll*. The quote from Robert Christgau's review of Petty's *Southern Accents* album comes from

Christgau's "Consumer Guide" column in *The Village Voice* (June 25, 1985). I got Petty's direct quotes from Bob Hilburn's *Los Angeles Times* piece "Tom Petty Tries His Hand at Southern Rock" (March 31, 1985).

CHAPTER 9

The sales figures for the Kentucky Headhunters' *Pickin' on Nashville* comes from two news stories: "Headhunters Rock Out on 'Ranch,' " by Ray Waddell (*Billboard*, July 3, 2000); and "Kentucky Headhunters Keep Rollin'," by Hugh Hart (*Chicago Tribune*, August 11, 1994). The background on the band comes from my interviews with Richard and Fred Young plus information on the band's Web site (www.ken tuckyheadhunters.com). Details about Metcalfe County, the Sulphur Well community, and the Beula Villa Hotel come from the Kentucky Historical Society Web site (www.history.ky.gov). Sales figures for the Georgia Satellites and Bon Jovi come from a wire story, "Richie Eyeing Beatle 'Record,' " by Scott Doggett (United Press International, February 12, 1987).

For the section on Steve Earle, Dwight Yoakam, and the so-called "smart country" movement, I looked to several sources, including Lauren St. John's Earle biography, *Hardcore Troubadour: The Life & Near Death of Steve Earle*; Bob Hilburn's interviews with Earle and Yoakam in the *Los Angeles Times* and Jack Hurst's "Getting Smarter: Better-Educated Performers Opening Up Country" in the *Chicago Tribune* (September 14, 1986). Steve Earle's comments on his family's attitudes regarding race come from *Hardcore Troubadour* (p. 34), as does his quote about his peers' views on hair length (p. 37). Other direct quotes by Earle come from Hilburn's early interview with the singer in the *Los Angeles Times* ("Steve Earle: Working-Class Songs from the Texas Soil," July 20, 1986). The sales and chart figures for *Guitar Town* come from Wade Jessen's "Country Corner" column in *Billboard* (June 24, 2000) and *Rolling Stone*'s "500 Greatest Albums of All Time" (December 11, 2003). Dwight Yoakam's background info comes from various sources, including VH1's Web site bio (www.vh1.com) and Holly George-Warren's passionately written liner notes to the box set *Reprise Please Baby: The Warner Bros. Years* (Rhino Records, 2002).

Most of the quotes from Warren Haynes come from interviews we did at the Bonnaroo Festival and over the phone, but one quote—about Haynes's father— comes from Tony Kiss's story in the *Asheville Citizen-Times*, "Warren Haynes Is Home for Christmas: After Years of Touring with the 'Biggies,' His Annual Christmas Jam Is Bigger than Ever" (December 17, 1999).

Phil Walden's comments on hitting rock bottom with alcohol and drugs comes from two stories in *The Atlanta Journal-Constitution*: "Capricorn: Phil Walden Tries Charting a New Course with Reborn Record Label," by Steve Dollar (November 26, 1991) and "Signs Right for Capricorn Records," by Maria Saporta (March 22, 1999). Some of the information on Walden's financial losses comes from Roni Sarig's cover story "Ramblin Clan," in *Creative Loafing* of Atlanta (July 25, 2001).

I gleaned the information on the 1988 presidential campaign and the first Bush years from a pile of reports in *Time, Newsweek, The Washington Post, The New York Times*, the *Los Angeles Times*, the *Chicago Tribune*, AP wire stories, and other sources that I got from doing Nexis searches.

At the end of the long section on the Kentucky Headhunters is a comment from

singer Doug Phelps on why his band appeals to country fans. That quote comes from an *Orlando Sentinel* story, "In Every Way, Headhunters Stand Out in the Crowd," by Parry Gettelman (October 5, 1990). Michael Stipe's comments in the last section of this chapter come from an interview I did with him for an *Option* magazine cover story, "What Are Friends For? Michael Stipe Supports His Pals" (Sept./Oct 1990).

CHAPTER 10

The opening anecdote about Chris Robinson of the Black Crowes comes from a recording of an interview I did with him for an article that appeared in *L.A. Weekly* in late 1992. I don't have a clue whether the quotes I've used here appeared in that story, because I don't have a copy of that story in my files. However, the quotes in this chapter were transcribed from my old tape of our confrontation that day. Other quotes in this section from Chris and Rich Robinson come from Kim Neely's *Rolling Stone* story "As the Crowes Fly: A Real Rock Band Wings Its Way to the Upper Regions of the Charts" (January 24, 1991).

Writer Gina Arnold's view of Nirvana's success in terms of punk-rock victory over mediocrity comes from her book *Route 666: On the Road to Nirvana* (p. 4), but her original so-called "We won" essay appeared in *Spin* magazine. The description of Kurt Cobain's hometown of Aberdeen, Washington, as a "redneck logging community" comes from Chris Mundy's story "Nirvana Spill Blood in Europe: Band Puts the Danger Back in Rock" in *Rolling Stone* (January 23, 1992).

Much of my discussion of the "politically correct" movement of the late '80s and early '90s comes from a series of essays in the book *Debating P.C.: The Controversy over Political Correctness on College Campuses*. Editor Paul Berman describes the history of PC in his introduction, "The Debate and Its Origins." The details on the "Nappy Hair" controversy come from numerous reports on the incident, chiefly an Associated Press story, "Black Writer Defends Her 'Nappy Hair,'" by Timothy Williams (December 9, 1998). Similarly, the details on the controversy over the term "niggardly" come from a variety of sources, mainly Sherry Jones's report in the Wilmington *Morning Star*, "Teacher Reprimanded for Word Choice" (September 4, 2002). The quote from Eric Frazier comes from his column in *The Charlotte Observer*, "If We Run from History, We Lose Its Many Lessons" (May 25, 2002).

My description of the Jeff Foxworthy video and his quotes come from Foxworthy's "Redneck Games," a track on a DVD included in his album *The Best of Jeff Foxworthy: Double Wide Single Minded* (Rhino Records, 2003). Background info on Foxworthy comes from All Music Guide's Web site (www.allmusic.com). The Lewis Grizzard quote comes from "The Official Lewis Grizzard Web Site" (www.lewisgrizard.com).

The information on David Duke's brief fling with the political mainstream (before he was hauled off to prison for mail fraud and tax evasion) comes from Tyler Bridges's *The Rise of David Duke*. I got the details on his fraud convictions from a report in *The Postal Bulletin*, the publication of the United States Postal Services: "David Duke Sentenced to 15 Months for Mail and Tax Fraud," by William A. Bonney (October 2003).

I got much of the section on the rise of black women in Congress from Ana Puga's March 20, 1994, story in *The Boston Globe*: "With 10 Black Women Serving in Congress, Washington Is Experiencing a Departure from Politics as Usual." The

direct quote from Keysville, Georgia, mayor, Emma Gresham, comes from that piece. The comments of Illinois congresswoman Carol Moseley Braun and Alabama senator Howell Heflin come from an April 16, 1995, report in the *Chicago Tribune Sunday Magazine*, by Dorothy Collin: "Power & Glory: Carol Moseley Braun Has Made Her Presence Felt in the U.S. Senate, but Even Her Achievements Are Controversial."

The quote about the Confederate flag from June Leake of the United Daughters of the Confederacy comes from an *Atlanta Journal-Constitution* story by Jim Auchmutey: "The Symbol of the Confederacy Still Haunts Ole Miss and the South: Does It Stand for a Heritage of Honor or the Horror of Slavery?" (September 29, 1991). The stories about racial unrest in Los Angeles and New York in the late 1980s and early 1990s come from a series of stories in *The New York Times*, *The Village Voice*, the *Los Angeles Times*, and *L.A. Weekly* by a team of great reporters too numerous to list by name.

Thanks to one of my real heroes of music journalism, Greil Marcus, for his keen insights into the Clinton/Elvis mystique compiled in his entertaining and informative collection of essays and whatnot, *Double Trouble: Bill Clinton and Elvis Presley in a Land of No Alternatives*. A *Boston Globe* story by one of my heroes of *political* journalism, Curtis Wilkie ("Perseverance: The Making of the Candidate," June 3, 1992), provided the metapoetic mix of himself and the great Theodore H. White in the account of Clinton's mythical childhood in Hope. Wilkie's piece gave more than just good quotes, though; it also provided great historical and social context. (Thanks, Curtis!) Cautiously, I used crazy rockabilly badass Ronnie Hawkins's account of the Clinton inauguration. (I siphoned off some of his more exaggerated and grandiose memories.)

Most of the section on Widespread Panic comes from my discussions with Phil Walden Jr. and producer Johnny Sandlin. The direct quotes from Panic percussionist Domingo "Sonny" Ortiz come from a story by Brenda Herrmann in the *Chicago Tribune*: "Spreading Panic: Southern Rockers Hope to Widen Their Horizons with a Tour" (October 19, 1992). I got much of my background info on the H.O.R.D.E. tours and other jam-band related details from the good people at www.jambands.com. (Those guys never sleep; at the 2003 Bonnaroo Music Festival, Dean Budnick and his team of reporters wrote and published a daily newspaper dubbed the *Bonnaroo Beacon* for the festival's makeshift town of eighty thousand freaks. *That's* Dead-ication!) The final section of this chapter is a variation on a few paragraphs from my southern rock piece for *The New York Times* in 1998. It summed up what I needed to say just fine.

POSTSCRIPT

Since I discovered the Drive-By Truckers' *Southern Rock Opera* while doing much of the initial footwork for this book, I decided to save the story of head Trucker, Patterson Hood, for my postscript. His album is as good a source as any book on southern rock.

The information on the city of Charlotte comes from the rich archives of *The Charlotte Observer*. I looked to former *Observer* reporter and editor Frye Gaillard's *The Dream Long Deferred* for background on the city's landmark school busing strategy; it's a wonderful book by a fine journalist who doesn't candy-coat Charlotte as some oasis of liberalism. (Thanks to my colleague Richard Maschal for turning me

on to this giant of southern journalists!) Finally, the touching story of Sam Fulwood III comes from the columnist's work as a reporter for the *Los Angeles Times,* where he created the paper's race-relations beat. The piece I quote comes from a perspective piece Fulwood wrote for the *Times,* "Rear-view Look at Busing Ruling: Trailblazer Goes Back to South in Wake of Judge's Order to End Race-Based Integration" (November 6, 1999).

★ Bibliography ★

Applebome, Peter. *Dixie Rising: How the South Is Shaping American Values, Politics, and Culture.* New York: Times Books/Random House, 1996.

Ballinger, Lee. *Lynyrd Skynyrd: An Oral History* (new edition). Los Angeles: XT377 Publishing, 2002.

Berman, Paul, ed. *Debating PC: The Debate over Political Correctness on College Campuses.* New York: Bantam Doubleday Dell, 1992.

Bertrand, Michael T. *Race, Rock, and Elvis.* Urbana and Chicago: University of Illinois Press, 2000.

Black, Earle, and Merle Black. *The Rise of Southern Republicans.* Cambridge, Mass.: Belknap, 2002.

Booth, Stanley. *Rhythm Oil: A Journey Through the Music of the American South.* London: Jonathan Cape, 1991.

———. *The True Adventures of the Rolling Stones.* Chicago: A Cappella Books (reprint), 2000.

Brant, Marley. *Freebirds: The Lynyrd Skynyrd Story.* New York: Billboard Books, 2002.

———. *Southern Rockers: The Roots and Legacy of Southern Rock.* Billboard Books, 1999.

Brewster, Bill, and Frank Broughton. *Last Night a DJ Saved My Life: The History of the Disc Jockey.* New York: Grove Press, 2000.

Bridges, Tyler. *The Rise of David Duke.* Jackson, Miss: University Press of Mississippi, 1994

Bryan, Bo. *Shag: The Legendary Dance of the South.* Beaufort, S.C.: Foundation Books, 1995.

Carter, Dan T. *The Politics of Rage: George Wallace, The Origins of the New Conservatism, and the Transformation of American Politics.* Baton Rouge: Louisiana State University Press, 2000.

Carter, Jimmy. *The Blood of Abraham: Insights into the Middle East.* Boston: Houghton Mifflin. 1985.

———. *An Hour Before Daylight: Memories of a Rural Boyhood.* New York: Simon & Schuster, 2000.

———. *Keeping Faith: Memoirs of a President.* New York: Bantam Books, 1982.

——. *Turning Point: A Candidate, a State and a Nation Come of Age*. New York: Times Books, 1992.

Cash, W. J. *The Mind of the South*. New York: Vintage Books, 1991.

Castaneda, Carlos. *The Teachings of Don Juan: A Yaqui Way of Knowledge* (The Original Teachings in a Deluxe 30th Anniversary Edition). Berkeley: University of California Press, 1998.

Conway, Cecelia. *African Banjo Echoes in Appalachia: A Study of Folk Traditions*. Knoxville: University of Tennessee Press, 1995.

Cox, Jacob D., and Brooks D. Simpson. *Sherman's Battle for Atlanta (Campaigns of the Civil War)* (a reprint of the 1882 book *Atlanta*). New York: Da Capo, 1994.

Davis, Stephen. *Atlanta Will Fall: Sherman, Joe Johnston, and the Yankee Heavy Battalions* (American Crisis Series, no. 3).

DeCurtis, Anthony, James Henke, and Holly George-Warren, eds. *The Rolling Stone Illustrated History of Rock & Roll*. New York: Random House, 1992.

Diamond, Sara. *Spiritual Warfare: The Politics of the Christian Right*. Boston: South End Press, 1989.

D'Souza, Dinesh. *Falwell: Before the Millennium*. Chicago: Regnery Gateway, 1984.

Duberman, Martin. *Stonewall*. New York: Plume, 1994.

Eagerton, John. *Speak Now Against the Day: The Generation Before the Civil Rights Movement in the South*. Chapel Hill: The University of North Carolina Press, 1994.

——. *The Americanization of Dixie: The Southernization of America*. New York: Harper's Magazine Press, 1974.

Fairclough, Adam. *Race and Democracy: The Civil Rights Struggle in Louisiana. 1915–1972*. Athens, Ga.: University of Georgia Press, 1995.

Foote, Shelby. *The Civil War: A Narrative* (vols. 1–3). New York: Vintage, 1986.

Fredrickson, Kari. *The Dixiecrat Revolt and the End of the Solid South, 1932–1968*. Chapel Hill: University of North Carolina Press, 2001.

Gaillard, Frye. *The Dream Long Deferred*. Chapel Hill: The University of North Carolina Press, 1988.

George-Warren, Holly, Patricia Romanowski, and Jon Pareles, eds. *The Rolling Stone Encyclopedia of Rock & Roll* (third edition). New York: Fireside, 2001.

Gillett, Charlie. *The Sound of the City: The Rise of Rock and Roll*. New York: Outerbridge & Dienstfrey, 1970.

Glazer, Tom, ed. *Songs of Peace, Freedom and Protest*. New York: David McKay Company, Inc, 1970.

Gold, Lewis. *Grand Old Party: A History of the Republicans*. New York: Random House, 2003.

Goldrosen, John, and John Beecher. *Remembering Buddy*. London: Pavilion, 1987.

Gray, Marcus. *An R.E.M. Companion: It Crawled from the South*. New York: Da Capo, 1993.

Guralnick, Peter. *Sweet Soul Music: Rhythm and Blues and the Southern Dream of Freedom*. New York: Harper and Row, 1986.

——. *Last Train to Memphis: The Rise of Elvis Presley*. Boston: Little, Brown, 1994.

Hinton, Brian. *Elvis Costello: Let Them All Talk*. London: Sanctuary Publishing, 1998.

Hirsch, Arnold R., and Joseph Logsdon, eds. *Creole New Orleans: Race and Americanization*. New Orleans: Louisiana State University Press (first edition), 1992.

Horowitz, David. *Radical Son: A Generational Odyssey*. New York: Free Press, 1998.

———, and Peter Collier. *Destructive Generation: Second Thoughts About the Sixties*. New York: Free Press, 1996.

———, eds. *Second Thoughts: Former Radicals Look Back at the Sixties*, Lanham, Md.: Madison Books, 1989.

Horwitz, Tony. *Confederates in the Attic: Dispatches from the Unfinished Civil War*. New York: Pantheon, 1998.

Kaufman, Burton. *The Presidency of James Earl Carter, Jr.* Lawrence: University of Kansas Press, 1993.

Kerner Commission. *Report of the National Advisory Commission on Civil Disorders*. New York: Bantam, 1968.

King, Jr., Martin Luther. *Where Do We Go from Here: Chaos or Community?*. Boston: Beacon Press, 1968.

Kingsbury, Paul, ed. *The Encyclopedia of Country Music*. New York: Oxford University Press, 1998.

Kolchin, Peter. *American Slavery: 1619–1877*. New York: Hill & Wang (10th-Anniversary Edition), 2003.

Kooper, Al. *Backstage Passes & Backstabbing Bastards: Memoirs of a Rock 'N Roll Survivor*. New York: Billboard Books, 1998.

Lewis, Catherine Heniford. *Horry County, South Carolina: 1730–1993*. Columbia: University of South Carolina Press, 1998.

Lomax, Louis E. *To Kill a Black Man: The Shocking Parallel in the Lives of Malcolm X and Martin Luther King Jr.* Los Angeles: Holloway House Books, 1987.

Malone, Bill C., and David Stricklin. *Southern Music/American Music* (revised edition). Lexington: The University Press of Kentucky, 2003.

Marcus, Greil. *Double Trouble: Bill Clinton and Elvis Presley in a Land of No Alternatives*. New York: Picador USA, 2000.

———. *Mystery Train: Images of America in Rock 'n' Roll Music*. New York: E. P. Dutton & Co., Inc., 1975.

Martin, William. *With God on Our Side: The Rise of the Religious Right in America*. New York: Broadway Books, 1996.

Miller, William Lee. *Yankee from Georgia: The Emergence of Jimmy Carter*. New York: Times Books, 1978.

Oates, Stephen B. *Let the Trumpet Sound: A Life of Martin Luther King, Jr.* New York: Harper Perennial (reprint), 1994.

Odom, Gene, and Frank Dorman. *Lynyrd Skynyrd: Remembering the Free Birds of Southern Rock*. New York: Broadway Books, 2002.

Palmer, Robert. *Rock & Roll: An Unruly History*. New York: Harmony Books, 1995.

Rebennack, Mac, et al. *Under a Hoodoo Moon: The Life of Dr. John the Night Tripper*. New York: St. Martin's Press, 1994.

Reed, John Shelton, and Dale Volberg Reed. *1001 Things Everyone Should Know about the South*. New York: Doubleday, 1996.

Romanillos, José L., and Marian Harris Winspear. *Vihuela de Mano and the Spanish Guitar: A Dictionary of the Makers of Plucked and Bowed Instruments of Spain (1200–2002)*. Guijosa, Spain: The Sanguino Press, 2002.

Rosen, Craig. *R.E.M. Inside Out: The Stories Behind Every Song*. New York: Thunder's Mouth Press, 1997.

Schumacher, Michael. *Crossroads: The Life and Music of Eric Clapton*. New York: Hyperion Press, 1995.

Short, Bob. *Everything Is Pickrick: The Life of Lester Maddox*. Macon: Mercer University Press, 1999.

Sick, Gary. *October Surprise: America's Hostages in Iran and the Election of Ronald Reagan*. New York: Random House/Times Books, 1992.

St. John, Lauren. *Hardcore Troubadour: The Life and Near Death of Steve Earle*. New York: Fourth Estate, 2003.

Stroud, Kandy. *How Jimmy Won: The Victory Campaign from Plains to the White House*. New York: William Morrow, 1977.

Sullivan, Denise. *Talk About the Passion: An Oral History*. Lancaster, Pa.: Underwood-Miller, 1994.

Thompson, Hunter S. *Fear and Loathing in Las Vegas and Other American Stories*. New York: Random House Modern Library Edition, 1996.

———. *Fear and Loathing: on the Campaign Trail '72*. New York: Warner Books (reprint), 1985.

———. *The Great Shark Hunt: Strange Tales from a Strange Time*. New York: Simon & Schuster (reprint), 2003.

Van-Zant, Lacy. *The Van-Zant Family: Southern Music Scrapbook*. Jacksonville, Fl: Lacy Van-Zant, 1995.

Ward, Brian. *Just My Soul Responding: Rhythm and Blues, Black Consciousness, and Race*. Berkeley, Calif.: University of California Press, 1998.

Watkins, Samuel R. *Co. Aytch: A Confederate's Memoir of the Civil War* (reprint). New York: Touchstone Books, 1997.

Whitburn, Joel. *Billboard Book of Top 40 Hits*. New York: Watson-Guptill Publications, 2000.

Wilkie, Curtis. *Dixie: A Personal Odyssey Through Events That Shaped the Modern South*. New York: Scribner, 2001.

Wilson, Charles Reagan, and William Ferris. *Encyclopedia of Southern Culture*. Chapel Hill: The University of North Carolina Press, 1989.

Witcover, Jules. *Party of the People : A History of the Democrats*. New York: Random House, 2003.

Wolfe, Thomas. *You Can't Go Home Again*. New York: Harper Perennial (reprint), 1998.

Woodward, C. Vann. *The Burden of Southern History*. Baton Rouge and London: Louisiana State University Press, 1960.

Wyman, Bill, and Richard Havers. *Bill Wyman's Blues Odyssey: A Journey to Music's Heart & Soul*. London; New York: DK Publishing, 2001.

X, Malcolm. *The Autobiography of Malcolm X*. New York: Grove Press, Inc., 1965.

★ Acknowledgments ★

In his "Letter from Birmingham Jail," Dr. Martin Luther King Jr. wrote that "human progress never rolls in on wheels of inevitability; it comes through the tireless efforts of men willing to be coworkers with God. . . ." To me, the very essence of God is the combined efforts of people working together in pursuit of something bigger, more loving, and more powerful than any individual vision. King, of course, was referring to something a bit more important than rock & roll, but his words can be applied to all human endeavors. I have been fortunate to have had many people guide me in positive ways throughout my life and career, helping me make whatever tiny contributions I've made and forgiving my countless self-centered transgressions. There's no way I could list all the people who inspired *Dixie Lullaby*—nor even thank any *one* of them sufficiently—but I'll do the best I can. My apologies to those I may have missed.

For their enduring love and support, I am eternally indebted to my mother and father, Joan and Richard Kemp, who always tried to show me how to be a southern gentleman; my sister, Cheri Ferguson, who opened my mind to new ideas and introduced me to rock & roll; my dear friend Megan Kingsbury, who believed in me even when I didn't believe in myself; and Dánica Coto, who came into my life like a new song and stuck by me through my writing, not just offering daily emotional and moral support but also reading drafts and chasing down books—all while getting her own breaking news stories on the front page of *The Charlotte Observer*. *Te amo, mi sol. Así de simple. Así de claro.*

In terms of my career and passion for music, no one has been more consistently supportive than Holly George-Warren, one of the most knowledgeable and conscientious editors in the field of music journalism and publishing. Holly not only initiated me into the world of *Rolling Stone*, she's been a part of my life from day one, having grown up just a short bicycle ride from my childhood home. She put up with me when I was an obnoxious adolescent and teen, showed me what rock & roll cool was all about, welcomed me to New York City in the late '80s, introduced me to some of my childhood music and literary heroes, helped me get my foot in more doors than the velvet-rope keepers at hip downtown nightclubs, and brought me in on several book projects. Words can't express my indebtedness to her.

This book wouldn't have gotten out of the gate without the hard work and commitment of the people who helped bring *Dixie Lullaby* to fruition. First among them is my agent and friend, David Dunton, who believed in the book, talked with me on a regular basis, read every draft, and offered valuable editorial suggestions. Thanks also to the folks at Simon & Schuster/Free Press: Wylie O'Sullivan, Tricia Wygal, Dominick Anfuso, and Kristen McGuiness, who trusted that a first-time author could pull off such an ambitious project and gave me the freedom and extra time to get it right. Thanks also to Patricia Romanowski, whose meticulous copyediting made the rough spots sing and whose expert editorial suggestions kept me accurate and honest. Attorney Robert Driscoll (an early subscriber to the sorely missed *Option* magazine!) made sure I didn't cross any legal lines.

I'm blessed to have had not just great editors on this book, but also friends (most of them editors or writers themselves) who have listened to me babble for hours at a time about the music and culture of the South, egged me on, read drafts, and helped me clarify and sharpen my ideas. They are my friends Andrew Huebner and Sarah Graham Hayes; Laura Sandlin and John Draper; Polly Paddock, Alison Powell, Jeff Whisnant, Mary Martin Niepold, and Jason Fine (who's been a loyal sounding board since our earliest years together at *Option* and *Rolling Stone*). Two colleagues at *The Charlotte Observer*, Mary Curtis and Michael Drummond, also read early drafts and offered helpful suggestions.

Other people have encouraged me along the way. Lee Barnes offered me a column to write about music at *The Daily Times News* of Burlington when I was supposed to be just reporting the crime beat; Scott Becker gave me carte blanche to make *Option* the best alternative music magazine it could be; Jann S. Wenner trusted me at the editorial helm of *Rolling Stone*'s music pages during a crisis in leadership; literary agent Sarah Lazin bugged me about writing a book before I'd even thought much about it; Jane Wenner (and the Wenner boys, Alex, Gus and Theo) kept pushing and nudging me, constantly asking how the book was going; and Mike Weinstein at *The Charlotte Observer* patiently allowed me the time to finish this project when I also had important duties to attend to at the paper. Thanks also to the recurrent words of support from my friends and onetime colleagues David Fricke, Barney Hoskyns, Andy Revkin, and Jim DeRogatis.

Many other editors have helped me hone my writing voice over the years; they include Richie Unterberger, David Sprague, Sue Cummings, Ira Robbins, Anthony DeCurtis, Mark Coleman, Bill Van Parys, Keith Moerer, Sid Holt, Nathan Brackett, Fletcher Roberts, Ashley Kahn, Shawn Dahl, Robert Levine, Matt Hendrickson, Tony Romando, and Carol Dittbrenner.

Obviously, *Dixie Lullaby* could not have happened without the people—friends, musicians, and otherwise—who freely gave of their time and shared their stories with me, both for this book and for the related articles and other projects I've worked on that inspired it. They are Bonnie Bramlett, Jeff Brown, Joseph "Red Dog" Campbell, Crystal Carver, Vic and Tina Chesnutt, Eric Clapton, Charlie Daniels, the late Rick Danko, Stephen J. Dubner, Donnah Dunthorn, Mike Farris, Jeffrey Foster, Patricia Fournier, Robert George, Jimmie Dale Gilmore, Sandy Gray, Emmylou Harris, Ronnie Hawkins, Warren Haynes, Brian Henneman and his Bottle Rockets, David Hood, Patterson Hood, Paul Hornsby, Linda and Harold Isbell, Jimmy Johnson, Richard Johnson, Carolyn Killen, Ed King, Leo Luther, Maria McKee, Hope

Nicholls, Martin Nicholson, Debbie Pickens, Aaron Pitkin, Mac Rebennack, Jason Ringenberg, Johnny Sandlin, Percy Sledge, Errol Stewart, Michael Stipe, Johnny Van Zant, Alan Walden, Phil Walden, Philip Walden Jr., Chip Womick, Tim Womick, Fred Young, and Richard Young. Thanks also to those with whom I corresponded but never got the chance to sit down and interview: Jimmy Hall, Levon Helm, Al Kooper, John Mayall, George McCorkle, and Bill Wyman. Many of these folks welcomed me into their homes, reminding me that southern hospitality is not a myth, nor is it dead.

A big question mark and semi-thanks to Gregg Allman, who began to talk with me for this book one afternoon at the Bonnaroo Music Festival but was cut off and quickly herded away by his handlers. (No thanks to the Allman Brothers Band's current manager, Burt Holman.)

I've had the privilege of knowing, talking with, and editing hundreds of talented writers, reporters, and critics over the years. Each one has taught me something new and different, but the following (whether they know it or not) helped expand my vocabulary, to one degree or another, with regard to issues raised in *Dixie Lullaby*: Gina Arnold, Jason Cohen, John Colapinto, Kandia Crazy Horse, the late Renee Crist, the late Chuck Dean, Jancee Dunn, Donna Gaines, Mikal Gilmore, Robert Gordon, Kathy Haight, Eddie Huffman, Tonya Jameson, Evelyn McDonnell, Sandy Masuo, Richard Maschal, Fred Mills, Woody Mitchell, Kevin Powell, Ann Powers, Kathi Purvis, Parke Puterbaugh, Ben Ratliff, Dudley Saunders, Craig Shaffer, Dean Smith, Debbie Stoller, Neil Strauss, Lawrence Toppman, Touré, Mim Udovitch, and Tom Waters. I'm deeply indebted to my former wife, Lorraine Ali, whose intelligent and intuitive criticism and commentary opened me to new ways of hearing music and seeing the world, but who also endured more heartache from me than she deserved. Thank you, Lorraine.

Several other people in various capacities of the music or journalism fields have been extremely helpful and gracious over the years. They include (but aren't limited to): James Austin, Bill Bentley, Nils Bernstein, Godfrey Cheshire, Jim Denk, Bobbie Gale, Brent Grulke, Kelvin Hart, Robert Hilburn, Regina Joskow, Kevin Kennedy, Rose McGathy, Meegan Ochs, Michael Ochs, Brenda Pinnell, Trent Roberts, Danyel Smith, Gary Stewart, Paula Szeigis, Tracy Thomas, Wendi Thomas, Ken Weinstein, Curtis Wilkie, Bob Williams, Don Williamson, and Fred Woodward.

I wouldn't be doing what I do if it weren't for all the songwriters, singers, rappers, guitar slingers, keyboard pounders, percussionists, horn players, turntable scratchers, and other musicians whose albums and performances got me through my childhood and kept me on a journey that's been fascinating, exhilarating, sometimes painful, and always unpredictable. I could list thousands from all over the world, but for the purposes of this book, I'll stick with the southern (or near southern) musicians who stand out as most meaningful to my life: Robert Johnson, Muddy Waters, Hank Williams, Little Richard, Chuck Berry, Elvis Presley, Jerry Lee Lewis, Johnny Cash, Otis Redding, Aretha Franklin, James Brown, Janis Joplin, Big Star, the Allman Brothers Band, Dr. John, Leon Russell, Lynyrd Skynyrd, Gram Parsons and Emmylou Harris, Willie Nelson and Waylon Jennings, Al Green, George Clinton, George Jones, R.E.M., Jason and the Scorchers, Uncle Tupelo, Steve Earle, Lucinda Williams, Alejandro Escovedo, the Goodie Mob, Gov't Mule, Drive-By Truckers, Ryan Adams, and OutKast. (Chief among honorary southerners, whether they'd appreciate that des-

ignation or not: the Rolling Stones, Bob Dylan, Neil Young, Bob Marley, the Grateful Dead, Phil Ochs, the Band, Little Feat, Television, Elvis Costello, the Clash, Public Enemy, Nusrat Fateh Ali Khan, Mekons, and Nirvana.)

Finally, in the late 1990s, right around the time I began working on my proposal for this book, I suffered some very rough years. I am indebted to several people at MTV Networks, who did their best for me during that period: Bill Brand, Jennifer Crisafulli, Bill Flanagan, Susan Horowitz, Judy McGrath, John Sykes, Shelly Tatro, and Mary Wahl. In a similar vein, a string of men in my life have been instrumental in helping me stay alive a day at a time since then; if it weren't for them, this book not only wouldn't have happened, it would be irrelevant. I am eternally grateful to Jim Fouratt, Drew Huebner, David Felton, Chuck Young, Dan Zanes, Steve Goldberg, Jay Spitz, Shane Doyle, Mace Perlman, Allen Hildreth, and Ted Sjolander. Also thanks to Bill W., Dr. Bob, and the power of good in this universe, which I choose to call God.

★ Index ★

★ About the Author ★

Mark Kemp has been writing about popular music and culture for two decades. He has served as music editor of *Rolling Stone* and vice president of music editorial for MTV Networks. In 1997 he was nominated for a Grammy for his liner notes to a CD retrospective of music by '60s protest singer Phil Ochs. Kemp lives in Charlotte, North Carolina, where he works as the entertainment editor at *The Charlotte Observer*.